THE LAW OF EVIDENCE
IN SCOTLAND

GREENS CONCISE SCOTS LAW

THE LAW OF EVIDENCE IN SCOTLAND

By

David Field, B.A. (Hons.) (Law),
Solicitor, Queensland, Australia,

Fiona E. Raitt, LL.B.,
*Solicitor, Senior Lecturer in Law, Department of Law,
University of Dundee*

W. Green / Sweet & Maxwell
Edinburgh
1996

First published 1988

Reprinted 1997

© 1996
W. Green & Son Ltd

ISBN 0 414 0104 18
A catalogue record for this book is available from the British Library

Typeset by Trinity Typesetting, Edinburgh
Printed and bound in Great Britain by Redwood Books, Wiltshire

PREFACE

It is eight years since any book on the Scots law of evidence was last published and this new edition of David Field's book aims to provide a comprehensive up-to-date account of the major statutory changes to the civil and criminal law including the far-reaching measures introduced by the Civil Evidence (Scotland) Act 1988 and the Criminal Procedure (Scotland) Act 1995. Several of the chapters have been re-structured, particularly those dealing with documentary evidence, corroboration and hearsay. The new material which has been added includes case law arising from the Children's Hearings referrals (which is making a significant contribution to the law on hearsay, corroboration and sufficiency), child witnesses and closed circuit TV, developments in DNA genetic profiling and distress as corroboration. The detailed legislative background to the Criminal Procedure (Scotland) Act 1995 (which came into force on April 1, 1996) has not been covered but the text footnotes cross-reference most of the 1995 statutory provisions discussed in the text with their derivations from the Criminal Procedure (Scotland) Act 1975.

The timetable for the production of this new edition was extremely tight and was effectively completed within four months. Despite this, every attempt has been made to make the whole text more accessible and "reader friendly" while carrying out the updating process.

I could not have kept to my timetable without the continuing support and encouragement from colleagues and friends. In particular, Pamela Ferguson, Liz Wilson and Suzanne Zeedyk tolerated bouts of my anti-social behaviour at periods of peak pressure, responding only with warmth and good humour. I owe a separate debt to Audrey Harrow who provided valuable assistance at the proof stage. I could not have delivered the corrected proofs without her help. I also wish to record my grateful thanks to Betty Bott and Lindsay Fowlis, both of whom found time at short notice and during hectic schedules to answer queries and offer helpful comments on parts of this book. Naturally though, all responsibility for errors rests with me.

Fiona E. Raitt
July 1996

CONTENTS

CONTENTS

TABLE OF CASES

TABLE OF STATUTES

TABLE OF STATUTORY INSTRUMENTS

CHAPTER 1

RELEVANCE, ADMISSIBILITY, WEIGHT AND SUFFICIENCY OF EVIDENCE

INTRODUCTION

An appropriate starting point for a textbook of the law of evidence is an **1–01** attempt to define what that area of law encompasses. One of the foremost modern writers in the law of evidence, William Twining, has defined the law as "a series of disparate exceptions to a single principle of freedom of proof".[1] This chapter sets out the key features underpinning the principle of freedom of proof. Much of the rest of this book is devoted to an examination of these "disparate exceptions" in operation.

The law of evidence in Scotland today remains firmly rooted in common **1–02** law but there is an increasing statutory influence, where procedural provisions frequently modify and shape the development of the rules of evidence. This area of law has a great many rules—the disparate exceptions referred to by Twining. One of the main reasons for having rules is to control what facts are able to be presented to a court. It would not be practicable for a court of law to consider every item of evidence which might conceivably have a bearing on the issues before it. Rules have therefore evolved to govern what facts will be admitted before the court. These rules are designed to promote justice during the course of the trial of an action, be it civil or criminal. These rules, when considered in aggregation, constitute a large proportion of what we call the law of evidence, a loosely compiled, confusing and occasionally contradictory set of principles which do not always form a harmonious pattern.

Without the law of evidence, all items of information no matter how **1–03** remote or however unreliable, unfair or misleading, would be put before the court. This could make the court process tiresome and time-consuming and in an action involving laypersons whether in a jury or a district court, or forming the majority in a tribunal, there would be much potential for confusion and conjecture. For these and other reasons, items of evidence which are undoubtedly relevant in the broad sense will often be excluded

---

[1] Twining, *Rethinking Evidence: Exploratory Essays,* p.178.

on the grounds that they are "inadmissible", and a study of the law of evidence is largely a study of those reasons.

1–04   We may therefore begin with the deceptively simple statement that in a court of law, all admissible evidence must first of all be relevant, but not all relevant items of evidence will be admissible.

RELEVANCE GENERALLY

1–05   Since no item of information may even be considered as potential evidence in a case until it is relevant to that case,[2] it is necessary first to establish what is meant by "relevance".

1–06   This creates an immediate problem, since relevance is not a fixed concept, and can only be expressed in general terms as a relationship which exists between two facts. Fact A is relevant to fact B when, in the light of collective human experience, the two tend to exist together. They are logically connected. When one of those two facts requires to be established in proof, then the existence of the other fact which is logically connected with it is potentially an item of evidence. As expressed in Walker and Walker, "Evidence is relevant if it is in some way logically connected with the matters in dispute..."[3] Since the whole process of defining relevance is somewhat akin to the thankless task of describing an elephant (almost impossible to describe, but instantly recognisable), a few illustrations may assist.

1–07   For example, it has been part of our common law for many years that the fact that an accused person is found to be in possession of recently stolen property in criminative circumstances is an admissible item of evidence in that person's subsequent trial for almost any crime of dishonesty relating to that property.[4] Why? Because it is part of human experience that persons who are found to be in possession of property shortly after its theft, and who cannot give an innocent explanation of such possession, tend to have been involved in some way in its dishonest appropriation, usually as thieves or resetters. Fact A (the possession of recently stolen property in criminative circumstances) is so logically related to fact B (the guilt of the person in possession) that it cannot be ignored, and is therefore relevant to the case. In the example quoted, the logical link between the two facts is so

---

[2]   Although it will probably have been assessed when preparing the case for trial.
[3]   *Law of Evidence in Scotland*, pp.5–6, quoted in *Inland Revenue Commissioners* v. *Stenhouse's Trustees*, 1993 S.L.T. 248.
[4]   For an example of this principle in action, see *Cassidy* v. *McLeod*, 1981 S.C.C.R. 270; see also Gordon, "The Burden of Proof on the Accused," 1968 S.L.T. (News) 29 and 37 at p. 40.

strong that it creates a presumption of guilt against the person in possession, which must then be rebutted by some innocent explanation.[5]

By the same process, if a man is charged with a crime, when assessing   **1–08**
his guilt or innocence, the facts cannot be ignored:

    (i)   that he was seen running away from the *locus* shortly after the commission of the crime;[6]

    (ii) that he made a statement admitting his guilt to police officers;[7] or

    (iii) that he attempted to bribe a prosecution witness.[8]

In all of these examples, the facts offered as evidence are relevant (*i.e.*   **1–09**
logically related to) the central issue in the case, namely the guilt or innocence of the accused. Of equal relevance, of course, to the same central issue will be items of defence evidence, such as the fact that the accused was 100 miles away from the *locus* at the time,[9] that he has never been in trouble before,[10] and that he gives evidence on oath that he knows nothing about it.[11] Whether or not all or any of these items of evidence will be regarded as admissible is, however, a separate consideration.

So far the examples quoted have been from criminal cases, but the basic requirement of all items of evidence—that they be relevant—is equally applicable to civil actions.

For example, in an action for damages arising from the negligent driving   **1–10**
of a motor vehicle, it is relevant to know how the vehicle was being driven shortly before and shortly after the collision which gave rise to the action.[12] Or, when it is alleged that a local highway authority ignored the known state of a road, in breach of its statutory duty, it is relevant to cite examples of other accidents on the same stretch of road in the weeks prior to the accident in question.[13]

In each of the cases cited, the item of evidence is relevant because of its   **1–11**
logical link with a fact in issue (*i.e.* respectively the care being taken by the

---

5   This presumption is dealt with more fully in paras. 3.113–3.119 *infra*, but certainly predates Alison, *Principles of the Criminal Law of Scotland*; see *ibid.*, p. 320.

6   *Teper v. R.* [1952] A.C. 480, dealt with more fully in paras. 8.20–8.33 *infra*.

7   For which see Chap. 14 *infra*.

8   Which might well constitute a separate offence in itself; see Gordon, *Criminal Law*, p. 1070.

9   An alibi defence which would require special notice to be given to the prosecution in terms of s. 78 (solemn proceedings) and s. 149 (summary proceedings) of the Criminal Procedure (Scotland) Act 1995.

10 Character evidence is generally admissible in favour of the accused; see *Slater v. H.M.A.*, 1928 J.C. 94 at p. 105, and paras. 13.23–13.26 *infra*.

11 The accused's right to give sworn testimony on his own behalf is dealt with more fully in paras. 11.05–11.65 *infra*.

12 Lord President Cooper in *Bark v. Scott*, 1954 S.C. 72 at p. 76.

13 *W. Alexander & Sons v. Dundee Corporation*, 1950 S.C. 123.

driver at the time of the accident, and the state of knowledge of the local authority concerning the condition of the road), and the resulting inference that one fact was probably accompanied by the other. As with criminal cases, the logical connection between the two facts is sometimes so strong in civil actions that it gives rise to a presumption or doctrine which the party against whom the first fact is proved is then obliged to counter with other evidence.[14]

1–12   It will now be appreciated why it is dangerous to generalise about relevance: it is the ultimate in moving targets. In general terms, facts which a party wishes to adduce as evidence must have a logical link with an issue raised by the case in hand. To complicate matters, there are different categories of issues, some of which are of greater significance than others. The next section considers these.

RELEVANCE TO THE ISSUES

1–13   During the course of a criminal trial or civil proof many issues will be raised, and these issues must themselves be relevant to the eventual outcome of the case. Those which are considered relevant are traditionally referred to as the *facta probanda*, and must be "logically connected with those matters in dispute between the parties",[15] and they are the issues which the parties are seeking to have resolved in their favour.[16]

1–14   In one sense there is only one ultimate issue (whether or not the accused is convicted, or which party succeeds in the civil action), but this simplistic view ignores the fact that the road to success in a court action is paved with several separate issues which together make up the case. These separate individual issues—the facts in issue—will be apparent from the written pleadings in a civil case and from the terms of the indictment or complaint in a criminal case. They are the *facta probanda* referred to above.

1–15   It is possible for a party (which term may be taken to include the prosecution and the accused in a criminal trial) to fail to establish a fact in issue in his or her favour and yet still succeed on the ultimate issue. Equally, but unusually, a party could prove every one of the points raised as facts in issue and still lose the case. This might occur, for example, when an accused offers no evidence in contradiction of the prosecution case, but is acquitted

---

[14] A clear example of this process is the so-called "presumption against donation *inter vivos*"; see *Grant's Trs.* v. *McDonald*, 1939 S.C. 448 and paras. 3.41–3.46 *infra*. The presumption rests upon the simple knowledge that people do not normally give away their property free of charge.

[15] Walker and Walker, *op. cit.*, n. 3, p. 5.

[16] When they are no longer in dispute, *e.g.* because they are admitted on the closed record, or form the subject of a joint minute between the parties, they cease to be live issues and no further evidence may be called which concerns only them.

following a successful submission of "no case to answer".[17] The court in such a situation has found the totality of the prosecution case insufficient to prove the accused's guilt beyond reasonable doubt.

Using the example of the criminal accused quoted above it can be seen that the facts in issue will include the fact that the accused was seen running away from the *locus* shortly after the commission of the crime, the fact that he confessed his guilt to police officers, his alibi and his denial of any knowledge of the incident. As listed they are of course contradictory, since two form part of the prosecution case while the other two are urged by the defence. Once they have been disentangled and assessed, the court will be in a position to give a ruling on the ultimate issue: the innocence or guilt of the accused. Exactly the same process obtains in a civil action, the ultimate issue being whether or not the pursuer succeeds in his or her claim.   **1–16**

The outcome of the ultimate issue will depend upon the effect of all the relevant evidence led in the case. In addition to direct evidence of a fact in issue, relevant evidence includes "evidence of a fact bearing on the probability or improbability of a fact in issue."[18] Such facts are known as *facta probationis*. For example, it may be extremely important for a court hearing testimony from a witness to know that this witness has previous convictions for perjury, since it affects his credibility as a witness and may result in his evidence being ignored. The fact that he has such previous convictions is an indirect issue, in the sense that it has no immediate bearing on the ultimate issue but may be highly relevant to a fact in issue (*i.e.* the acceptability or otherwise of the evidence given by that witness). Before it will be accepted as relevant to it, it must be logically connected with it. Such evidence is often described as circumstantial evidence.   **1–17**

Referring back to the examples used above to establish what is meant by relevance, it follows that the question of how a motor vehicle was being driven at the time of the accident[19] is part of the *facta probanda*, whereas how it was being driven shortly before or after an accident only has a bearing on the facts in issue and is therefore part of the *facta probationis*. Equally, the fact that an accused person attempted to bribe a prosecution witness, and the suggestion that he is of previous good character, are not in themselves directly in issue at the trial. They are however highly relevant in that either they cast light on the reliability of the accused as a witness or they are indicative of the sort of person who is on trial.   **1–18**

---

17 For which concept see paras. 2.25–2.44 *infra*. The statutory procedure was first introduced in 1980 and is now contained in the s. 97 (solemn proceedings) and s. 160 (summary proceedings) of the Criminal Procedure (Scotland) Act 1995.

18 Walker and Walker, *op. cit.*, n. 3. *N.B.* that when the fact sought to be proved is insufficiently relevant to a primary issue to justify its tendency to confuse matters, it will be rejected as an inadmissible "collateral" issue, for which see paras. 13.01–13.04 *infra*. See also *Swan v. Bowie*, 1948 S.C. 46 at p. 51.

19 See n. 11 *supra*.

1–19   There is an additional complication, in that *facta probanda* are sometimes concerned solely with the admissibility of an item of evidence. If, for example, it is accepted for the moment that a confession made by an accused person to police officers will only be admissible if made "voluntarily",[20] then it follows that any evidence which the court receives on the circumstances in which a confession came to be made will be relevant. Initially, the evidence relating to the circumstances will be considered to see if the confession is admissible. If it is then decided to admit the confession as an item of evidence, the circumstances in which it was taken become relevant when assessing the reliability of that confession, *i.e.* the weight to be attached to it.[21] In both cases the circumstances surrounding the confession constitute *facta probationis*, relevant to first, the admissibility of, and second, the weight to be attached to the confession.

1–20   A common example of a similar process in a civil action is the general practice of admitting, as probative of the facts which they contain, extracts of certain documents kept by public officials.[22] Before such an extract will be admissible, its public nature and the status of the keeper must be established by evidence. Such items of evidence are therefore relevant as *facta probationis* in establishing the admissibility of *facta probanda*, namely the information contained in the extracts.

1–21   The question of relevancy is therefore quite complex. An item of evidence need only be relevant to one of the facts in issue in order to have passed this first hurdle. What is then required is for the court to establish that it is also "admissible", *i.e.* that it is not excluded on one of the many grounds upon which relevant evidence is withheld from the court.

ADMISSIBILITY

1–22   The mere fact that an item of evidence is relevant does not automatically guarantee that the court will even consider it, let alone that it will attach any great weight to it. The American jurist Wigmore suggested that, "Admissibility signifies that the particular fact is relevant and something more—that it has also satisfied all the auxiliary tests and extrinsic policies."[23]

1–23   It is perhaps misleading to refer to "auxiliary" tests or "extrinsic" policies, as that might suggest that the issue of admissibility is somehow of lesser

---

[20] This concept is explored more fully in paras. 14.03–14.44 *infra*.
[21] A concept explored in paras. 1.37–1.43 *infra*.
[22] This topic is explored more fully in paras. 8.05–8.56 *infra*. An example would be an extract of a lighthouse keeper's log, which may be used to establish weather conditions at a particular time and place.
[23] Wigmore, *Evidence*, Vol. 1, p. 296.

importance. In fact, the tests and policies to which Wigmore refers are the very nucleus of the law of evidence.

In practice it is usually not too difficult to decide whether or not an item   **1–24**
of evidence is relevant. The item is either relevant to one of the issues in the case or it is not. It is, however, a totally different matter when it comes to assessing the admissibility of that same item.

Certain items of evidence, although relevant, are unacceptable in a court   **1–25**
of law. This may be because they are unreliable or because they are potentially misleading, and on occasions simply because the public interest requires that the information in question should remain undisclosed. In many cases the actual fact which the party wishes to establish by evidence would be perfectly acceptable, and what is being objected to is the form in which it is sought to produce this evidence. These various considerations have a common root—the desire to ensure that every issue before a court is considered fairly and accurately.

(1) Unreliability

Taking first the objection that an item of proposed evidence could be   **1–26**
unreliable, the following major exclusionary rules apply.

(a) *Hearsay*[24]

It may well be highly relevant to know what a particular witness A saw   **1–27**
or heard, but in criminal cases, (and until 1989 in civil cases), such information must come from A and not someone else—B—to whom A recounted the experience. For this reason the hearsay rule generally prohibits the evidence of A being given by B.[25] The exceptions to this rule arise when there is some additional factor which makes B's evidence of what A experienced more reliable than it would otherwise have been.

(b) *Opinion*[26]

Unless the witness is an expert on the matter in hand, all that the court   **1–28**
requires from him or her is an accurate statement of *fact*, namely what was seen, heard, etc. It does not require—and will not accept—the witness's *opinion* of how these facts should be interpreted, since interpretation of facts is for the court. Thus, the witness may say "The car was travelling fast," but not "The car was exceeding the speed limit."

---

[24] Dealt with in full in Chap. 8 *infra*.
[25] The general rule is subject to various exceptions dealt with in Chap. 8 *infra*.
[26] Dealt with in full in Chap. 16 *infra*.

(c) *Involuntary confession*[27]

1–29   A confession which is involuntary, although arguably still relevant, is likely to be less reliable than one freely volunteered, and its relevance may be far outweighed by its prejudicial effect on the accused during the trial. It will therefore normally be excluded.

(2) **Tendency to mislead**

1–30   Among the items of evidence normally rejected on the grounds that they are potentially misleading are the following.

(a) *The previous misdeeds of the accused*[28]

1–31   As a general rule, a criminal court is only concerned to establish, whether on the occasion libelled, the accused committed the offence(s) libelled. It is not concerned with what may or may not have been done by the accused on a previous occasion. While it would often be relevant to know that the person now charged with an offence has several previous convictions for the same offence, it is regarded as misleading and unjustifiably prejudicial to the accused to raise the issue. The exceptions which exist to this rule arise when another factor exists which makes the relevance of the accused's previous misdeeds so compelling that it outweighs the prejudicial effect of that evidence. For example, when the accused claims to have no such previous convictions, or the manner of commission of the present offence is strikingly similar to that known to have been employed by the accused on previous occasions. The latter is the basis of the so-called *Moorov* doctrine examined in more detail in paragraphs 7.66–7.81 *infra*.

(b) *Unsworn precognitions*

1–32   The contents of an unsworn precognition given on an earlier occasion cannot be put to a witness giving testimony in court. (Unlike the precognition sworn by a witness on oath before a sheriff[29] which is in effect a sworn statement anyway). Precognitions are excluded because the court is required to consider only what the witness is now saying on oath, and not what he or she is alleged to have said earlier to the precognoscer. Such evidence would inevitably carry less weight and to allow it would be to undermine the value our legal system places on sworn oral testimony.[30]

---

[27] Dealt with in full in Chap. 14 *infra*.
[28] For which see Chap. 13 *infra*.
[29] Which is dealt with more fully in paras. 10.74–10.87 *infra*.
[30] The question of "weight" is considered in paras. 1.37–1.43 *infra*.

(3) **Public policy**

There are also other items of evidence which, although no doubt relevant, are denied to the court on general grounds of public policy. Each exclusion proceeds upon its own rationale, and among the more commonly encountered in practice are the following. **1–33**

(a) *Confidentiality*[31]

A witness can be relieved of the duty of answering a particular question or series of questions on the ground that it relates to a matter which is regarded in law as confidential between that witness and someone else. Whether or not the privilege of confidentiality exists, or applies to a particular situation, is a matter of decided public policy.[32] **1–34**

(b) *Crown privilege*[33]

From time to time a Government department or agency will claim that disclosure of certain information, usually contained in a document which one of the parties is attempting to recover, is contrary to the public interest. When successful it results in certain often highly relevant, or even conclusive evidence being denied to the court. In 1992 this issue became the focus of much public concern following the collapse of the highly publicised Matrix Churchill trial. In those proceedings, various businessmen narrowly escaped conviction and likely imprisonment when certain government documents essential to their defence were withheld on the ground of public interest. A wide ranging public enquiry was set up under Lord Justice Scott which considered, *inter alia*, the way in which this privilege should operate.[34] **1–35**

This is not an exhaustive list of examples of relevant evidence being deemed inadmissible, but they are among the most important. They illustrate that there are many areas of the law in this field in which evidence which would otherwise be deemed relevant is excluded from a court. **1–36**

WEIGHT AND SUFFICIENCY OF EVIDENCE

The "weight" of an item of evidence is simply the degree of reliance which the court places upon it. Weight must be distinguished from admissibility of evidence. The latter is a matter for the judge, while the former as a question **1–37**

---

[31] Dealt with in full in Chap. 12 *infra*.
[32] *e.g.* it applies between solicitor and client, but not between doctor and patient.
[33] Dealt with in full in Chap. 12 *infra*.
[34] Report of the Inquiry into the Export of Defence Equipment and Dual-use Goods to Iran, HMSO, 1996, otherwise known as the Scott Report.

of fact is a matter for "the tribunal of fact"[35]. There is no pre-assessment of weight and no legal rules governing it. The tribunal of fact has to assess the evidence for itself, using what one judge[36] described as "rules of common sense." In so doing it has a wide discretion.

1–38   This same guiding principle also underlies the reluctance of appeal courts to interfere with a judgment on purely factual grounds. It is frequently pointed out that since the court of first instance was the only one to see the witnesses, hear their evidence, and observe their demeanour, all inferences from this must be theirs alone. The only time when an appeal court will interfere is where no reasonable court could have reached the conclusion it did on the evidence before it.[37]

1–39   The weight to be attached to a *single* item of evidence, and the weight which is given to a party's entire evidence, are two separate considerations. If at the end of the day a party's case has failed to produce sufficient evidence *as a matter of law* for it to succeed, then the case will be lost. Sufficiency of evidence is a question of law.[38]

1–40   There are many situations in which, as a matter of law, a party's evidence must reach a certain minimum standard of persuasion before it will succeed. It is traditional to refer to such standards of persuasion as being a "sufficiency" of evidence to support a finding by a court.[39] It is possible in certain situations for a party to produce sufficient evidence in law to prove the case, but the other party still succeeds because his or her evidence is more convincing.

1–41   It is also possible for a party to produce the only evidence in a case, and still find that this evidence is *insufficient* in law to justify a decision in their favour. This is what happens in criminal cases when a judge or sheriff rules that there is "no case to answer,"[40] or where a trial judge refuses to allow a

---

[35] *i.e.* the judge, sheriff or magistrate when there is no jury, and the jury when there is. In the case of a tribunal, it will be a majority decision by the members of that tribunal.

[36] Lord Blackburn in *Lord Advocate* v. *Lord Blantyre* (1879) 6 R.(H.L.) 72 at p. 85.

[37] *Thomas* v. *Thomas*, 1947 S.C.(H.L.) 45 at p. 47. For a clear statement of this principle in action in a criminal case, see *Webb* v. *H.M.A.*, 1927 J.C. 92. For recent examples, see *Cocker* v. *Tudhope*, 1987 G.W.D. 4–109 and *Loftus* v. *H.M.A.*, 1987 G.W.D. 5–139. But see also the Criminal Procedure (Scotland) Act 1995, s. 107 which sets out new requirements for leave to appeal in solemn cases. Appellants will need to provide adequate specification of their grounds for appeal in order to obtain leave to appeal.

[38] See, for example, *Donaghy* v. *Normand*, 1992 S.L.T. 666.

[39] Walker and Walker, *op. cit.,* n. 3, p. 402. See, for example, *White* v. *Mackinnon*, 1987 G.W.D. 4–110. For a discussion and application of sufficiency, see *F.* v. *Kennedy*, 1988 S.L.T. 404.

[40] For which see n. 17 *supra*: see *Lockhart* v. *Crockett*, 1987 S.L.T. 551 and *Wallace* v. *McLeod*, 1986 S.C.C.R. 678.

particular point to go to the jury because insufficient evidence has been led to justify it.[41]

Whether or not a party's case is sufficient is a question of law, and more **1–42** than one principle may be involved. It may be, for example, that there is no conviction in a criminal case because there is a lack of corroboration.[42] It may alternatively be the case that a vital ingredient of a party's case in a civil action has not been established,[43] or it may be held that taking a party's case as a whole, an insufficient volume of acceptable evidence has been proved to permit a decision to be made in their favour.

This final possibility introduces the concept of the burden of proof, which **1–43** takes up the next chapter.

---

[41] *e.g.* on an indictment libelling assault to severe injury and to the danger of life, a failure to adduce sufficient evidence to establish that the victim's life was in danger will normally result in the prosecution, at the suggestion of the judge, deleting any reference to danger to life before the charge to the jury: see Renton and Brown, *Criminal Procedure*, para. 10–58.
[42] Corroboration is dealt with in Chap. 7 *infra*.
[43] *e.g.* "failure to take reasonable care" in a reparation action.

CHAPTER 2

BURDENS OF PROOF

INTRODUCTION

2–01 A burden of proof may be defined in general terms as an obligation which rests upon the party who seeks to have a particular issue decided in their favour to adduce sufficient evidence to support their contention. This preliminary definition is deliberately wide because it is required to cover more than one burden of proof.

2–02 There are, in Scots law, two well defined and distinct burdens of proof,[1] namely:

2–03 (i) *the persuasive burden*: the burden of satisfying a court to the appropriate standard of proof on a particular issue; and

2–04 (ii) *the evidential burden*: the burden of adducing enough evidence on a particular issue to warrant the court at least considering it.

2–05 Each of these burdens exists in respect of every issue in a case, is fixed by law, and never shifts from whichever party it is allocated to at the commencement of the hearing. They are, however, vastly different in their purpose and function, and must be considered separately.

THE PERSUASIVE BURDEN

2–06 If party A is asking a court to make a particular finding of fact (*e.g.* that B owes him money) then he must produce some evidence to that effect or he will fail in his action. To this extent, therefore, A clearly carries a burden of proof on that issue. At the same time, if it is B's contention that he did indeed at one time owe A money but has since repaid it, then it is clear that B bears a burden of proof on the separate issue of repayment.

2–07 However, B is under no obligation to begin discharging this burden (*i.e.* to begin leading evidence to show that the debt has been repaid) until A has proved to the satisfaction of the court that the money was "due and resting owing" in the first place—unless of course B has admitted that fact on

---

[1] See Macphail, *Evidence*, Chap. 22.01. The terminology employed is that recommended by him.

record. The two burdens are clearly connected, and occupy sequential positions in the development of the overall action.

On each and *every issue* in a case, there is a burden of proof which **2–08** attaches to one or other of the parties. If no evidence at all is led on that issue, or if the evidence leaves the matter finely balanced, then the party relying on that issue as part of his case will lose, at least on that issue. As was seen in paragraphs 1.13–1.21 *supra*, a legal action, be it civil or criminal, is in effect a series of related issues, and it follows from this that in the course of the trial of any action with more than one issue, these persuasive burdens of proof are distributed among the parties in accordance with the issues raised.

The actual distribution of these burdens in a case, as between the parties, **2–09** is always a matter of law, since it is the substantive law which determines what each party must prove in order to succeed in any given case. Thus in the simple example above, if A wishes to secure decree for the repayment of money due to him, it is incumbent upon him to produce evidence of the existence of the debt. However, even if he does so, he will not obtain decree if the court is satisfied that the money has been repaid, hence the obligation placed upon B to prove repayment once the existence of the debt has been established.

In reality, of course, judgment will be given on the totality of the evidence **2–10** produced, and one would not expect to be able to identify, in the course of the hearing, a moment at which A sits back having discharged his burden and waits for B to set about discharging his. But in the process of coming to a decision, the sheriff or judge will require to analyse the evidence in this way.[2]

In a criminal case, it is now well established that it is for the prosecution **2–11** to prove the guilt of an accused person,[3] and only rarely does the law place upon the accused the obligation to produce exculpatory evidence.[4] On this basis, the burdens of proof on each issue in a criminal case are fairly rigidly distributed, with a high proportion of them resting with the Crown.

In England, these persuasive burdens, allocated as they are by the **2–12** operation of law, are described as "legal burdens."[5] However, this description

---

[2]   See, *e.g.* the analytical approach taken by Lord Denning in *Brown* v. *Rolls Royce*, 1960 S.C.(H.L.) 22 at p. 27.

[3]   This point is fully explained in paras. 2.61–2.78 *infra*.

[4]   Two such exceptions arise in relation to the defences of insanity and diminished responsibility, which are for the accused to prove if he wishes to escape the normal consequences of his criminal actions: see paras. 2.63–2.67 *infra*.

[5]   See Cross and Tapper, *Evidence*, p. 121.

[6]   The existence of more than one burden of proof has been acknowledged only relatively recently in Scotland: see Gordon, "The Burden of Proof on the Accused", 1968 S.L.T. (News) 29. Walker and Walker, *Law of Evidence in Scotland*, Chap. 7 writing in 1964 referred throughout to "the burden of proof" as if there were only one.

has not found favour in Scotland,[6] where the name given to the main burden of proof on each issue is the "persuasive" burden.[7]

2–13   When a party bears the persuasive burden on an issue, he or she must satisfy the court on that issue to the required degree or "standard"[8] of proof, or lose that issue. Whether or not the entire case is then lost depends upon how crucial that issue is to the overall case. As Walker and Walker put it[9]: "if on any issue of fact, no evidence is led, or the evidence leaves the matter in doubt the party upon whom the burden of proof rests has not discharged it, and accordingly fails on that issue."

2–14   A party may fail to discharge the persuasive burden on an issue without any evidence at all having been led in replication by the other party (to counter the evidence already led). This may be, for example, because the evidence is "insufficient"[10] in law, or because it fails to come up to the requisite standard.[11] Alternatively, the party with the persuasive burden may find that the court prefers the evidence of the other party. Or the other party's evidence may have created sufficient doubt on the matter to prevent the party with the persuasive burden from discharging it to the required standard.[12]

THE EVIDENTIAL BURDEN

2–15   As was indicated above, the evidential burden may be defined as the burden of adducing sufficient evidence on a particular issue to allow the court to begin considering it as a live issue.[13] In the example quoted in paragraph 2.06, for instance, A cannot expect the court even to begin considering the possibility that B owes him money unless and until he produces *some* credible evidence of the existence of the debt. Without at least this, his case would be a "non-starter." Once he *has* produced some such evidence, and the court is prepared to consider the possibility that a debt exists, he will hope to go on to reinforce the point with further evidence.

2–16   The same item of evidence may of course achieve both objectives at once, but often a stage can exist in connection with *any* issue at which the court has accepted that some evidence exists, but is looking for more before it will regard the persuasive burden as having been discharged.

---

[7]   See Renton and Brown, *Criminal Procedure*, para. 18–02, and Macphail, *op. cit.,* n. 1, Chap. 22.03. See also Gordon, *op. cit.,* n. 6, p. 29.

[8]   The issue of "standards of proof" is dealt with in paras. 2.102–2.131 *infra.*

[9]   *op. cit.,* p. 65, referring to what they regarded as the only burden of proof, now referred to as the "persuasive" burden; see also *Brown* v. *Rolls Royce*, n. 2 *supra.*

[10]   For the concept of sufficiency, see paras. 1.37–1.43 *supra.*

[11]   The issue of "standards of proof" is dealt with in paras. 2.102–2.131 *infra.*

[12]   A good example of this process is the "reasonable doubt" which many an acquitted person has been able to leave in the minds of the magistrate, sheriff or jury.

[13]   See Macphail, *op. cit.,* n. 1, Chap. 22.01.

The most appropriate description for this second major burden is still **2–17** the "evidential" burden,[14] and it may be more formally defined as the burden of adducing sufficient evidence on an issue to warrant its consideration by a court.[15]

The evidential burden is, like the persuasive burden, fixed by law[16] upon **2–18** a particular party, and the general rule is that the party bearing the persuasive burden on any given issue also bears the evidential burden. This is both logical and just, since one would expect the party who is required to convince the court on a particular issue to have to set the ball rolling, as it were, with some evidence pointing in that direction. However, a special problem is created by the position of an accused in a criminal trial who raises a specific[17] defence.

As will be seen in paragraphs 2.61–2.101 *infra*, it is for the accused to **2–19** discharge the evidential burden on any specific defence which is offered to a charge (*i.e.* any defence other than a general denial of guilt), but thereafter, with the exception of the defences of insanity and diminished responsibility, it is for the Crown to discharge the persuasive burden on that *same* issue. In other words, the evidential and persuasive burdens on, for example, the defence of self-defence are divided between the defence and the prosecution. Once there is *some* credible evidence to suggest that the accused acted in self-defence, it is for the Crown to prove that he or she did not.[18]

The failure to distinguish carefully between the two major burdens in **2–20** cases in which they rest with different parties has led to several successful appeals in criminal cases. Surprisingly, these cases have not resulted in a clear distinction being laid down for future reference,[19] but the distinction between the two burdens has been implicit in each appeal judgment.

For example, in *Campbell* v. *Mackenzie*,[20] the accused in a drink-driving **2–21** case sought to explain away the analyst's certificate showing his blood/

---

[14] A description in general use in England: see Cross and Tapper, *op. cit.*, n. 5, p. 121. Although the existence of this second burden has been recognised in Scotland, and is implicit in several recent criminal appeal judgments (see *Earnshaw* at n. 20 *infra*), the use of the term "evidential burden" seems still to be confined to academic works; see Gordon, *op. cit.*, n. 6, and Renton and Brown, *op. cit.*, n. 7, para. 18–02. See also Macphail, *op. cit.*, n. 1, Chap. 22.01 and 22.03.

[15] Or, in the words of Sheriff Macphail: "The burden of adducing sufficient evidence to require an issue to be considered by the trier of fact when he comes to decide whether the legal burden has been discharged" (*op. cit.*, n. 1, Chap. 22.01).

[16] For discussion of the actual distribution, or "incidence," of the burdens of proof, see paras. 2.45–2.101 *infra*.

[17] *N.B.* not necessarily a "special" defence, for which see paras. 2.68–2.73 *infra*.

[18] See *Lambie* v. *H.M.A.* at n. 69 *infra*. Note that this evidence need not necessarily come from the accused or the defence witnesses, but may come from the prosecution evidence: see *Ritchie* v. *Pirie*, at n.21 *infra*.

[19] Nor have the terms "persuasive" and "evidential" been attached to these burdens.

[20] 1981 S.C.C.R. 341; see also *Earnshaw* v. *H.M.A.*, 1981 S.C.C.R. 279, and *McGregor* v. *Jessop*, 1988 S.L.T. 719.

alcohol level to be higher than that permitted by law at the time of the taking of the sample. He claimed that he had consumed enough alcohol between the time of his driving and the taking of the sample to account for the excess reading. The sheriff ruled that since it was the accused who was raising the "defence" of post-accident drinking, it was for him to prove it on a balance of probabilities—the appropriate standard of proof for an accused who bears the persuasive burden on an issue. On appeal, although the conviction was upheld on other grounds, it was clearly pointed out that in such cases, once the accused has raised the issue (*i.e.* discharged the evidential burden) it is for the Crown to disprove it beyond reasonable doubt (*i.e.* to discharge the persuasive burden).

2–22 In an earlier case on the same point,[21] Lord Justice-Clerk Wheatley had made it clear that the sort of evidence required to raise such a defence, which the Crown then have to disprove beyond reasonable doubt, can come from any source, and not necessarily the accused. In his words:

> "The onus of proving the case beyond reasonable doubt rests with the prosecution, and remains on the prosecution throughout, and whether that has been done depends upon all the evidence before the court, whether adduced by the prosecution or by the defence, and on the view which the court takes of it."[22]

2–23 In short, the persuasive burden of convincing the court on the issue of a defence raised by an accused (other than insanity or diminished responsibility) rests with the Crown, but not until some evidence has been adduced which might suggest such a defence. Since this evidence is, however, hardly likely to come from the prosecution witnesses,[23] it is incumbent upon the accused to provide the evidence. In this respect the accused bears the evidential burden—and *only* the evidential burden—on the issue of a specific defence. The Crown bear the responsibility for discharging the persuasive burden beyond reasonable doubt and in the process of doing so would need to negate the issues raised by the accused.

2–24 The evidential burden is therefore simply the burden of ensuring that enough evidence is before the court to allow it to consider the issue at all. Such evidence will normally come from the party bearing the evidential burden, but it need not, even in a criminal case.

THE TACTICAL BURDEN

2–25 As has been seen, the two major burdens—the persuasive and evidential burdens—may be said to apply to each and every issue in a case, and to be

---

[21] *Ritchie* v. *Pirie*, 1972 J.C. 7; see also *Tudhope* v. *Miller*, 1978 J.C. 26.
[22] *ibid.*, at p. 17.
[23] Although if it did, it would have precisely the same effect, *per Ritchie, supra.*

fixed as a matter of law.[24] In particular, they do not shift from one party to another in the course of hearing the evidence on a particular issue. The party who bears the persuasive burden on an issue at the outset will still bear it at the close of the evidence. The party who bears the evidential burden on that same issue (usually, as noted in paragraph 2.18 *supra*, the party bearing the persuasive burden) will have discharged it once that issue is being actively considered by the court.

However, most cases consist of more than one issue,[25] and the persuasive **2–26** burdens on these issues may well be allocated between the parties in a sequential pattern. Taking the original example of a simple debt action by A against B, it will be recalled that B's obligation to begin proving that the debt was in fact repaid did not arise until A had adduced some evidence of the existence of the debt. It may well be, for reasons stated earlier, that this evidence may not of itself win the case for A, or indeed even prove to the appropriate standard of proof that the debt ever existed.[26] However, once A has discharged the evidential burden on the issue of the existence of the debt, B would need to counter with evidence that the debt is in fact discharged by repayment. B may not necessarily lose the case if he does not, but prudence suggests that he should.

The procedure adopted in the Scottish courts does not reveal this process **2–27** very clearly. Each party leads his witnesses in turn, and each in turn is open to cross-examination, until at the end of the hearing the court is left with a mixture of conflicting testimonies which it then has to untangle and assess. Neither an impartial observer, nor indeed the lawyers on either side, could identify the moment at which party B in the example given would need to begin leading evidence of his own.[27] Nevertheless the court, when assessing the evidence as a whole, will very often require to establish whether or not issue X has been established before being obliged to go on to consider issue Y.

---

[24] In the manner explained in paras. 2.45–2.101 *infra*.

[25] For example, in a criminal case, in which it is well established that the prosecution must prove the accused's guilt beyond reasonable doubt, it is incumbent upon the Crown to prove both the *actus reus* and *mens rea*. Most forms of *actus reus* involve more than one issue (*e.g.* the accused's presence at the locus, his actions, his subsequent possession of incriminating items *etc.*). In civil cases the persuasive burden is normally only relevant when the court is unable to make up its mind on an issue: *Thomas v. Thomas* 1947 S.C.(H.L.) 45.

[26] *i.e.* A may fail to discharge the persuasive burden on that issue.

[27] The introduction of a plea of "no case to answer" in both solemn and summary criminal proceedings (under s. 19 of the Criminal Justice (Scotland) Act 1980) and now contained in ss. 97 and 160 of the Criminal Procedure (Scotland) Act 1995 for solemn and summary proceedings respectively), has, however, made it possible for the defence lawyers in criminal cases to ascertain whether or not the Crown has discharged the evidential burdens on the crucial issues, thus requiring the accused to lead evidence in his own defence.

2–28   For this reason, it is sometimes asserted that once A has established a particular issue "the burden of proof shifts" to B. This misleading statement may be challenged on more than one ground, but in particular it fails to indicate *which* burden, and it suggests that a burden which is fixed by law can transfer to another party. If it is accepted that each issue carries with it its own persuasive and evidential burdens which are fixed from the outset,[28] then neither of these may be said to "shift".

2–29   And yet, clearly, something significant happens once party A discharges either of the burdens on an issue and requires B to lead evidence in replication. It places what might be termed a "tactical" obligation on B to begin leading some evidence of his own, or run the risk that the court will be persuaded by the unchallenged evidence it has heard. As Lord Justice-Clerk Grant put it in *McIlhargey* v. *Herron*[29] explaining a principle equally applicable to a civil action:

> "I am not … suggesting that any fact in a criminal prosecution can be established merely by failure to cross examine, and there are many cases where wise defending counsel asks as few questions in cross as possible. On the other hand, the silent defender does take a risk, and, if he fails to challenge evidence given by witnesses for the Crown by cross-examination or, in addition, by leading substantive evidence in support of his challenge, he cannot complain if the Court not merely accepts that unchallenged evidence but also, in the light of all the circumstances, draws from it the most unfavourable and adverse inferences to the defence that it is capable of supporting."[30]

2–30   In many cases, all that party B requires to do once party A appears to have discharged the evidential burden on an issue is to cross-examine so as to challenge, contradict or weaken that evidence, *i.e.* to take action so as to prevent A from discharging the persuasive burden on the *same* issue. On other occasions, however, his only course of action is to introduce another issue entirely (on which he will normally bear both the evidential and persuasive burdens) which will neutralise the issue which A has raised. Once A has discharged the persuasive burden on his issue, this is the *only* course of action which B can take.

2–31   Thus, in the example quoted, once A has produced evidence of the existence of the debt, B has no interest in denying that the debt existed.[31]

---

[28]   This suggestion is justified by reference to authority, in paras. 2.45–2.101 *infra*.
[29]   1972 J.C. 38.
[30]   *ibid.*, at p. 42; see also *O'Donnell* v. *Murdoch Mackenzie & Co.*, 1967 S.C.(H.L.) 63, in which the opinion was given that when a defender in a civil case calls no evidence, only the most favourable inferences should be drawn from the pursuer's evidence. This principle was also followed in *Davidson* v. *Duncan*, 1981 S.C. 83.
[31]   And, in practice, may well have admitted it on record.

He is more interested in proving that it has been repaid. He therefore leaves the first issue alone, and begins leading evidence of the repayment, which A in his turn must counter if he wishes to win the case. What is being observed in such a situation is a succession of *different* issues (which may not, of course, be presented to the court in quite such a tidy sequence). When one issue is succeeded by another on which a different party bears the burdens, it is indeed tempting to speak of a "shifting" of the burden of proof. And if one is referring simply to what one might call the "tactical burden,"[32] then undeniably something is shifting between one party and another in the sense that "if the trial were to stop at any particular time the jury would be entitled, and indeed likely, to find for one side, and ... if the other side wish to avoid such a finding it behoves them to produce counter evidence."[33]

Put in such a way, the concept of a "shifting" of a burden is harmless **2–32** enough. Unfortunately, until fairly recently Scots law recognised only one burden of proof, namely what was identified in paragraphs 2.06–2.14 *supra* as the persuasive burden, and there is a danger that any reference to a shifting of "the" burden of proof will be taken to mean a shift in the persuasive burden.[34]

Nor is this an imaginary danger. In *Tallis* v. *H.M.A.*[35] the trial sheriff **2–33** directed the jury in the following terms:

> "the situation may arise, ladies and gentlemen, that the Crown puts forward such a strong case that it is only if you are satisfied with the explanation given by the accused, that you would be entitled to acquit him and again that may very well be the situation here you feel, but again it is a matter for you to make up your minds about, ladies and gentlemen."[36]

On appeal, it was said of this charge that it was a "serious misdirection in law," in that it was a "plain indication to the jury that in certain circumstances the onus of proof shifts to the accused and unless he can discharge it by an explanation which satisfies the jury, *i.e.* of his innocence, then conviction must follow."

---

[32] A term recognised under English law; see Cross and Tapper *op. cit.*, n. 5, p. 127, where it is also described as a provisional burden. See also its use by Gordon, *op. cit.*, n. 6 at p. 37.

[33] Gordon, *op. cit.*, n. 6, at p. 37.

[34] See Macphail, *op. cit.*, n. 1, Chap. 22.03 who acknowledges this problem and does not use the term. Also, Walker and Walker, *op. cit.*, n. 6, paras. 77–79.

[35] 1982 S.C.C.R. 91. See similarly, *McDonald* v. *H.M.A.*, 1989 S.C.C.R. 559 where a conviction was quashed after a sheriff suggested in his charge to the jury that, in relation to the doctrine of recent possession, it was for the accused to prove his or her innocence. As to the need for precision in explaining the burden of proof to a jury, see *Craddock* v. *H.M.A.*, 1994 S.L.T. 454.

[36] *Tallis supra*, at p. 99.

2–34   As will be seen in paragraphs 2.63–2.67 *infra*, the only common law circumstances in which any persuasive burden (which was the "onus" referred to in *Tallis*) rests with the accused, arise when he himself raises the defence of either insanity or diminished responsibility. On all other issues in a criminal trial, the persuasive burdens rest and remain with the Crown. At no stage, and in no circumstances can this burden ever shift to the accused, and if at the end of the day the court has any reasonable doubt, that doubt must work in favour of the accused and lead to an acquittal because the Crown have failed to discharge the persuasive burden. This was the fatal error which the sheriff made in *Tallis*, in assuming that the force of the Crown evidence could in some way transfer the persuasive burden to the accused, so that it was suddenly for him to prove his innocence.

2–35   At the same time, it must be recognised that any accused who remains silent in the face of cogent Crown evidence enhances the chances of conviction, because "the silent defender does take a risk."[37] What shifts to the accused once the Crown have produced a strong case against him, is of course the *tactical* burden of explaining it away. If the accused fails to rise to the challenge, then he has failed to prevent the Crown from discharging the persuasive burden. This is because "there are certain cases in which the proved facts may raise a presumption of guilt, and in which, in the absence of some explanation by the person accused—where the person accused is the one person who can know the real truth—a jury may be entitled to proceed to draw an inference of guilt".[38]

2–36   In the case from which this excerpt from the charge to the jury is taken, the accused was convicted of a fraudulent attempt to pose as the husband of a deceased lady whose estate was to be distributed, claiming that he had married her some years earlier in a form of ceremony witnessed by certain named persons. He failed to call any of these persons as witnesses, and he chose not to give evidence himself, and it is hardly surprising that the Crown succeeded in discharging the persuasive burden. In this case too, Lord Justice-Clerk Aitchison said (in relation to the standard of proof), "If an explanation had been given, it might have thrown doubt upon the Crown case—it might have satisfied you or it might have made you think that it was unsafe to find the case established...."[39]

2–37   As will be seen in paragraph 3.01, a party to a case (even a criminal case) may be relieved of the need to lead any further evidence on an issue

---

[37] *McIlhargey, supra,* at p. 42.

[38] Lord Justice-Clerk Aitchison in *H.M.A.* v. *Hardy*, 1938 J.C. 144, this passage was approved in *Mochan* v. *Herron*, 1972 S.L.T. 218, in which the sheriff, in his stated case to the High Court, added at p. 219: "If the appellant had an innocent explanation he was fully entitled to exercise his right to remain silent about it, in which case, however, I could see no objection to the court drawing its own conclusion from such evidence as was before it, which is what I did." The conviction was upheld.

[39] *H.M.A.* v. *Hardy supra,* at p. 147.

because of the operation of a presumption. All that this means is that the presumption takes the place of any further evidence which might have been required to be led, and places a tactical burden on the other party to counter the effect of that presumption with evidence of his own. For example, as was seen in Chapter 1, an accused who is found in possession of recently stolen property in "criminative" circumstances, and is charged with theft has, in most cases, a good deal of explaining to do if he is to avoid a conviction. But this does not mean that the traditional burden that rests upon the Crown to prove the guilt of the accused beyond reasonable doubt has suddenly transformed itself into a burden on the accused to prove his innocence. It simply means that if the accused does not come up with something convincing, the prosecution will have had their work done for them by the presumption.[40] The burden of proof has not shifted—it is simply about to be discharged, unless the accused produces some evidence of his own to explain his possession in non-criminative terms.

The distinction between the persuasive burden (borne throughout by the Crown except in the exceptional cases already noted and the statutory situations referred to *infra*) and the tactical burden which a strong Crown case places on an accused person, is far from a mere academic one when there exists at the end of the day a "reasonable" doubt. However miserably an accused person otherwise fails to discharge the tactical burden, he must be acquitted if there is such a doubt, because the persuasive burden has not been discharged by the Crown. However much the prosecution strive to discharge the persuasive burden, the accused must still be acquitted if, from whatever source, there appears a reasonable doubt, even if the accused remains positively mute from the start of the trial to its conclusion. **2–38**

In distinguishing between the persuasive and tactical burdens, and in arguing that the persuasive burden on an issue never shifts from one party to another, the examples have so far been taken from criminal law, because it is in this context that the greatest danger lies in confusing the two. But the problem can also arise under civil law, where a failure to allocate correctly a persuasive burden at the end of the evidence (*i.e.* by mistakenly believing that it has somehow shifted to the other party) can clearly result in injustice. **2–39**

In *Brown* v. *Rolls Royce*[41] the pursuer had worked for the defenders as a machine-oiler, during the course of which he had contracted industrial dermatitis. He claimed damages for negligence, based on the fact that the employers had not provided him with the same barrier cream which other employers supplied in similar circumstances. The employers admitted this fact, but claimed in replication that they had been persuaded by medical **2–40**

---

[40] In the present example, of guilt, arising from the circumstances of possession.
[41] 1960 S.C.(H.L.) 22.

advice that the barrier cream in question was not effective. They further claimed that the provision of good washing facilities, which they had made available, was an effective precaution against dermatitis.

2–41   The defenders lost their case at first instance and the employers appealed to the Court of Session. They won by a majority ruling after a dissension among their Lordships as to where "the burden of proof" rested. The employee then appealed to the House of Lords, who upheld the Court of Session judgment, but Lord Denning had much to say about their approach to the question of the burden of proof, namely that:

> "This difference of opinion shows how important it is to distinguish between a *legal* burden[42] properly so called, which is imposed by the law itself, and a *provisional* burden[43] which is raised by the state of the evidence. The legal burden in this case was imposed by law on the pursuer. In order to succeed, he had to prove that the defenders were negligent, and that their negligence caused the disease ... In order to discharge the burden of proving negligence, the pursuer proved that 'barrier cream was commonly supplied by employers to men doing such work as the pursuer was doing.' This was a cogent piece of evidence and raised no doubt a 'presumption' or a '*prima facie*' case, in this sense, that if nothing more appeared, the Court might well infer that the defenders were negligent, and in that sense it put a burden on the defenders to answer it. But this was only a provisional burden which was raised by the state of the evidence as it then stood. The defenders might answer it by argument, as indeed they did ... In this way, a provisional burden may shift from one party to the other as the case proceeds or may remain suspended between them. But it has no compelling force. At the end of the day the Court has to ask itself—not whether the provisional burden is discharged—but whether the legal burden has been discharged, that is to say: Has the pursuer proved that the defenders were negligent?"[44]

2–42   The effect of the tactical burden in civil cases is well illustrated by the facts of *Inglis* v. *L.M.S.*,[45] a case in which the parents of a young boy sued a railway company for negligence in causing his death. It was proved for the pursuers that the boy had fallen through the door of a moving train, and that there had been no interference with the door handle by either the boy or any other of the passengers in the carriage. In awarding damages to the pursuers, the court found that once the facts were proved, the onus transferred

---

[42] *i.e.* The term in English law for the persuasive burden.
[43] *i.e.* The term in English law for the tactical burden.
[44] *ibid.*, at pp. 27–28.
[45] 1941 S.C. 551, in which the burden was never referred to as such. See paras. 3.120–3.130 *infra* for the issues of *res ipsa loquitur* which this case raised.

to the defenders in the sense that it was for them to acquit themselves of the inference that the door had been insecurely fastened when it left the station.[46] The suggestion was that the railway company had been negligent, a fact already prima facie proved by the pursuers' evidence, and confirmed by the defenders' silence on the matter. It was, in the terminology we have adopted, always for the pursuers to discharge the persuasive burden, but their evidence had passed a tactical burden to the defenders which they had then failed to discharge.

By remaining silent, the defenders had allowed the pursuers' **2–43** interpretation of events to seem the more probable, so that the latter were able to discharge the persuasive burden on a balance of probabilities, the standard applicable in a civil case. There was never any question of that burden shifting from the pursuers to the defenders. If, at the end of the evidence, the defenders' version of the facts had seemed more probable, or the pursuers' evidence had been insufficient to tip the scales of probability, then the pursuers would have lost.

When, therefore one speaks of a "shifting" of a burden during the course **2–44** of a trial, be it civil or criminal, one is referring, not to either the persuasive or evidential burdens, which are fixed by law on the parties to whom they are allocated, but to the tactical burden which arises once party A has adduced sufficient evidence to make it at least a possibility that the court will find in his favour on the case as a whole unless party B produces some contradictory evidence of his own.

THE INCIDENCE OF THE BURDENS OF PROOF IN CIVIL CASES

The "incidence" of the burdens of proof is the term used to describe the **2–45** way in which the two major burdens which were identified in paragraphs 2.02–2.04 *supra* are allocated between the parties to the case. Bearing in mind that each case will normally consist of more than one issue, and that the burdens of proof fall to be allocated on each and every issue, the following rules may be observed in civil cases. Criminal cases are dealt with in paragraphs 2.61–2.101 *infra*.

Although the point may sometimes be confused by requirements of court **2–46** practice and procedure,[47] the general rule with respect to both the persuasive and evidential burdens of proof, is this. The burdens rest with the party who will lose on that issue if no other evidence is led,[48] or if at the end of the day there is an equal balance in the persuasiveness of the evidence led

---

[46] *ibid.*, Lord Moncrieff at p.563.
[47] Particularly, *e.g.* on the question of which party should begin leading evidence first. See below and Maxwell, *The Practice of the Court of Session*, p. 264, and Macphail, *Sheriff Court Practice*, paras. 8.56–7.
[48] Walker and Walker, *op. cit.*, n. 6, para. 75, quoting Dickson, *Evidence*, para. 25.

by both parties on that issue. This is another way of saying that the party who raises an issue must prove it. In the earlier example, A, who asserts that B owes him money, must produce the necessary evidence of this, and therefore the persuasive and evidential burdens on this issue rest with him.

2–47   To this extent, therefore, it ought to be possible in a civil action to examine the closed record, list the remaining live issues,[49] and allocate the burdens of proof according to which party is making which assertion. It is, regrettably, not always as simple as this.

2–48   In some cases, for example, a party appears to be asserting a negative (*e.g.* that the defender has failed to honour a contract, or that the pursuer failed to take reasonable care for his own safety) and it can seem that a party is being asked to prove a negative. However, if it is "the substance and not the grammar,"[50] which is considered such averments are positive and not negative.

2–49   For example, in order to show that the pursuer in a negligence action failed to take reasonable care for his own safety (the essence of a defence of "contributory negligence") the defender will require to produce positive evidence of the pursuer's behaviour. This might be a failure to follow safety procedures, or failure to look both ways at a road crossing. A party cannot transfer a burden of proof simply by employing some ingenious device of the English language to convert a positive averment into a negative one. For this reason, an averment, whether phrased in the positive or the negative, will normally impose the burdens of proof on the party making it.

2–50   The incidence of the burdens of proof can also sometimes be obscured by a procedural ruling which requires one of the parties to lead his evidence first. The general rule[51] is that in the absence of any specific interlocutor before proof it is for the pursuer to lead. This reflects the fact that in most cases the pursuer must discharge the burdens of proof on at least some of his averments before the defender is required to prove anything. Thus, in the original example, A had to prove the existence of the debt before B was required to prove that it had in fact been repaid. There will be occasions, however, when the defender should lead,[52] if for example an issue has been raised on the record which if proved, would end the case without the need to hear evidence from the pursuer. In such a case the burdens of proof remain where the averments have placed them—it is simply the case that the court has altered the order in which the parties set about discharging them.

---

[49] *i.e.* those not admitted on the record.
[50] Walker and Walker, *op. cit.,* n. 6.
[51] For which see MacLaren, *Court of Session Practice*, p. 554, Maxwell, *op. cit.*, n. 47, Dobie, *Sheriff Court Practice*, p. 182, and Macphail, *loc.cit.*
[52] This may have important implications for the conduct of the proof.

Another problem surrounds the operation of presumptions.[53] These have **2–51** the effect of relieving a party of the need to prove anything further once the facts upon which a presumption is based have been established. If the facts upon which the presumption is based are admitted on the record, it is for the party against whom that presumption operates to lead evidence immediately so as to counter its effect. This may well create the impression that the burden of proof has somehow shifted to that party. However, for reasons explained in paragraphs 2.25–2.44 *supra*, this is not the case. It is simply that the party making use of the presumption has employed it in the discharge of the burdens. This places a tactical burden upon the other party to lead evidence in replication, and to lead off with his or her witnesses. Exactly the same process obtains when, in the absence of any presumption, the opponent simply admits certain facts on the record, thus relieving the asserting party of the burden of proving them. Also, where two presumptions conflict, it will be the party who seeks to overcome the stronger of the two presumptions who will be required to bear the burdens of proof.[54]

The position may also be complicated by the operation of a statute, which **2–52** may, for defined and limited purposes, allocate the burdens of proof. For example, section 30(2) of the Bills of Exchange Act 1882[55] states that once it is proved that the acceptance, issue or subsequent negotiation of a bill is affected by fraud, duress, force and fear or illegality, then the burden of proof is upon the "holder" to show that, subsequent to the incident complained of, value in good faith has been given for the bill. This is in contrast to the normal position, under which the holder is presumed to be the "holder in due course" (*i.e.* to have taken the bill in good faith and for value) until the contrary is proved.[56]

Similarly, a statute may provide that a court must be "satisfied" that a **2–53** particular event happened, or that a particular state of affairs exists, or alternatively that such an issue must "appear to the court" to be so. In such a case the burdens of proof fall upon the party who is relying on, or asserting, the point.

For example, in *Kerrigan* v. *Nelson*[57] the court was considering the effect **2–54** of a section in the Rent and Mortgage Interest Restrictions (Amendment)

---

[53] Dealt with in full in Chap. 3, *infra*.

[54] See *Penman* v. *White*, 1957 S.C. 338, a case involving the presumption against donation.

[55] One of several sections in this Act which reallocate the persuasive burden, see also ss. 13, 21(2) and (3), 32(5), 63(3) and 65(4).

[56] See generally, Gloag and Henderson, *Introduction to the Law of Scotland*, para. 23.18.

[57] 1946 S.C. 388; for other examples of the same process see *McLaughlin* v. *Caledonia Stevedoring Co.*, 1938 S.C.(H.L.) 31, *Moore* v. *Harland & Wolff*, 1937 S.C. 707 and *McCallum* v. *Arthur*, 1955 S.C. 188.

Act 1933[58] which entitled a court to grant an ejectment order against a domestic tenant where it could be shown that the landlord reasonably required the premises for his own occupation, but which contained a proviso which prevented the court from issuing such an order where "the Court is satisfied" that greater hardship would be created by granting the order than by refusing it. It was held that the "onus of proof" (*i.e.* the persuasive burden) on the issue of greater hardship rested with the tenant.

2–55   Finally, there is the problem posed by statutory sections which create a right, or establish some other position, but subject to some proviso, excuse, exemption or qualification. As will emerge below, the position in criminal cases would appear to be that it is for the person relying on such a proviso, etc., to prove that it applies to him. The position is not authoritatively settled under civil law, partly because of conflicting early dicta,[59] but in the most recent case on the point, it seems to have been taken for granted that the principle applies equally in civil cases.

2–56   In *Nimmo* v. *Alexander Cowan & Sons Ltd*[60] the House of Lords was considering, for the purposes of an accident claim by a papermill worker, the effect of section 29(1) of the Factories Act 1961, which requires that every place at which any person has to work shall be kept safe "so far as is reasonably practicable." It was held that it was for the defender to aver, and subsequently to prove, that the premises were so safe once the pursuer had shown that they were not safe in general terms, since the effect of the words quoted was to create a qualification which it is for the employer to bring himself within. In the course of what was in fact a dissenting judgment on other grounds, Lord Wilberforce referred to "the orthodox principle (common to both the criminal and the civil law) that exceptions, etc., are to be set up by those who rely on them."[61]

2–57   So far it has been assumed that the party bearing the persuasive burden will also bear the evidential burden, and in the vast majority of cases this will be so, since the party who will lose an issue if no evidence is led is logically the one who should begin leading it. However, in certain exceptional cases, what are essentially practical considerations may dictate that the two burdens be separated.

2–58   The only clear example of this process arises in those cases in which a fact which requires proof one way or the other lies exclusively (or, to use

---

[58] A similar rule to which may now be found in the Rent (Scotland) Act 1984 s. 11(3) and Sched. 2, Pts. I and III.

[59] Notably those in *Coul* v. *Ayr County Council*, 1909 S.C. 422 at p. 424, and *Brydon* v. *Railway Executive*, 1957 S.C. 282 at p. 290.

[60] 1967 S.C.(H.L.) 79.

[61] *ibid.*, at p. 109. See also Macphail, *Evidence*, Chap. 22.28, in which he calls for clarification on the point for the purposes of the civil law. The Scottish Law Commission, Memo. No. 46, para. V.13, rejected this proposal, recommending that each statute should be interpreted according to its own wording.

the accepted legal term, "peculiarly") within the knowledge of one of the parties. In such a case, although it will require very little evidence to enable a party without the knowledge to place a burden on the party with such knowledge, the former still bears the initial burden of leading evidence. This seems, from the few decided cases on the subject, to be a rare exception to the general rule that the party bearing the persuasive burden on an issue also bears the evidential burden on that same issue.

In *McClure, Naismith, Brodie and Macfarlane* v. *Stewart*[62] a solicitor **2–59** was asked by a client to secure a loan on a patent he was taking out. The solicitor had another client who was persuaded to lend £5,000 on the patent, which was then found to be invalid because it had been anticipated. The creditor client sued the solicitor concerned, alleging that the solicitor had known of the invalidity of the patent, but had failed to communicate that fact to him in time.

It was held that where one party (in this case the creditor) is obliged to **2–60** make a negative averment (*i.e.* the failure to communicate with him), the proof or otherwise of which lies peculiarly within the knowledge of the other party (*i.e.* the solicitor), then that other party, who is asserting the affirmative, must prove it. But he is not obliged to do this unless and until the party asserting the negative has at least produced some evidence (in this case that he had received no communication from the solicitor). This is another way of saying that the persuasive burden on the issue (in this case the issue of communication) rests with the person with the knowledge of the facts, but he is not obliged to begin discharging it until the party without the knowledge has discharged the evidential burden.[63]

THE INCIDENCE OF THE BURDENS OF PROOF IN CRIMINAL CASES

(1) **General rule**

The general rule concerning the incidence of the burdens of proof in a **2–61** criminal case was succinctly and authoritatively stated by Lord Justice-Clerk Thomson in *Mackenzie* v. *H.M.A.*[64] as being that: "The presumption of innocence is a fundamental tenet of our criminal procedure. It follows that the burden of proof rests on the Crown to displace this presumption." This is essentially another way of saying that the Crown bear both the persuasive and evidential burdens on every issue in a case which tends to

---

[62] (1887) 15 R.(H.L.) 1.
[63] See also *Cruickshank* v. *Smith*, 1949 J.C. 134 at pp. 151–152. The significance of these cases is not, of course, that the pursuer is asserting a negative, but that the facts are almost exclusively within the knowledge of the defender. See also *Burns* v. *Royal Hotel (St Andrews) Ltd.*, 1958 S.C. 354.
[64] 1959 J.C. 32 at pp. 36–37.

prove the guilt of the accused of the crime(s) libelled in the complaint or indictment.

2–62   These burdens remain with the Crown throughout the trial, and virtually never shift to the accused,[65] which is why at the end of the trial any "reasonable doubt" which remains in the minds of the jury or sheriff must be exercised in favour of the accused.[66] However, the position is confused by the existence of various exceptions to the general rule. They fall into three main categories which to a greater or lesser extent place a burden on the accused. These categories are the special defences of insanity and diminished responsibility; other special defences; and certain statutory provisions.

(2) **Insanity and diminished responsibility**

2–63   Insanity and diminished responsibility are known in criminal law as special defences. It has been firmly established at least since the days of Hume[67] that when an accused person seeks to assert that he was insane at the time of the offence,[68] the persuasive burden of proof is upon him. So also is the evidential burden, although there may of course be sufficient evidence of the accused's insanity from other sources to discharge this burden.

2–64   The clearest modern statement of the law on this point is that of Lord Justice-Clerk Thomson in *H.M.A.* v. *Mitchell*,[69] who directed a jury in the following terms: "There is a special defence in this case, and the special defence is that at the time of the act charged the accused was insane and not responsible for his actions, and you have got to consider then … whether this defence is made out … on this issue the burden of proof is on the defence, because in our law there is a presumption that a man is sane."[70]

2–65   There remains, however, the problem situation (albeit a fairly rare one) in which the sanity of an accused is questioned by the Crown. This could happen, for example, if the accused has raised a defence of diminished responsibility, and the Crown wish to counter it by asserting that in fact the accused should be committed to a mental hospital.[71] There is no clear and

---

[65] See, *e.g.* Lord Justice-General Normand's judgment in *Lennie* v. *H.M.A.*, 1946 J.C. 79 at p. 80. See also *Owens* v. *H.M.A.*, 1946 J.C. 119, and Renton and Brown, *op. cit.*, n. 7, para. 18–02. *N.B.* also *Tallis* v. *H.M.A.* in para. 2.33 *supra*.

[66] As explained in paras. 2.102–2.107 *infra*.

[67] I, 43.

[68] The same rule would seem to apply to insanity in bar of trial, which is a procedural matter outwith the scope of this book; see Renton and Brown, *op. cit.*, n. 7, para. 20–05.

[69] 1951 J.C. 53 at pp. 53–54; see also *Lambie* v. *H.M.A.*, 1973 J.C. 53 at p. 58.

[70] No significance should be attached to the fact that insanity is a "special" defence, since it is "special" only in procedural terms.

[71] For which procedure see Renton and Brown, *op. cit.*, n. 7, para. 20–17.

authoritative ruling on this point, but dicta and commentary suggest that the persuasive burden of proving insanity in such a case will rest with the Crown.[72]

Despite the historical and procedural differences between insanity and **2–66** diminished responsibility,[73] the latter has always been regarded as a form of "partial insanity"[74] and it makes sense that the evidential implications of a plea of diminished responsibility should be the same as those for insanity. Thus in *Carraher* v. *H.M.A.*[75] Lord Russell directed the jury that: "If the Crown have established here that the accused did this thing ... it is not for the Crown to go further and show that the accused was fully responsible for what he did. It is for the accused to make good his defence of partial irresponsibility . ."

In other words, the persuasive burden on the issue of diminished **2–67** responsibility is upon the accused, as also is the evidential burden. This is in the sense that it will normally be for the accused to raise enough of a suggestion that he was not fully responsible for his actions to warrant the judge leaving that possibility for the jury's consideration.

(3) **Special defences**

The special rules applicable to insanity defences have already been **2–68** examined. The remaining "special defences", as they are called, are alibi, self-defence and incrimination (impeachment).[76]

A number of cases, in particular, *Lennie* v. *H.M.A.*,[77] *Owens* v. *H.M.A.*[78] **2–69** and *H.M.A.* v. *Cunningham*,[79] have created confusion in this area and it is important to keep in mind the context in which such defences are regarded as "special." In *Lambie* v. *H.M.A.*,[80] Lord Justice-General Emslie stated that "The only purpose of the special defence is to give fair notice to the

---

[72] See Macphail, *op. cit.,* n. 61, Chap. 22.06, quoting *H.M.A.* v. *Harrison* (1968) 32 J.C.L. 119, and The Scottish Law Commission, Memo. 46, para. V.03. For a discussion of the standard and onus of proof in a plea of insanity in bar of trial see *Jessop* v. *Robertson,* 1989 S.C.C.R. 600.

[73] For which see Gordon, *Criminal Law*, Chap. 11.

[74] And was described as such in *H.M.A.* v. *Braithwaite*, 1945 J.C. 55. Alison described a person suffering from diminished responsibility as being "partially deranged" (I, 652).

[75] 1946 J.C. 108 at pp.112–113. This passage was adopted in *Braithwaite, supra*. The categories of special defences are probably now closed, Renton and Brown, *op. cit.,* n. 7, and *Sorley* v. *H.M.A.,* 1992 S.L.T. 867.

[76] See Renton and Brown, *op. cit.,* n. 7, para. 7–21. Since *H.M.A.* v. *Cunningham*, 1963 J.C. 80 it is assumed that somnambulism is no longer (if it ever was) a special defence, and as such belongs in the category of "specific" defences referred to *infra*. Similarly, automatism is not a special defence: *Ross* v. *H.M.A.*, 1991 S.L.T. 564.

[77] 1946 J.C. 79.

[78] 1946 J.C. 119.

[79] 1963 J.C. 80.

[80] 1973 J.C. 53 at pp. 58–59.

Crown and once such notice has been given the only issue for a jury is to decide, upon the whole evidence before them, whether the Crown has established the accused's guilt beyond reasonable doubt."

2–70   *Lambie* was a classic example of a potentially fatal misdirection to a jury on the subject of the special defence. The defence in question was incrimination, and although the trial judge made it clear to the jury that the Crown were required to prove the accused's guilt, he withdrew the special defence from them on the ground that it was not supported by corroborated evidence.[81]

2–71   The misunderstanding arose from a long–established practice of regarding the special defence, (i) as a defence in itself, which it was for the accused to prove; and (ii) as a possible source of "reasonable doubt" which might lead to an acquittal. Whatever historical reasons there may have been for such a distinction,[82] at the end of the day the accused requires only a reasonable doubt to secure an acquittal, and it is misleading and potentially dangerous to direct a jury in terms which suggest that the accused must bear the persuasive burden of proof on a special defence. As Gordon put it,[83] when referring to special defences: "their being special has nothing to do with the question of their proof: a defence is not made special in order to confer on the accused the privilege of persuading the jury of its truth; it is made special in order to confer on the Crown the right to object to evidence being led about it without prior notice."

2–72   Unfortunately the appeal court in *Lambie* did not refer as such to the evidential and persuasive burdens, but the authoritative opinions which followed this case take from it the conclusion that the special defence has no special evidential implications, and that therefore, as with all "specific" defences raised by an accused (*i.e.* defences which are something more than a flat denial of guilt), the evidential burden rests with him, but that once he has discharged that burden, it is for the prosecution to disprove the defence he raises, *i.e.* to discharge the persuasive burden on that issue. Thus, to quote Renton and Brown:

> "There is no duty on the prosecution to refute any specific defence until it is raised in evidence by the accused or arises out of the evidence led for the Crown, but once a specific defence, whether or not technically 'special,' has been raised, it is for the prosecution to exclude it beyond reasonable doubt. The only burden laid on the

---

[81]   On the need for which generally see Chap. 7 *infra*. In the event in *Lambie* the appeal court held that taken as a whole the charge to the jury narrowly avoided amounting to a misdirection. The appeal was sustained on a different ground.

[82]   These are examined by Gordon, *op. cit.*, n. 6.

[83]   *op. cit.*, n. 6, p. 30.

defence is what is sometimes called the 'evidential burden,' the onus of raising the issue. The 'persuasive burden' remains on the Crown."[84]

The correct way for a trial judge to approach any specific defence raised by an accused is respectfully suggested to be that laid down by Lord Justice-General Cooper in *Crawford* v. *H.M.A.*[85] who ruled, in the context of a plea of self-defence that:

> "[It] is the duty of the presiding Judge to consider the whole evidence bearing upon self-defence and to make up his own mind whether any of it is relevant to infer self-defence as known to the law of Scotland. If he considers that there is no evidence from which the requisite conclusion could reasonably be drawn, it is the duty of the presiding Judge to direct the jury that it is not open to them to consider the special defence. If, on the other hand, there is some evidence, although it may be slight, or even evidence about which two reasonable views might be held, then he must leave the special defence to the jury subject to such directions as he may think proper."

The case of *Gilmour* v. *H.M.A.*[86] illustrates the importance of an accurate **2–73** charge to the jury. The accused had raised special defences of alibi and incrimination. The sheriff directed the jury that "there is no special burden on the accused to prove his special defence—corroboration is not necessary…" The appeal court described this charge to the jury as "quite unsatisfactory" and "defective" because of the failure to explain to the jury that, "if what is raised by the special defence leaves them with any reasonable doubt, the accused must be given the benefit of that doubt."[87]

(4) **Statutory provisions**

The general rule concerning the incidence of the burdens of proof in a **2–74** criminal case (*i.e.* that they are both borne by the Crown) is also subject to

---

[84] *op. cit.*, n. 7, para. 18–02. Macphail, *op. cit.,* n. 1, Chap. 22.08, took the implication of *Lambie* to be that, in the case of the special defences other than insanity and diminished responsibility, "the persuasive burden of proof remains on the Crown and the only duty on the defence is to discharge the evidential burden of raising the issue in such a way that it has to be left to the jury." Another effect of *Lambie* became apparent in *McAvoy* v. *H.M.A.*, 1982 S.C.C.R. 263 and *Fraser* v. *H.M.A.*, 1982 S.C.C.R. 458. in which it was held that, with the exception of the defence of insanity, there is no need for any direction to be given to a jury on any requirement for a corroborated case to support such a defence. *Lambie* was also followed in *Mullen* v. *H.M.A.*, 1978 S.L.T. (Notes) 33 and *Donnelly* v. *H.M.A.*, 1977 S.L.T. 147.

[85] 1950 J.C. 67 at p. 69. See also the direction given to trial judges in *Dunn* v. *H.M.A.*, 1986 J.C. 124.

[86] 1989 S.L.T. 881.

[87] At p. 882K.

statutory exceptions. Perhaps the most obvious are those which require the accused to show that he had some lawful justification or excuse for what he did,[88] or which require him to prove that he had no knowledge of some vital fact essential to the commission of the offence.[89] A common example arises under sections 4(3) and 5(2) of the Road Traffic Act 1988, whereby an accused may escape conviction for being in charge of, or driving, a motor vehicle under the influence of drink or drugs if he "proves" that at the material time there was no likelihood of his driving while he remained in such a condition.

2–75   The difficulty in such cases is that of establishing exactly what burden the accused bears, since there appears to be no general rule of universal application to these isolated and unrelated statutory impositions. However, despite the absence of a general rule, the courts when interpreting such statutory provisions appear to conclude that their effect is to impose a persuasive burden on the accused.[90] This is hardly surprising, given the relatively recent emergence of the evidential burden in Scots law, but Macphail has criticised it as a general practice,[91] and suggested[92] that all burdens falling upon an accused should be evidential only.

2–76   There is another general statutory provision which has also created some confusion and uncertainty. Sections 66 and 312(v) of the Criminal Procedure (Scotland) Act 1975 (now re–enacted in substantially similar terms in paragraph 16 of Schedule 3 to the Criminal Procedure (Scotland) Act 1995),[93] provides as follows:

> "Where, in relation to an offence created by or under an enactment any exception, exemption, proviso, excuse, or qualification, is expressed to have effect whether by the same or any other enactment, the exception, exemption, proviso, excuse or qualification need not

---

[88] Such as the Prevention of Crime Act 1953, s. 1(1) of which makes it an offence to carry an offensive weapon in a public place "without lawful authority or reasonable excuse, the proof whereof shall lie on him" (*i.e.* the accused).

[89] *e.g.* Misuse of Drugs Act 1971, s. 28(2). See also Licensing (Scotland) Act, 1976, s. 126

[90] See, *e.g. Neish* v. *Stevenson*, 1969 S.L.T. 229 for the imposition of such a burden on the accused in a drink/driving case involving a defence of "no likelihood of driving," in terms of s. 1(2) of the Road Safety Act 1967. And, *King* v. *Lees*, 1993 S.L.T. 1184, which held there was a persuasive burden on the accused to prove his statutory defence, though the court said the evidence led need not be corroborated. See also *Grieve* v. *Macleod*, 1967 J.C. 32, in which the accused in a complaint under s. 1 of the Prevention of Crime Act 1953 lost his appeal because the court was not satisfied that it was "reasonable" for an Edinburgh taxi driver to protect himself from customers with a length of rubber hose. The persuasive burden was clearly regarded as being his. For a critical discussion of these issues see Sheldon, "Hip Flasks and Burdens", 1993 S.L.T. (News) 33.

[91] See Macphail, *op. cit.*, n. 1, Chap. 22.19.

[92] *op. cit.*, n. 1, Chap. 22.23.

[93] See Renton and Brown, *op. cit.*, n. 7, para. 13–52.

be specified or negatived in the indictment or complaint, and the prosecution is not required to prove it but the accused may do so."

This provision was encountered in *Earnshaw* v. *H.M.A.*,[94] in the context **2–77** of the defence of "reasonable excuse" for failure to provide a blood or urine sample in a drink/driving case.[95] Its predecessor in summary cases was section 16(*d*) of the Summary Jurisdiction (Scotland) Act 1954, which was also considered in *Nimmo* v. *Alexander Cowan & Sons Ltd* (for which see paragraph 2.56 *supra*), an action for personal injuries sustained as the result of an alleged breach of statutory duty under the Factories Act 1961. In that case the opinion was given that where it applied, its effect was to require the person claiming such an excuse to "prove the facts by which they contend that they are excused."[96]

In the case of *Gatland* v. *Metropolitan Police Commission*[97] it was held **2–78** that an accused in such a situation bears the persuasive burden, and there seems little doubt that this is also the position under Scots law. In practice, the greatest difficulty encountered in connection with the statutory provisions now contained in paragraph 16 of schedule 3 to the 1995 Act would seem to be that of establishing when it applies.[98]

(5) **Miscellaneous**

There are two important categories of case in which the operation of the **2–79** law is said to shift the persuasive burden to the accused. They may be considered separately before a more general comment is made.

(a) *Facts peculiarly within the knowledge of the accused*

It was noted, when dealing with the incidence of the burdens of proof **2–80** in civil cases, that when certain facts are "peculiarly within the knowledge of" one of the parties, the court takes the view that the party with that knowledge bears the persuasive burden on that issue, but that the other party must at least generate sufficient evidence to make it a live issue (*i.e.* must discharge the evidential burden).[99] The objection to applying such a rule to a criminal case in which the person with the knowledge is the accused is, of course, that it conflicts with what is generally referred to as

---

[94] For which see n. 20 *supra*.
[95] But the court did not consider the application of s. 66 in depth as the Crown conceded they had the persuasive burden of proof. See also *Kennedy* v. *Clark,* 1970 J.C. 55.
[96] 1967 S.C.(H.L.) 79 at p. 114. This point is considered further in paras. 7.58–7.65 *infra*.
[97] [1968] 2 Q.B. 279, an English case based on the equivalent of para. 16 of Sched. 3 to the 1995 Act.
[98] See Renton and Brown, *loc. cit.*
[99] See, in particular, *McClure, Naismith, Brodie and Macfarlane* v. *Stewart*, in paras. 2.59–2.60 *supra*.

"the presumption of innocence," and requires an accused to prove his own innocence in the face of little more than prima facie evidence from the Crown.

2–81 Nevertheless it has a lengthy pedigree as a statement of general application in criminal cases,[1] but from the days before the existence of more than one burden of proof was recognised. For this reason, when Walker and Walker refer to "the onus" which rests upon an accused who has all the facts upon an issue peculiarly within his own knowledge, it may not be safe to conclude that they are referring to what is now known as the persuasive burden.

2–82 In fact, in *Mochan* v. *Herron*,[2] in which the sheriff applied the above passage from Walker and Walker to a situation in which the accused remained totally silent in the face of cogent prosecution evidence, and thus in effect allowed that evidence to rule the day, the terms of the sheriff's stated case (on which he was upheld by the appeal court) made it clear that he regarded it as one of those cases in which the evidence for the Crown placed a tactical burden[3] on the accused, which he had failed to discharge.

2–83 Significantly, one of the cases he founded on as supporting his ruling was *H.M.A.* v. *Hardy*,[4] another case in which the court was impressed by the fact that the accused offered not one single word in his own defence, and clearly failed to discharge the tactical burden placed on him by the Crown evidence. The wording of the passage from Walker and Walker refers to an onus on the accused in the context of his silence in the face of Crown evidence on facts of which he is manifestly well aware, and in a position to clarify.

2–84 The case on which Walker and Walker founded, *Cruickshank* v. *Smith*,[5] was one in which a statute required it to be shown whether or not the accused had a legal right to be fishing where he was. It was held that "the burden of proof" on the issue rested with the Crown, but that they need only produce prima facie evidence of illegal fishing for the onus to pass to the accused to show that he was fishing lawfully. The failure to recognise the existence of two burdens (one evidential and the other persuasive) leaves the case open to two interpretations.

---

[1] Notably by Dickson, *Evidence,* para. 32, and Walker and Walker, *Law of Evidence in Scotland,* para. 83(c) in which it is stated that: "When the facts proved by the Crown raise a presumption of the guilt of the accused person, unless other facts or another explanation of the facts are put forward, the onus of establishing these other matters rests upon the accused. This is especially the case where the facts are peculiarly within the accused's own knowledge." See also *Irving* v. *Jessop,* n. 8 *infra.*

[2] 1972 S.L.T. 218; see also n. 36 *supra* and *Donaghy* v. *Normandy,* 1992 S.L.T. 666.

[3] For which see paras. 2.25–2.44 *supra. N. B.* that the term "tactical burden" was not used as such.

[4] 1938 J.C. 144. See also paras. 2.25–2.44 *supra,* where this case is more fully considered.

[5] 1949 J.C. 134.

The first (what one might call the "orthodox" view, taken by Walker and   **2–85**
Walker and adopted in *Mochan* v. *Herron*) is that the accused bears the
persuasive burden whenever the facts are peculiarly within his knowledge,
and the Crown merely have the evidential burden of producing a prima
facie case against him. The alternative view might be that both the evidential
and persuasive burdens in such cases rest throughout with the Crown, but
that once they have discharged the evidential burden, the tactical burden
takes over, and "the silent defender takes a risk."[6]

Macphail has argued[7] that it would be dangerous to rely on any general   **2–86**
rule which places a persuasive burden on an accused whenever exculpatory
facts are peculiarly within his knowledge. In effect the rule would apply in
every case, on the basis that only the accused really knows whether or not
he is guilty. His view finds support from Sheriff Kermack in *McNeill* v.
Ritchie,[8] who observed: "I interpret the effect in Scots law of a fact being
peculiarly within the knowledge of the accused as requiring him to produce
evidence of that fact and not as requiring him to substantiate it by full legal
proof."

To do so would be to invert the presumption of innocence into a   **2–87**
presumption of guilt based on a prima facie case for the Crown. At the
highest then, the burden placed upon an accused with facts peculiarly within
his knowledge is probably only a tactical one.

(b) *The doctrine of possession of recently stolen goods*

Reference has already been made to the so-called presumption of guilt   **2–88**
which arises when an accused person is proved to have been found in
possession of recently stolen property in "criminative" circumstances,[9] and
it is noted again in Chapter 3 when examining presumptions more fully. Its
relevance in the present context is that it is popularly believed to shift the
persuasive burden from the Crown to the accused once the qualifying facts
are proved.

Gordon[10] in fact regards it merely as a cogent item of circumstantial   **2–89**
evidence,[11] and puts forward a strong argument that it is historically unsound

---

[6] Lord Justice-Clerk Grant in *McIlhargey* v. *Herron*, 1972 J.C. 38 at p. 42, dealt with at
     length in para. 2.29 *supra*.
[7] Macphail, *Evidence*, Chap. 22.15.
[8] 1967 S.L.T. (Sh.Ct.) 68. See too *Irving* v. *Jessop*, 1987 S.L.T. 53 which supports the view
     that the Crown need only produce a prima facie case.
[9] In paras. 1.05–1.12 *supra*.
[10] In Renton and Brown, *Criminal Procedure*, para. 18.02, and Gordon, "The Burden of
     Proof on the Accused," 1968 S.L.T. (News) 29 at pp. 40–43, in which he describes this
     doctrine as: "The clearest example of the tendency to discuss a tactical burden of proof in
     terms which suggest that it is a persuasive burden."
[11] In which view he is supported by Macphail, *op. cit.*, n. 7, Chap. 22.13.

to regard the presumption as placing a persuasive burden on an accused found in such circumstances. The fact remains that this is the effect which the doctrine is regarded as having. In the leading case[12] it was clearly stated by Lord Justice-General Cooper[13] that, provided three conditions were met— possession of stolen goods; a short interval between theft and discovery; and other criminative circumstances—the full effect of the rule was "in shifting the onus from the prosecution to the accused, and raising a presumption of guilt which the accused must redargue or fail."

2–90   However, it is still open to argument whether the "onus" in question is the full persuasive burden, or merely the tactical burden which an accused person bears in the face of the cogent evidence required in order to establish the presumption. There can be no doubt that the accused found in possession of property shortly after it was stolen, in circumstances suggestive of guilt, has in popular parlance "a lot of explaining to do," in order to argue away a formidable body of circumstantial evidence. If this is not done then a conviction is neither unexpected nor unfair, and in many cases it will make little difference whether the conviction arises from a failure to discharge the persuasive burden or a failure to discharge the tactical burden.

(c) *General*

2–91   The problem only becomes a live and practical one, in either situation, when at the end of the day there remains a "reasonable doubt" on the evidence, but not enough doubt to tip the scales of probability.[14] If the accused bears the persuasive burden of proving his innocence, he must be convicted if he fails to convince the court on a balance of probabilities. If, on the other hand, he bears only the tactical burden, and the Crown retains the persuasive burden, then a reasonable doubt will be enough to secure his acquittal.

2–92   There is obviously a need for clarification in both areas (*i.e.* those cases in which facts are said to be peculiarly within the knowledge of the accused and cases arising from possession of recently stolen property), and Macphail,[15] in recommending clarification, clearly came down in favour of the burden placed upon the accused being only evidential in nature. An alternative approach might be to leave both the persuasive and evidential

---

[12] *Fox* v. *Patterson*, 1948 J.C. 104, followed in many subsequent cases, including *Simpson* v. *H.M.A.*, 1952 J.C. 1; *Brannan* v. *H.M.A.*, 1954 J.C. 87; *McSorley* v. *H.M.A.*, 1975 S.L.T. (Notes) 43, and *Cassidy* v. *McLeod*, 1981 S.C.C.R. 270.

[13] *Fox* v. *Patterson*, *supra*, at p. 108. The same assertion was made in *Cameron* v. *H.M.A.*, 1959 J.C. 59 at p. 63, and *Cryans* v. *Nixon*, 1955 J.C. 1 at p. 6.

[14] Which, as will be seen in paras. 2.102–2.111 *infra*, is the quantum or standard of proof required to discharge the persuasive burden when it is borne by an accused.

[15] *op. cit.*, n. 7, Chaps. 22.13 and 22.16. His recommendation *quoad* recently-stolen property was endorsed by the Scottish Law Commission, Memo. No. 46, para. V.07.

burdens in both cases with the Crown, and allow the tactical burden to take its course. This would preserve the presumption of innocence, but allow the court to react accordingly to a failure on the part of the accused to give an explanation when one is naturally called for.

(6) **Summary**

It may be helpful to summarise this complex section into several general statements concerning the incidence of the burdens of proof in criminal cases.   **2–93**

(a) *Persuasive burden*

The general rule in criminal cases is that the persuasive burden on all issues, rests with the Crown throughout the trial. The only situations in which a persuasive burden on an issue will be borne by the accused are: **2–94**
    (i) when he raises the defences of insanity and diminished responsibility;   **2–95**
    (ii) when a statute imposes upon him a burden of proof which may be interpreted as being a persuasive one;   **2–96**
    (iii) when facts are peculiarly within his knowledge, or when it is proved that he was in possession of recently stolen property in criminative circumstances. Arguably the burden borne by an accused in such cases is only a tactical one, or perhaps only evidential.   **2–97**

(b) *Evidential burden*

The general rule in criminal cases is that the evidential burden on all issues rests with the Crown throughout the trial. The only situations in which an evidential burden on an issue will be borne by the accused are: **2–98**
    (i) when a specific defence is raised (*i.e.* a defence other than a general denial of guilt). In all other cases, once the accused has discharged the evidential burden, the Crown must go on to prove the accused's guilt (*i.e.* to discharge the persuasive burden on the defence raised by the accused). *N.B.* that the term "specific defence" is wider than the term "special defence", which is special only in a procedural sense; and in the cases of insanity and diminished responsibility the accused also bears the persuasive burden;   **2–99**
    (ii) when a statute imposes upon an accused a burden which may be interpreted as being only evidential in nature;   **2–100**
    (iii) pending clarification, in those cases referred to in (a)(iii) above.   **2–101**

THE STANDARDS OF PROOF ON THE PERSUASIVE BURDEN

The phrase "standard of proof" is used to describe the amount and quality of evidence required to discharge a burden of proof. There are basically two such standards in use in connection with the persuasive burden of proof, namely proof "beyond reasonable doubt" in a criminal case, and proof "on the balance of probabilities" in a civil action.   **2–102**

(1) **The general rule**

2–103   When referring to "the standard of proof", commentators, textbook writers and judges are normally alluding to the persuasive burdens, and it has been said that: "It is now clear that there are only two standards of proof known to the law of Scotland; proof beyond reasonable doubt, and proof upon the balance of the probabilities on the evidence."[16]

2–104   In a criminal case, therefore, it is traditional for juries to be directed by the trial judge that the prosecution must establish the guilt of the accused beyond reasonable doubt, since this is the standard of proof required whenever the Crown bears the persuasive burden.

2–105   The concept of beyond reasonable doubt cannot be rigidly defined. But it is understood as meaning the sort of doubt which a reasonable person would entertain, something more than a fanciful possibility,[17] and "more than a merely speculative or academic doubt."[18] As an English Lord Chief Justice put it, in a case in 1949[19]:

> "Once a judge begins to use the words 'reasonable doubt' and to try to explain what is a reasonable doubt and what is not, he is much more likely to confuse the jury than if he tells them in plain language 'It is the duty of the prosecution to satisfy you of the prisoner's guilt.'"

2–106   So far as concerns the standard of proof applicable to persuasive burdens in civil cases, there is generally less confusion and sheriffs and judges only rarely have to explain the concept of balance of probabilities to a jury. In civil cases it is simply that in order to win on a particular issue, the party bearing the persuasive burden must persuade the court that his version of the facts is more probable than that of his opponent's.[20] As Macphail has explained[21]: "What is being weighed in the 'balance' is not quantities of evidence but the probabilities arising from the acceptable evidence and all the circumstances of the case."

---

[16] Macphail, *op. cit.*, n. 7, Chap. 22.29. quoting *inter alia Brown* v. *Brown*, 1972 S.C. 123 and *Lamb* v. *Lord Advocate*, 1976 S.L.T. 151.

[17] See Lord Justice-Clerk Cooper in *Irving* v. *Minister of Pensions*, 1945 S.C. 21 at p. 29, something more than "a strained or fanciful acceptance of remote possibilities." See also *H.M.A.* v. *McGinlay*, 1983 S.L.T. 562 and *Tudhope* v. *Craig*, 1985 S.C.C.R. 214.

[18] Lord Justice-Clerk Thomson in *McKenzie* v. *H.M.A.*, 1959 J.C. 32 at p. 37.

[19] *R.* v. *Kritz* [1950] 1 K.B. 82 at p. 90. Lord Justice-Clerk Thomson, in *McKenzie* v. *H.M.A.*, *supra,* warned that "it is desirable to adhere so far as possible to the traditional formula and to avoid experiments in reformulation."

[20] Provided there is a sufficient case in law. For the concept of the "sufficiency" of evidence see paras. 1.37–1.43 *supra*.

[21] *op. cit.*, n. 7, at Chap. 22.30. See also Lord Jamieson in *Hendry* v. *Clan Line Steamers*, 1949 S.C. 320 at p. 328.

So far, then, the position is clear. The Crown in a criminal case must **2–107** discharge its persuasive burdens beyond reasonable doubt, while the party bearing the persuasive burden on an issue in a civil case must discharge it on a balance of probabilities. But this does not cover every persuasive burden, and other considerations must now be examined.

(2) **The accused in a criminal case**

As was seen in paragraphs 2.61–2.101 *supra* there are situations in which **2–108** an accused person bears a persuasive burden on a particular issue, and the question arises as to the standard of proof which must be employed in order to discharge it.

Dealing first with the common law situation (*i.e.* the defences of insanity **2–109** and diminished responsibility), the point was clearly settled so far as insanity is concerned in *H.M.A.* v. *Mitchell*,[22] when Lord Justice-Clerk Thomson directed a jury that:

> "the burden of proof is on the defence, because in our law there is a presumption that a man is sane. But you must keep clearly in mind that the burden in the case of an accused person is not so heavy a burden as the burden which is laid on the Crown ... the Crown has to prove its case beyond reasonable doubt ... Where, however, the burden of proof is on the accused, it is enough if he brings evidence which satisfies you of the probability of what he is called upon to establish ... it is a question of the balance of probabilities."

In some situations a statute places a persuasive burden upon an accused. **2–110** For example, in *Robertson* v. *Watson*,[23] a prosecution under Sale of Milk Regulations, milk found to have been adulterated was presumed to have been adulterated by the accused unless and until he proved otherwise. In formally directing himself on the appropriate standard of proof required for the accused to discharge the persuasive burden thus placed upon him, Lord Justice-General Cooper stated[24]:

> "I adopt, as an accurate statement of Scots law of general validity the rule laid down in *R.* v. *Carr-Briant*[25] that, when (as in this instance) some matter is presumed against an accused person unless and until

---

[22] 1951 J.C. 53 at p. 54. The same standard was established for the defence of diminished responsibility in *Carraher* v. *H.M.A.*, 1946 J.C. 108 at p. 113, and *H.M.A.* v. *Braithwaite*, 1945 J.C. 55, in which Lord Justice-Clerk Cooper at p. 58 directed the jury that: "If you think the balance of probability to be in favour of that defence, you must sustain it."

[23] 1949 J.C. 73.

[24] *ibid.*, p. 88.

[25] [1943] K.B. 607, an English case which is still the leading authority on the same point in England.

the contrary is proved, the burden of proof on the accused is less than that required at the hands of the prosecutor in proving the case beyond reasonable doubt, and that this burden may be discharged by evidence satisfying the jury or the Court of the probability of that which the accused is called upon to establish."

2–111   The authorities are confusing on the point, but it is thought that if an accused bears a persuasive burden on an issue, either because he is peculiarly in possession of the necessary facts or because he has been found in possession of recently stolen property in criminative circumstances,[26] then he need only discharge such a burden on a balance of probabilities. Certainly it is difficult to see why he should be required to produce evidence of a higher standard on an issue such as this than he would be required to produce on, *e.g.* the issue of his sanity. In any case, it is arguable that the principle expounded in *Robertson* v. *Watson* is of general applicability to any situation in which some fact is presumed against an accused unless the contrary is proved as *R.* v. *Carr-Briant* has been taken to be in the English courts. In *Farrell* v. *Moir*[27] it was held that an accused who bore the persuasive burden of showing "special reason" why he should not be disqualified for drunken driving need only discharge it on a balance of probabilities.[28]

(3) Special cases

2–112   Over the years, problems have arisen in selecting the appropriate standard of proof (*i.e.* beyond reasonable doubt or on the balance of probabilities) where an action which is essentially non-criminal in nature nevertheless gives rise to such important issues that it is argued that a higher standard of proof should be required than a mere balance of probabilities. It has even been suggested that some third, intermediate, standard should apply. Each such case must be examined separately.

(a) *Divorce and judicial separation*

2–113   Prior to 1976, a party seeking a decree of divorce or separation who was claiming adultery, sodomy or bestiality on the part of the alleged guilty spouse was (in the absence of an extract conviction, where appropriate) required to prove the allegation beyond reasonable doubt.[29] However, the

---

[26] Both of which were considered more fully in paras. 2.79–2.90 *supra*.
[27] 1974 S.L.T. (Sh.Ct.) 89.
[28] See paras. 7.58–7.65 *infra*, and for an analysis of the confusion created in this area see Sheldon, "Hip Flasks and Burdens", 1993 S.L.T. (News) 33.
[29] An example of such a case being *Burnett* v. *Burnett*, 1955 S.C. 183; see also *Brown* v. *Brown, infra*.

Divorce (Scotland) Act 1976, ss. 1(6) and 4(1), reduced the applicable standard on the issue of adultery to one on a balance of probabilities. This is also the appropriate standard for all other grounds of divorce or separation, including unreasonable behaviour. In cases of unreasonable behaviour it is frequently averred that the defender behaved in a manner, *e.g.* assault, which would constitute a crime. For the purposes of the civil action the standard of proof is on a balance of probabilities. This is so even if a spouse is alleging sodomy and bestiality, which are also criminal offences.[30]

(b) *Declarator of death*

Under the Presumption of Death (Scotland) Act 1977, a court may grant **2–114** a declarator that a person is dead when that person has not been known to be alive for a period of at least seven years. This provision is dealt with more fully in Chapter 3, but section 2(1) of the Act specifically states that the appropriate standard of proof is that on a balance of probabilities. This overrules the previous leading authority of *McCeachy* v. *Standard Life Assurance Co.*,[31] in which it was agreed by the parties that the standard of proof on the persuasive burden borne by the pursuer was proof beyond reasonable doubt.

(c) *Breach of interdict and other contempts of court*

An action for an alleged breach of interdict raises an interesting problem, **2–115** since the possible sanctions following upon proof of such a breach include criminal penalties.[32] The concurrence of the Lord Advocate is required before such an action may be raised since it is possible criminal proceedings may arise out of the act complained of as a breach of interdict and these would pre-empt any civil action. Despite the possibility of criminal sanctions, proceedings for breach of interdict are civil proceedings within the meaning of section 1(1) of the Civil Evidence (Scotland) Act 1988 and corroboration is unnecessary.[33] But since the proceedings have criminal implications the question arises as to what is the appropriate standard of proof. In *Gribben* v. *Gribben*,[34] it was held that where a wife raised an action alleging a breach by her husband of an interim interdict to prevent him from molesting her, she was required to prove the breach beyond reasonable doubt.

---

[30] See, *Hastie* v. *Hastie*, 1985 S.L.T. 146, in which it was held that a false allegation of *inter alia* an incestuous relationship contributed to the irretrievable breakdown of a marriage on a balance of probabilities.

[31] 1972 S.C. 145.

[32] See Robinson, *The Law of Interdict*, Chap. 16.

[33] *Byrne* v. *Ross*, 1993 S.L.T. 307.

[34] 1976 S.L.T. 266, following *Eutectic Welding Alloys Ltd.* v. *Whitting*, 1969 S.L.T. (Notes) 79.

2–116   Breach of interdict is a breach of a court order and as such is a contempt of court. It is thought that proof beyond reasonable doubt is also the appropriate standard of proof for all cases of alleged contempt of court, of which breach of interdict is only one example. This is because it is punishable as a crime, by admonition, censure, fine or imprisonment.[35]

2–117   A helpful dictum in this connection is that issued in *Morrow* v. *Neil*,[36] a rare action of lawburrows[37] brought by a widow in a tenement flat who was apprehensive of further assaults by her neighbours. Sheriff Macphail held that the question of the standard of proof fell to him to determine because it had never been raised before. He acknowledged that since the case of *Brown* v. *Brown*[38] he had only two standards of proof to choose from, and that in an action for contravention of lawburrows, which bears a similarity to an action for breach of interdict and requires the concurrence of the procurator fiscal, the appropriate standard would probably be proof beyond reasonable doubt.

(d) *Fatal accident inquiries*

2–118   Whatever doubts may have existed before, it is now settled by statute that the appropriate rules of evidence, including standard of proof, for a fatal accident inquiry are "as nearly as possible those applicable to an ordinary civil cause."[39]

(e) *Allegations of crime in a civil action*

2–119   For various reasons, one of the parties to a civil action may set out to prove facts which will indicate that the other party has committed a crime. Were that same crime to be libelled against him in a criminal court, the prosecution would be required to prove those facts beyond reasonable doubt. The question then arises whether or not a party in a civil action should be required to prove these allegations of criminal behaviour to the same standard.

---

[35] See Macphail, *op. cit.,* n. 7, Chap. 22.37, and *H.M.A.* v. *Airs*, 1975 S.L.T. 177, in which all contempts of court were judged to be essentially the same in nature. The Scottish Law Commission also opted for proof beyond reasonable doubt in such cases (Memo. 46, para. V.18). *Gribben* was followed in *Inland Revenue* v. *Ruffle*, 1979 S.C. 371, *quoad* a tax penalty.

[36] 1975 S.L.T. (Sh.Ct.) 65.

[37] Essentially a civil action brought by someone fearing harm to either himself or his family. The defender is required to find caution for good behaviour, with the threat of imprisonment unless he does so. The circumstances of any breach may also be made the subject of criminal charges: see Walker, *Delict*, p. 500, and Stair Memorial Encyclopaedia, *The Laws of Scotland*, Vol.13, paras. 901–926.

[38] 1972 S.C. 123, dealt with more fully below.

[39] *i.e.* proof on a balance of probabilities: Fatal Accidents and Sudden Deaths Inquiry (Scotland) Act 1976, s. 4(7).

The position has shifted considerably since 1964 when, taking the general **2–120**
tenor of the authorities as they then stood, Walker and Walker[40]
acknowledged that the question had not been authoritatively considered
very often, but that the criminal standard (*i.e.* proof beyond reasonable
doubt) had been said to apply.[41] Since then the point has been considered in
a number of cases. In *Buick* v. *Jaglar*,[42] the defender in an action for
repayment admitted a course of embezzlement from the pursuer, but disputed
the amount to be repaid. Sheriff Wilkinson distinguished between cases in
which the guilty party admitted the criminal conduct (which is therefore no
longer a live issue anyway) and those in which such conduct is "altogether
disputed." He concluded that "if a higher standard of proof applies in
Scotland it is clear that that standard is restricted in its application and it
does not apply to all civil allegations of crime."[43] Sheriff Wilkinson also
noted that English law only required proof on a balance of probabilities.[44]
And many technical crimes such as breaches of the Road Traffic Acts and
Factories Acts were held to have been committed, for the purposes of a
civil action, on a balance of probabilities.[45]

In his recommendations to the Scottish Law Commission,[46] Sheriff **2–121**
Macphail confirmed the frequency with which, as a matter of practice,
allegations of statutory crimes are accepted on a balance of probabilities in
actions for damages for personal injuries, and also quoted the authority of
King v. *Patterson*,[47] in which it was held that it was for the defender to
show "on a balance of probabilities, that the conviction was wrong and that
the presumption of negligence has been rebutted."[48] His recommendation
was that it should be made clear that in all cases in which crime is alleged
in the course of a civil action, the standard of proof will be on a balance of
probabilities, adding that: "The nature of the offence with which the court
was concerned would cause variations in the amount of evidence required
to tilt the balance of probability, but would not alter the standard of proof."[49]

---

[40] *Law of Evidence in Scotland*, para. 85.
[41] By Lord Neaves in *Arnott* v. *Burt* (1872) 11 M. 62 at p. 74.
[42] 1973 S.L.T. (Sh.Ct.) 6. See also *Sloan* v. *Triplett*, 1985 S.L.T. 294 at p. 297 and *Wilson* v. *Price* 1989 S.L.T. 484, where the same opinion was expressed in the Outer House.
[43] *ibid.*, p. 7.
[44] By virtue of *Hornal* v. *Neuburger Products* [1957] 1 Q.B. 247. See also *R.* v. *Hants C. C., ex p. Ellerton* [1985] 1 W.L.R. 749.
[45] See, *e.g. Nimmo* v. *Alexander Cowan & Sons,* 1967 S.C.(H.L.) 79, considered in para. 2.77, in which Lord Reid at p. 97 said of the pursuer's burden of proving a breach of s. 29(1) of the Factories Act 1961 that: "It is true that the standard of proof is lower in a civil case, so that the Pursuer only has to show that it is probable that an offence was committed."
[46] *op. cit.*, n. 7, Chap. 22.34.
[47] 1971 S.L.T. (Notes) 40, considered more fully in Chap. 3.
[48] *ibid.*, p. 40.
[49] *op. cit.*, n. 7, Chap. 22.34. See the opinion of Lord Cowie in *Ashcroft's C.B.* v. *Stewart* (O.H.) 1988 S.L.T 163. The Scottish Law Commission, Memo. 46, para. V.16 accepted his basic proposal, but see *Lennon* v. *Co-operative Insurance Society, infra.*

2–122   The position has now been authoritatively settled in the five bench decision in *Mullan* v. *Anderson*.[50] In this case the widow of a man who had been murdered raised an action for damages against the man who had been acquitted of the murder. In her pleadings she alleged that the defender had indeed murdered her husband. The question arose as to what was the appropriate standard of proof. The appeal court reviewed many of the earlier cases and affirmed that there was a "well established principle that in civil cases the standard of proof required of a pursuer is that he prove his case on a balance of probabilities."[51]

(f) *Legitimacy*

2–123   There is, as will be seen in Chapter 3, a statutory presumption of legitimacy arising either from the marriage of the parents, or from the fact that the husband has acknowledged paternity. This arises under section 5 of the Law Reform (Parent and Child) (Scotland) Act 1986, and that same section provides that the presumption may be rebutted by evidence on a balance of probabilities.

2–124   This therefore resolves the problems created by the older case authorities[52] to the effect that the appropriate burden of proof was beyond reasonable doubt.

(g) *Children's Hearings*

2–125   Children's Hearings were set up by the Social Work (Scotland) Act 1968. Their principal function is to determine whether a child is in need of compulsory measures of care under any of the grounds mentioned in section 32 of the 1968 Act.[52a] Compulsory measures of care may be deemed appropriate because of the child's offending behaviour or because the child is at risk from external factors and requires protection. Children's Hearings generate frequent applications to the Sheriff Court for proof of the grounds of referral. The grounds have to be clearly established and the standard of proof to be applied is the civil standard of balance of probabilities except in a case of a referral under section 32(g) of the Act where the criminal standard of proof beyond reasonable doubt applies. The justification for the lower standard of proof for the remaining ten grounds is the primacy of the

---

[50] 1993 S.L.T. 835.
[51] At p. 842D.
[52] *e.g. Imre* v. *Mitchell*, 1958 S.C. 439 at p. 462; *Brown* v. *Brown*, 1972 S.L.T 143 at p. 145, *S.* v. *S.*, 1977 S.L.T. (Notes) 65 and *Docherty* v. *McGlynn*, 1985 S.L.T. 237. *N.B.* that in *A.* v. *C.*, 1984 S.L.T. (Sh.Ct.) 65, it was held that the appropriate standard of proof of paternity in an affiliation action is also on a balance of probabilities.
[52a] The provisions in the 1968 Act are to be replaced by similar provisions in the Children (Scotland) Act 1995, Chapters 2 and 3, (not yet in force).

protection of the child. In Lord Justice-Clerk Ross's view, "it is still a justification even if the person concerned is ultimately acquitted of the offence in the criminal courts."[53]

(h) *Additional standards of proof ?*

It has sometimes been suggested that there are special types of cases **2–126** which require the application of a standard of proof different from the standard of proof beyond reasonable doubt or proof on a balance of probabilities. In *Anderson* v. *Lambie*,[54] a civil action for reduction of a probative deed was said by Lord Reid to place "a heavy onus" on the pursuer. In that case, the House of Lords held that the pursuer "has proved his case beyond reasonable doubt."[55] Lord Keith said that the onus was one which would leave "no fair and reasonable doubt upon the mind."[56] This terminology is suggestive of the appropriate standard in criminal cases and is confusing in the context of civil cases (especially where no criminal conduct is alleged), but it is likely these terms were used to emphasise the degree of persuasion required of a pursuer in such an action.

In *Sereshky* v. *Sereshky*,[57] an action for reduction of a deed for forgery, **2–127** Lord Weir said that the standard of proof was less than that required in a criminal case but "must be proved to a very high degree of probability having regard to the criminal implications involved."

In *Lennon* v. *Co-operative Insurance Society*[58] Lord Kincraig held, in a **2–128** case involving an insurance claim following a fire in a boarding house which it was alleged that the insured had started himself, that since the insurance company was alleging facts which amounted to an accusation of wilful fire-raising on the part of the insured, there was a "much higher onus" on the company. However, the onus was still one which was to be discharged on a balance of probabilities. This affirms the argument of Lord Weir in *Sereshky, supra,* that any difference in the standard of proof relates to the quality and sufficiency of the evidence rather than the standard itself.

There have been several other cases where an intermediate standard has **2–129** been suggested, particularly where the proceedings are considered "quasi-criminal". For example, cases involving malpractice in returns to the Inland Revenue,[59] and cases concerning alleged assault. In *Guest* v. *Annan*[60] a

---

[53] *Harris* v. *F.*, 1991 S.L.T. 242 at p. 246C.
[54] 1954 S.C.(H.L.) 43.
[55] At p. 63.
[56] At p. 69.
[57] 1988 S.L.T. 426 at p. 427E.
[58] 1985 S.L.T. 98.
[59] *Inland Revenue* v. *Ruffle,* and *Irving* v. *Minister of Pensions, supra.*
[60] 1988 S.C.C.R. 275.

conviction for excessive chastisement of a child—in effect an assault—
was quashed because the sheriff had used the words, "on balance ... I
convict." The language was suggestive of the application, incorrectly, of
the civil standard in a criminal case.[61]

2–130   The cases were reviewed by Lord Penrose in *Rehman* v. *Ahmad,*[62] an
action brought under section 8(1) of the Law Reform (Miscellaneous
Provisions)(Scotland) Act 1985. This section provides for an application to
the court to be made to rectify the terms of an agreement under certain
limited circumstances. The statute makes no specific provision regarding
the applicable standard of proof, but must be read in the general context
that the courts will not look lightly behind the terms of any written document
to determine the parties intentions.

2–131   Lord Penrose noted that the earlier cases which considered the possibility
of an intermediate standard all involved allegations of criminal conduct in
civil cases where no person was exposed to criminal penalties. He declined
to apply an intermediate standard saying: "It is clear that the reason for
adopting the intermediate position was in each case the nature of the
allegations, and the present case raises no issues of that kind."[63]

The Standards of Proof on the Evidential Burden

2–132   There is virtually no direct authority on the standard of proof required to
discharge the evidential burden. This is no doubt due partly to the failure of
the courts formally to note its existence as a separate burden of proof,[64] and
partly to the fact that since it is not a matter on which a court normally
requires formally to direct itself, or on which a judge has to advise a jury,
there is little opportunity in practice for formulae to be laid down for future
adoption.

2–133   In criminal cases, as has been seen in paragraphs 2.61–2.101 *supra*, on
most issues the Crown bears both the persuasive and evidential burdens. It
was also noted in paragraphs 2.102–2.107 *supra* that the standard of proof
required in order to discharge the persuasive burden is proof beyond
reasonable doubt. As a result, the standard of proof necessary to discharge
the evidential burden on the same issue could, in theory, be any standard
lower than proof beyond reasonable doubt.

---

[61] See also *Ward* v. *Chief Constable of Strathclyde*, 1991 S.L.T. 292, an action of damages for
injuries allegedly sustained when mounted police cantered into a crowd. The appropriate
standard was balance of probabilities, but it was observed that it would be difficult for a
pursuer to overcome evidential hurdles and demonstrate want of probable cause and malice
on the part of the police.

[62] 1993 S.L.T. 751

[63] At p. 745J.

[64] See paras. 2.15–2.24 *supra*.

What the Crown are seeking to do when attempting to discharge the **2–134** evidential burden on an issue, is to produce sufficient evidence to justify the court considering that issue. To avoid a conviction the accused then needs to raise sufficient doubt over that evidence to create a "reasonable doubt" in the minds of those deciding the issue. If a reasonable doubt is raised it will prevent the Crown discharging the persuasive burden. Before that stage is reached though the Crown must produce enough evidence to make the issue a "live" one.

The court will be more likely to accept as true an item of evidence from **2–135** the prosecution which the accused has not bothered to refute, since "the silent defender does take a risk."[65] This risk may be so serious as to allow a single unchallenged item of evidence from the prosecution to discharge not only the evidential burden but also the persuasive burden on that issue.[66] As a result, in such cases the standard of proof required to discharge the evidential burden may be no more than prima facie evidence.

Thus in *Tudhope* v. *Miller*,[67] Lord Justice-Clerk Wheatley, when **2–136** considering the evidential implications of an analyst's certificate under section 6(1) of the Road Traffic Act 1972[68] observed as follows:

> "the position is that the Crown had established a *prima facie* case under reference to the appropriate certificate, and there had been a failure to adduce evidence before the court of a sufficiently definite and conclusive nature to invalidate the evidential value of that certificate. That being so, there was but one course for the Sheriff to follow, and that was to find the respondent guilty."

In effect the Crown had provided prima facie evidence of the accused's guilt, which was enough to discharge the evidential burden. This evidence, having been left unchallenged by the accused, had been sufficient to discharge the persuasive burden also.

On the other hand, it may be that vigorous cross-examination by the **2–137** defence of a witness called by the Crown to give the evidence which is

---

[65] Lord Justice-Clerk Grant in *McIlhargey* v. *Herron* 1972 J.C. 38.
[66] Although a further item of separate evidence in corroboration will be required before a conviction may be entered: see Chap. 7.
[67] 1978 J.C. 26 at p. 27. See also *Mochan* v. *Herron*, 1972 S.L.T. 218 at p. 219, in which the High Court upheld the sheriff's ruling that when the Crown produce simply a prima facie case arising from possession of recently stolen property in criminative circumstances, this will be sufficient to discharge even the ultimate burden (*i.e.* the burden of proving the accused's guilt) if the accused offers no innocent explanation. In a rare commentary on the standard of proof required of the Crown when discharging an evidential burden, the Judicial Committee of the Privy Council, in *Jayasena* v. *R.* [1970] A.C. 618 at p. 624, said that the evidence required is "such evidence as, if believed, and if left uncontradicted and unexplained, could be accepted by the jury as proof."
[68] Now s.5 of the Road Traffic Act 1988.

intended to discharge the evidential burden will result in the sheriff or judge having the gravest doubt as to the acceptability of that evidence. The court may ultimately rule that the evidence cannot be considered or that it should be withdrawn from the jury. To this extent, therefore, the quality of evidence required to discharge the evidential burden may vary according to the strength with which it is contested. In order to overcome a strong defence challenge, the prosecution may require evidence which tilts the balance of probabilities simply in order to discharge the evidential burden.

2–138   It will also be recalled that when an accused bears the persuasive burden on an issue, then only evidence on a balance of probabilities is required in order to discharge that burden.[69] It follows from this that something less than evidence on a balance of probabilities will be sufficient to warrant the issue which is raised being considered by the court (*i.e.* for the accused to discharge the evidential burden).

2–139   In *Crawford* v. *H.M.A.*[70] Lord Justice-General Cooper, in speaking of the duty of a trial judge when directing a trial jury on the issue of self-defence, said that while such an issue must be withdrawn from them if there is *no* evidence to support it: "If, on the other hand, there is some evidence, although it may be slight, or even evidence about which two reasonable views might be held, then he must leave the special defence to the jury subject to such directions as he may think proper."

2–140   This means that where an accused bears both the evidential and persuasive burdens on any issue, that issue must be left to the jury once the accused has adduced what amounts to only prima facie evidence,[71] and thereby discharged the evidential burden. This is equally applicable where the accused bears the evidential burden, but the persuasive burden rests with the Crown once he has discharged it.[72] At the end of the day a "reasonable doubt" is enough for an acquittal, and Lord Justice-General Cooper's reference to "some evidence, although it may be slight", may well amount to a reasonable doubt and be sufficient to discharge the evidential burden.

2–141   In civil cases, as was seen above, the appropriate standard of proof to discharge the persuasive burden is normally proof on a balance of probabilities, and obviously the standard required to discharge the evidential burden on the same issue (which will normally be borne by the same party who bears the persuasive burden) will be something less than this.

2–142   In *Inglis* v. *L.M.S.*[73] the parents of a boy killed when he fell from the doorway of a moving train were held to have passed a tactical burden[74] to

---

[69] See, in particular, *H.M.A.* v. *Mitchell*, at para. 2.64 *supra*.
[70] 1950 J.C. 67 at p. 69, referred to at para. 2.72 *supra*.
[71] Assuming, of course, that it is not totally discredited in cross-examination by the Crown.
[72] For which see paras. 2.102–2.131 *supra*.
[73] 1941 S.C. 551, referred to in paras. 2.42–2.43 *supra*.
[74] For which see paras. 2.25–2.44 *supra*.

the defenders once it was shown that no one, including the boy, had interfered with the door handle. It was held that this was prima facie evidence of negligence on the part of the defenders, in the face of which the ensuing silence on the part of the defenders served to discharge the persuasive burden. Had the defenders countered with some evidence of their own, the court would undoubtedly have considered all the evidence in its totality. This suggests that by producing a prima facie case, the pursuers had discharged the evidential burden, and that this is the appropriate standard of proof for the discharge of an evidential burden in civil cases.

Similarly, in *Brown* v. *Rolls Royce*[75] the House of Lords held that once **2–143** the pursuer in a case involving the contracting of industrial dermatitis had raised what amounted to a prima facie case, then "if nothing more appeared, the Court might well infer that the defenders were negligent."[76] Again, the court was referring to the effect of a tactical burden, but was making the point in passing that a prima facie case is enough, in a civil action, to call for a reply. In short, a prima facie case will discharge the evidential burden.

It can therefore be argued that, with one exception, the standard of proof **2–144** required to discharge an evidential burden on any given issue is always at a lower level than the standard required to discharge the persuasive burden on the same issue.

Where the persuasive burden must be discharged beyond reasonable **2–145** doubt then the standard required to discharge the evidential burden, when it rests with the Crown, may be as high as a balance of probabilities, unless the accused chooses to remain silent on the matter, and thus invoke the operation of a tactical burden. Where the persuasive burden requires only evidence on a balance of probabilities for its discharge then the evidential burden on the same issue may be discharged by evidence which is really only prima facie in nature.

The one exception arises in those criminal cases in which the persuasive **2–146** burden rests with the Crown, but the evidential burden falls on the accused. Although the evidence required to discharge the persuasive burden is proof beyond reasonable doubt, the evidential burden may be discharged by the accused by means of prima facie evidence only.

Whether or not such a generalised statement is a correct assessment of **2–147** Scots law on the subject must remain a matter of debate until the standard of proof on evidential burdens is authoritatively quantified.

THE STANDARDS OF PROOF ON TACTICAL BURDENS

A tactical burden is essentially a floating burden. It needs to be discharged **2–148** only when the other party has adduced evidence which calls for a reply.

---

[75] 1960 S.C.(H.L.) 22, considered more fully in paras. 2.25–2.44 *supra*.
[76] *ibid.*, at p. 27.

There is no fixed standard of proof for the discharge of a tactical burden. It is instead a matter of adducing stronger evidence than that adduced by the other party.

CHAPTER 3

PRESUMPTIONS

INTRODUCTION

Even though a party may bear a burden of proof on a particular issue, there **3–01** are four situations where there may be no need to lead all or some direct evidence in discharge of that burden. These situations arise:

    (i) when a presumption operates in favour of a party;
    (ii) when the matter is "judicially noted";
    (iii) when as between the parties it is said to be "*res judicata*";
    (iv) when the point is formally admitted by the other party at the outset.

Judicial notice, facts which are *res judicata* and formal admissions form **3–02** the subject of the next three chapters. This chapter concentrates on presumptions.

PRESUMPTIONS DEFINED

A presumption may be defined as a process by which Fact A is offered as **3–03** proof of Fact B.[1] Or, to put it another way, a party offers to the court certain facts from which that court is invited to conclude that other facts must also exist.

To use one example to which reference has already been made in each **3–04** of the previous chapters, (and which is expanded in paragraphs 3.113–3.119 below), the fact that an accused person charged with a crime of dishonesty was found, in "criminative" circumstances, in possession of recently stolen property is sufficient to bring into operation a presumption that he is guilty of a crime of dishonesty in respect of that property. Fact A (the possession, etc.) gives rise to a suggestion that Fact B (the accused's guilt) is established.

In practice, presumptions may be found in a wide variety of contexts, **3–05** and may arise either under statute or as the result of common law. In many

---

[1] See Cross and Tapper, *Evidence*, at p. 136. Walker and Walker, *Law of Evidence in Scotland*, at p. 50, describe it as "an inference as to the existence of one fact from a knowledge of the existence of another fact."

cases they have little more to recommend them than practical convenience, public policy or long usage, and in some cases they fail to reflect modern attitudes and practices. They are also so numerous that it is impossible to refer to them all in this chapter, and reference should be made to standard reference works on the substantive law for a full list.

3–06   Presumptions fall into three general categories, according to their effect on the evidence, if any, which falls to be heard once the particular presumption has been invoked. This chapter aims to distinguish between these three categories by reference to some of the principal examples from each.

3–07   The three categories are as follows:

(1) Irrebuttable presumptions of law

3–08   These are, in reality, fixed principles of law which cannot be "rebutted", or argued away by means of evidence to the contrary. On some occasions they amount to legal fictions, but once the basic facts which give rise to the presumption are proved, the presumed fact is thereby automatically proved. They are said to be "irrebuttable" because no evidence, however strong, can contradict them, and they are presumptions of "law" because they can only arise from an authoritative law-making source namely statute or common law.

(2) Rebuttable presumptions of law

3–09   Like the first category of presumption, these are the creation of law, in the sense that they have been laid down for future reference for the courts to follow. However, unlike the first category, they may be countered by evidence which shows that in the particular case it is unsafe to arrive at Fact B purely on the basis of Fact A. They are therefore "rebuttable."

(3) Rebuttable presumptions of fact

3–10   This final category of presumption arises not from the operation of some established legal principle, but as the result of the process of common sense and human experience. It is this human experience which suggests that, in the normal course of things, Fact A usually means Fact B, but because this is not invariably the case the court will listen to rebutting evidence. There is only one major distinction between a rebuttable presumption of fact and an item of circumstantial evidence,[2] and this is considered in paragraphs 3.95–3.104 below.

3–11   In distinguishing the three types of presumption from each other, two primary considerations arise. The first is whether the presumption has a

---

[2] Examined more fully in paras. 9.46–9.51, *infra*.

legal or a factual basis. The second is whether or not it is "rebuttable", *i.e.* can evidence be led to negative its operation. In practice the latter is more important. Each type of presumption is now examined more closely to consider the various ways in which a presumption may be rebutted.

IRREBUTTABLE PRESUMPTIONS OF LAW

GENERAL PRINCIPLE

It might be accurate to describe "irrebuttable presumptions of law" as **3–12** "irrevocable conclusions of law", since this is in effect what they are. For a variety of reasons often connected with considerations of public policy, proof of certain facts leads to certain conclusions being drawn. These conclusions brook upon proof of certain basic facts, which brook no argument, however powerful the potential rebutting evidence.[3] As Walker and Walker explain, "in some cases they resemble fictions of law."[4]

Strictly speaking, such presumptions have no place in the law of evidence, **3–13** since they arise as points of substantive law and are not even arguable. But they can affect the outcome of a trial. In extreme cases they prevent any trial of an action taking place at all, because the party against whom such a presumption operates knows in advance that there is no prospect of persuading the court, by means of evidence, to take a different view from that prescribed by law. For example, a procurator fiscal faced with a birth certificate showing an accused person to be only seven years of age can proceed no further by way of criminal proceedings.[5]

3–14

In short, faced with Fact A the court *will*, as a matter of law, reach Conclusion B. Some of the more common examples of this process are now considered.

EXAMPLES OF IRREBUTTABLE PRESUMPTIONS OF LAW

(1) **Nonage as a bar to criminal trial**

By virtue of section 41 of the Criminal Procedure (Scotland) Act 1995,[6] **3–15** "it shall be conclusively presumed that no child under the age of eight years can be guilty of any offence." This "conclusive presumption", is based upon the principle that a child under eight is deemed incapable of forming the necessary *mens rea* for the commission of a crime. The effect is, of course, that no charge may be brought.

---

[3] See, for example, *G.'s Trs.* v. *G.*, in para. 3.24 *infra*.
[4] Walker and Walker, *op. cit.*, n. 1, p. 51. where they are referred to by their Latin title of presumptions *juris et de jure*.
[5] See paras. 3.15–3.24 *infra*.
[6] Formerly ss. 170 and 369 of the Criminal Procedure (Scotland) Act 1975.

(2) **Lack of sexual consent by a girl under 12**

3–16　　At common law, since at least the days of Hume,[7] a girl aged under 12 has been regarded as being incapable of giving the necessary "consent" to intercourse which would reduce a charge of rape to one of a less serious sexual nature. The origin of this rule has been said to be a "legal presumption" that a girl so young cannot give effective consent in a matter so serious.[8] The offence with which an accused is charged in such a case is described by Gordon[9] as one of "constructive rape."

3–17　　The reality of the situation in modern times is more accurately reflected by section 3 of the Sexual Offences (Scotland) Act 1976, which provides an alternative charge of sexual intercourse with a girl under 13; section 15 of the Act allows the jury in a rape trial involving a girl of such age to convict the accused of the section 3 alternative.

(3) **Capacity in the law of contract**

3–18　　Since September 25, 1991, when the Age of Legal Capacity (Scotland) Act 1991 came into force, a child aged 16 years and over is deemed to have legal capacity. The Act is not retrospective. Prior to it a boy under 14 and a girl under 12[10] were deemed incapable of giving the consent necessary for the formation of a legally binding contract, and any contracts by a pupil had to be entered into through the medium of his or her tutor. The presumption of the pre-1991 position was reflected in the fact that any purported contract by a pupil would be regarded as a nullity.[11]

(4) **Previous convictions in a defamation action**

3–19　　As is explained in paragraphs 5.101–5.112 *infra*, for the purposes of any defamation action a conviction is regarded as conclusive evidence of the commission of the offence. This is in terms of section 12 of the Law Reform (Miscellaneous Provisions) (Scotland) Act 1968.

(5) **Prescription**

3–20　　Prescription is a process whereby legal rights may be both created and extinguished by the passage of time, and such creation and extinction is achieved by the application of a conclusive legal presumption once the qualifying facts have been established.

---

[7]　Who seems to have regarded effective consent as being commensurate with the onset of puberty in a girl: see Hume, I, 303.

[8]　See, *e.g. Chas Sweenie* (1858) 3 Irv. 109 at pp. 138 and 147.

[9]　*Criminal Law*, para. 33–14.

[10]　The ages again reflecting the legal view of the age of puberty: see Stair I, iv, 35.

[11]　*McGibbon* v. *McGibbon* (1852) 14 D. 605.

The modern law is contained in the Prescription and Limitation (Scotland) **3–21** Act 1973, which deals with both "positive" and "negative" prescriptions.[12]

The negative prescriptions serve to extinguish certain obligations after **3–22** they have been enforceable for either five years or 20 years,[13] and have been neither claimed by the creditor nor acknowledged by the debtor. On proof of these facts, the court has no alternative but to declare the obligation extinguished, since it is conclusively deemed to be so by statute.

The effect of the positive prescription is to establish conclusively a party's **3–23** right to an "interest in land". This can arise where such a right is either founded upon a recorded title accompanied by 10 years' continuous possession, or proceeds upon 20 years of such possession either in certain special cases, or where there is no foundation writ which the party claiming title would ordinarily be required to register. Once the party has established these facts, and there is no evidence of any "judicial interruption" of the qualifying period of possession (*e.g.* by court action), then the effect of section 1 of the 1973 Act is to exclude "all inquiry into the previous titles and rights to the lands."[14] In short, a ten-year "prescriptive" title is valid against the whole world, and provides a good example of an irrebuttable presumption of law.[15]

(6) **Age of child-bearing in a woman**

The Court of Session, in *G.'s Trs.* v. *G.*,[16] laid down the irrebuttable **3–24** presumption that, in any case in which the interests of a person other than a possible unborn child are affected, a woman is capable of child-bearing at any age.[17]

---

[12] For a detailed discussion see Gloag and Henderson, *Introduction to the Law of Scotland*, Chap. 15.

[13] ss. 6 and 7 respectively of the 1973 Act; the appropriate period depends upon the nature of the obligation.

[14] See Gloag and Henderson, *op. cit.*, n. 12, Chap. 15.11. So final is the effect of this presumption that it forms the basis of the modern conveyancing practice of seeking only a 10 year prescriptive progress of titles when confirming that the seller has title to the subjects of the disposition. *N.B.* that the foundation writ may be challenged on the grounds that it is *ex facie* invalid, or was forged.

[15] The presumption being that the title is valid. It would seem to proceed upon what Lord Chancellor Halsbury, in *Clippens Oil Co. Ltd.* v. *Edinburgh and District Water Trs.*, 1903 6 F.(H.L.) 7, referred to at p. 8 as: "that principle of presumption in favour of long-continued use or possession, from which the presumption arises that such use or possession was lawful in its origin."

[16] 1936 S.C. 837.

[17] For an example of a similar presumption of a man's ability to father a child see *Munro's Trustees* v. *Monson,* 1965 S.L.T. 314.

CONCLUSION

3–25 Every irrebuttable presumption of law, once invoked, has the effect of excluding all further argument on the subject, and numerous additional examples may be encountered under statute.[18] However, as with all presumptions, the qualifying facts[19] must be established first, so that in many cases a party must appear before a court in order to establish the facts necessary for the operation of the presumption in his favour. Needless to say, if the agent for the other party is in no position to refute the facts, then he need waste neither his time nor his client's money in attempting to scale what is an insurmountable legal barrier.

REBUTTABLE PRESUMPTIONS OF LAW

GENERAL PRINCIPLE

3–26 This category of presumption which is also known as a presumption *"juris tantum"*,[20] is just as much the creation of law as the type considered in the previous section. The major difference between the two is the fact that the presumption *juris tantum* is not conclusive. It may be set aside by clear evidence which shows that it is unsafe to draw the conclusion which would normally flow from the basic facts adduced in order to invoke it. However, unless some rebutting evidence is produced, the conclusion almost certainly will be drawn. The effect of a presumption *juris tantum* is therefore to place a burden of disproof[21] on the party against whom it operates.

3–27 Like their irrebuttable counterparts, presumptions *juris tantum* come from any valid legal source. They may even arise through commercial custom,[22] and have on occasions developed from what were for many years previously, mere presumptions of fact. All that is required to convert a presumption of fact into a presumption of law is that it be adopted in the *ratio* of a judgment, and thereby laid down for future courts to follow.

3–28 Most of the best-known presumptions *juris tantum* are in practice judge-made, as the succeeding examples show. This does not mean, however,

---

[18] *e.g.* Companies Act 1985, s. 13(7) of which makes a certificate of incorporation "conclusive" evidence of (i) the existence of the company from the date thereof, and (ii) compliance with all the statutory formalities of incorporation: see Gloag and Henderson, *op. cit.,* n. 12, Chap. 51.7. For a further example, see the Bills of Exchange Act 1882, s. 38, which gives the holder in due course a title to a bill of exchange which is free from any defect in the title of prior parties to it: see Gloag and Henderson, *ibid.,* para. 23.18.

[19] *i.e.* what Cross and Tapper call the "basic facts"—see n. 1 *supra.*

[20] Walker and Walker, *op. cit.,* n. 1, para. 54.

[21] Which may be persuasive, evidential or tactical, depending upon the circumstances: see paras. 2.01–2.05 *supra.*

[22] The presumption arising from *apocha trium annorum* provides a good example.

that they cannot also be found in considerable numbers under statute, and an established example of a statutory presumption *juris tantum* is that found in section 13 of the Bills of Exchange Act 1882, under which a bill of exchange, and any acceptances and endorsements thereon, are presumed, until the contrary is proved, to have been executed on the dates which they bear.[23]

Increasing use is being made of statutory presumptions *juris tantum* to resolve uncertainty in many areas of law. For example, the Family Law (Scotland) Act 1985 contains two such presumptions which are designed to settle arguments over the division of moveable property upon the break-up of a marriage. Section 25 states that in the case of "household goods obtained in prospect of or during the marriage other than by gift or succession from a third party, it shall be presumed, unless the contrary is proved,[24] that each (party) has a right to an equal share in the goods in question."[25] **3–29**

Section 26 attempts to do the same for what used to be called the "wife's *praepositura*",[26] by enacting that in the case of "money derived from any allowance made by either party for their joint household expenses or for similar purposes, or ... any property acquired out of such money, the money or property shall, in the absence of any agreement between them to the contrary, be treated as belonging to each party in equal shares."[27] **3–30**

Having seen something of the general nature of presumptions *juris tantum*, it is now possible to look in more detail at some of the more common examples. **3–31**

OMNIA PRAESUMUNTUR RITE AC SOLEMNITER ESSE ACTA

This formidable-sounding phrase (which is usually referred to by its shortened name *omnia praesumuntur*) means simply that there is a general **3–32**

---

[23] This is a statutory example of the principle known for short as *omnia praesumuntur*, and is examined more fully in paras. 3.32–3.40 *infra*.

[24] A clear indication that the presumption is rebuttable, and that it imposes a persuasive burden on the other party.

[25] The section goes on, interestingly, to exclude as rebutting evidence the fact that while the parties were married and cohabiting, the goods in question were purchased from a third party (*e.g.* a shop) by either party alone or by both in unequal shares. Any alternative legal view would, of course, circumvent s. 26.

[26] Repealing and replacing a somewhat similar provision under the Married Women's Property Act 1964; the new provision envisages a situation in which the wife makes an allowance to the husband, and both Acts replaced a previous common law ruling that money given to a wife for household expenditure remained the property of the husband in so far as it was not spent.

[27] Other examples of modern presumptions *juris tantum* are provided by s. 11 of the Law Reform (Miscellaneous Provisions) (Scotland) Act 1968, considered in paras. 5.69–5.74 *infra;* s. 10 of the same Act, considered in paras. 5.108–5.112 *infra*, and s. 280(9) of the Criminal Procedure (Scotland) Act 1995, considered in para. 7.44 *infra*.

presumption that where an act is performed in accordance with normal procedure, it is an act lawfully and properly done. In the words of Lord Chancellor Halsbury in *Bain* v. *Assets Co.*,[28] "every intendment should be made in favour of what has been done as being lawfully and properly done."

3–33   The case from which this quotation comes illustrates the essentially practical considerations which lie behind the presumption. It was alleged that 20 years previously, a contributory to a Glasgow bank which had been liquidated under court supervision had not made a full disclosure of his assets, and that his discharge ought therefore to be set aside. The court was mindful of the time which had elapsed since then, and held that the essential validity of the discharge, since it proceeded from a lawful process which had not subsequently been challenged, could not be questioned without clear proof that it had been falsely obtained. The burden of proof was on the party seeking to set it aside to show that there had not been a full disclosure at the time, and since he had failed to do so, he lost the action and the discharge stood.[29] It was, in short, presumed to be valid until the contrary was proved.

3–34   The time factor has also been regarded as important in other cases, such as *Sutherland* v. *Barbour*,[30] in which the proprietor of a tenement comprising inter alia a shop and a house, sought a building warrant for an extension of his property to the street line. It was argued against him that to do so would violate the terms of a feu charter under which the land had originally been conveyed with a burden to erect a building in accordance with a plan annexed thereto. There was, by the date of the hearing, no copy of the plan available, but the court held that since the building had been erected many years before, it must be presumed to have complied in its finished state with the plan, and that therefore any further building would violate the plan. It was said to be for the applicant to produce the plan in order to show that he would not be violating it, and since he had failed to do so, he lost the application.[31]

3–35   In all cases involving the presumption *omnia praesumuntur*, the use of a valid process is taken to be evidence of the validity of the action taken under that process. Thus, where a person purports without challenge to act in an official capacity, he is presumed to have been duly appointed,[32] while a decree duly recorded in old judicial records will be presumed to have been validly and properly pronounced.[33]

---

[28] (1905) 7 F.(H.L.) 104 at p. 106.
[29] Clearly in this case the challenging party bore the persuasive burden.
[30] (1887) 15 R. 62.
[31] Again the persuasive burden appears to have been imposed on the party against whom the presumption operated.
[32] As in *Marr* v. *Procurator Fiscal of Midlothian* (1881) 8 R.(J.) 21, in which the presence on the bench of an interim sheriff substitute was taken to be evidence of his appointment.
[33] *Duke of Atholl* v. *Lord Advocate* (1880) 7 R. 583 at p. 589.

In *Hamilton* v. *Fyfe*,[34] H was convicted under a local authority Closure **3–36** Order of keeping his shop open for longer than permitted under the Order, which under the Shop Hours Act 1904 had the effect of a statute once it was confirmed by the then Secretary for Scotland. H argued that the order was invalid because certain procedures required by law prior to the making of the order had not been complied with, but the court refused to investigate this on the grounds that any earlier irregularity had been "entirely superseded" by the official confirmation. Since no one had objected prior to the confirmation, the order must be taken to have been made *solemniter*.

The principle applies even to regular business or office practices, which **3–37** may be used to set up a presumption that they were followed on a particular occasion simply because they are normally followed.[35]

The doctrine of *omnia praesumuntur* also lies behind the principle that a **3–38** "probative" writ, which gives the appearance of being in accordance with required form, may be presumed to have been validly executed. This aspect of the law of evidence is now largely regulated by the provisions of the Requirements of Writing (Scotland) Act 1995 and is dealt with in Chapter 9.

Finally, the principle applies in cases of disputed marriage, whereby the **3–39** essential validity of the marriage may be presumed from the performance of the formalities of a wedding ceremony leading to the issue of an authorised certificate.[36]

The whole rationale of the principle *omnia praesumuntur* is perhaps **3–40** best summarised in the words of Lord Simons in *Morris* v. *Kanssen*,[37] who pointed out that: "The wheels of business will not go round unless it is assumed that that is in order which appears to be in order."

PRESUMPTION AGAINST DONATION

The presumption against donation[38] proceeds from the observable fact that **3–41** people do not as a rule give away their money or possessions to strangers. Therefore, when it is claimed by A that B gave him something as a gift, the courts tend to be sceptical and to look for some other explanation for the transfer of the property.

Since at least the days of Stair,[39] there has been a legal presumption **3–42** against the transfer of moveable property by free gift. In relation to donation

---

[34] 1907 S.C.(J.) 79.
[35] *Edinburgh District Council* v. *MacDonald* 1979 S.L.T. (Sh.Ct.) 58.
[36] *Burke* v. *Burke* 1983 S.L.T. 331.
[37] [1946] A.C. 459 at p. 475.
[38] Which, as will be seen below, is largely a presumption based upon human experience.
[39] I,viii,2, who described it even then as "a rule in law ... whatsoever is done, if it can receive any other construction than donation, it is construed accordingly."

inter vivos, McBryde states that "there is a strong presumption against outright donation. By contrast there is less of a presumption against the revocable gift constituted by *donatio mortis causa.* "[40]

3–43   The presumption against donation *inter vivos,* may only be rebutted by clear evidence of (i) actual delivery by the donor to the alleged donee, and (ii) *animus donandi,* or intention on the part of the donor to gift the property in question. However, it may be that, if necessary, comparatively "weak evidence of delivery may be eked out by unmistakable evidence" in support of the other.[41] In addition, it would seem to be incumbent on the party seeking to rely on the presumption to indicate to the court what the *real* nature of the transaction is alleged to have been, since:

> "Donation, undoubtedly, is not to be presumed; but, on the other hand, it is not to be rejected, unless some other tangible solution consistent with the whole facts of the case can be suggested; and the want of any such alternative amounts to real proof in its favour."[42]

3–44   There are few modern cases to illustrate this presumption,[43] but a relatively recent one indicates the sort of circumstance in which it might still be invoked. In *Grant's Trustees* v. *MacDonald,*[44] the court was required to examine the motivations behind a grant of money by an elderly lady who lived alone and bedridden. She had an estate of some £6,000, £2,000 of which she placed on deposit receipt and endorsed over to a neighbour with the words: "I give this money in deposit receipt for £2,000 to Mrs M for anything she has had to get for me, and to do with as I have instructed her." Before Mrs Grant's death, Mrs M made no attempt to have the money transferred to herself, but upon Mrs G's death she claimed it as a gift to herself by the deceased.

3–45   The court had before it no tangible evidence of any other motivation on the part of the deceased than to provide for her own requirements before death, and to leave her neighbour the balance of the money for herself. It was therefore held that the presumption had been overcome by lack of evidence of any other arrangement which was fully consistent with the facts. The neighbour was therefore held to be entitled to the money.

---

[40] *The Law of Contract in Scotland,* p. 18.

[41] *MacPherson's Exrx.* v. *Mackay,* 1932 S.C. 505 at pp. 514–515.

[42] Lord Jeffrey in *British Linen Co.* v. *Martin* (1849) 11 D. 1004 at p. 1011, an interesting example of the rebuttal of a presumption by negative evidence.

[43] Which may often be found entangled with other presumptions, such as that whereby services performed by A or B are presumed to have been intended to be paid for by B (see *e.g.* *Turnbull* v. *Brien,* 1908 S.C. 313—board and lodging) and that under which a loan of money attracts interest (*Smellie's Exrx.* v. *Smellie,* 1933 S.C. 725).

[44] 1939 S.C. 448, or *Macaulay* v. *Milliken,* 1967 S.L.T. (Notes) 30, an action of debt where the alleged debtor claimed donation.

The presumption has no application to heritable property, in respect of **3–46** which infeftment or physical possession under habile title are conclusive.[45]

APOCHA TRIUM ANNORUM

This term means "discharges for three years". According to old authority, **3–47** when a particular debt or obligation is to be repaid on a termly basis then the possession by the debtor of receipts for payment for three consecutive terms raises a presumption that all prior instalments due have in fact been paid.[46] The principle rests upon the assumption that no creditor would allow a debtor to honour three consecutive recent debts without either demanding payment of an earlier debt or in fact "ascribing" payment to that earlier debt.[47] The presumption will not apply unless and until there are three separate receipts—one single document containing a receipt for three previous payments will not suffice, at least not according to the older authorities.[48]

Few of the leading cases are less than 100 years old and it is uncertain **3–48** how far this presumption has survived into the machine age of computerised banking, standing orders, direct debits and electronic credit control. In one of the most recent of these cases[49] their Lordships appear to have been prepared to accept not only the oral evidence of the creditor to the effect that she had not understood what she was signing, but also a single document containing five receipts in one, which appears to have failed as an item of evidence only because it was not stamped.

For these reasons, it may not prove in future to be a very reliable **3–49** presumption.

PRESUMPTIONS ARISING FROM POSSESSION OR DESTRUCTION OF DOCUMENTS

Over the years there has been a rich harvest of presumptions relating to **3–50** possession of both property and the titles to property, and their destruction. Possession of heritable property is, as has been seen,[50] now largely a matter of recorded title and prescription. And possession of moveable property gives rise to a factual presumption of ownership which is dealt with in paragraphs 3.105–3.112 below. This section, therefore, concentrates on the

---

[45] For which see paras. 3.15–3.24 *supra*, and the presumption created by prescription.

[46] Stair, I,xviii,2, but limited by the Institutional writers to annual or biannual payments.

[47] For which process see Gloag and Henderson, *op. cit.*, n. 12 Chap. 14.7.

[48] Dickson, *Evidence*, para. 177.

[49] *Cameron v. Panton's Trs.* (1891) 18 R. 728.

[50] In paras. 3.15–3.24 *supra*.

remaining legal presumptions which surround the possession and destruction of documents which constitute evidence of title to property.

3–51   One may begin with the old presumption[51] that when a deed granted by A to B is found to be in the possession of B, it has been duly delivered.[52] Except where the document in question is alleged to be held in trust by the grantee for the grantor, the presumption may be rebutted by any form of evidence acceptable to the court,[53] and the evidence required will obviously vary according to the circumstances.

3–52   In *Semple* v. *Kyle*[54] the court was faced with evidence of delivery by K to S of a cheque drawn by K and payable to S, a classic case for the application of the presumption. It was argued for S that he was therefore entitled to the value of the cheque as the holder in due course. The court held the presumption to have been rebutted by oral testimony from K that he had only delivered the cheque on condition that he received a cheque from a named third party to cover the amount in question. This was held to be effective against any indorsee who was not a holder in due course, which S clearly was not.

3–53   The presumption is based on the belief that the grantor would not voluntarily place such a document outwith his control unless he had in fact intended to make an effective delivery of it to the grantee.[55] The evidence which is normally heard in rebuttal will be of some condition attached to the delivery (*e.g.* that the alleged grantee was in fact only intended to be a custodier) which demonstrates that the grantor did not intend to lose control over it. Alternatively, of course, it may be evidence of fraud on the part of the alleged grantee.

3–54   The same underlying principle—that the grantee is the only person who, by his actions, can retain or demit control of his own document—gives rise to a second presumption. This is where a document which is known to have been made by A and to have been in his custody is not discovered after his death, it is presumed that he destroyed it *animo revocandi*.[56] The same is true of an undelivered deed which is so found, but in a mutilated condition. An obvious type of document to fall into this category is a will. In an action to prove the tenor of the will to show that it may be regarded as still valid and effective, the terms of the original

---

[51] Described as "strong" by Walker and Walker, *op. cit.,* n. 1, para. 66, and referred to by Stair, 1,vii,14 and Erskine, III,ii,43.

[52] A fact which may be crucial in establishing transfer of the property itself from A to B: see Gloag and Henderson, *op. cit.,* n. 12, Chap. 37.9, and Chap. 3.41–3.46 *supra* particularly *Grant's Trs.* v. *MacDonald*, 1939 S.C. 448.

[53] Or, to use the formal term, *prout de jure*. See Walker and Walker, *op. cit.,* n. 51.

[54] (1902) 4 F. 421.

[55] Which in many cases is tantamount to an effective delivery of the rights evidenced in the document. See Gloag and Henderson, *op. cit.,* n. 12.

[56] *i.e.* literally "with intent to revoke it."

will can be proved by other means. This could include the continued existence of a draft.

In *Clyde* v. *Clyde*,[57] C made a will in favour of his nephew, and deposited **3–55** it with his solicitors. Twelve years later it was returned to him at his request, and seven years after that he died. There was no trace of the will among his papers, but his nephew—who was also his business partner—gave evidence that the two parties had remained on good terms, and that the deceased had never evinced any intention of altering or revoking his will. It was held[58] that these facts were not sufficient to rebut the presumption that A had destroyed the will *animo revocandi,* and that he had therefore died intestate.

In assessing how much evidence must be adduced to rebut the **3–56** presumption much will depend, however, upon the nature and purpose of the document. In particular, where the document is normally one which would be destroyed after its purpose has been served (*e.g.* a bill of exchange, cautionary obligation or revoked will), then: "the presumption is that such destruction or cancellation took place in the exercise of his power of revocation, and that presumption can be obviated only by very clear evidence to the contrary."[59]

One of the most transient types of document is an obligation of debt **3–57** such as an IOU or a bond of caution, and there is yet a third presumption attached to this type of document. It is to the effect that if the document of obligation is found in the hands of the debtor, cautioner or other obligant, it is presumed that the debt or obligation which it evidenced is discharged. It is based upon a similar consideration to the two previous presumptions considered in this section, namely that the creditor has control, and would not otherwise have relinquished possession of the document which evidenced the debt or obligation.

It is obviously for the creditor seeking to enforce the document of which **3–58** he has lost possession to explain how this came about. This must be done in terms which are fully consistent with the facts and which are sufficiently convincing to override the strong suggestion that the debt or obligation was discharged.[60]

---

[57] 1958 S.C. 343.
[58] Relying on *Bonthrone* v. *Ireland* (1883) 10 R. 779, a case in which the presumption was confirmed as a "legal" (*i.e.* persuasive) one, but in which it was not required anyway because the court accepted the corroborated evidence of the deceased's daughter (who stood to gain the entire estate on an intestacy) that she had, before her father's death, destroyed the will on his instructions.
[59] Lord Guthrie in *Clyde* v. *Clyde, supra* at p. 345.
[60] *Henry* v. *Miller* (1884) 11 R. 713 at p. 716 suggested that proof would not be restricted to writ or oath if an allegation of fraud was made. The Requirements of Writing (Scotland) Act 1995 now render that irrelevant as proof would not be restricted anyway.

3–59 The presumption has in fact been extended further, and now applies to all situations in which a creditor in a written obligation cannot produce the document of debt, whether it is in the hands of the debtor/obligant or not. It is for the creditor to overcome the presumption that the debt or obligation evidenced by the document has been discharged.[61]

Presumption of Continuance

3–60 There is a general common law presumption[62] that conditions which are proved to have existed at one time may be presumed to have continued in existence. There are a variety of applications of this general presumption.[63] Two specific applications of the general rule will now be considered in detail, namely the presumption of continued life and the presumed continuance of a person's domicile of origin.

(1) **Presumption of continued life**

3–61 At common law, there is a general presumption that human life extends for a period of between 80 and 100 years, and that, in the absence of specific indications to the contrary, a person may not be presumed dead until he has reached at least the lower of these two ages. To this general rule there are now two statutory exceptions. Under the Succession (Scotland) Act 1964, where a person dies in a "common calamity"; and, under the Presumption of Death (Scotland) Act 1977 where a person disappears for at least seven years. These are dealt with in paragraphs 3.72–3.86 below, as a separate presumption of death. However, since there could be circumstances in which neither statutory provision will apply,[64] the common law rule may still have relevance.

3–62 One of the clearest statements of the common law rule may be found in *Secretary of State* v. *Sutherland*,[65] a case in which Mrs S's right to a pension depended upon the validity of her marriage to S, a point which was in turn dependent upon whether or not a previous husband was still alive. If he were still alive, he would have been 72 at the date of the hearing, but evidence was given that he had deserted Mrs S 44 years previously, and had not been heard of for the past 40 years. Mrs S had heard a rumour to the effect that he had died many years before, but she had not bothered to investigate.

---

[61] *Walker* v. *Nisbet*, 1915 S.C. 639 at p. 641.
[62] Noted by Dickson, *Evidence*, para. 114(5) and Walker and Walker, *op. cit.,* n. 1, para. 69.
[63] Which may be found in Walker and Walker, *op. cit.,* n. 1, but some of which have been overtaken by statutory changes, notably in the area of divorce law and practice.
[64] *e.g.* if a person has not been missing for seven years, and the case is not one involving succession.
[65] 1944 S.C. 79.

The underlying law was neatly summarised by Lord Moncrieff,[66] who **3–63** ruled that:

> "[While] in a case in which there are no special features our common law assumes life will continue up to the age of eighty years[67] or even longer, it is always a jury question in each particular case whether or not the presumption of continuance of life has been displaced. The considerations which influence a finding for or against that presumption have long been well established; either there must be direct proof of something amounting to a proper *casus amissionis*, or there must at least be facts and circumstances indicating such a break in the continuing relations of the absentee as would have been wholly out of character with his conduct had he been in life."

In the present case there was no reason why Mrs S would have seen her first husband, and indeed, in the words of Lord Normand, they "had every motive for avoiding one another." The wife therefore failed to discharge the onus of proof placed upon her of proving that he was dead, and therefore failed in her claim for pension rights as the widow of the second "husband". It was also held that the presumption of death after seven years' absence which could be invoked under the Divorce (Scotland) Act 1938[68] in no way diminished her burden of proof, since it was relevant only on a direct application for declarator of death and dissolution of marriage.

An illustration of the sort of circumstances in which the common law **3–64** presumption may be rebutted is afforded by *Greig* v. *Merchant Company of Edinburgh*.[69] G brought an action against the trustees of a fund for declarator that she was entitled to a widow's annuity because her husband must be presumed dead. In 1893 he had begun drinking heavily, his business had collapsed and he had been sequestrated. The parties had been judicially separated in 1896, and he had then left Scotland to lead a somewhat unsettled life. Until 1900 he had made spasmodic appearances in Scotland, always in reduced circumstances, in poor health and in a drunken condition. He had last been seen in 1901, after which nothing more had been heard of him despite extensive inquiries. By the date of the original action (1918) he would have been 61.

The court granted declarator to the effect that the husband was presumed **3–65** to have died as at December 31, 1910,[70] on the grounds that "the reasonable result from all the evidence is that he did not survive 1910."[71]

---

[66] At pp. 85–86.
[67] The period suggested by the Institutional writers; Lord President Normand at p. 84 referred to "a period of between eighty and a hundred years."
[68] And is now subsumed under the 1977 Act—see paras. 3.83–3.86 *infra*.
[69] 1921 S.C. 76.
[70] An unusually specific choice of date, which contrasts with the normal practice under statute in such circumstances: see 1977 Act and *O'Halloran*, both at paras. 3.72–3.86 *infra*.
[71] Lord Justice-Clerk Scott-Dickson at p. 84.

3–66　　These cases must, of course, be considered now in the light of subsequent statutory changes explained in paragraphs 3.72–3.86 below.

(2) **Presumption of continued domicile of origin**

3–67　　There is a well-established common law rule[72] that a person's domicile of origin (*i.e.* the domicile acquired at birth) is presumed to continue as his domicile for legal purposes until he is shown to have acquired another domicile not only by residence (*facto*) but also by intentionally abandoning that domicile of origin (*animo*). The burden of proof[73] rests with the party seeking to rebut the presumption and rely upon the new domicile.

3–68　　One of the best illustrations of the presumption in use is *Liverpool Royal Infirmary* v. *Ramsay*.[74] B had died in Liverpool, leaving a will which was valid under Scots law but not English. It therefore fell to be decided which jurisdiction applied. This in turn raised the question of his domicile at the date of his death. He had been born in Glasgow and had spent the first 45 years of his life there, but had moved to Liverpool to be nearer to his family. He remained in Liverpool for 37 years until his death at the age of 82, even after the last remaining member of his family had died, but there was evidence to suggest that his continued residence in Liverpool was largely the product of lethargy.

3–69　　Referring to the presumption of continued domicile of origin, Lord MacMillan[75] said that: "The acquisition of a domicile of choice is a legal inference which is drawn from the concurrence of evidence of the physical fact of residence with evidence of the mental fact of intention that such residence shall be permanent." Lord Thankerton[76] put it in more practical terms by ruling that:

> "the appellant undertakes the burden of proving that [B] acquired an English domicile *animo et facto*; his long residence establishes the *factum*, but there remains the question of the *animus*. It seems clear on the authorities that mere length of residence by itself is insufficient evidence from which to infer the *animus*, but the quality of the residence may afford the necessary inference."

3–70　　It was held that, on the facts, B's prolonged absence in England did not rebut the presumption that his domicile was still Scotland because there was insufficient evidence of the abandonment of the domicile *animo*.

3–71　　A disputed will is one obvious context in which the question of domicile can arise, but it can also be used by the living as a defence against litigation,

---

[72] Noted by Dickson, *op. cit.*, n. 62, para. 27, and Walker and Walker, *op. cit.*, n. 1, para. 69.
[73] Obviously the persuasive burden.
[74] 1930 S.C.(H.L) 83.
[75] At p. 89.
[76] At p. 88.

using the simple assertion that the court has no jurisdiction over the defender. For an example of this process, see *McLelland* v. *McLelland*.[77]

PRESUMPTION OF DEATH

As was explained in paragraphs 3.60–3.71, the presumption of death is **3–72** entirely statutory, the common law preferring a presumption of continued life at least until a person has reached the age of 80. There are, however, occasions upon which the common law presumption is either inconvenient or inequitable or both, and Parliament has intervened to provide a practical alternative. These occasions are identifiable under two main statutory provisions.

(1) **Succession (Scotland) Act 1964, s. 31**

At common law, when two persons perished in what is referred to as a **3–73** "common calamity",[78] there was no presumption as to which of them died first. If, for example, father and son died in a house fire or an air crash, there would be no presumption that the son had survived the father, so as to regulate the problems of succession which might thereby arise.

That such a rule could clearly defeat the testamentary intentions of the **3–74** parties is obvious from a perusal of the authorities, and some of the cases governed by the old common law rule. In *Drummond's Judicial Factor* v. *H.M.A.*,[79] for example, a man, his wife and two children were killed when their house was completely destroyed by enemy bombing. There was no evidence to show if any of the victims had lived longer than the others, and at the time of the tragedy the husband was 41 and his wife 39. Both died intestate,[80] the wife leaving in her estate some 250 war savings certificates, and legal argument ensued as to whether these fell into the husband's estate or to the Crown as *ultimus haeres*.

In finding in favour of the Crown, the court held that there was no **3–75** presumption under Scots common law as to survivorship among those killed in a common calamity. Survivorship was held to be solely one of fact. In order to prove survivorship, some factual evidence was required.[81]

---

[77] 1942 S.C. 502. See also *Labacianskas* v. *Labacianskas*, 1949 S.C. 280 for a case in which the presumption was invoked along with a statutory presumption of death.

[78] *i.e.* circumstances (*N.B.* not necessarily the same incident) in which two people are found to be dead such that it is impossible to tell which, if either, died first.

[79] 1944 S.C.(H.L.) 298.

[80] Although in the circumstances, the case would probably not have been decided differently had they left wills bequeathing their estates to members of their immediate family. Since the court was not prepared to presume survivorship by anyone in the absence of evidence, the children could not possibly inherit, whether the parents died testate or not, because not even the children could be presumed to have survived either parent.

[81] *Ross* v. *Martin*, 1955 S.C.(H.L.) 56.

3–76   It was to prevent the potentially harsh operation of the common law that section 31 of the 1964 Act was enacted for the limited purpose of regulating succession. Under the section, where two persons have died in circumstances indicating that they died simultaneously, or rendering it uncertain which of them (if either) survived the other, then there is a presumption that they died in order of seniority, that is, that the younger survived the elder. To this rule there are two exceptions, so that in either of these exceptional cases the old common law rule will prevail, and no survivorship will be presumed.

3–77   First of all, where the two persons in question were husband and wife, there is a statutory presumption[82] that neither survived the other. This means in practice that neither of the two inherits the estate of the other, and cannot thereby pass on that estate, together with his or her own, to persons who may not be within the immediate family. Were the facts of *Drummond's Judicial Factor* v. *H.M.A.* to arise again, therefore, the result would be the same notwithstanding the 1964 Act.

3–78   The other exception arises when the older person (*i.e.* the one presumed to have died first) has left a testamentary provision in favour of the younger (*i.e.* the presumed survivor), whom failing to some third party, and that younger person has died intestate. In such a case, for the purposes of that testamentary provision only, there is a presumption that the older person survived the younger, so as to prevent the older person's testamentary wishes being thwarted by the legacy passing in the younger person's intestacy. By virtue of this exceptional presumption, the legacy will pass to the third party as if the younger person had died first.

3–79   It will have been noted that the presumption only applies where two people die in circumstances which render it "uncertain" which of them survived the other. If there is evidence that one of them survived the other, then section 31 does not apply at all, not even the exceptions to it. If, for example, in the case of husband and wife it can be shown by evidence that one seems to have survived the other, then the court is not bound by the statutory presumption that neither survived the other.

3–80   This point emerged clearly in *Lamb* v. *Lord Advocate*,[83] a case in which a sister was claiming under the intestacy of a lady who died in a house fire along with her husband. The husband had been bedridden at the time of the fire, and his wife had rushed out into the street to summon assistance. As

---

[82] *per* s. 31(1).

[83] 1976 S.L.T. 151, referred to in para. 2.103 *supra*. See too, the implications which the case had for a possible intermediate burden of proof upon the party seeking to rebut the presumption raised by s. 31. At first instance Lord Grieve had indicated the standard of proof required was "evidence which, albeit short of establishing certainty, is sufficiently reliable to warrant a definite conclusion...", at p.155. This was rejected as a test by the Inner House.

she did so, there was an explosion in the house which turned it into an inferno. The wife rushed back into the house in a vain attempt to reach her husband, but died in the attempt. The husband was 69 and the wife 66.

The sister argued that there was evidence to show that the husband must **3–81** have died first, and that therefore his wife must have inherited his estate under his will, albeit for a brief period only. When the wife died, it was further argued, her estate contained the estate left to her by the husband, and the sister was entitled to this. On behalf of the Lord Advocate, it was argued that since it was uncertain which died first, section 31(1) applied. The husband died without heirs (having no other family) and therefore his estate fell to the Crown as *ultimus haeres*.

The position was explained by Lord Wheatley[84] thus: **3–82**

> "Section 31 was introduced to clarify the position, by way of legal presumptions, when a pursuer had failed to prove survivance. But if a pursuer can establish survivance, the section does not begin to apply. There is then no uncertainty … the question is one for determination by proof and not by presumption. There is nothing … which I can find to suggest that the answer to the question would be determined otherwise than by the normal standard in civil proceedings in Scotland, namely on a balance of probabilities on all the evidence."

It was held that the pursuer had established, on a balance of probabilities, that the husband had died first, and that the sister was therefore entitled to claim from the wife's estate. It was also held *obiter* that when a section 31 presumption applies, it requires evidence on a balance of probabilities to rebut it. However, since, as was pointed out in this case, the presumption only applies where by definition there is no clear evidence one way or the other, it is hardly likely that a court will ever require to apply that standard. Either there is evidence of survival, in which case the presumption does not apply, or there is not, in which case it does.

(2) **Presumption of Death (Scotland) Act 1977**

By virtue of section 1 of this Act, any person "having an interest"[85] may **3–83** apply to the court for declarator that a person who is missing is in fact dead. This may be for any legal purpose, and not just the limited one of divorce,[86]

---

[84] At p. 153.
[85] Which can include the Lord Advocate, for the public interest, *per* s. 17.
[86] Which was the case under the now repealed Divorce (Scotland) Act 1938, s. 5. Prior to the 1977 Act, there had been several statutes which created, for their own limited purposes, a presumption of death, but there was little commonality, and even less universality, between such provisions, and the 1977 Act was intended as an all-purpose provision.

and the pursuer must produce either evidence which points to the conclusion that the missing person has died, or evidence to the effect that he or she "has not been known to be alive for a period of at least seven years."

3–84   In either case, the court need only be persuaded on a balance of probabilities,[87] and may thereafter grant declarator. Where the court is satisfied that the missing person died, the declarator must include a finding as to the date and time of death. Where this is uncertain, it may simply find that he died at the end of the period of time during which he must be presumed to have died. Where the court is satisfied merely that the missing person has not been known to be alive for a minimum of seven years, the declarator must simply state that the missing person died at the end of the day occurring seven years after the date on which he was last known to be alive.[88]

3–85   At the same time, the court is empowered to determine the domicile of the missing person as at the time of his death, determine any question relating to any interest in property raised by his death, and appoint a judicial factor on the estate of the "deceased."[89] Once the appeal period has expired, the decree is, in terms of section 3, "conclusive" of the matters contained in it, and is "effective against any person[90] and for all purposes including the dissolution of a marriage to which the missing person is a party and the acquisition of rights to or in property belonging to any person." Even if the person in question is subsequently found to have been alive at the date specified in the decree as being the date of death, the marriage stays dissolved by virtue of the decree.[91] Section 13 of the Act also provides a defence to a bigamy charge where the accused can show that at no time during the period of seven years ending with the date of the second marriage had he "any reason to believe that his spouse was alive." This is, of course, in the absence of any decree, *per* section 2.

3–86   The decree may be varied or recalled at any time by any person having an interest.[92]

---

[87]   *ibid.*, s. 2.

[88]   Under the 1938 Act, the courts had refused to be drawn at all on the date of death: see *O'Halloran, Petr.*, 1974 S.L.T. (Notes) 19. For the view taken under another previous statute, the Presumption of Life (Limitation) (Scotland) Act 1891, s. 3, see *Tait* v. *Sleigh*, 1969 S.L.T. 227 at p. 228.

[89]   *ibid.*, s. 2. See *Labacianskas* v. *Labacianskas*, 1949 S.C. 280.

[90]   *i.e.* it is a judgment *in rem*.

[91]   See Clive, *The Law of Husband and Wife*, p. 651.

[92]   This is the effect of s. 4, and may be necessary, *e.g.* when the missing person turns up, or fresh evidence is available which makes it more likely that he is still alive, or varies the date at which he may be presumed to have died. However, a dissolved marriage cannot be revived, and a variation or recall made more than five years after the original cannot affect property rights: *ibid.*, s. 5.

PRESUMPTION OF LEGITIMACY

Prior to 1986, the common law recognised three different presumptions, **3–87** each of which sought to uphold the legitimacy of a child born to a married woman, but each of which related to a different set of facts. These in turn depended upon the chronological relationship between the conception, the birth and the marriage of the mother to the putative father. They were as follows:

(1) **Child conceived and born during marriage**

The common law has long recognised a presumption that a child **3–88** conceived and born in wedlock is the legitimate child of the parties to the marriage.[93] It is described by the Latin phrase *pater est quem nuptiae demonstrant*, and at common law the presumption was so strong that it required evidence beyond reasonable doubt to rebut it.[94]

(2) **Child conceived before marriage but born during it**

When the child in question is born during wedlock but conceived before **3–89** it, a similar presumption applies at common law to that relating to a child both conceived and born during wedlock. The position was confused in earlier cases by the principle of legitimation *per subsequens matrimonium*, a straightforward principle of substantive law whereby, when there is no dispute that the husband of the subsequent marriage is the father of the child, the child is legitimated by the subsequent marriage.[95]

(3) **Child born during the marriage**

When it is not disputed that the child in question is that of the husband, **3–90** any such child born before the marriage will also be legitimated *per subsequens matrimonium*.[96] The only remaining problem case was that in which it was disputed that the child was that of the man who subsequently married the mother after its birth.

Section 5 of the Law Reform (Parent and Child) (Scotland) Act 1986, **3–91** largely replaced these common law presumptions with a statutory one which provides that:

> "(1) A man shall be presumed to be the father of a child —

---

[93] Stair, III,iii,42; Erskine, I,vi,49.

[94] See paras. 2.123–2.124 *supra*, and the authorities quoted at n. 52 thereof.

[95] A common law principle which was confirmed and expanded under the Legitimation (Scotland) Act 1968, under which the principle still applies even if the parties were not free to marry at the time of the conception.

[96] Which, as indicated above, had the effect of legitimising an illegitimate child.

(*a*) if he was married to the mother of the child at any time in the period beginning with the conception and ending with the birth of the child;

(*b*) where paragraph (*a*) does not apply, if both he and the mother of the child have acknowledged that he is the father and he has been registered as such in any register kept under section 13 … or section 44 … of the Registration of Births, Deaths and Marriages (Scotland) Act 1965 or in any corresponding register kept under statutory authority in any part of the United Kingdom other than Scotland."

Subsection (1)(*a*) clearly covers the first two of the old common law presumptions, and by virtue of subsection (2), the new presumption applies equally to void, voidable and irregular marriages. Most importantly, however, subsection (4) provides that: "Any presumption under this section may be rebutted on a balance of probabilities," with the result that all the old case law[97] which established the burden of proof as being that beyond reasonable doubt is now redundant. Even when the husband denies that he is the father of the child, it will be presumed that he is (once the facts come within section 5(1)(*a*)), until it is proved otherwise on a balance of probabilities.[98]

3–92   The only situation in which there is now no presumption of legitimacy, either at common law or under the 1986 Act, is that in which the husband marries the mother of the child after its birth and fails to comply with the provisions of section 5(1)(*b*). The law on this point remains as it was laid down in *Brooks' Exrx.* v. *James*.[99]

3–93   The court in this case found itself in the difficult position of having to examine events which occurred almost 100 years previously, in which a woman (A) married a man (M) at a time when she already had an illegitimate child (W) aged three, and was seven months pregnant with another child (J) which was duly born after her marriage to M. No one was disputing the legitimacy of J, which could presumably have been proved by means of the normal presumption which arose when a man married a pregnant woman. The parties had freely admitted that J was M's child.[1] But it was argued successfully that the presumption could not apply when the child (W) was already born at the date of the marriage. As Lord Reid put it:[2]

"There is undoubtedly a presumption that a child born during marriage is the child of the husband. But there can be no presumption that, if a

---

[97] See paras. 2.123–2.124 *supra*, and the authorities quoted at n. 52 thereof.
[98] Such evidence may take the form of blood tests which can be used to provide a genetic fingerprint through DNA techniques. See s. 6 and paras. 9.06–9.20 *infra*.
[99] 1971 S.C.(H.L.) 77; see also paras. 8.45–8.49 *infra*.
[1]   And legitimation therefore flowed naturally *per subsequens matrimonium*.
[2]   *ibid.*, at p. 81.

man marries a woman who has an illegitimate child, that child is his child … Suppose a man marries a woman who has an illegitimate child of twelve, it would be absurd to presume that the child is his: that would have to be proved on a balance of probability."

There is, therefore, no presumption of legitimacy in such a case, and the court must instead look for positive evidence of legitimacy, because the burden of proof is now on the party seeking to prove that a child born out of wedlock is in fact the child of the subsequent husband. In reaching the conclusion that W was indeed the legitimate son of M, the court made use of another presumption, namely that of "common reputation."[3] This was on the basis that:

"Where, owing to the passage of time or for other good reasons, there is no other evidence at all, then common reputation ought to be regarded as prima facie evidence displacing the onus of proof … all the information we have points to (W) having been (M)'s son, and there is nothing pointing the other way."[4]

The presumption created by section 5(1)(b) is a totally new one, which had no forerunner at common law, under which an entry in the appropriate register was only one adminicle of evidence.[5] The new presumption based on a register entry does not apply if the presumption created by section 5(1)(a) does, so that if Mrs A has a child while she is married to A, but it is registered in the name of B, A will still be presumed to be the father of that child. However, the register entry would perhaps serve to rebut that presumption on a balance of probabilities, particularly if A did not assert paternity.

3–94

REBUTTABLE PRESUMPTIONS OF FACT

INTRODUCTION

Rebuttable presumptions of fact[6] arise, not from any established principle of law, but from the facts of particular cases. As such they are difficult to

3–95

---

[3] Which has a similar underlying rationale to marriage by "cohabitation and repute," the only form of irregular marriage now recognised by law; see Clive, *Husband and Wife*, p. 48. *N.B.* that marriage by cohabitation with habit and repute is another presumption *juris tantum*. See too, Wilkinson and Norrie, *The Law Relating to Parent and Child in Scotland*, p.133 n. 81 re "reputation of paternity."

[4] Lord Reid, *ibid.*, at p. 81. The onus of proof in this instance appears to have been only on a balance of probabilities.

[5] Walker and Walker, *Law of Evidence in Scotland*, pp. 33 and 61.

[6] Referred to by Walker and Walker, *op. cit.*, n. 5, para. 56, as presumptions *hominis vel judicis*.

classify, do not make particularly reliable precedents, and are distinguishable from the single items of circumstantial evidence[7] of which they are composed only by the fact that, as presumptions, they impose a burden of proof (and not necessarily a persuasive burden) on the party against whom they operate. This party then needs to produce some evidence in rebuttal, or the issue will almost certainly go against him or her. In the case of a single item of circumstantial evidence, on the other hand, there is no guarantee that the court will rely upon it, even if it goes unchallenged.

3–96 The main distinction between a rebuttable presumption of law and an equivalent one of *fact* is that the former is usually invoked by the production of relatively few facts which are required by law, and which are well identified in advance, whereas the latter may require a whole battery of facts of an imprecise nature before the court will be persuaded that a presumption has come into operation.

3–97 For example, as was seen in paragraphs 3.87–3.94, the legitimacy of a person X may be presumed by the relatively simple process of adducing evidence that he was born during the continuance of his parents' marriage. The point is universally recognised, and it is a simple question of whether or not the establishing facts can be proved. Once they are, then the presumption must be invoked, although it may of course be rebutted.

3–98 By comparison, a party seeking to advance their case to the point at which a presumption of fact comes into play does not know precisely which facts will have this effect, or how many different types of fact may require to be established. This is because presumptions of fact only come into operation after a certain stage has been reached on the amassed facts, at which the obvious inference from them cannot be ignored.

3–99 This process cannot simply be dismissed as the combined effect of various items of circumstantial evidence all pointing in the same direction.[8] Unlike circumstantial items taken singly, the facts which together invoke the presumption of fact also impose a burden of proof on the party against whom they operate. From that point onwards, that party will almost certainly lose on that issue if there is no rebuttal.[9] It is the aggregation of a mass of facts, virtually all of them circumstantial to the main issue, which leads to the operation of a presumption of fact.

3–100 The process of isolating and defining presumptions of fact is not assisted by two particularly common misuses of the word "presumption", namely in references to "the presumption of innocence" and "the presumption of sanity".

---

[7] Which are considered more fully in paras. 9.46–9.51, *infra*.

[8] There can be no doubt that the constituent facts which combine to invoke the presumptions are themselves normally circumstantial in nature.

[9] For examples of the process in action, see *Pickup* v. *Thames Insurance Co*. (1878) 3 Q.B.D. 594, esp. at p. 599, and *Klein* v. *Lindsay*, 1911 S.C.(H.L.) 9.

It is a commonplace for juries to be advised at the outset of a judge's **3–101** charge to them that there is "a presumption of innocence" which operates in favour of the accused.[10] This is simply another way of explaining that the persuasive burden of proving guilt rests with the prosecution. There are no basic facts which require to be proved before an accused person may be said to begin the trial with a "clean sheet". Rather, it is for the prosecution to prove the accused's guilt if they can.

By the same token, when one speaks of a "presumption of sanity", this **3–102** merely reflects the requirement of law that an accused person who wishes the court to believe that he was insane at the time of the commission of the offence has the persuasive burden of proof to demonstrate this.[11] In *H.M.A. v. Mitchell*,[12] Lord Justice-Clerk Thomson advised the jury that on the issue of insanity, "the burden of proof is on the defence, because in our law there is a presumption that a man is sane."

In the case of neither the "presumption of innocence" nor the **3–103** "presumption of sanity" does the party relying on the so-called presumption require to prove any qualifying facts before the presumption will operate. These two presumptions are not, therefore, presumptions of the type which can change the course of a trial once it is under way. This chapter is not concerned with the normal operation of the pre-ordained burdens of proof, but with the inferences to be drawn from facts adduced during the trial.

As with the previous classes of presumption, one may learn more of the **3–104** nature and effect of rebuttable presumptions of fact by examining some of the more common of them in operation.

THE PRESUMPTION ARISING FROM POSSESSION OF MOVEABLE PROPERTY

It has already been seen[13] how possession of heritable property for the **3–105** requisite period of time, together with a recorded title, forms the basis of a positive prescription which operates as an irrebuttable presumption of law. Since moveable property is not normally subject to registration of title, there cannot be the same documentary evidence of ownership as there is in the case of heritable property. Therefore the mere fact of possession is regarded as some evidence of ownership, but is more easily rebutted.

---

[10] This famous phrase may be found enshrined in some of the more famous leading cases on criminal evidence, such as *Slater* v. *H.M.A.*, 1928 J.C. 94 and *Lambie* v. *H.M.A.*, 1973 J.C. 53.

[11] One of those rare occasions upon which a persuasive burden is borne by an accused; see paras. 2.61–2.101 *supra*.

[12] 1951 J.C. 53, also referred to in paras. 2.61–2.101 *supra*.

[13] In paras. 3.15–3.24 *supra*.

3–106   There is accordingly a common law presumption that the person in possession of moveable property is the rightful owner.[14] The party seeking to assert that he is the true owner, against whom the presumption operates must show, "not only that the moveables once belonged to [him] but that his possession terminated in such a way that the subsequent possessor could not have acquired a right of property in them."[15]

3–107   It is clearly not enough for the party seeking to rebut the presumption to show that he or she once owned the property. Evidence must be led to eliminate any possibility that the present possessor could have acquired lawful title to it in the interim. This may be done in a variety of ways. For example by showing that the goods were stolen from the pursuer, or proving that the present possessor is merely a custodier in the course of a business and has no right of lien over the property.[16]

3–108   It is very common today for a person to be in legitimate possession of goods which he or she does not own. This can arise in connection with hire purchase, auction sales and contracts involving repair or storage. As Gloag and Henderson point out,[17] "the mere fact that the true owner has allowed another to be in possession of his property will not preclude him from asserting his right as against those who purport to have acquired the property or rights over it from the possessor."

3–109   The separation of ownership from possession has become very marked in recent years, and the modern context in which the presumption arising from possession of moveable property must be judged is perhaps best illustrated by the case of *George Hopkinson* v. *Napier & Sons*.[18] H, a Glasgow furnishing store, sold furniture to a married couple under a hire-purchase agreement. The furniture was delivered to their home, but a few months later another finance company (N) obtained decree against the couple for a different debt entirely. N sought to poind the items on hire-purchase from H, on the basis of the so-called "doctrine of reputed ownership."[19] It was held that in the absence of some personal bar operating against the true owner, the fact of possession merely established a factual presumption of

---

[14]   Lord President Cooper in *George Hopkinson Ltd.* v. *Napier & Sons*, referred to *infra*. See also Stair, II,i,42, Erskine, II,i,24 and Dickson, *Evidence*, para. 150.

[15]   Dickson, *op. cit.*, n. 14, para. 150, quoted with approval in *Prangnell O'Neil* v. *Lady Skiffington, infra*.

[16]   Lord Cockburn in *Anderson* v. *Buchanan* (1848) 11 D. 270, who observed (at p. 284) that the presumption was one "liable to be rebutted, and perhaps liable to be rebutted easily."

[17]   *Introduction to the Law of Scotland*, Chap. 37.3. Note, however, the general exception to this rule (*per* Factors (Scotland) Act 1890) which gives "ostensible authority" for sale, pledge or other disposition, to a "mercantile factor".

[18]   1953 S.C. 139.

[19]   A variant of the presumption now under consideration, whereby if A allows B to possess his property as apparent owner, he cannot assert his true ownership as against a third party who has relied on that apparent ownership when extending credit to B.

ownership which was capable of being rebutted, as it was in this case. Lord President Cooper[20] warned that:

> "I do not think that it is an overstatement of the position to-day to say that any creditor proposing to poind the furniture in an average working-class dwelling is put on his inquiry as to whether the furniture is the property of his debtor or is only held by him upon some limited title of possession."

Nevertheless, the presumption may still operate successfully even today, **3–110** as is evident from the ruling in *Prangnell-O'Neill* v. *Lady Skiffington*.[21] The pursuer had lived with the defender, with only one gap of some 18 months, for the period from 1968 to 1979. He left following a deterioration in their relationship. The defender refused to allow him back into her home, although she handed over to him a number of items of moveable property which she did not deny were his. The pursuer then raised an action against the defender for the return of various other items of moveable property which he claimed were his but of which she maintained possession.

It appears not to have been disputed that the items in question had at one **3–111** time been the property of the pursuer. It was equally not in dispute that by the time of the raising of the action, the *de facto* possession of those items rested with the defender. Even counsel for the pursuer conceded that, in the words of Lord Hunter,[22] "the defender starts with a presumption in her favour of ownership of the articles still in dispute, that presumption, which is one of fact, being based on her possession of the said articles as at the date when the present action was raised."

The court therefore required the pursuer to show that (i) he had once **3–112** been the owner of the disputed items, and (ii) he had parted with possession of them in such a way that the defender could not now assert ownership. In fact, although prepared to accept that he had proved (i), the court was firmly of the opinion that he had not proved (ii), because he could not even show that he had retained possession of the items in question until the parties had finally separated. On this point, the court accepted the finding of fact from the court below that the pursuer's evidence was no more persuasive than that of the defender, and that therefore, the matter being finely balanced, the defender won by virtue of the presumption.[23]

---

[20] At p. 147.

[21] 1984 S.L.T. 282.

[22] At p. 284.

[23] Clearly the court was of the opinion that the presumption imposed a persuasive burden of proof on the pursuer: see paras. 2.06–2.14 *supra*.

PRESUMPTION OF GUILT FROM POSSESSION OF RECENTLY STOLEN
PROPERTY

3–113 It was noted in both preceding chapters that when a person is found, in "criminative circumstances", in possession of recently stolen property, this is sometimes said to give rise to a "presumption of guilt." This presumption operates against that person on any charge of dishonesty relating to that property. However, what is really meant by this is that the prosecution have produced "a state of facts from which it is reasonable to infer guilt."[24] The presumption is therefore at best a factual one, which at most casts a tactical burden upon the accused who takes a high risk of conviction unless rebutting evidence is produced.[25] Given this reservation, one may now examine those factors which bring the presumption into play.

3–114 The underlying rationale for the presumption was observed by Alison to be that:[26]

> "Possession of the stolen property recently after the theft is the circumstance of all others which most strongly militates against a panel[[27]]; and, unless explained by him in some way consistent with his innocence, almost always leads with sensible juries to conviction."

In the light of cases decided since the days of Alison,[28] it is unwise to take his words too literally, but they illustrate the important principle that in such circumstances "the silent defender does take a risk."[29]

3–115 The leading case is generally accepted as being that of *Fox* v. *Patterson*.[30] F was a scrap metal dealer charged with reset of scrap metal bought in the course of his business from a man who could not subsequently be traced. F had obtained a receipt from the man, and had thereafter resold the metal with no attempt to conceal what he was doing. He sold it for a fair price, had it weighed on a public weighbridge, and upon discovering that it was stolen, made an offer of repayment to his customer. At his trial F was convicted of reset, and appealed.

3–116 Lord Justice-General Cooper[31] said of the presumption which had led to his conviction:

---

24 Renton and Brown, *Criminal Procedure*, para. 18–02.
25 See paras. 2.25–2.44 *supra*, and Gordon, "The Burden of Proof on the Accused," 1968 S.L.T. (News) 29 at p. 40.
26 *Principles of the Criminal Law of Scotland*, p. 320.
27 A now somewhat outmoded term for the accused in a solemn trial.
28 Notably *Wightman and Collins* v. *H.M.A., infra.*
29 Lord Justice-Clerk Grant in *McIlhargey* v. *Herron*, 1972 J.C. 38 at p. 42, referred to more fully in para. 2.29 *supra*. See also *McHugh* v. *H.M.A.*, 1978 J.C. 12, referred to more fully in paras. 11.50–11.65 *infra*.
30 1948 J.C. 104.
31 At p. 107.

"When applied with due regard to its limitations, the rule of recent possession of stolen goods is salutary and sensible: but, if its limitations are not observed, the cardinal presumption of innocence may easily be transferred into a rash assumption of guilt."

He reiterated that mere recent possession was not enough. In addition to that, the court required some "other criminative circumstances." And he said of these constituent factors: "Even when they concur, the weight of the resulting presumption, and the evidence required to elide it, will vary from case to case."[32] In the present case the appeal court held there was not even sufficient evidence of possession on the part of the accused shortly after the theft, let alone any evidence that he had attempted to conceal his actions. Therefore, there could not have been any "criminative circumstances" such as to invoke the presumption, and the conviction was set aside.

It seems from the authorities that the three constituent factors of the **3–117** presumption (*i.e.* possession, brevity of time since the theft, and criminative circumstances) may be used to complement each other, in the sense that strong evidence of recent possession may compensate for relatively weak additional evidence of criminative circumstances, and vice versa. Thus, as Lord Justice-Clerk Thomson put it in *Cryans* v. *Nixon*[33]:

"The necessity for the presence of other criminative circumstances arises because the degree and character of possession may vary greatly, and the fact of possession may be so bare as not by itself to be incriminating. Of course, the fact of possession may be in the circumstances so suspicious that very little in the way of incriminating circumstance may be enough … Very different considerations may rule according to whether a stolen article is found in an accused's pocket or in his back garden."

The case in question was a good illustration of this principle, since the stolen property had been found hidden in premises occupied by the accused, but to which others had free access. The accused, when questioned by the police, had simply stated that he knew nothing about it. Given the fact that the only evidence against him at that stage was bare possession, then the presumption could not be invoked.[34]

---

[32] At p. 108.

[33] 1955 J.C. 1 at p. 5. *N.B.* that the necessary possession must occur in a personal capacity, and not, *e.g.* as an employee: *Simpson* v. *H.M.A.*, 1952 J.C. 1. For a recent case in which possession two and a half months after the theft was held not to be "recent", see *MacLennan* v. *Mackenzie*, 1988 S.L.T. 16.

[34] Nor may the accused's silence when cautioned and charged, or thereafter, be said to constitute criminative circumstances: see *Wightman and Collins* v. *H.M.A.*, 1959 J.C. 44. A failure to answer preliminary police questions, or a false explanation, may however be sufficient— see *Cryans* v. *Nixon, supra* at p. 6.

3–118　　The necessary criminative circumstances may come from all manner of sources. In *Cameron* v. *H.M.A.*,[35] for example, the criminative circumstance which secured the accused's conviction was the fact that he ordered his wife to throw the stolen property out of the window only seconds before the police knocked on his door. In *Cassidy* v. *McLeod*,[36] on the other hand, it came from an overpowering collection of circumstantial items.

3–119　　The presumption may be invoked in respect of any offence involving theft, including aggravated theft,[37] and whether the accused is charged as actor or art and part.[38] It will also support a conviction for reset.[39]

PRESUMPTION OF NEGLIGENCE: *RES IPSA LOQUITUR*

3–120　In an action arising from the alleged negligence of the defender, the courts can, in some circumstances, infer negligence on the part of the defender from the facts adduced in proof by the pursuer. While this could be regarded as a "shifting of the burden of proof" from pursuer to defender,[40] or the imposition of a "tactical burden" of disproof on the defender,[41] the practical outcome is that if the defender does not produce evidence to show that despite appearances he was not negligent, he will almost certainly have decree pronounced against him.

3–121　　It is extremely difficult to generalise about presumptions of fact, and the so-called "presumption of negligence" is almost impossible to define. It can be seen as merely the operation of a natural principle which ensures that when one party produces a cogent case which prima facie points the finger of blame at the other, then that other party needs to adduce evidence to dispel the presumption created. A few examples will illustrate how widely the principle operates.

3–122　　In *Inglis* v. *L.M.S.*[42] the railway company were found liable for the death of a young boy after offering no evidence to counter the suggestion of negligence on their part. The presumption of negligence had been raised when the boy was proved to have fallen through the carriage door of a moving train, the handle of which had not been interfered with in any way by anyone in the carriage, including the boy. Likewise, in *Gunn* v. *McAdam & Son*[43] a railway company was held liable for the negligence of its

---

[35] 1959 J.C. 59.

[36] 1981 S.C.C.R. 270.

[37] *Christie* v. *H.M.A.*, 1939 J.C. 72; *Cameron* v. *H.M.A.*, *supra*.

[38] *Christie*, *supra*.

[39] *Christie* and *Cameron*, *supra*.

[40] The description given to the process by Walker and Walker, *op. cit.*, n. 5, para. 79.

[41] The more likely effect of such evidence: see paras. 2.25–2.44 *supra* esp. *Brown* v. *Rolls Royce*.

[42] 1941 S.C. 551, and see para. 2.142 *supra*.

[43] 1949 S.C. 31. Lord President Cooper said of the facts of this case at p. 38 that they were "clamorously calling for some explanation from [the defenders]."

employees who had removed a block from under the wheel of a bogie which had been standing on an incline. The bogie careered down the incline and collided with a trolley whose operator was killed—a clear indication of negligence which was never rebutted by defence evidence.

Another illustration of this process can be seen in *Fleming* v. *C. & W.* **3–123**
West.[44] The proprietors and occupiers of a house sued an electrical contractor for damages in respect of a fire which caused severe damage in the roof area. The fire broke out within 30 minutes of the defenders' workmen having completed the installation of an electric immersion heater in the water storage tank in the roof area. Before leaving, the workmen had declared the heater to be in satisfactory working order, and the technical evidence showed that the fire had begun in the roof area.

In repelling the defenders' plea to the relevancy of the pursuers' averments **3–124**
of negligence, Lord Stewart said of the facts of the case that: "the pursuers here have averred enough to raise a prima facie presumption of negligence on the part of the defenders' servants and thus to entitle them to a proof of their averments, even though they have not specified in detail the cause of the fire."[45]
Although the inference might well be "displaced for any number of reasons," said Lord Stewart, there was enough of a relevant case to allow the parties a proof.

There have been many other examples of the process in action over the **3–125**
years,[46] and each one may be taken as laying down a precedent only for future cases whose facts correspond. In fact, there would probably be no need to consider the concept of a "presumption of negligence"[47] at all were it not for one variant of it which has emerged in the past 100 years. This is the so-called doctrine of *res ipsa loquitur*. The development of this "doctrine" or principle has created considerable confusion.[48]

The doctrine emerged with the judgment of Erle C.J. in *Scott* v. *London* **3–126**
and St Katherine Docks Co.,[49] who, in dealing with a case in which a barrel had fallen from the window of a warehouse owned and operated by the defenders, offered this observation:

"There must be reasonable evidence of negligence. But where the thing is shown to be under the management of the defendant and his

---

[44] 1976 S.L.T. (Notes) 36.
[45] At p. 37.
[46] *e.g. Craig* v. *Glasgow Corpn.*, 1919 S.C.(H.L.) 1 (pedestrian knocked down when vehicle had enough time to slow down or stop) and *Moffat* v. *Park* (1877) 5 R. 13 (damage from a water pipe which was 30 years old and had been repaired six times in the previous 12 months).
[47] Which, after all, is only a collection of unrelated cases in which the proved facts militated strongly against the defender, and which has no apparent general principle behind it.
[48] Walker and Walker, *op. cit.*, n. 5, suggested, at para. 80, the maxim should cease to exist because if construed literally it tends to mislead.
[49] (1865) 3 H. & C. 596 at 601. His definition of *res ipsa loquitur* was adopted into Scots Law in *Milliken* v. *Glasgow Corpn.*, 1918 S.C. 857 at p. 867.

servants, and the accident is such as in the ordinary course of things does not happen if those who have the management use proper care, it affords reasonable evidence, in the absence of explanation by the defendants, that the accident arose from want of care."

Taken at face value, and limited to cases in which, in truth, "a thing tells its own story",[50] it is no more than a particular application of the general principle already noted. This is that the facts may point the finger so strongly at the defender that the court will inevitably look to him for an explanation of what happened which is at least consistent with a lack of negligence on his part. Unfortunately, it appears to have developed as something else, and to have been used as authority for the statement that once something which is involved in an accident is shown to have been under the control of the defender, it is for him to show that he used all reasonable care. This inverts the normal operation of the burdens of proof.

3–127 In more recent years the doctrine has been relegated to its rightful place in the general approach to a negligence action. This is best expressed in the words of Lord Moncrieff in *O'Hara* v. *Central S.M.T. Co.*[51]: "The characteristic of such cases is, or in my opinion ought to be, that the action or conduct which is charged as negligent has not been open to observation by witnesses, and so must be spoken to by according a voice to the subsequent event itself."

3–128 A good example of such a situation is afforded by the leading modern authority on *res ipsa loquitur*, *Devine* v. *Colvilles Ltd.*.[52] In this case a workman at Ravenscraig steelworks was injured after leaping 15 feet from a platform on which he had been working. He did so because of a violent explosion nearby which placed him in a state of fear and alarm for his own safety. The cause of the explosion was unexplained, but was known to have resulted from a fire in a hose conveying oxygen to a converter. The oxygen came from a plant operated by British Oxygen, and the defenders maintained that in the circumstances they could not be held to blame. However, further evidence established that responsibility for filtering impurities from the oxygen stream lay with the defenders, who could not prove that their filters were working properly. Even after accepting the opinion of the court below (the Court of Session) that "the maxim [of *res ipsa loquitur*] is of limited ambit",[53] their Lordships nevertheless had no doubt that this was a situation in which it applied. In the words of Lord Guest[54]:

---

[50] The literal translation from the Latin.
[51] 1941 S.C. 363 at p. 388.
[52] 1969 S.L.T. 154.
[53] Lord Guest, at p. 154.
[54] At pp. 154–155.

"The res which is said to speak for itself was the explosion. I must say that, without evidence to the contrary, I should have thought it self evident that an explosion of such violence that causes fear of imminent danger to the workers does not occur in the ordinary course of things in a steel works if those who have the management use proper care ... [The appellants] are absolved if they can give a reasonable explanation of the accident and show this explanation was consistent with no lack of care on their part."

On the facts the defenders had failed to do so, said the court, because they had failed to show that the filters for which they were responsible had been working properly. In the words of the Lord Justice-Clerk in the court below[55]:

"I accept their explanation of how the explosion happened, but I am unable to see how that explanation rebuts the presumption of negligence raised against them. It explains how the explosion probably occurred, but on exculpation, even at the best for the reclaimers, it is silent. The res has the last word as well as the first."

It would seem, therefore, that *res ipsa loquitur* will only normally operate **3–129** where (i) there is no direct evidence of how an accident happened, and (ii) the fact that the cause of the accident was something within the exclusive management and control of the defender. This becomes the starting-point for the court. If the defender can rebut the inevitable inference of mismanagement which arises from such facts, all well and good, but if he cannot, then indeed "the res has the last word."

The presumption will not, however, apply when there is some direct **3–130** evidence of what happened,[56] or where the offending item was not in the exclusive management or control of the defender.[57]

---

[55] Reported at p. 155, and adopted by their Lordships in the House of Lords.
[56] See, *e.g. O'Hara* v. *Central S.M.T., supra.*
[57] *McLeod* v. *Glasgow Corpn.*, 1971 S.L.T. 64; *Murray* v. *Edinburgh D.C.*, 1981 S.L.T. 253; *Carrigan* v. *Mavisbank Rigging Co.*, 1983 S.L.T. 316.

CHAPTER 4

JUDICIAL KNOWLEDGE

INTRODUCTION

4–01 "When a court takes judicial notice of a fact, as it may in civil and criminal cases alike, it declares that it will find that the fact exists, or direct the jury to do so, although the existence of the fact has not been established by evidence."[1]

4–02 This approach is permissible whenever the points in issue "are matters which can be immediately ascertained from sources of indisputable accuracy, or which are so notorious as to be indisputable."[2] Into this latter category come a whole host of common observations (*e.g.* that the streets of Edinburgh are busy during the rush hour, or that New Year's Day falls on January 1) which are so notorious that the judge or sheriff simply takes note of them when assessing evidence of which they are part, without even formally noting that this is what has been done.

4–03 In practice, therefore, many facts are judicially noted by the courts without any formal record being made of the process in action. On some occasions, however, a judge or sheriff will take the time to acknowledge on the record what is being done, while in others there is an obligation to refer to some recognised work of authority on the subject because, although the point at issue is beyond dispute, it is not within the immediate knowledge of the judge or sheriff.

4–04 Although the process and the legal consequences[3] are the same in both cases, it has become traditional to approach the subject by dividing judicial knowledge into two sections, one dealing with judicial notice without inquiry, and the other with judicial notice after inquiry.

---

[1] Cross and Tapper, *Evidence*, p. 69. This definition is an equally valid description of the process under Scots law. *N.B.* the terminology, also used under Scots law, whereby a fact which is within "judicial knowledge" is "judicially noted".

[2] Walker and Walker, *Law of Evidence in Scotland*, para. 52.

[3] *i.e.* that the fact judicially noted may not be argued in evidence, but must be taken as proved.

JUDICIAL NOTICE WITHOUT INQUIRY

As has already been noted, a fact which may be judicially noted without **4–05** inquiry is one which is "notorious," or well-known to everyone. It is just as much a product of everyday human experience of life as the factors which give rise to a factual presumption and to circumstantial evidence, but with judicial notice the observed fact is normally final, and may not be attacked by any contrary evidence.

A fact which is judicially noted without inquiry is perhaps the closest **4–06** that any court, civil or criminal, will ever come to absolute certainty on any point, and in most cases will be so incontrovertible that the party against whom it operates will not even attempt to argue it away. It is impossible to compile even the beginnings of a comprehensive list of the sorts of facts which the courts will judicially note without inquiry, but a few examples are offered.

Over the years, the courts have shown themselves willing to take notice **4–07** of the consequences of basic laws of mechanics which result in skids, collisions and physical injuries.[4] Only where it is alleged that something unusual occurred, or that "freak" conditions prevailed, will the parties request that the court consider the testimony of expert witnesses.[5]

In *Ballard* v. *North British Ry. Co.*,[6] for example, the court was **4–08** considering a claim for damages arising from the fact that, while on a steep incline leading on to the quayside at Tayport, a railway wagon broke loose from a defective coupling, raced down the incline and crashed on to the deck of a ship. Although it was proved that the defect in the coupling was a latent one,[7] the court nevertheless found the defenders liable because they had placed too much strain on it, by first of all approaching the incline too fast and then braking too hard. As Viscount Haldane put it,[8] in explaining how the court had come to this conclusion: "Of the character of such an operation, it is said that Judges must take notice of their own knowledge as men experienced in the affairs of life."

A good example of the way in which judges make use of their experience **4–09** "as men experienced in the affairs of life" without necessarily

---

[4] Notably in run-of-the-mill cases arising from accidents involving motor vehicles. It would, for example, be expected that a judge would accept without further need for proof the fact that, in icy conditions, a motorist should travel at a lower speed than normal.

[5] Dealt with in Chap. 16. *N.B.*, however, that such witnesses frequently base their own opinions on works of reference which then become part of their testimony as items of "received knowledge" on the subject—see, *e.g. Davie* v. *Magistrates of Edinburgh*, paras. 4.58 and 16.32–16.42 *infra*.

[6] 1923 S.C.(H.L.) 43, a case in which *res ipsa loquitur* was applied; see paras. 3.120–3.130 *supra*, and especially n. 52.

[7] And therefore not necessarily the responsibility of the defenders.

[8] At p. 49.

acknowledging that they have done so, is *Carruthers* v. *Macgregor*,[9] a claim in respect of an allegedly faulty building, in which an argument ensued as to whether cracks which appeared in the walls of a house were caused by poor quality concrete flooring or the use of unseasoned timber in the roof. Lord Blackburn observed,[10] almost casually:

> "The walls being rigid, it is of course obvious that any shrinkage of the roof beams and rafters, by drawing the top of the walls inwards, might produce the same effects as would be produced by an expansion of the concrete floor forcing the base of the walls outwards."

4–10   Equally it is regarded as one of the functions of a judge to know the ordinary meanings of words, whether they appear in contracts, defamatory statements, confessions or whatever, and only when it is alleged that a word was being used in an unusual, or technical, context will expert evidence be admissible to assist the court. One manifestation of this principle is the "parole evidence rule" under the law of contract, which denies to the parties, as a general rule, the opportunity of contradicting the apparently clear wording of a written contract.[11]

4–11   In practice the courts make use of everyday knowledge in an impressive variety of contexts, occasionally earning themselves a rebuke on appeal when they have gone too far and made use of knowledge which is strictly speaking "expert".[12] It is impossible to classify such permissible uses of general knowledge as have been employed, but among the remaining examples are *Kelly* v. *Glasgow Corporation*,[13] a case in which the Court of Session more than doubled the award of damages given by the Lord Ordinary in respect of the death of a mother of five knocked down by a Glasgow bus. The appeal court reminded trial judges of their duty to keep always in mind the falling value of money. And in *Hennigan* v. *McVey*,[14] the court reminded itself of the unreliable nature of a wild boar.

4–12   The courts also, as a matter of routine, take account of the habits of children, and the fact that special precautions must be taken to protect them from dangers which would be obvious to adults.[15] In *Manson* v. *H.M.A.*,[16] a

---

[9]   1927 S.C. 816.

[10] At p. 819.

[11] See *Inglis* v. *Buttery* (1878) 5 R.(H.L.) 87 at p. 90, and, generally paras. 9.36–9.45 *infra*. See also *Tancred, Arrol & Co.* v. *Steel Co. of Scotland* in para. 16.21 *infra*.

[12] See paras. 4.54–4.61 *infra*.

[13] 1949 S.C. 496; 1951 S.C.(H.L.) 15.

[14] (1881) 9 R. 411.

[15] See, *e.g. Taylor* v. *Glasgow Corporation*, 1922 S.C.(H.L.) 1, a successful claim for compensation against the operators of Glasgow Botanic Gardens by the father of a seven-year-old boy who died from the effects of eating poisoned berries.

[16] 1951 J.C. 49 at p. 52, considered more fully in para. 10.51 *infra*.

criminal court took judicial notice of the fact that witnesses in criminal trials are often subject to intimidation.

JUDICIAL NOTICE AFTER INQUIRY: GENERAL

When a matter is noted after judicial inquiry, it is one which, although **4–13** incontrovertible, a judge or sheriff nevertheless cannot be expected to carry around in his or her head. Thus, while an undoubted function of any occupant of the bench is to "know" Scots law on any matter which may be placed before the court, it is not unreasonable for there to be a requirement to consult authoritative books on the subject, or to peruse case reports or statutes.

Similarly, in some cases it is necessary for a judge or sheriff to consult a **4–14** reference book or other learned tome before judicially noting that the matter in hand is beyond argument. When judicial notice is taken after inquiry, then the court is merely refreshing its memory on some point which it is taken to "know" anyway, and of which it merely requires reminding. It is a different matter if the subject is the province of a specialist, and is contested, since then the more appropriate course is to hear expert testimony and receive it as oral evidence.[17] Nor may the judge or sheriff simply read a textbook and judicially note its findings.[18]

Given, then, that there is a dividing line between being reminded of the **4–15** obvious and taking unchallenged expert opinion as if it were fact, which books may the courts use in order to assist them in the pursuit of judicial knowledge? It is now well established that they may employ a dictionary, as in *Inland Revenue* v. *Russell*,[19] in which by reference to the *Oxford Dictionary* the Court of Session satisfied itself that a person could be the "stepchild" of another for the purposes of the Finance Acts, even though that person's natural parents were still alive.

No doubt other unimpeachable sources of pure reference may also be **4–16** employed without any great danger, for example, Ordnance Survey maps for measurements of distance and marine charts for ocean depths. However, although a text may be commonly regarded as a reference book, that does not necessarily raise its contents to the status of being within judicical knowledge. For example, the courts have held that the fact that there is a Highway Code is within judicial knowledge, but the stopping distances given in it are not and cannot be referred to without leading evidence.[20]

Further problems arise when what is employed is in itself a disputable **4–17** work, on whose contents there can be more than one opinion. An example

---

[17] See Chap. 16 *infra*.
[18] See paras. 4.54–4.61 *infra*, esp. *Davie* v. *Magistrates of Edinburgh*.
[19] 1955 S.C. 237. See also *Edinburgh Corporation* v. *Lord Advocate*, 1923 S.C. 112.
[20] *Cavin* v. *Kinnaird*, 1994 S.L.T. 111. See also Macphail, *Evidence*, Chap. 11.35A.

of this type of work is the medical or scientific textbook which, while it may be the summation of all contemporary wisdom when it is first published, rapidly becomes overtaken by new research.[21] Such areas ought perhaps to be reserved for expert testimony, where textbooks and other academic research can be used as a secondary source and "spoken to" by the witness. There remain, though, occasions when judges consider it appropriate to form their own opinions.

4–18 An example of this was seen in the consideration of the normal, or likely, period of human gestation. In *Preston-Jones* v. *Preston-Jones*[22] Lord Normand observed:

> "If the only period to be considered were the period of gestation, I have myself no doubt that ordinary men and women would unhesitatingly say that a 360-days gestation is beyond the limits of what is possible, and a court of law could so decide without evidence. So far at least judicial knowledge may be allowed to reach."

4–19 As will be seen in paragraphs 4.54–4.61, the appeal courts have on occasions stepped in to prevent the judges from becoming instant experts on matters which ought not to be left to judicial knowledge. For the only matters which should be judicially noted even after inquiry are undisputed items of common knowledge. Care should therefore be taken before assuming that any standard work of reference may be employed in place of an expert witness.

With this *caveat*, some of the items which are most frequently judicially noted after inquiry are now examined.

ACTS OF PARLIAMENT

4–20 It has been accepted for many years that the provisions of Acts of Parliament need not be proved in court, but may be judicially noted.[23] The point is now succinctly established by the Interpretation Act 1978, s. 3 of which states,

---

[21] For example, great strides were made in the field of blood grouping in the years after the Second World War, during which period nuclear physics also emerged as a separate science. Textbooks on either subject published prior to, say, 1945 would today be greatly out of date.

[22] [1951] A.C. 391 at p. 406. But see *Williamson* v. *McLelland*, 1913 S.C. 678, in which the court ignored the expert medical evidence in order to rule that a child born to a woman only 306 days after intercourse with the pursuer could not be his.

[23] As is required anyway of any Scots judge or sheriff, all of whom are required to have judicial knowledge of the entire law of Scotland, from whatever source. See paras. 4.30–4.33 *infra*. *N.B.* Until recently, the courts were not allowed to investigate the history of an Act as a Bill, either through the pages of Hansard or by means of prior White Papers: see *MacCormick* v. *L.A.*, 1953 S.C. 396 at p. 411. By virtue of the decision in *Pepper* v. *Hart* [1993] A.C. 593, the courts are permitted to examine Hansard for the relevant debates where the construction of a statute is ambiguous or obscure or the literal meaning would lead to an absurdity.

"Every Act is a public Act to be judicially noticed as such, unless the contrary is expressly provided by the Act."[24] Section 3 is stated[25] to apply to all Acts passed subsequent to January 1, 1979, and to all Acts[26] passed after 1850. In practice, judicial notice is also taken of public Acts passed by the United Kingdom Parliament from 1707 to 1850, and of public Acts of the Scottish Parliament prior to 1707.[27] Only when the actual contents of a statute are in dispute[28] will the court call for authentication, in the form of a copy bearing to be printed by the Queen's Printer or under the authority of H.M. Stationery Office.[29]

STATUTORY INSTRUMENTS

There is some uncertainity about whether statutory instruments[30] are within judicial knowledge, and therefore not requiring to be proved in court. The authority for such an assumption is not altogether unchallengeable,[31] and the main supporting authority quoted by Walker and Walker[32] is best regarded as a special case relying on its own peculiar facts.   **4–21**

In *MacMillan* v. *McConnell*,[33] a publican was prosecuted for liquor offences under (i) the Defence of the Realm Regulations 1915, and (ii) an Order of the Central Control Board (Liquor Traffic) for Scotland West Central Area. Neither of these two was produced by the fiscal, and the sheriff felt himself unable to convict. It was held by the High Court that a conviction should have been entered, since the production of the relevant legislation was unnecessary because under the wartime legislation which had produced both the Regulations and the Order, they were to be regarded as equivalent to statutes. The key passage appears at page 47, where it was   **4–22**

---

[24] This, in turn, is derived from the Interpretation Act 1889, s. 9, and s. 21(1) of the 1978 Act defines "Act" so that it "includes a local and personal or private Act." "Subordinate legislation" means Orders in Council, orders, rules, regulations, schemes, warrants, bye-laws and other instruments made or to be made under any Act.

[25] *ibid.*, s. 22(1) and Sched. 2.

[26] For the definition of which, see n. 24 *supra*.

[27] Walker and Walker, *op. cit.*, n. 2, para. 194, relying on the somewhat generalised authority of *McMillan* v. *McConnell*, 1917 J.C. 43 and *Herkes* v. *Dickie*, 1958 J.C. 51, considered more fully in para. 4.29 *infra*. However, it is unlikely that this practice will ever be challenged in future.

[28] *e.g.* where it is alleged that the copy produced contains a misprint.

[29] Walker and Walker, *op. cit.*, n. 2.

[30] Which term has since 1948 included Orders in Council (Statutory Instruments Act 1946, s. 1(1)) and Acts of Sederunt and Adjournal (*ibid.*, s. 1(2)). Acts of Sederunt and Adjournal passed prior to that date also appear to have had statutory effect, first under the Act 1540, c. 10, and then under the Rules Publication Act 1893, s. 4.

[31] See Macphail, *op. cit.*, n. 20, Chap. 11.02, who concludes that there is a need for a U.K. statute to put the point beyond doubt in all cases.

[32] *op. cit.*, n. 2, para. 198(*c*).

[33] 1917 J.C. 43.

held that: "The Law, indeed, is presumed to be known to everyone. A statute or order having the force of statute[34] is not produced to prove what the law is, but merely to refresh the memory of the Judge or lieges."[35]

4–23　　There are, however, stronger authorities for the current practice of regarding a statutory instrument as being the equivalent of an Act of Parliament. For example, in *Sharp* v. *Leith*[36] the accused had been convicted of the illegal movement of cattle, contrary to the Foot and Mouth Disease Order 1892, and local authority regulations which were made under the Order and given the status of statutory instruments by that Order. In rejecting an appeal based on the ground that neither the Order nor the regulations had been produced in court, Lord McLaren ruled:[37]

> "When an Act of Parliament authorises the making of Regulations, it points out the manner in which proof of such regulations is to be given, but where there is no dispute as to the existence and substance of the order or regulations,[38] it is, in my opinion, quite unnecessary, and would be quite out of place to adduce such proof. I agree that ... if any mistake has been made in setting out the terms of the Regulations, or doubt as to the power of the Board to impose them, we should be quite willing to hear argument on these points, but it is a different proposition altogether to say that an Order having the force of an Act of Parliament[39] must be produced as a matter of evidence under a complaint charging a person with having contravened it."

4–24　　A firmer authority is *Hutchison* v. *Stevenson*,[40] in which following a conviction under the Sale of Food and Drugs Act of 1895 of an offence of selling milk which did not comply in quality with Regulations issued under that Act for quality control purposes, the accused appealed on the ground that the Regulations themselves had not been adduced in evidence as a production. In the process of quashing the appeal on the totally unconnected ground that the correct sampling procedure had not been followed, Lord McLaren stated[41] that:

---

[34]　*N.B.* that the court was not ruling that all statutory instruments are the equivalent of statute, but merely stating their effect when they are.

[35]　Quoting the authority of Dickson, *Evidence*, s. 1105.

[36]　(1892) 20 R.(J.) 12.

[37]　At pp. 15–16.

[38]　Where there is, then in practice it is customary to call for a Stationery Office copy: see Documentary Evidence Act 1868, s. 2 and 1882, s. 2, and Walker and Walker and Macphail, *op. cit.*, nn. 2 and 20.

[39]　Which again seems to be begging the important question of whether or not a statutory instrument does have the force or status of an Act of Parliament if the "enabling Act" does not give it such force or status.

[40]　(1902) 4 F.(J.) 69.

[41]　At p. 72.

"The production of these regulations seems to me like the production of an Act of Parliament in order to satisfy the Judge as to the existence of the law on the particular point. The regulations are not part of the proof of the contravention of the law, and therefore they are not documents necessary for the proof of the prosecutor's case."

As will have been noticed from these leading authorities, the most likely **4–25** context in which it may be argued that an item of delegated legislation such as a statutory instrument should be produced in court is in the course of a summary prosecution. The position is clear in relation to statutory instruments which are relied upon in a summary prosecution. Section 154 (2) of the Criminal Procedure (Scotland) Act 1995, states that:

"Any order by any of the departments of state or government or any local authority or public body made under powers conferred by any statute, or a print or copy of any such order, shall when produced in a summary prosecution be received in evidence of the due making, confirmation and existence of such order without being sworn to by any witness and without any further or other proof."

There is a proviso which allows any such order to be challenged on the grounds that it was made *ultra vires* of the authority which made it, or "on any other competent ground". Section 154(2) is a comprehensive provision which affirms those common law authorities which held statutory instruments to be of equivalent status to an Act of Parliament.[42] As Renton and Brown observe[43]: "Orders etc. which do have statutory status form part of the general law of the land and need not be produced. All statutory instruments fall into this class. In other cases it is a question for the court whether the particular order or regulation does have statutory force."

While the position in relation to summary criminal cases may be clear, **4–26** it remains unclear whether judicial notice may be taken of statutory instruments in civil cases, or in solemn criminal cases.[44] For this reason, Macphail[45] recommended that:

"it may be desirable to enact in a United Kingdom statute a provision to the effect that judicial notice shall be taken of all statutory instruments, and that in case of doubt as to their terms they may be established by reference to a Stationery Office copy."

---

[42] See the cases referred to at nn. 36 and 40 *infra*.
[43] *Criminal Procedure,* para. 14–62.
[44] Since s. 154(2) of the 1995 Act applies only in summary cases. In practice it is rare for a case involving the breach of a statutory instrument to be placed on indictment, and in many cases the enabling statute under which it was made provides for summary prosecution only.
[45] *op. cit.,* n. 20, para. 11.02.

4–27   There have been a number of cases concerning the status of the breathalysing equipment used by the police in cases where drivers are alleged to have been driving with excess alcohol.[46] In *Valentine* v. *McPhail*[47] the appeal court held that it was within judicial knowledge to know that the Camic device was a breathalyser of a type approved by the Breath Analysis Devices Approval (Scotland) Order 1983. It was not therefore necessary to produce the Order as evidence to prove the Camic was an approved device.[48]

4–28   The position regarding the legal status of local authority bye-laws is distinct and separate. Such bye-laws are another form of delegated legislation, but they do not normally arise directly "under powers conferred by any statute."[49] When they do not acquire statutory status by virtue of an enabling Act they must be produced in court as an item of evidence, and are not, for example, covered by section 154 of the 1995 Act.[50]

4–29   The leading authority is that of *Herkes* v. *Dickie*,[51] a case in which a burgh licensing court made bye-laws which required all public houses in their area to close at 1 p.m. on New Year's Day. A licensee was convicted of a contravention of these bye-laws, but appealed on the ground that the bye-law in question had not been produced in court. Even counsel for the prosecutor had to concede that they should have been, and Lord Cameron[52] gave his opinion that:

> "While it can never be suggested that a public general statute requires to be produced or proved in criminal proceedings, it has never, so far as I know, been argued that there is any such general presumption in favour of bye-laws of limited personal and local application made by a local authority ... In my opinion, the extent to which such local orders or bye-laws prove themselves is a question to be decided in each case in light of the statutory provisions which authorise the making of such orders or bye-laws and lay down the method by which their existence and validity is to be established in any legal proceedings."

Scots Law

4–30   In paragraphs 4.20–4.29 above, we considered the extent to which judges, sheriffs and stipendiary magistrates are expected to be aware of the effect

---

[46] *McIlhargey* v. *Herron*, 1972 J.C. 38.

[47] 1986 S.L.T. 598.

[48] This case overruled the decision of *Knox* v. *Lockart*, 1985 S.L.T. 248. For a discussion of the problems implicit in the judgment, see Sheriff Gordon's commentary on the case at 1986 S.C.C.R. 326.

[49] See 1995 Act, s. 154(2), *supra*.

[50] See Renton and Brown, *op. cit.*, n. 43.

[51] 1958 J.C. 51. See also *Johnston* v. *MacGillivray*, 1993 S.L.T. 120.

[52] *ibid.*, pp. 58–59. See also Lord Patrick at p. 55. This case is also considered in another context in para. 4.57 *infra*.

of statutory law in so far as it forms part of the law of Scotland. It would seem that the same is true of any order having statutory effect. Such matters are deemed to be within judicial knowledge, and therefore require no proof.[53]

This statement has never been challenged in the Scots courts, and both **4–31** statutes and judicial precedents are quoted daily in our courts without need for proof. The practice of quoting at length from statutes and case reports is officially simply a process whereby the court's memory is refreshed. It is the duty of all those who appear in the courts to bring to the courts' attention *all* the relevant law on the matter in hand, whether it is favourable to their case or not. The judgment of the House of Lords in *Glebe Sugar Refining Corporation* v. *Greenock Harbour Trustees*[54] reinforced this duty:

> "It is not, of course, in cases of complication possible for their **4–32**
> Lordships to be aware of all the authorities, statutory or otherwise
> which may be relevant to the issues which in the particular case require
> decision. Their Lordships are therefore very much in the hands of
> counsel, and those who instruct counsel, in these matters, and this
> House expects, and indeed insists, that authorities which bear one
> way or the other upon matters under debate shall be brought to the
> attention of their Lordships by those who are aware of these
> authorities. This observation is quite irrespective of whether or not
> the particular authority assists the party which is so aware of it."

Whenever a matter may be said, therefore, to be one of Scots law, the **4–33** Scots courts are taken to be aware of it without need for proof, simply a need for the refreshment of judicial memory. The extent to which a point of law is within judicial knowledge is therefore coterminous with the extent to which the point comes under Scots law.[55] Clearly this will be true of any statute which covers Scotland, and any decision reached by a Scots court, and this latter category will include even the House of Lords, as the supreme court of appeal for all civil cases from Scotland.[56]

---

[53] Walker and Walker, *op. cit.*, n. 2, para. 53(b): Scots law, including Scottish judicial decisions in the House of Lords and the lower courts, and the practice and procedure of the Scottish courts, are within judicial knowledge, and evidence regarding these matters is excluded." See also Macphail, *op. cit.*, n. 20, Chap. 2.02.

[54] 1921 S.C.(H.L.) 72 at p. 77.

[55] The extent to which, in the case of judicial precedent, the court will be bound by it will of course depend upon the relative positions of the two courts (*i.e.* the trial court and the court which laid down the precedent) in the hierarchy of Scots courts.

[56] For the precise status of the House of Lords in this context, see *Orr-Ewing* v. *Orr-Ewing* (1884) 11 R. 600, in which it was also established that the Scots courts must defer to rulings of the House in English or Irish cases in which the point of law involved is analogous to the law of Scotland. The same is believed to be true of rulings of the Judicial Committee of a similar nature.

Foreign Law

4–34   Judges of the Scottish courts are expected to take judicial notice of all Scots law, from whatever source. This will occasionally encompass the judgments of the House of Lords, on points not only of Scots law but also points from other jurisdictions which are the same as Scots law. This does not, generally, oblige the Scots courts to note judicially any point of "foreign" law. Foreign law is regarded in the Scots courts as a question of *fact* to be proved like any other.

4–35   There is, however, a rebuttable presumption of law[57] to the effect that foreign law[58] is the same as Scots law on any given point. The burden of proving that the foreign law is in fact different rests upon the party relying on that assertion.[59] The same party must also prove as a matter of evidence what that law is, and must do so by means of evidence.[60] A variety of methods may be used,[61] but the important point in the present context is that foreign law may not, as a general rule, be judicially noted.

4–36   In *Duffes* v. *Duffes*[62] the Court of Session refused to declare incompetent a divorce petition against the defender on the alleged grounds, (i) that he was domiciled in the American state of Ohio; and (ii) that he had obtained a divorce decree against the pursuer in the Ohio courts in 1970 which was valid in Scotland. In the course of granting a proof Lord Emslie felt himself obliged to follow "the rule that questions of foreign law are, in the Court of Session, questions of fact, which must be focused in averment ... It may be that there is such a rule of reciprocity as the defender maintains, but I cannot notice it judicially in procedure roll where it is not admitted by the parties."[63]

4–37   To this general rule, there are two broad categories of exception. First of all, as has already been noted, the House of Lords in civil cases is the highest Scottish court, and it may judicially note the laws of all the jurisdictions which also send appeals to it. For example, it would be perfectly competent when hearing a Scottish appeal for the House of Lords to note judicially

---

[57]   For the general nature of such presumptions, see paras. 3.26–3.31 *supra*.

[58]   Which term encompasses the law of any jurisdiction outwith Scotland (see Walker and Walker, *op. cit.,* n. 2, para. 415) and includes English law (see *Orr-Ewing* v. *Orr-Ewing* in para. 4.33 and n. 56 *supra*).

[59]   Anton, *Private International Law*, p. 773; see also *Bonner* v. *Balfour Kilpatrick Ltd.*, 1974 S.C. 223 and *Emerald Stainless Steel Ltd.* v. *South Side Distributions Ltd.*, 1982 S.C. 61.

[60]   *Cf.* Anton, *op. cit.*, n. 59, p. 774: "The rule that foreign law must be proved by evidence is always applicable in the Scottish courts." Since any point of law discovered is for the purposes of that case a fact, it may not be founded on as a precedent for any future action: see *Killen* v. *Killen infra*.

[61]   *e.g.* remit of consent to a foreign lawyer, the hearing of expert testimony, or a stated case to a Dominions court.

[62]   1971 S.L.T. (Notes) 83.

[63]   At p. 84.

and incorporate in its judgment a point of English law which did not conflict with Scots law.

This process may be observed in operation in reverse in *Elliot* v. *Joicey*,[64] **4–38** an action raised in the English courts over a will made by a domiciled Scots woman. It was held by the House of Lords that in the circumstances her will fell to be interpreted under Scots law, but that:

> "No doubt in the courts below[65] the law of Scotland is a matter of fact and must be vouched there by evidence or admission. But in your Lordships' House the law of Scotland is a matter not of fact but of law, for this House is the *commune forum* of both England and Scotland, and your Lordships have judicial knowledge of the laws of both countries."[66]

Secondly, there is a group of situations in which, by virtue of various **4–39** statutory requirements, Scottish courts are obliged to take judicial notice of foreign law, mainly English.

First of all, in *Commissioners for the Special Purposes of the Income* **4–40** *Tax* v. *Pemsel*,[67] it was held that when dealing with income tax cases, the Scottish courts are obliged to apply the English law of charities. The same duty is also imposed upon them in any other context in which the English charity laws are stated by statute to apply to Scottish cases.[68]

Secondly, and also for the sake of uniformity, when sitting in their **4–41** capacity as judges in the Courts-Martial Appeal Court, Scottish judges are required to adopt the criminal law and procedure of England, as well as its laws of evidence, since these are the basis of courts-martial hearings.[69]

Finally, under the Maintenance Orders (Reciprocal Enforcement) Act **4–42** 1972, and for various purposes,[70] the Scottish courts are required to note the law operating in any country from which a maintenance case originates which has a reciprocation agreement with Scotland, and to make a decision in conformity with the law of that country.[71]

---

[64] 1935 S.C.(H.L.) 57.
[65] *i.e.* the English courts below the House of Lords.
[66] Lord MacMillan, at p. 68.
[67] [1891] A.C. 531.
[68] An example is the Consumer Credit Act 1974, s. 189, which requires the definition of "charity" to be as it is under the Income Tax Acts. In *Scottish Burial Reform Society* v. *Glasgow Corporation*, 1967 S.C.(H.L.) 116, when dealing with a claim for rate exemption under the Local Government (Financial Provisions etc.) (Scotland) Act 1962, Lord Reid observed (at p. 122) of the effect of s. 4: "It is well settled that that means that we have to apply the English law of charities."
[69] See Courts-Martial (Appeals) Act 1968, s. 2(1)(*b*) which provides for the appointment of Scottish judges to sit in such appeals. And, see *Hendry*, 1955 S.L.T. (Notes) 66.
[70] *e.g. per* s. 7 for the confirmation of a provisional maintenance order, and *per* s. 9 for the revocation of a registered maintenance order.
[71] *Killen* v. *Killen*, 1981 S.L.T. (Sh.Ct.) 77.

E.C. Law

4–43 In addition to taking judicial notice of Acts of the United Kingdom Parliament, and Scots law from whatever source, the Scottish courts must also now take notice of legislation emanating from the E.C. Thus, by virtue of the European Communities Act 1972, s. 2(1):

> "All such rights, powers, liabilities, obligations and restrictions from time to time created or arising by or under the Treaties, and all such remedies and procedures from time to time provided for by or under the Treaties, as in accordance with the Treaties are without further enactment to be given legal effect or used in the United Kingdom shall be recognised and available in law, and be enforced, allowed and followed accordingly."

4–44 Section 3 goes on to require all Scottish courts to treat questions of Community law as questions of law, and not questions of fact which require to be proved as items of foreign law (see paragraphs 4.34–4.42 *supra*). The same section requires such courts to take judicial notice of "the Treaties, of the Official Journal of the Communities and of any decision of, or expression of opinion by, the European Court on any such question as aforesaid: and the Official Journal shall be admissible as evidence of any instrument or other act thereby communicated of any of the Communities or of any Community institution."[72]

4–45 In the English Court of Appeal, in *H.P. Bulmer Ltd.* v. *J. Bollinger S.A.*,[73] Lord Denning, in typical fashion, said of the Treaty of Rome that it "is like an incoming tide. It flows into the estuaries and up the rivers. It cannot be held back. Parliament has decreed that the Treaty is henceforth to be part of our law. It is equal in force to any statute."

4–46 Under section 2(1) of the Civil Jurisdiction and Judgments Act 1982, judicial notice must be taken of the E.C. Conventions which gave rise to the 1982 Act, which have the force of law in Scotland. A similar provision is laid down for decisions of the European Court on Conventions, per section 3(2).

History and Current Affairs

4–47 It can be competent for the courts to take judicial notice of matters of historical fact or contemporary custom. In some cases[74] the courts are able

---

[72] *ibid.*, subs. (2). Even those instruments not published in the Official Journal may be proved, *per* subss. (3), (4) and (5), by production of a certified true copy.

[73] [1974] Ch. 401, at p. 418.

[74] *e.g.* when noting the identity of the current U.K. Prime Minister, or the existence of a national stoppage such as the 1984 miners' strike.

to do so without reference to standard works, and without the need for any sort of inquiry, but certain cases demand some preliminary research. In *Read* v. *Bishop of Lincoln*[75] the House of Lords had to consider whether or not the mixing of communion wine with water was a practice at variance with the law of the Church. It was held that when the judge's own historical knowledge on such matters proved inadequate, reference might be made to historical reference works, since "where it is important to ascertain ancient facts of a public nature the law does permit historical works to be referred to."[76]

In *Renouf's Trs.* v. *Haining*,[77] the question in issue was the validity of a **4–48** clause in a will which provided for payment of the salaries of two "native missionaries" to preach "the Gospel of Jesus Christ my Lord among the heathen." It was alleged that the clause fell for lack of specification, since it did not identify any particular branch of the Church from which such missionaries might be chosen. Lord Guthrie, in holding that it was not too vague in its purpose, combined history with current affairs in the course of his finding that: "Judicial knowledge involves acquaintance not only with ancient history but with present day conditions."[78]

In *MacCormick* v. *Lord Advocate*[79] the Court of Session found itself in **4–49** the unique situation of being petitioned, by two members of the Scottish Covenant Association, to interdict Her Majesty's Government from describing the present Queen as "Elizabeth II." It was argued for the pursuers that this royal title allegedly contravened an article of the Treaty of Union of 1707, and was inconsistent with both historical fact and political reality. Lord President Cooper began by judicially noting the fact that the Queen had used this title when taking the statutory oath in relation to the rights and privileges of the Church of Scotland, and that so far as he was concerned that was enough to settle the issue. He stated she had been confirmed in that title, and it was now too late for challenge. He based his judicial knowledge on his examination of the appropriate entry in the Books of Sederunt after the signed oath had been presented to the Court of Session.[80]

ECONOMIC AND BUSINESS AFFAIRS

Judicial knowledge can also be applied in the world of business and **4–50** commerce, in which the Scots courts have never found difficulty in

---

[75] [1892] A.C. 644.
[76] Lord Halsbury, at p. 653.
[77] 1919 S.C. 497.
[78] At pp. 510–511.
[79] 1953 S.C. 396.
[80] Lord Russell, at p. 115, also took judicial notice of the fact that at every Coronation since 1707, the incoming monarch had been proclaimed in his or her royal styles and title, and this practice had never been challenged. His Lordship did not therefore feel that the present court was in any position to raise a challenge.

displaying a lively awareness of economic reality. Many of the most common examples[81] pass unnoticed and unrecorded in court proceedings, and only rarely will a case report contain a record of the court having consulted some indisputable source of reference before coming to a conclusion.

4–51   In *Naismith* v. *Assessor for Renfrewshire*[82] the rateable values of all properties in Renfrewshire were increased by a flat rate of 20 per cent., regardless of individual circumstances. In an appeal against this policy, the Court of Session held that the failure of the assessor to lead evidence in justification of the increase in the particular case was fatal to his defence of the appeal. It was held that although the court could take into account various known facts such as the increase in the value of houses since the 1914–18 war and the general rise in living costs, it could not apply it on a flat-rate basis to all cases, since it was conceivable that some properties had actually gone down in value. Lord Hunter,[83] speaking of an Act of 1919 which allowed landlords to increase the "standard rents" for properties, gave his opinion that: "It is a matter of general knowledge that the increases made lawful by the latter Act are within the increases which the operation of economic causes consequent upon the war would in the ordinary case have justified landlords in exacting."

4–52   The introduction of new business methods can also become a matter of judicial knowledge, as in *Muirhead & Turnbull* v. *Dickson*,[84] in which the Court of Session was called upon to decide whether the payment of instalments of 15 shillings per week in respect of a piano arose under a contract of hire or a contract of hire purchase. The Lord President, referring to the relatively recently-emerged form of business finance known as hire-purchase, said of it[85]: "It is a form of contract which has become common enough in modern times, and it was judicially inquired into and noticed in the case of *Helby* v. *Mathews*."[86] A few years later, when examining the repayment provisions of a hire-purchase contract in *Taylor* v. *Wylie & Lochhead*,[87] the Lord President said: "It is quite evident that, according to the ordinary business view, the instalments will be so calculated as to provide for interest on so much of the principal as is not paid. All that, I think, may be taken to be common judicial knowledge of this class of agreement."

---

[81]   *e.g.* allowances for inflation, knowledge of contemporary industrial trends and awareness of underlying economic conditions such as unemployment.

[82]   1921 S.C. 615.

[83]   At p. 624.

[84]   (1905) 7 F. 686.

[85]   At p. 691.

[86]   [1895] A.C. 471, a House of Lords case in which the term "hire purchase" seems not actually to have been used. The term was, however, employed in *Lee* v. *Butler* [1893] 2 Q.B. 318, a case noted in *Helby* v. *Mathews*.

[87]   1912 S.C. 978 at p. 983.

It was observed in the *Lord Advocate's Reference No.1 of 1992*[88] that it **4–53** could not be said to fall within judicial knowledge that the Halifax Building Society was a building society within the meaning of the Building Societies Act 1986.

LIMITATIONS ON THE USE OF JUDICIAL KNOWLEDGE

There are limitations to the use and application of judicial knowledge. Judges **4–54** and sheriffs should not attempt to make use of their own personal experience of a particular matter where direct evidence is available which might have a bearing on the subject. Judicial notice is only supposed to be taken of matters which are beyond dispute, and not those which are in issue between the parties.

The danger of invoking personal knowledge was highlighted in *Gibb* v. **4–55** *Edinburgh and District Tramways*.[89] In this case, the pursuer was seeking damages for injuries sustained when her dress was caught on an unguarded section of a tramcar which lay beneath the tramcar and between the front and back wheels. It was averred by her that it should have been guarded. On appeal, after noting his own surprise that a tramcar might be so designed as the present one was averred to be, the Lord President in a sense corrected himself, by adding[90]:

> "I do not think one is entitled to use what, of course, one cannot help having—one's knowledge of the construction of ordinary tramway cars, and then making oneself into a jury to pronounce a judgment one way or the other upon whether a certain thing is an ordinary and reasonable precaution, the absence of which means fault and negligence ... I think it can only be done by the tribunal that is to try the facts of the case."

Even when one is the "tribunal of fact" in a case,[91] it is still not the **4–56** function of judicial knowledge (which merely notes the existence of a matter beyond dispute) to usurp the function of evidence on a contested matter. In *Dyer* v. *Wilsons and Clyde Coal Co. Ltd*[92] an arbitrator sat to hear a claim by a workman who, despite injuries, had been declared fit for light duties. The workman argued that he should in fact receive a full disablement allowance because there was no such work to be had in the district, citing in evidence the considerable efforts he had made to obtain it. The arbitrator, without hearing this evidence in full, found against the workman on the

---

[88] 1992 S.L.T. 1010.
[89] 1912 S.C. 580.
[90] At p. 583.
[91] *i.e.* the jury, or the sheriff or judge in a non-jury trial.
[92] 1915 S.C. 199.

basis that from his own personal knowledge, there was such work available in the area. In overturning this finding on the grounds of a fundamental flaw in procedure, Lord Skerrington[93] summed up the view of the Court of Session as follows:

> "The arbitrator ... pronounced a decision upon the merits based not on evidence but on his own local knowledge. I do not say that such local knowledge could not be used as an element in the proof: but the arbitrator used his local knowledge as the sole evidence in the case."

4–57   Reference has already been made (in paragraph 4.29 *supra*) to the case of *Herkes* v. *Dickie*,[94] in which it was held that local bye-laws could not be judicially noted unless they had statutory force, or were otherwise provable without the giving of evidence. The bye-laws in question (which it was held could not be judicially noted) had been made by the local burgh licensing court. The magistrate who sat in judgment over the case, and who was a member of that licensing court, had been prepared to note the existence of the bye-laws and their content from the fact that he had helped to draft them. Lord Patrick, in rejecting such an approach, reminded the court that "if any matter requires to be proved in a criminal prosecution, the want of proof of the matter cannot be mended by the private knowledge of the Judge."[95]

4–58   On occasions, judges seeking to make use of personal knowledge have gone so far as to supplant or supplement expert testimony. In *Kennedy* v. *Smith*,[96] it was held that a judge might not form his own unaided opinion of the likely effect of one and a half pints of lager on a man who was not a regular drinker and who had had an empty stomach at the time. Likewise, in *Davie* v. *Magistrates of Edinburgh*[97] an expert witness, giving evidence on the effect of shock waves in blasting operations, made reference to a section of a pamphlet which he claimed supported his view. The Lord Ordinary rejected the expert testimony, and in doing so adopted other parts of the same pamphlet to which the expert had not referred. In disapproving this course of action, the Court of Session ruled[98] that "the Court cannot ... rely upon such works for the purpose of displacing or criticising the witness's testimony."

4–59   The same has been held to be the case when judges have sought to turn themselves into witnesses by examining productions or scenes of incidents for themselves and forming their own conclusions. It is one thing for a

---

[93] At p. 204. See also the Lord President at p. 203.
[94] 1958 J.C. 51.
[95] At p. 56.
[96] 1976 S.L.T. 110.
[97] 1953 S.C. 34, referred to more fully in Chap. 16.
[98] At p. 41.

court to take a "view" of something in order more easily to understand the evidence which they are about to hear, but it is not competent for this to occur independently of such evidence, so that in effect the court is taking its own view regardless of what the witnesses have to say.[99]

Finally, a matter which may be judicially noted without difficulty in a particular locality, or at a particular time, may require further inquiry, or even expert testimony, in a different locality or only a few years later. In *Oliver* v. *Hislop*,[1] for example, the accused was charged with an offence under a local statute which made it an offence to be caught salmon fishing by means of a "cleek." No evidence was led as to what a "cleek" was, and whether or not such a definition corresponded with the article which had been found in the accused's possession, and the sheriff felt himself unable to note judicially what a "cleek" was. On appeal, Lord Justice-Clerk Cooper held that[2]: **4–60**

> "I do not consider that a Border sheriff, through whose territory the Tweed flows, requires, or ought to require, to be instructed by expert or other evidence as to the meaning of the terms which have been employed in the statutory regulation of the river for a period of close on ninety years."

Similarly, the fact that knowledge can change over time was acknowledged by Lord Sorn,[3] who ruled that: **4–61**

> "It seems to me that the learned Sheriff-substitute was too diffident in refraining from using what I really think must have been within his own knowledge. The word "cleek" has a dictionary meaning and it is also used in section 16 of the Act in a way which shows that in this locality and in this river it bears the meaning of what today would be more usually referred to as a gaff."

Had these cases been heard in a city court, those involved would be forgiven if they wished to consult a dictionary or hear evidence on the precise nature of a cleek or a gaff.

---

[99] See *e.g. Hattie* v. *Leach* (1889) 16 R. 1128 and *McCann* v. *Adair*, 1951 J.C. 127.
[1] 1946 J.C. 20.
[2] At p. 24.
[3] At p. 27.

CHAPTER 5

RES JUDICATA

INTRODUCTION

5–01 The rule of evidence known under the shortened title of *res judicata* was summarised by Walker and Walker[1] as: "When a matter has been the subject of judicial determination by a competent tribunal, the determination excludes any subsequent litigation in regard to the same matter between the same parties on the same grounds." It operates as a procedural bar to any further court action on the matter, and "is based upon considerations of public policy, equity and common sense, which will not tolerate that the same issue should be litigated repeatedly between the same parties on substantially the same basis."[2]

5–02 The effect of the rule is that a party wishing to reopen an issue which has already been litigated between him and another party is denied the right to lead any evidence on it. In the words of Walker and Walker[3]: "the result of a successful plea of *res judicata* is that evidence is neither necessary nor admissible with regard to the issues previously determined." The rule is one which has considerable overlap with the law of procedure and specialist texts on that subject will provide a more detailed study.[4]

5–03 The doctrine is most frequently encountered in civil cases, although, as will be seen, it finds application in criminal cases also, as a plea in bar of retrial for the same offence. There is also a limited form of *res judicata* applicable between civil and criminal cases. The remainder of this chapter observes these three main divisions.

GENERAL RULE IN CIVIL CASES

5–04 The conditions to be satisfied before a plea of *res judicata* will be accepted

---

[1] Walker and Walker *Law of Evidence in Scotland*, para. 50, quoting Dickson, *Evidence*, para. 385.
[2] Lord President Cooper in *Grahame* v. *Secretary of State for Scotland*, 1951 S.C. 368 at p. 387.
[3] *op. cit.*, n. 1.
[4] For example, Maxwell, *Practice of the Court of Session*, Macphail, *Sheriff Court Practice*.

in a civil action were summarised in *Esso Petroleum Co.* v. *Law*[5] as follows: "There must have been an antecedent judicial decree of a competent tribunal, pronounced *in foro contentioso* between the same parties (or their authors) relative to the same subject-matter and proceeding on the same grounds."

From this summary may be extracted the following elements, all of which **5–05** require further examination:

    (i)   an antecedent decree pronounced *in foro contentioso*;
    (ii) a competent antecedent tribunal;
    (iii) the same subject-matter;
    (iv) the same grounds of action; and
    (v) the same parties.

The next five sections are taken up with this examination.

ANTECEDENT DECREE *IN FORO CONTENTIOSO*

A decree "*in foro*"[6] is: "any decree pronounced in a cause after defences **5–06** have been lodged. It includes, therefore, every kind of decree— interlocutory, interim and final—other than a decree in absence.[7]

Because a decree in absence does not constitute a decree *in foro* it cannot **5–07** constitute the basis of a later plea of *res judicata*. This is for the reason given in *Lockyer* v. *Ferriman*,[8] that "there has been no appearance for the defender." Even if an appearance is initially entered, it is well established that a decree is not pronounced *in foro* where no defences are subsequently lodged, since such a case is not regarded as a "defended" one.[9]

If there are no defences lodged, and no appearance entered by the **5–08** defender, no plea of *res judicata* may be based on any resulting decree. This applies even if the court, prior to decree, makes a full inquiry into such averments as it has before it. In *Paterson* v. *Paterson*,[10] a judge found that there was insufficient evidence before him of a wife's impotence to grant declarator of nullity of marriage. The wife had never entered an appearance so the resulting decree of dismissal was a decree in absence.

---

[5] 1956 S.C. 33, *per* Lord Carmont at p. 38; see also Maxwell, *op. cit.,* n. 4, p. 196, and Walker and Walker, *op. cit.,* n. 1, para. 51(a).
[6] The shortened form of the phrase normally used.
[7] Maxwell, *op. cit.,* n. 4, p. 617. For the purposes of the sheriff court, it has been defined by Dobie (*Sheriff Court Practice*, p. 249) as: "A decree granted after both parties have been heard, and where both have been represented in the course of the process," a definition adopted by Sheriff Macphail in *McPhee* v. *Heatherwick*, 1977 S.L.T. (Sh.Ct.) 46 at p. 47, for which see also *infra* and para. 5.20 *infra*.
[8] (1876) 3 R. 882 *per* Lord Gifford at pp. 911–912.
[9] *Esso Petroleum* v. *Law*, *supra*.
[10] 1958 S.C. 141.

This finding allowed a second action for the same declarator to be raised by the husband, who alleged that he had additional evidence.

5–09 However, once the defender has entered an appearance *and* lodged defences, then any resulting decree (including one granted by default) will be regarded as *in foro*, and a suitable base for a subsequent plea of *res judicata*.[11]

5–10 Any decree of absolvitor, for whatever reason granted, will be sufficient to support the plea, even if the court has had ample opportunity to examine the facts of the case.[12]

5–11 In *Young* v. *Young's Trustees*[13] the first action concerned a claim by a son to be entitled to the benefit of certain shares issued to his mother, but allegedly held in trust for him. He also claimed against the trustees of his mother's estate for an accounting in respect of their intromissions with the shares. The action was settled out of court, and decree of *absolvitor* was granted to the trustees. It was then discovered that certain bonus shares had been issued on the original shares, and the son brought an identical action in respect of these. It was held that the subject-matter in the second case was the same as that litigated in the first.[14] The court also held that the original *absolvitor* was a valid foundation for a plea of *res judicata*, even though it had been granted without the court having applied its mind to the issues involved. It was, said the court, a similar situation to a decree by default.[15]

5–12 In *Glasgow and South Western Ry.* v. *Boyd and Forrest*[16] it was held that *res judicata* will apply to a decree of absolvitor of consent, while in *Hynds* v. *Hynds*[17] it was held that:

> "It is not material that the judicial determination should have proceeded upon a compromise, consent or joint minute … Therefore the fact that the defender was assoilzied by the court interponing authority to a joint minute does not alter the finality or quality of the decree of absolvitor."

---

[11] *Forrest* v. *Dunlop* (1875) 3 R. 15. See also Maxwell, *op. cit.*, n. 4.

[12] Walker and Walker, *op. cit.*, n. 1, para. 51(a). They are supported in this view by Maxwell, *op. cit.*, n. 4.

[13] 1957 S.C. 318.

[14] A point taken up in paras. 5.26–5.36 *infra*.

[15] This case was approved in *McPhee* v. *Heatherwick, supra,* and effectively put an end to a long line of conflicting authorities on the precise status of decrees of absolvitor following an out-of-court settlement; these are listed in Walker and Walker, *op. cit.*, n. 12.

[16] 1918 S.C.(H.L.) 14.

[17] 1966 S.C 201, *per* Lord Cameron at p. 202, quoting *Young* and *Boyd and Forrest* as his authorities. See also Lord President Emslie in *Luxmore* v. *Red Deer Commission*, 1979 S.L.T. (Notes) 53 at p. 54.

In *McPhee* v. *Heatherwick*,[18] Sheriff Macphail was faced with a previous **5–13** finding in the small debt court in which the "defences" consisted of an oral admission of liability. He ruled that it was not material that the defence was an admission of liability, because:

> "in Scottish legal practice a defence consists of *answers* to a statement of facts which form the ground of action, and these answers may be either negative in content, as is usually the case, or affirmative, as where the defender admits liability."

In summary, therefore, it would seem that any decree pronounced **5–14** following the lodging of defences will be sufficient to support a subsequent plea of *res judicata*, even if it follows upon a joint minute, a settlement out of court, or the consent of one of the parties to decree. It makes no difference that the court was precluded from examining the factual issues raised by the action, or that a party failed to pursue the action beyond the lodging of defences. Nor does it make any difference that the "defences" consisted of no more than a flat admission of liability. A decree of absolvitor will always found a subsequent plea of *res judicata*, and the same effect may be obtained by other decrees regarded as being of a similar nature. The significant point is that the defender has been given an opportunity to be heard in all such cases.

A decree *in foro* may, however, be set aside where it is obtained by fraud **5–15** or collusion between the parties. In such a case it will cease to be a decree *in foro*.[19]

It should be noted in conclusion that a decree of dismissal is not a decree **5–16** *in foro*.[20]

Competent Antecedent Tribunal

Before a plea of *res judicata* will be upheld, it must be shown that the **5–17** decree *in foro* which is founded upon was issued by a "competent tribunal." This will normally be a court of law, and in Scottish civil cases the only available courts are the sheriff court, the Court of Session and the House of Lords.

It has never been doubted that the Court of Session and the House of **5–18** Lords are "competent tribunals" for this purpose, and that therefore any decree *in foro* emanating from them has sufficient status to found a plea of *res judicata*. For many years, there was doubt as to whether or not *res judicata* was a competent plea in the Court of Session when it was founded

---

[18] *Supra.*
[19] See *Lockyer* v. *Ferriman, supra* at p. 911.
[20] *Duke of Sutherland* v. *Reed* (1890) 18 R. 252.

upon a decree of the sheriff court,[21] but in *Murray* v. *Seath*[22] the door was opened to recognition of sheriff court decrees in the higher courts.

5–19   In *Hynds* v. *Hynds*[23] the Court of Session, in a divorce action raised by a wife on the grounds of her husband's alleged cruelty, saw no objection to the competency of a plea of *res judicata* based upon an earlier action for separation and aliment raised in the sheriff court on the same grounds.[24]

5–20   In *McPhee* v. *Heatherwick*[25] the sheriff said of the cases before *Murray* v. *Seath* that:

> "They belong to an age when the sheriff court enjoyed a lesser jurisdiction and, perhaps, prestige, than it does today ... I am of the opinion that, provided the necessary conditions are fulfilled, a competent decree in the small debt court[26] can sustain a plea of *res judicata* in the Court of Session."

5–21   A decree-arbitral issued by an arbiter is binding upon the parties both in point of law and in point of fact. The position was explained in *Farrans* v. *Roxburgh County Council*[27] to be that once a decree-arbitral has been given, "that decision is as good as a decree of court of a type which founds *res judicata*."

5–22   A ruling by a "tribunal" in the narrow sense of the word[28] may well be sufficient to found a plea of *res judicata* in the mainstream civil courts. Generally tribunals have exclusive jurisdiction over the matters remitted to them, subject to an appeal on a point of law only. For example, an appeal from a decision of an industrial tribunal lies first to an employment appeal tribunal and then to the Court of Session,[29] while appeals in cases relating to social security go via a commissioner to the Court of Session.[30]

5–23   The legislation which establishes such tribunals normally takes great care to ensure that a case which comes before a tribunal cannot be raised elsewhere, particularly not in a more traditional court such as the sheriff court. Because of this privative jurisdiction granted to tribunals, it is unlikely

---

[21] In *Duke of Sutherland* v. *Reed, supra,* the Court of Session was able to sidestep the issue, which was stated by the court to be uncertain.

[22] 1939 S.L.T. 348 at p. 352.

[23] 1966 S.C. 201.

[24] Although it refused the plea on the grounds that the "subject-matter" of the two actions was different: see paras. 5.26–5.36 *infra*. See also *Anderson* v. *Wilson*, 1972 S.C. 147, in which *Hynds* v. *Hynds* was approved. This case is reconsidered in paras. 5.57–5.74 *infra*.

[25] 1977 S.L.T. (Sh.Ct.) 46 at p. 47; considered also in para. 5.13 *supra*.

[26] The predecessor of the Small Claims Court.

[27] 1969 S.L.T. 35, *per* Lord Stott at p. 36.

[28] *i.e.* a judicial body such as an industrial or a social security tribunal, which exist outside the traditional court structure.

[29] See Employment Protection (Consolidation) Act 1978, ss. 135 and 136.

[30] Social Security Administration Act 1992 s. 24.

that a case litigated before a tribunal could competently arise in the same form elsewhere, so that the question of whether a ruling by a tribunal would be *res judicata* in, say, the sheriff court is unlikely to arise in practice.

In *Turner* v. *London Transport Executive*[31] it was held that since an **5–24** industrial tribunal deals with statutory cases of unfair dismissal, while the traditional courts handle common law claims of wrongful dismissal, there could be no question of a wrongful dismissal claim being barred by the previous hearing of an unfair dismissal action by a tribunal arising from the same dismissal.[32]

Finally there is the problem posed by foreign decrees,[33] and the unsettled **5–25** question of whether, once a case has been the subject of an equivalent decree *in foro* issued by a foreign court, the matter may be raised afresh in a Scottish court, always assuming that the latter has jurisdiction. Walker and Walker[34] are of the opinion that a foreign decree may found a plea of *res judicata* in the Scottish courts, but offer no authorities other than the various statutes under which foreign decrees may be *enforced* by Scottish courts.[35] However, the effect of such statutory provisions is that in cases in which they apply, the party against whom the judgment operates will normally be unable to contest the obligation thus created, but will be bound by the original judgment, and the practical outcome is the same as a plea of *res judicata* by the enforcing party.[36]

SAME SUBJECT-MATTER

For the operation of the rule of *res judicata*, the "matter to be litigated"[37] **5–26** in the present case must have been litigated between the same parties on a previous occasion. Some illustrations may help.

---

[31] [1977] I.C.R. 95.

[32] A similar point arose in *Clink* v. *Speyside Distillery Company Ltd.*, 1995 S.L.T. 1344 where it was held that findings by an industrial tribunal related to statutory remedies and were of a different character to common law claims under the contract of employment. A plea of *res judicata* was not therefore well founded.

[33] *i.e.* decrees issued by any court outwith Scotland.

[34] *op. cit.*, n. 12.

[35] See, *e.g.* para. 4.42 *supra* for the provisions of the Maintenance Orders (Reciprocal Enforcement) Act 1972, which require the Scottish courts to apply the laws of a foreign country when making a maintenance order against any person resident in Scotland. This is not an example of *res judicata*, however.

[36] *N.B.* that s. 10 of the Presumption of Death (Scotland) Act 1977, which makes provision for the recognition in Scotland of a declaration by a foreign court that a person domiciled or habitually resident in that country is dead, only states that such a declaration shall be "sufficient evidence of the facts so declared." The presumption is clearly rebuttable, and there can be no question of it being *res judicata* of any action in Scotland relating to the same death (*e.g.* in respect of Scottish property).

[37] See *Hynds* v. *Hynds*, *infra*.

5–27   In *Hynds* v. *Hynds*,[38] a wife raised a divorce action in the Court of Session on the grounds of her husband's cruelty. She had earlier raised an action for separation and aliment in the sheriff court, based on the same grounds, and a joint minute between the parties in that case had led to the husband being assoilzied of consent. It was held that since the decree in the first action, had it been granted, would have kept the marriage intact, whereas the present action was raised with the intention of having the marriage dissolved, the two actions were not the same, and *res judicata* could not therefore apply. As Lord Cameron put it[39]:

> "I do not think that it alters the position that the point to be decided in evidence[40] may be the same, *i.e.* has the defender been guilty of cruelty in law towards his wife ... a difference in the matter to be litigated, even if the *media concludendi* are identical, is sufficient to differentiate the subject-matter of the proceedings between the parties and to prevent them being regarded as identical ... Having regard to the differences in the nature of the rights which are in dispute in the two actions ... and the marked differences in the remedies sought and their effect if granted, I think there is no identity of subject-matter between the two actions here."

5–28   Another similar case is *Ryan* v. *McBurnie*,[41] in which an earlier action between the driver of a car and the operators of a bus, arising from a collision between the two vehicles, had led to the award of damages to the car driver. A passenger in the bus then raised an action for damages against the car driver, who pleaded *res judicata* on the general ground that the matter in issue (*i.e.* the liability for the accident) had already been litigated. It was held that the two actions were different, since the first dealt with the injuries of the car driver (and the duty of care of the bus driver to him) while the second dealt with the injuries of the passenger (and the duties of care of both drivers to her).[42]

5–29   On the basis of cases such as these, it could be thought that the "subject-matter" of a case was confined to the narrow legal remedy sought by the pursuer. But there is authority for a broader approach to the problem and to ask simply: "What did the previous case decide?" The start of this process may be detected as early as *Glasgow and South Western Ry.* v. *Boyd and*

---

[38] 1966 S.C. 201; see also paras. 5.06–5.25 *supra*. See too, *Rorie* v. *Rorie*, 1967 S.L.T. 75, in which *Hynds* was followed in an even clearer case in which the earlier sheriff court action had been for adherence and aliment, rather than separation and aliment.

[39] At pp. 203–4.

[40] *i.e.* the *medium concludendi*, the subject of paras. 5.37–5.56 *infra*.

[41] 1940 S.C. 173, considered in para. 5.60 *infra*, on the issue of the identity of the parties.

[42] See also *Mitchell's Trs* v. *Aspin*, 1971 S.L.T. 29, in which it was held that the issues created by the liferent of a share in an estate enjoyed by one daughter of the testator were not the same issues as arose in the case of another liferent enjoyed by another daughter.

Forrest,[43] in which Lord Shaw, dealing with the question of an action for the reduction of a document, rejected the suggestion that a pursuer might systematically exhaust all available legal remedies in such a case, one by one in separate cases, by ruling that:

> "I am not prepared ... to assent to the proposition, for instance, that an action of reduction, grounded on fraud, and failing, can be competently succeeded by another action of reduction with reference to the same document and founded on the same facts, but the ground of action being, not fraud, but, say, force and fear, or error arising from innocent misrepresentation."

In *Grahame* v. *Secretary of State for Scotland*,[44] Lord President Cooper referred to: **5–30**

> "a tendency which can be detected in earlier Scottish cases to concentrate too narrowly upon the precise terms of the conclusions of a summons or of pleas in law which was corrected in the third *Boyd and Forrest* appeal, in which we were directed to look at the essence and reality of the matter rather than the technical form, and simply to inquire—What was litigated and what was decided?"

This approach was adopted in *McPhee* v. *Heatherwick*,[45] in which, in an   **5–31**
earlier small debt action, a motorcyclist involved in an accident with a car had obtained damages under a decree by consent in respect of the value of his crash helmet and the amount payable under an excess clause in his insurance policy. The motorcyclist's insurers, unaware of the earlier action, raised a further action against the car driver in the name of the motorcyclist, on the same ground but concluding for the cost of replacing the motorcycle. In holding that the two actions related to the same subject-matter, the sheriff adopted the broad approach suggested in *Grahame*, and concluded[46] that:

> "In my opinion, what was litigated in the small debt action was the question whether the pursuer was entitled to reparation from the defender for patrimonial loss sustained through the alleged fault of the defender—in causing the accident ... What was decided was that the pursuer's contentions were correct and that the defender should pay to the pursuer the sum sued for plus expenses. In the present action the pursuer raises exactly the same question ... In each case he sues for pecuniary loss covered by the same infringement of his

---

[43] 1918 S.C.(H.L.) 14 at p. 30. See also Lord Kinnear in *Edinburgh and District Water Trs.* v. *Clippens Oil Co.* (1899) I F. 899 at p. 909.
[44] 1951 S.C. 368 at p. 387.
[45] 1977 S.L.T. (Sh.Ct.) 46, also considered in paras. 5.13 and 5.20 *supra*.
[46] *ibid.,* at p. 47. See also *Farrans* v. *Roxburgh County Council*, 1969 S.L.T. 35.

patrimonial interests; and the rule is that damages which arise from one and the same cause of action must all be assessed and recovered in one action."

5–32   The test of "what was litigated and what was decided?" was referred to by the Sheriff in *McSheehy* v. *McMillan*[47] a road traffic accident which the sheriff agreed was "on all fours" with the facts in *McPhee*. He held however that the subject-matter of the second litigation differed from the prior litigation. The distinction was that in the second litigation the pursuer insurance company sought to recover the costs of repairing their insured's car. This differed from the prior litigation which had been concerned only with the recovery by the insured of his uninsured losses.

5–33   A more narrow approach of the test of "what was litigated and what was decided?" was also applied in *Bacon* v. *Blair.*[48] This case arose from a collision between two cars. An earlier court had found that the driver of one car A had been 25 per cent contributorily negligent during the course of his action for damages against the driver of the second car B. In a second action, brought by C, who was the owner of the car driven by B, it had been held that A was fully liable for C's costs. The present (third) action was then brought by A against B for relief against the damages awarded against him in the second action. B argued that the entire issue of liability for the accident was now *res judicata*. However, the court held that:

> "There is no identity of subject-matter between the present action and the earlier action between the same parties, since no claim was made in the earlier action for loss which the pursuer [A] had to pay to [C] in respect of damage to his car ... The subject-matter of the present action has not been litigated."[49]

5–34   Certainly, in cases involving a multiplicity of claims arising from one incident, the courts do not always seem prepared to take a broad approach and to conclude that the first action must be taken to have resolved, for all time, the question of who was to blame. Instead, the various duties owed by the parties to each other will be treated as separate issues. Thus in *Anderson* v. *Wilson*[50] the Court of Session preferred to rely on the authority of *Ryan* v. *McBurnie*,[51] and said of it that it was,

> "adverse to the general proposition that, where there is a multiplicity of potential claims arising out of the one motor accident, the decision

---

[47]   1993 S.L.T. (Sh.Ct.) 11 at p. 13.
[48]   1972 S.L.T. (Sh.Ct.) 11.
[49]   *ibid.*, at p. 13.
[50]   1972 S.C. 147, the facts of which are examined in para. 5.65 *infra*.
[51]   1940 S.C. 173, considered in para. 5.60 *supra*, on the issue of the identity of the parties.

on apportionment of liability reached in relation to one such claim constitutes *res judicata* as regards the other claims."[52]

In reference to the apparently broad test laid down in *Grahame*,[53] Lord **5–35** Keith[54] in *Anderson*, said: "I do not regard Lord Cooper's observations as an invitation to decide questions of *res judicata* on a broad equitable basis or otherwise than in accordance with established principles."

A large part of the reason for the confusion between these two lines of **5–36** authority lies in the requirement that before *res judicata* will succeed as a plea, the *media concludendi* of both cases must be the same, and this additional factor must now be considered.

SAME *MEDIA CONCLUDENDI*

The *media concludendi* of a case may be defined as "the grounds of action **5–37** in fact and law",[55] or "the point[s] to be decided in evidence?"[56] As such they represent the narrow factual issues raised by a case. They may be distinguished from the "subject matter" of a case, in that while the latter deals with the overall legal relationship between two or more parties (*e.g.* whether A is entitled to a divorce from B, whether C is liable to pay damages to D and so on), the *media concludendi* are the facts in issue in each case. As was seen in *Hynds* v. *Hynds*,[57] the question of whether or not a husband has been "cruel" to his wife is a *medium concludendi* (being both a question of fact and a conclusion in law), but one which may arise in two cases with a different subject matter (*e.g.* separation and divorce).

It is essential that the *media concludendi* is the same for the operation of **5–38** *res judicata*.[58] An earlier case will only be *res judicata* of a second case when both the subject-matter and the *media concludendi* are the same in both cases. If the subject matter is different, then even though the *media concludendi* are the same, the earlier case is not *res judicata* of the second.[59] By the same token, even if the subject-matter of both cases is the same the earlier case will not support a successful plea of *res judicata* if the *media concludendi* are different. It is this latter point which must be examined more fully in this section.

---

[52] *Anderson v. Wilson, supra,* at p. 151.
[53] 1951 S.C. 368 at p. 387.
[54] At p. 150.
[55] Maxwell, *Practice of the Court of Session*, p. 197. See also Lord Shaw in *Glasgow and South Western Ry. Co.* v. *Boyd and Forrest*, 1918 S.C.(H.L.) 14 at p. 28, who defined them as "the reality and substance of the thing disputed between the parties."
[56] *Hynds* v. *Hynds*, 1966 S.C. 201, *per* Lord Cameron at p. 203.
[57] *ibid.*.
[58] For a recent example, see *Gibson & Simpson* v. *Pearson*, 1992 S.L.T. 894.
[59] As was seen in *Hynds* v. *Hynds, supra,* and paras. 5.26–5.36 generally.

5–39   It was well expressed by Lord Kinnear in *North British Ry. Co.* v. *Lanarkshire and Dunbartonshire Ry. Co.*,[60] who said:

> "I take it to be clear that in order to support a plea of *res judicata* it is necessary to show not only that the parties and the subject-matter in two suits are identical, but also that the two suits present one and the same ground of claim, so that the specific point raised in the second has been as directly raised in the pleadings and concluded by the judgment in the first."

5–40   In *Malcolm Muir Ltd* v. *Jamieson*,[61] a moneylending contract for the sum of £60 provided for the repayment of the capital sum plus interest of approximately £30. A clause in the contract provided that in the event of default, the debtor was to repay the whole sum plus interest calculated from the date of default. An earlier action under the default clause was held to be incompetent since the clause was unenforceable due to the rate of interest charged thereunder being higher than that permitted by law. The creditors therefore raised a second action for the principal sum plus 12 instalments of interest at the permissible statutory rate of interest, but the debtor pleaded that the first action was *res judicata* of the second. The plea was rejected on the grounds that the first case had dealt with the pursuer's right to charge a higher interest rate, while the present dealt only with the lawful interest in terms of the contract. The *media concludendi* were therefore different.

5–41   In *Matuszczyk* v. *National Coal Board*,[62] on the other hand, it was held that common law negligence and breach of statutory duty leading to common law liability to an employee involved the same *media concludendi*.

5–42   However, a line of authority beginning with *Glasgow and South Western Ry.* v. *Boyd and Forrest*[63] has complicated matters by apparently authorising the application of *res judicata* to those cases in which the *media concludendi* of the second case *could* have been raised by the pursuer in the previous action, but were not. The case itself was a complex one involving a contract for the construction of a section of railway line which turned out to be more expensive for the contractors than had originally been anticipated because of a misleading geological survey by the railway's own engineer.

5–43   The present case was the third in a series, all based on the same facts, and in a previous action the House of Lords absolved the railway company on a claim by the contractors that the contract was not binding upon them because of fraud by the railway company, and essential error. The present case which came before the House of Lords was an action raised by the contractors in an attempt to secure extra payment under an arbitration clause

---

[60] (1897) 24 R. 564 at p. 572. See also *Boyd and Forrest*, *supra*, *per* Lord Shaw at p. 31.
[61] 1947 S.C. 314. See also *Edinburgh Water Trs.* v. *Clippens Oil Co.* (1899) 1 F. 899.
[62] 1955 S.C. 418.
[63] 1918 S.C.(H.L.) 14, also dealt with in para. 5.29.

in the contract. It was held that the present action was *res judicata* because it was an issue which could easily have been included by the contractors in their pleadings in the previous action.

The effect of the ruling in *Glasgow and South Western Railway* would **5–44** seem to be that a pursuer, in raising an action for the first time, must take care to include in it every issue of law which can reasonably be associated with it, otherwise a later court may uphold a plea of *res judicata*, not on *media concludendi* which were raised, but on those which might have been raised.

This point was taken up in *McPhee* v. *Heatherwick*,[64] in which, it will be **5–45** recalled, an action for compensation for loss of a crash helmet in an accident was followed by a second action by the same party's insurers for the loss of the motorcycle. In applying the principle that "damages which arise from one and the same cause of action must all be assessed and recovered in one action,"[65] the sheriff went on to observe that: "The rule may be thought to be particularly apt in a case such as this, where the damages claimed in the second action could have been claimed at the time when the first action was raised." Thus, not only was the subject-matter the same in both cases but the grounds of action were also, and could not be duplicated.

The same principle was clearly under consideration in *Bacon* v. *Blair*,[66] **5–46** when it was suggested that the owner of a car, who had in an earlier action sued the driver of a second car, could have included in his claim for damages a sum to represent the amount which a later court found him liable to pay to the owner of the second car. The application of the general principle to the facts of the case in hand was finally rejected by the sheriff, who ruled:

"I do not think it is enough for the defender to say that the pursuer 'could have' included the loss which he has incurred to the owner of the other car in his original claim for damages against the driver of the other car or that he knew from correspondence of [that] claim."[67]

The reason for this was that:

"without the gift of second sight he was not to know with certainty that (contrary to his own contention) he would be found partly to blame for the accident. It is, moreover, hard to see how he would have quantified his liability for expenses in the court of first instance and in an uncertain number of courts of appeal."

The ruling of Lord Shaw in *Boyd and Forrest* (*supra*) to the effect that **5–47** multiple claims on the same issue were not possible where the new reasons

---

[64] 1977 S.L.T. (Sh.Ct.) 46, the facts of which were considered in para. 5.31 *supra*.
[65] At p. 47.
[66] 1972 S.L.T. (Sh.Ct.) 11, the facts of which appear in para. 5.33 *supra*.
[67] At p. 13.

were legal, but were possible when they were factual, was another way of referring to the principle of *res noviter*,[68] which operates in such a way as to cancel out the effect of a plea of *res judicata*.

5–48   The extent of this principle is well described by Lord Blackburn in *Phosphate Sewage Co.* v. *Molleson*,[69] who offered the opinion that it "is nearly equivalent to saying that you were taken by surprise, and have since discovered material evidence." This was a case where the pursuers sought to reopen a case in the Scottish courts (having lost an earlier one there) and having had in the interim secured a favourable decree in the English courts. Lord Chancellor Cairns[70] rejected the action, on the grounds that the first Court of Session ruling was *res judicata* of the present action because:

> "it is perfectly clear, upon the statement of the present appellants themselves, that this fact was within their knowledge before their proof was led in the former action, and they were just as free to have had the record opened and to have had it stated as if it had come to their knowledge before the record was closed."

5–49   Finally, it should be noted that the operation of *res judicata* is sometimes obscured by the effect of another procedural bar known as "competent and omitted", which prevents a pursuer from putting forward, as a new *medium concludendi*, a ground of action which he could have pled in an earlier case between the same parties in which he was the defender, but did not.

5–50   The operation of "competent and omitted," and its rationale, were well summarised by Lord Milligan in *Rorie* v. *Rorie*[71] as follows:

> "The plea of 'competent and omitted' is designed to deal with a situation where a defender who has been unsuccessful in an action seeks to have the decision in that action reversed on the ground that he had not put forward in the first action all the defences which he might have done. The purpose of the doctrine is to avoid endless litigation."

The way in which it does so is to set up a procedural bar against a party who seeks to reopen the case on the narrow technical ground that, because the issue was not raised by him in the previous action, *res judicata* cannot apply. Any *medium concludendi* which is deemed to have been competent

---

[68] In effect, "new facts".
[69] (1879) 6 R.(H.L.) 113 at p. 121.
[70] At p. 117.
[71] 1967 S.L.T. 75 at p. 78. See also Beaumont, "Competent but Omitted", 1985 S.L.T. (News) 345.

and omitted in the previous action will be given no consideration in assessing whether or not the first action is *res judicata* of the second.[72]

To summarise this complex topic, the following general statements may be made. **5–51**

(i) A successful plea of *res judicata* requires that the *media concludendi* of the previous case and the present one be identical. **5–52**

(ii) The *media concludendi* may be identified as the legal and factual issues in a case which lead to a legal conclusion. **5–53**

(iii) The principle may extend to cover all the *media concludendi* which the pursuer could have raised in the previous case, whether or not this was done. **5–54**

(iv) The *media concludendi* will not be regarded as identical if the present claim introduces new facts (*res noviter*) which were not available to the pursuer in the previous action. **5–55**

(v) The *media concludendi* will not be regarded as different if the allegedly new ground of action raised is one which was "competent and omitted" in an earlier action between the parties in which the present pursuer was the defender.[73] **5–56**

SAME PARTIES

A prerequisite of a successful plea of *res judicata* is that the action now brought should have been litigated before by the same parties in the same capacities. If, for example, a previous action was by A against B, then it will be *res judicata* of any subsequent action by A against B, or B against A,[74] but will not operate so as to prevent a subsequent action by A against C, or B against D, unless the new party is in some way *legally* associated with the former one. **5–57**

For example, where one of the parties to a previous action is the agent of a party to the present action, and acting in that capacity at the time, the principal cannot reopen the action, since he or she was represented earlier. If, on the other hand, the agent is acting in a personal capacity in the first action, its outcome will not be binding upon the principal, who was not represented in it. The same would be true where the intending party in the second action has the same "interest" to protect as a party in the earlier action. **5–58**

---

[72] For a case in which a plea of "competent and omitted" was upheld, see *Glasgow Shipowners* v. *Clyde Navigation Trs.* (1885) 12 R. 95. For a more recent case in which it was repelled, see *Cantors Properties (Scotland) Ltd.* v. *Swears & Wells Ltd*, 1978 S.C. 310.

[73] *N.B.* that it will not apparently operate where the present pursuer was also the pursuer in the earlier action *Edinburgh Water Trs. supra.*

[74] Subject always to the other essential ingredients of *res judicata* being present.

5–59   This principle was applied in *Glasgow Shipowners* v. *Clyde Navigation Trustees,*[75] so as to prevent a shipowners' association from reopening an issue concerning the extension of certain piers with the trustees of navigation on the Clyde. In an earlier action between the trustees and a riparian owner, the interests of the shipowners had been represented by the trustees themselves. The present action was said[76] to have been rendered "*res judicata* in a litigation in which the proper interests of navigation were duly represented."

5–60   Similarly, a potential party will be excluded from further litigation where that party is the assignee, successor or other representative of a former litigant in the same issue. This point was considered in *Ryan* v. *McBurnie,*[77] in which an initial action for damages by the driver of a car against the operators of a bus which had collided with his car was followed by an action against the car driver for personal injuries by one of the passengers in the bus, who assigned her right to sue to the bus company, which brought the action in her name. As well as concluding that the two actions were not identical,[78] the court made the following observations concerning the identities of the parties, in answer to the defender's argument that the real pursuer was the bus company:

> "When it is asked who are the parties to this action, you do have regard to the realities and the substance of the action. It is for that reason that the doctrine *assignatus utitur jure auctoris* must be applied, because it is the cedent's claim that is truly the subject of the litigation, and, for the purpose of determining whether the parties are the same as in the former action, you must treat the cedent as the real pursuer in the present case."[79]

In short, had Ryan been the party in the former case, she could not have brought the present action by hiding behind the bus company. Equally, the bus company could not have brought the present action on its own behalf had the issue involved been the same as in the previous case.

5–61   In *Allen* v. *McCombie's Trs.,*[80] one of two beneficiaries under a trust deed raised an action against the trustees in the estate for the restoration of trust funds allegedly lost by improper investment. It was held that intimation of the action should be given to the other beneficiary, because the outcome

---

[75] (1885) 12 R. 695. See also *Macfie* v. *Scottish Rights of Way Society* (1884) 11 R. 1094, where it was held that an earlier action for declarator of a public right of way raised by a member of the public was *res judicata* as regards other members of the public.

[76] *per* Lord Shand at p. 701.

[77] 1940 S.C. 173, considered more fully in para. 5.28 *supra.*

[78] On which point the case is considered in para. 5.28 *supra.*

[79] *per* Lord President Normand at p. 177.

[80] 1909 S.C. 710.

of the action would be *res judicata* against her also. One beneficiary was taken to be able to represent the interest(s) of the other(s).

The principle that a previous judgment is *res judicata* of a second action **5–62** by the same parties concerning the same subject-matter and *media concludendi* is extended so as to cover all potential future litigants to the same issue (whether or not they were parties to the original case) whenever the original decree was one "*in rem*". This may be defined as being: "A judgment of a court of competent jurisdiction determining the status of a person or thing, or the disposition of a thing (as distinct from a particular interest in it of a party to the litigation)".[81] Its effect is that it is conclusive evidence for and against all persons whether parties, privies or strangers, of the matters actually decided."[82]

Obvious judgments *in rem* are decrees of divorce or nullity of marriage,[83] **5–63** declarators of paternity and death, and the award of confirmation on the estate of a deceased. The same effect is obtained by the reduction of a deed or contract, which will be void so far as concerns not only the parties to it, but also anyone else having an interest in the subject-matter.

Where, however, a particular previous finding was not *in rem*, and the **5–64** parties to the present case are not the same as those in the previous case, the doctrine of *res judicata* will not be extended so as to debar a party from reopening an issue which has not been previously litigated, and by which that party is not bound. This rule can be seen in operation in road traffic accidents which sometimes give rise to multiple claims. Where there has been a decree in an earlier court establishing the proportions of liability for the accident that finding will not be *res judicata* in another case arising from that accident, but involving different parties.[84]

The leading case is *Anderson* v. *Wilson*,[85] which arose out of a collision **5–65** between a minibus and a car. In an earlier action in the sheriff court, brought by a passenger in the minibus, the court had found both drivers to blame, and had apportioned liability between the employer of the bus driver and the judicial factor on the estate of the car driver. In a subsequent action in the Court of Session five other passengers sued both drivers for damages.

The court took for granted that the original action was not *res judicata* **5–66** as between the new pursuers and the defenders, but it was argued that at least the question of the liability of the two drivers *inter se* had been settled for all time. Counsel for the employer of the bus driver urged the court to regard "the true issue to be simply what person or persons were to blame

---

[81] Halsbury's *Laws of England* (Hailsham, ed.), vol. 13, p. 405.
[82] *Lazarus-Barlow* v. *Regent Estates Co. Ltd.* [1949] 2 K.B. 465 at p. 475.
[83] See, *e.g. Administrator of Austrian Property* v. *Von Lorang*, 1926 S.C. 598 at p. 622, 1927 S.C.(H.L.) 80; and *Murray* v. *Murray* (O.H.) 1957 S.L.T. 41.
[84] See paras. 5.37–5.56 *infra*.
[85] 1972 S.C. 147.

for the accident, and, if more than one person were to blame, in what proportions they were to blame."[86] The court was asked to adopt the approach suggested by Lord President Cooper in *Grahame* v. *Secretary of State for Scotland*[87] and to ask simply, of the first case: "What was litigated and what was decided?"

5–67   Lord Keith, however, was not prepared to follow this line of reasoning because he felt that it "would involve some departure from, or at least significant extension of, the principles which have hitherto governed *res judicata* in the law of Scotland."[88] Nor did he regard "Lord Cooper's observations as an invitation to decide questions of *res judicata* on a broad equitable basis or otherwise than in accordance with established principles."[89] He therefore approved for jury trial all the issues raised by the present action, including the proportions of liability for the accident.

5–68   It would seem therefore, under Scots law as presently formulated, that provided that the true identity of one of the parties to a subsequent case is different from those in an earlier case, no finding of fact from that earlier case will be *res judicata*.[90] This creates an obvious risk "that in comparatively simple cases different courts will reach different decisions on the same issues of fact and the same evidence."[91]

5–69   The Law Reform (Miscellaneous Provisions) (Scotland) Act 1968 provides a statutory example of a finding in civil proceedings being of value in a "*res judicata*" context. In relation to a subsequent court action section 11 states:

5–70   (1)"In any civil proceedings —

> (a) the fact that a person has been found guilty of adultery in any matrimonial proceedings, shall ... be admissible in evidence for the purpose of proving, where to do so is relevant to any issue in those civil proceedings, that he committed the adultery to which the finding relates, whether or not he offered any defence to the allegation of adultery and whether or not he is a party to the civil proceedings; but no finding other than a subsisting one shall be admissible in evidence by virtue of this section."[92]

5–71   Subsection (2) goes on to make the finding probative "unless the contrary is proved", which clearly places a persuasive burden on the party seeking

---

[86]   At p. 150.
[87]   Referred to more fully in para. 5.30 *supra*.
[88]   At p. 153.
[89]   At p. 150.
[90]   Unless, of course, the previous finding was *in rem*.
[91]   Macphail, *Evidence,* Chap. 11.28 and the discussion in *Scottish Law Commission Memorandum,* No. 46, para. K. 24. The Commission were not in favour of extending the principle of *res judicata*.
[92]   *ibid.,* subs. (1).

to disprove the point, who may not of course be the party to whom the finding relates. The subsection also renders admissible in the subsequent proceedings, as evidence of "the facts on which the finding was based", "the contents of any document which was before the court, or which contains any pronouncement of the court" in the earlier proceedings. The definition of "matrimonial proceedings" for the purpose of section 11 is extended so as to cover proceedings in the English, Welsh or Northern Irish courts, so that both presumptions apply to any competent United Kingdom findings.

Leaving aside the implications of the section so far as concerns the law on presumptions,[93] the section does create a situation in which a finding from an earlier hearing will have evidential effect in a subsequent case in which the parties are different. If, for example, A is found to be the father of X in paternity proceedings brought by X's mother, B, then when A dies, X may use the finding against other claimants on A's estate. **5–72**

Another potential use of the section is in a case in which A has been found guilty of adultery with Mrs B in an action for divorce raised by B. That finding may then be relied upon in an action for divorce by Mrs A against A, based on the *same* act of adultery. **5–73**

Section 11 may also be applied where the parties in the present case are the same as in the previous case. Where, for example, a wife wishes to rely upon a decree of judicial separation on the grounds of her husband's adultery as evidence in pursuance of a subsequent divorce action.[94] **5–74**

RES JUDICATA IN CRIMINAL CASES

As a general rule,[95] the two parties in a criminal case will always be the Crown and the accused, and the *media concludendi* (*i.e.* the guilt or innocence of the accused) are always the same. As a result, in practice the application of *res judicata* in a criminal case is limited to the question of whether, when a previous trial of an accused is followed by another, the "subject-matter" is the same and has been fully litigated. If so, then *res judicata* will apply; if not, then it will not. When *res judicata* does apply, the accused is said to have "tholed his assize."[96] **5–75**

(1) **Matter fully litigated**

It was noted, when examining the application of the principles of *res judicata* to civil cases, that a civil action dismissed as irrelevant or **5–76**

---

[93] These are dealt with more fully in Chap. 3 *supra*.

[94] Which is not *res judicata* because the subject-matter is different in the two cases: see *Hynds* v. *Hynds per* para. 5.27 *supra*. *N.B.* s. 3(1) of the Divorce (Scotland) Act 1976, which has the same effect for other grounds of separation/divorce.

[95] *i.e.* leaving aside the question of private prosecution, which is considered at the end of this section.

[96] See generally Renton and Brown, *Criminal Procedure*, paras. 9–26 to 9–30.

incompetent will not be regarded as having created a decree *in foro* sufficient to form the basis of a later plea of *res judicata*.[97] This same principle applies in criminal cases, at least where the matter is being raised subsequently before a superior court. An indictment dismissed as irrelevant by a sheriff court can be raised again in the High Court.[98]

5–77   The position is different where the issue claimed to be *res judicata* is raised in the same court. It has been held that the prosecution could not proceed in the sheriff court on a libel which had already been rejected as irrelevant in the sheriff court.[99]

5–78   In a criminal case, the equivalent of a decree *in foro* in a civil case, is a finding of guilt, a formal admission of guilt, or a finding of not guilty or not proven.[1] In each case this would be following upon the service on the accused of a complaint or indictment libelling a specific offence or a list of offences. The same result is achieved by a desertion *simpliciter*,[2] which, whether it comes from a Crown motion or from the court *ex proprio motu*, has the effect of terminating the Crown criminal process in respect of those particular charges for all time.[3]

5–79   When an accused pleads not guilty and proceeds to trial, *res judicata* will not apply[4] unless and until "the trial, properly conducted, has concluded in a determination of the issue of guilt or innocence."[5]

---

[97] Paras. 5.06–5.16 *supra*.

[98] *George Fleming*, (1866) 5 Irv. 289, in which the Crown were allowed to proceed on the basis that "the justiciary court could not be held bound by the decision of an inferior judge" at p.292.

[99] *Longmuir* v. *Baxter* (1858) 3 Irv. 287 which was followed in *McNab*, Petitioner, *H.M.A.* v. *McNab*, 1994 S.C.C.R. 633.

[1] *N.B.* that in all cases the court must be one of "competent jurisdiction", *i.e.* it must be a district court, a sheriff court or the High Court, and must be acting within its jurisdiction. For criminal jurisdiction generally, see Renton and Brown, *Criminal Procedure*, paras. 1–04 and 1–05. But it would also seem that the accused can plead tholed assize when he has been tried by an English court in a case in which a crime could also have been charged in Scotland (*e.g.* a fraud by an English based company advertising in Scotland); see Renton and Brown, *ibid.*, para. 9–27.

[2] *N.B.* not a desertion *pro loco et tempore*, which is a desertion of the diet but not of the right of the prosecutor to reraise the charge(s) against the accused; see Renton and Brown, *op. cit.*, n. 1, para. 10–15 and *Herron* v. *McCrimmon*, 1969 S.L.T. (Sh.Ct.) 37 at p. 39. However, formal intimation of abandonment has the same effect as a Crown desertion *simpliciter*; see Renton and Brown, *ibid.*, paras. 9–32 to 9–34; *Thom* v. *H.M.A.*, 1976 J.C. 48; *H.* v. *Sweeney*, *infra*; and *Lockhart* v. *Leighton*, 1985 S.L.T. 549.

[3] See Renton and Brown, *op. cit.*, n. 1, paras. 10–16 and 10–17 and Criminal Procedure (Scotland) Act 1995 s. 81(3). *N.B.* that desertion on a Crown motion does not rule out the possibility of a private prosecution: see *infra*.

[4] *i.e.* the accused will not be regarded as having "tholed his assize."

[5] *i.e.* a verdict of guilty has been pronounced: Lord Justice-General Emslie in *Dunlop* v. *H.M.A.*, 1974 J.C. 59 at p. 67. He need not apparently be sentenced. See *Milne* v. *Guild*, 1986 S.L.T. 431, which is authority for this view at least in relation to summary cases.

When an accused pleads guilty before the trial has commenced,[6] a **5–80** different rule apparently applies, and the accused has not tholed his assize until he has been sentenced.[7] In fact, it may now be the case that the principles of *res judicata* do not apply until that sentence has actually been recorded, following the ruling in the High Court in *Tudhope* v. *Campbell*.[8]

(2) Subject-matter the same

The remaining question concerning the applicability of a plea of *res* **5–81** *judicata* to a criminal trial is whether or not the subject matter of the proposed new trial is the same as that for which the accused has already stood trial. Macdonald[9] states that before the plea of tholed assize will be upheld, the previous trial "must have been for the same crime, depending upon the same evidence, and not for what is truly another crime."

This was interpreted by Lord Justice-Clerk Grant in *H.M.A.* v. *Cairns*[10] **5–82** as meaning: "It is identity of the charges and not of the evidence that is the crucial factor." In that case, C had on an earlier occasion stood trial on a charge of murder by stabbing M, and following his own sworn testimony, in which he denied the stabbing, the charge was found not proven. The Crown then served an indictment for perjury upon him, libelling that he had falsely denied the stabbing at the earlier trial.

The defence objected to the new indictment on the ground that C had **5–83** already stood trial (tholed his assize) on the question of the stabbing. It was held that the new indictment was competent and that *res judicata* was not applicable, because the two charges (*i.e.* murder and perjury) were wholly different in nature, and the two crimes were allegedly committed on different dates and at different places.

It is also well established that the same facts may give rise to different **5–84** charges in different trials where events have occurred which alter the nature of the crime. For example, when a trial for assault is followed by the death of the victim, an accused may be re-indicted for murder or culpable homicide.[11]

---

[6] *i.e.* before the jury is sworn in, or before the first witness is sworn in a summary case; see Renton and Brown, *op. cit.,* n. 1, para. 18–67 (solemn cases) and Criminal Procedure (Scotland) Act 1995, s. 152 (summary cases). This will also include a plea of guilty at a specially convened diet under s. 76 of the Criminal Procedure (Scotland) Act 1995 (previously s. 102 of the 1975 Act). See Renton and Brown, *ibid.,* Chap. 8.

[7] Renton and Brown, *op. cit.,* n. 1, para. 9–27; see *Herron* v. *McCrimmon, supra* at p. 39.

[8] 1979 J.C. 37 at p. 41.

[9] *Criminal Law of Scotland*, p. 272. Lord Justice-General McNeill in *Fraser* (1852) 1 Irv. 66 at p. 73 gave as his test whether or not the present charge was one that the accused was "in jeopardy of" at the previous trial.

[10] 1967 J.C. 37 at p. 41. For a recent application of this same principle see *H.M.A.* v. *M., infra.*

[11] See, *e.g.* Macdonald, *op. cit.,* n. 9; *Stewart* (1866) 5 Irv. 310 and *O'Connor* (1882) 5 Couper 206. For a recent application see *Tees* v. *H.M.A.,* 1994 S.L.T. 701.

5–85   But unless there has been some material change of circumstance which gives rise to a charge which was not available to the prosecution at the earlier trial, they cannot bring a second charge after the completed trial for the first, "for the same facts, under a new denomination of the crime."[12] So, if the prosecution fail to secure a conviction for robbery against D, they cannot recharge him with separate charges of assault and theft arising from the same alleged incident. On the other hand, where an indictment is dismissed as irrelevant for lack of specification a fresh indictment libelling the same offences may be competent, and not *res judicata*, provided there is a material difference in the way the charges are expressed.[13]

5–86   If a plea of *res judicata* is to be avoided, either the facts in the new trial must be different from those in the first, or the charge which is now based on those facts must have been one upon which the prosecution could not have obtained a conviction at the earlier trial. There is an evident parallel here with the distinction between the "subject-matter" and the *"media concludendi"* which were identified when examining *res judicata* in civil cases.

5–87   In criminal cases, in terms of section 118 (solemn proceedings) and section 185 (summary proceedings) of the Criminal Procedure (Scotland) Act 1995, the High Court may, on appeal, dispose of the case by setting aside the verdict of the trial court and granting authority to the Crown to bring a new prosecution, and in both cases the effect of the statutory provision is that a plea of tholed assize will not be available to the defence.[14]

(3) Private prosecutions

5–88   While *res judicata* is an effective bar to any further prosecution when it is based upon a final verdict following a competent trial, or a plea of guilty followed by sentence, it does not operate as a bar to a private prosecution in cases in which the Crown have deserted simpliciter, or by a formal intimation of abandonment. Such a course of action operates as a personal bar only against the Crown, and no one else.[15]

5–89   Although private prosecutions are extremely rare they can arise. The most recent successful example was the highly publicised case of

---

[12] Hume, II, 466. See *H.M.A.* v. *M.*, 1986 S.C.C.R. 624, in which the material difference between the first indictment and the second was said to be a narrower "latitude" of time, and a different wording of the charges. A plea of tholed assize was rejected.

[13] *H.M.A.* v. *M*, 1986 S.C.C.R. 624, where the Lord Justice-Clerk said at p.630 that the second libel should be "word for word the same as in the first." This case approved the dicta of Lord Deas in *Longmuir, supra*.

[14] See Renton and Brown, *op. cit.*, n. 1, para. 11–45.

[15] *N.B.* that where desertion simpliciter is by the court *ex proprio motu*, it binds all future parties, subject to the Crown's right of appeal by a bill of advocation. See *Mackenzie* v. *MacLean*, 1981 S.L.T. 2.

H. v. *Sweeney,*[16] in which three youths were indicted in the High Court by the Lord Advocate on charges of rape and assault. Subsequently, on the advice of a psychiatrist who stated that the alleged victim would be unable, for several months, to withstand the rigours of a trial, the Lord Advocate sent a letter to each accused informing them that no further proceedings were to be taken against them.

The victim subsequently applied to the High Court with a bill for **5–90** "criminal letters" to allow her to raise a private prosecution on the same charges. The case was almost unique in the sense that not since 1829 had an application for leave to prosecute privately been made in a case in which the Crown had formally abandoned charges against an accused.[17] The case therefore raised directly the question of the effect of a Crown abandonment on subsequent private proceedings.

In granting the bill, and therefore allowing the private prosecution to **5–91** proceed, Lord Justice-General Emslie ruled[18] that: "the only effect of desertion of a diet simpliciter on the prosecutor's motion is to disable that prosecutor from taking fresh proceedings against the accused upon the same charge or charges."

Lord Cameron added[19] that: "the abandonment of the prosecution by the **5–92** Crown in no way excluded the right of a private prosecutor to seek at the hands of this court the issue of criminal letters in her own name."

Another application for a private prosecution occurred in 1995 in the **5–93** case of *C* v. *Forsyth.*[20] It was unsuccessful and highlighted the very substantial procedural obstacles facing a complainer in such circumstances.

RES JUDICATA: CIVIL AND CRIMINAL CASES *INTER SE*

On the face of it, it is unlikely that *res judicata* could operate between civil **5–94** and criminal cases since the parties to each action are normally different, and, to a lesser extent, the same issues will not arise in the same "cause of action." For these reasons, the older authorities[21] recognised a general rule that the doctrine could not apply between civil and criminal cases.

The older case authorities also follow the same theme, allowing in civil **5–95** actions what were in substance retrials of issues which had already been

---

[16] 1983 S.L.T. 48, the so-called "Glasgow Rape case". See Harper and McWhinnie, *The Glasgow Rape Case.*
[17] In all other such cases, the Crown had simply declined to proceed at all.
[18] At p. 55. *N.B.* that earlier his Lordship impliedly equated desertion simpliciter with the formal abandonment which had occurred in this case, and the two must therefore be taken as having the same effect so far as concerns a subsequent right of private prosecution.
[19] At p. 52.
[20] 1995 S.L.T. 905.
[21] *e.g.* Hume, 1171, 479 and Dickson, *Evidence,* para. 3.5; see also Walker and Walker, *Law of Evidence in Scotland,* para. 51(c).

considered in criminal cases. Thus, in *Wood* v. *North British Ry. Co.*,[22] a cab operator who had already been convicted of a breach of the peace by resisting his removal from the forecourt of Edinburgh Waverley Station was allowed to raise a civil action for damages for assault and illegal arrest against the police officer responsible for his removal.

5–96   The clearest statement of what is still the general rule came in *Wilson* v. *Bennett*,[23] in which W, who had earlier been convicted of an assault on a police officer, then raised a civil action against the same officer in respect of an alleged assault upon him immediately before the incident which had led to his conviction. The two issues were clearly not the same anyway, but in rejecting the defence plea that the whole incident was now *res judicata* by virtue of the earlier conviction, Lord Traynor[24] gave a more general opinion that "a conviction or judgment in a criminal court is not a *res judicata* effectual to bar an action or claim in a civil action arising, or alleged to arise, out of the same circumstances."

5–97   That general rule may be modified in circumstances in which an earlier conviction before a criminal court may have evidential relevance in a later civil action. These circumstances fall into two broad categories. First, where the earlier action does, as an exception to the general rule, operate so as to resolve the matter for all time. And second, where the earlier action creates a presumption of guilt.

(1) Finding of guilt res judicata of later civil action

5–98   The main exceptions to the general rule are statutory, but even at common law there is some authority for regarding a previous finding of guilt as being *res judicata* of a particular issue where it is reraised in a later civil action between the same parties. Since it is rare for a private individual to be a party to a criminal case, such cases will clearly not arise often, but where they do, all the necessary ingredients are present for a successful plea of *res judicata*.

5–99   In *Young* v. *Mitchell*,[25] a servant had earlier brought a criminal complaint of illegal dismissal against his former employer under the Master and Servant Act of 1867,[26] and the charge had been found not proven. The servant then raised a civil action based on precisely the same facts. In holding that the criminal case was *res judicata* of any subsequent civil action, the Lord President stated[27]: "I think that a judgment in a criminal complaint may be

---

[22] (1899) I F. 562. See also *Faculty of Procurators of Glasgow* v. *Colquhoun* (1900) 2 F. 1192.
[23] (1904) 6 F. 269.
[24] At p. 271.
[25] (1874) I R. 1011. See also *Kennedy* v. *Wise* (1890) 17 R. 1036.
[26] Which authorised such an action.
[27] At p. 1013.

res judicata in a civil action, provided the parties are the same, the ground of action the same, and the remedy sought the same."[28]

The general principle is, it is submitted, just as applicable to a case in **5–100** which a common law crime is prosecuted privately by the victim[29] in a case in which the Crown have declined to proceed.[30] If, having obtained a conviction for, say, assault, the victim then raises a civil action for damages in compensation for the same assault, the conviction may be regarded as *res judicata* of the question of whether or not the assault occurred, unless the view is taken that the "remedy" sought is not the same.

(2) **Presumption of guilt from previous conviction**

The Law Reform (Miscellaneous Provisions) Act 1968 provides for two **5–101** situations in which a conviction in previous criminal proceedings will create a presumption of guilt in later civil proceedings.

The first situation is created by section 12 which states that: **5–102**

"In an action for defamation in which the question whether a person did or did not commit a criminal offence is relevant to an issue arising in the action, proof that, at the time when that issue falls to be determined, that person stands convicted of that offence shall be conclusive evidence that he committed that offence; and his conviction thereof shall be admissible in evidence accordingly."

The obvious use for this provision arises when, say, a newspaper **5–103** publishes an item describing someone as "a convicted thief", or even simply "a thief", and the person concerned challenges the writer to prove that he actually committed the offence. This is what happened in several well-publicised cases involving English offenders,[31] and the Law Reform Committee, in its 15th Report,[32] recommended a corresponding change in the law which in Scotland found expression in section 12.

The effect is that a conviction is regarded in later defamation **5–104** proceedings[33] as conclusive of guilt of the offence to which it relates, and subsection (2) provides that once the conviction itself has been proved:

---

[28] The classic formulation of the prerequisites of *res judicata:* see para. 5.04 *supra.*

[29] Which Walker and Walker, *op. cit.,* n. 21, regarded as "rare," and limited to cases in which "the proceedings in the criminal court were of a quasi-civil character and the parties in both proceedings were the same."

[30] A possibility which may be stronger following *H.* v. *Sweeney,* dealt with in paras. 5.89–5.92 *supra.*

[31] See, *e.g. Hinds* v. *Sparks* [1964] Crim.L.R. 717 and *Goody* v. *Odhams Press* [1967] 1 Q.B. 333.

[32] *N.B.* that another recommendation of the committee, that acquittal of an offence should also be regarded as conclusive evidence of innocence, was rejected.

[33] But no other type of action, *e.g.* damages for unlawful arrest.

> "the contents of any document which is admissible as evidence of the conviction, and the contents of the complaint, information, indictment or charge-sheet on which that person was convicted, shall, without prejudice to the reception of any other admissible evidence for the purpose of identifying the facts which constituted that offence, be admissible in evidence for the purpose of identifying those facts".

The conviction may be by any court in the United Kingdom, or any court-martial.[34]

5–105   There is a very good practical reason for authorising the production of documents such as copy complaints. It is not always obvious from the bare record of a conviction what exactly the accused did. For example an extract conviction for a breach of the peace encompasses a wide range of criminal behaviour. Where a newspaper article refers to a person as being a "Peeping Tom",[35] the journalist may find it difficult to make use of section 12 as a defence to a defamation action if armed only with an extract conviction showing that the pursuer committed a breach of the peace, with no further specification.

5–106   An example of this problem in practice is the English case of *Levene* v. *Roxhan*,[36] in which a newspaper article alleged that L, by means of a bogus bomb-scare telephone call, had caused a four-hour shutdown of Victoria Station. The court in the subsequent libel action refused to consider an extract conviction which stated merely that L had been convicted of maliciously abstracting electricity belonging to the Postmaster-General.

5–107   Another potential barrier to the effective use of section 12 may be the difficulty of proving that the extract conviction relates to the person who is now the pursuer in the defamation action. This is a problem frequently encountered in criminal cases in which it is essential to the present charge to prove that the accused has a previous conviction.[37]

5–108   The second situation is created by section 10 of the 1968 Act which was intended to obviate the need in civil proceedings of proving the conduct which led to a criminal conviction. It states that:

> "In any civil proceedings the fact that a person has been convicted of an offence by or before any court in the United Kingdom or by a court-martial there or elsewhere shall ... be admissible in evidence for the purpose of proving, where to do so is relevant to any issue in those proceedings, that he committed that offence, whether he was so convicted upon a plea of guilty or otherwise and whether or not he

---

[34] *ibid.*, subs. (3). *N.B.* that certified copies are allowed under subs. (2) by virtue of subs. (4).
[35] A species of breach of the peace identified in *Raffaeli* v. *Heatly*, 1949 J.C. 101.
[36] [1970] 1 W.L.R. 1322.
[37] *e.g.* on a charge of driving while disqualified; see *Herron* v. *Nelson*, 1976 S.L.T. (Sh.Ct.) 42.

is a party to the civil proceedings; but no conviction other than a subsisting one shall be admissible in evidence by virtue of this section."

Subsection (2)(a) goes on to state that where the person in question is **5–109** proved to have been convicted of an offence then "he shall be taken to have committed that offence unless the contrary is proved." This places a persuasive burden on the person concerned[38] of proving that, despite the conviction, he was in fact innocent. As with section 12, documents such as complaints, indictments and charge-sheets are admissible to show the real nature of the offence,[39] and extracts may be used.

Frequent use is made of section 10 in cases such as actions for damages **5–110** arising from a road accident in which the defender has been convicted of a motoring offence arising from the same accident. Similarly, in a divorce action a wife pursuer may seek to prove the criminal behaviour towards her of her husband by reference to relevant convictions. Once again, however, the pursuer may face difficulties in identifying the precise nature of the offence, and showing that the person named in the conviction is the defender.[40] Although not settled, it is likely that the standard of proof on a defender who tries to prove his innocence is on a balance of probabilities.[41]

Problems remain, though, for a pursuer who is relying on section 10 in a **5–111** subequent civil action. The pursuer will require to link the present defender with the previous accused and to demonstrate the two incidents are the same. In some cases in may be easier to prove *de novo* the defender committed the act in question.

In a civil action involving the application of section 10 the parties may **5–112** rely on the provisions of section 1 of the Civil Evidence (Scotland) Act 1988 which removed the requirement for corroboration in civil cases.[42]

---

[38] For which see para. 2.06–2.14 *supra*.

[39] *e.g.* in the case of an "assault," that it was in fact an assault upon his wife, which may be an essential factor in a separation or divorce action. This provision may be even more important when the convicted person is not a party to the present proceedings.

[40] See, *e.g. Caldwell* v. *Wright*, 1970 S.L.T. 111 and *Andrews* v. *Andrews*, 1971 S.L.T. (Notes) 44.

[41] See *King* v. *Patterson*, 1971 S.L.T. (Notes) 40. See also Macphail, *Evidence,* Chap. 11.05–21 and the English cases quoted there. The matter seems not to have been authoritatively settled under Scots law.

[42] For which see paras. 7.87–7.89 *infra*.

Chapter 6

JUDICIAL ADMISSIONS

Introduction

6–01 A matter which has been judicially admitted is one which is to be taken as proved just as if a witness had given unchallenged evidence on the point. According to Walker and Walker[1]: "judicial admissions are in themselves, and without anything more, conclusive against the party making them, for the purposes of the action in which they are made."

6–02 The reason behind the rule is that there is little point requiring a party to lead evidence on a particular issue if the other party is prepared to admit it. Judicial admissions cannot be used for any other purpose, and they must be taken subject to any explanations or qualifications which accompany them, but their effect is to relieve the other party of the need to lead any evidence on the fact or facts admitted.

6–03 This is another aspect of the law of evidence which encroaches into the law of procedure, and the civil law position will be considered separately from that of the criminal law.

JUDICIAL ADMISSIONS IN CIVIL CASES

6–04 In the course of a civil action, there are basically three procedures in which a fact or set of facts may be judicially admitted formally by one of the parties, and usually without any objection from the other. These arise:

(i)   in the closed record adjusted between the parties;
(ii) by means of oral admissions at the bar; and
(iii) in a minute of admissions.

However, a party may be taken to have *impliedly* admitted a fact, either by remaining silent when it is arguable that he or she should not have done, or by virtue of a partial averment in the written pleadings. Moreover, since January 1, 1994 the Sheriff Court Rules provide for the service of Notices

---

[1] *Law of Evidence in Scotland*, para. 48(*a*), quoting Stair, IV,xlv,5 and Erskine, IV,ii,33.

to Admit by one party on another seeking agreement of a specified fact or the authenticity of a document. This procedure is designed to expedite the judicial process and avoid time spent on the unnecessary proof of non-contentious issues.[2]

FORMAL ADMISSIONS

(1) **In the closed record**

The closed record is intended to be the final statement by the parties of those matters which require to be litigated, and "the closing of the record marks the borderline between pleading and Proof."[3] It has been said that: "Admissions on record ... are, no doubt, equivalent to proof; but averments have no factual significance unless and until they are proved."[4]   **6–05**

Put another way, what party A chooses to concede in the closed record in response to averments from party B, will be held as proved against A. But what a party avers, with no admission from the other party, must be proved.   **6–06**

Lee v. *N.C.B.*,[5] is the leading case on the subject in relation to civil cases. It was an action for damages by a labourer in respect of personal injuries which he alleged he had sustained as the result of a breach of statutory duty by his employers, and the failure of a colleague to act with reasonable care towards him. The only evidence of any of this came from the pursuer himself but in corroboration of his evidence[6] he sought to rely on certain of the defender's averments concerning the actions of his colleague. In rejecting the suggestion that a simple unadmitted averment by one party could ever constitute proof for the other party, Lord Sorn[7] ruled that: **6–07**

> "It would introduce the greatest confusion into our practice should we countenance the view that a pursuer in order to supply deficiencies in his evidence, could select passages from his opponent's averments, construe them as a representation of certain facts, and then treat the result as if it was a judicial admission."[8]

---

[2]   The receiving party can counter with a Notice of Non-admission: rule 29.14 of the Sheriff Court (Ordinary Cause) Rules 1993. An equivalent rule for the Court of Session is contained in rule 36.6 of the Rules of the Court of Session 1994.

[3]   Maxwell, *Practice of the Court of Session*, p. 202.

[4]   Lord Sorn in *Lee* v. *N.C.B.*, 1955 S.C. 151 at p. 160.

[5]   *ibid.*. See also *Stewart* v. *Glasgow Corporation,* and *Wilson* v. *Clyde*, both *infra*.

[6]   Such corroboration would not be required today: see paras. 7.87–7.89 *infra*.

[7]   *ibid.*.

[8]   See also *Lennox* v. *N.C.B.*, 1955 S.C. 438.

(2) **Oral admissions at the bar**

6–08 "In practice admissions are frequently made orally by counsel or solicitors at the bar, and are acted upon by the parties and by the court."[9] Although in theory such admissions are not as formal as those contained in the closed record, they have the same effect. The other party is therefore relieved of the duty of proving the point and the fact admitted finds its way into the formal record of the Proof, either in the form of a minute noted by the court as being of consent,"[10] or in the notes of evidence.

6–09 Whereas an admission contained in the closed record will be regarded as final, and as the equivalent of proof, oral admissions at the bar may be rescinded if they are proved to be incorrect.[11]

(3) **Minute of admissions**

6–10 "A minute lodged in process by a party, or by the parties jointly, is a competent method of recording admissions and is the appropriate method of bringing them to the notice of a jury, who are denied access to the written pleadings."[12]

6–11 In both Court of Session civil jury trials and proofs, this procedure is formally recognised by rules 36.7 and 37.4 of the Rules of the Court of Session 1994, and in all forms of action in the sheriff courts, and is in fact positively encouraged.[13] It is particularly prevalent in non-contentious issues such as the medical evidence in actions for personal injuries, in which the extent of the injuries is not disputed, but the cause of them is. Equally it is common in actions of divorce, nullity or separation, in which agreements between the parties on questions relating to children or the financial arrangements may be incorporated in a joint minute under rule 49.27 of the Rules of the Court of Session.[14]

6–12 In matrimonial cases there are frequently joint minutes relating to financial provision on divorce. The general position is governed by s. 16(1)(b) and s. 16(2)(b) of the Family Law (Scotland) Act 1985. These sections govern the court's power to set aside or vary an agreement or any term in an agreement made by the parties to resolve the question of financial

---

[9] Walker and Walker, *op. cit.,* n. 1, para. 48(c).

[10] Referred to as such in the interlocutor following the proof.

[11] See *Whyte* v. *Whyte* (1895) 23 R. 320.

[12] Walker and Walker, *op. cit.,* n. 1, para. 48(b).

[13] Macphail, *Evidence,* Chap. 2.14.

[14] See also s. 16 of the Family Law (Scotland) Act 1985 *infra,* which allows joint minutes of agreement on financial provision in divorce. For cases involving the use of substantial joint minutes, see *Johnstone's Exrs.* v. *Harris,* 1977 S.L.T. (Notes) 10 and *Ross* v. *B.R.B.,* 1972 S.L.T. 174. See also *Ribble Paper Mills* v. *Clyde Paper Mills,* 1972 S.L.T. (Notes) 25.

provision. The power can only be exercised on granting decree of divorce or within such period as the court may specify.[15]

In actions relating to children it is competent to enter into joint minutes **6–13** purporting to settle the action and setting out the terms of the agreement between the parties in relation to the children. Prior to the Children (Scotland) Act 1995 some reference was generally made to one of the parties having custody and the other access to the child(ren). The intention behind the 1995 Act is to abandon those terms in favour of "residence" and "contact",[16] and to encourage people to think in terms of parental "responsibilities" rather than "rights". The Child Support Act 1991 has caused a similar shift in attitude since many disputes about aliment are now dealt with through the statutuory procedures of that Act.

As a general rule, whatever is jointly admitted will normally be taken as **6–14** final, with no opportunity of reopening the issue.

IMPLIED ADMISSIONS

In addition to the possibility of a party formally and expressly admitting **6–15** certain facts as part of the pleadings, or in the course of a proof, there is some authority to the effect that admissions may be made by implication. This could occur in two ways: either by a party remaining silent in the face of an averment from the other party which could easily be denied, or by a party making averments about some fact which, taken in context, operates as an admission of some fact averred by the other party.

(1) **Admission by silence**

In relation to this concept of admission by silence Walker and Walker[17] **6–16** commented:

> "Both in the Court of Session[18] and in the sheriff court[19] an averment made by one party of a fact within the knowledge of the other party is held by implication to be admitted if it is not denied by the other

---

[15] In addition to this general power, the court can set aside or vary an agreement in terms of s. 16(1)(a) and s.16 (3) respectively of the 1985 Act. See *Milne* v. *Milne,* 1987 S.L.T. 45 and *Horton* v. *Horton,* 1992 S.C.L.R. 197.

[16] s.2(1) of the Act.

[17] *op. cit.,* n. 1, para. 48(d).

[18] Quoting Act of Sederunt, July 11, 1828, s. 105. The current provisions are in rule 36.6 of the Rules of the Court of Session 1994.

[19] Quoting Sheriff Court Rules 1907, r. 44, now r. 45 of the Rules as amended by S.I. 1983 No. 747, for actions commenced between September 1, 1983 and December 31, 1993. For actions commenced on or after January 1, 1994 see S.I. 1993 No. 1956 rule 9.7. The terms of these two rules are slightly different.

party. The words 'not admitted' are not the equivalent of a denial for this purpose."[20]

6–17   The Sheriff Court Ordinary Cause Rules 1993 provide, at rule 45, that, "Every statement of fact made by one party shall be answered by the other party, and if a statement made by one party of a fact within the knowledge of the other party is not denied by that other party, the latter shall be held as having admitted the fact so stated." Rule 45 will only apply when the fact in question is within the other party's undoubted knowledge, without the need for any sort of inquiry or investigation.

(2) Admission from partial averment

6–18   If party A makes an averment which is capable of being interpreted as consistent with an averment made by party B, then it is arguable that A's averment may be taken as an implied admission of B's averment. However, there would seem to be two lines of authority on the point.

6–19   What may be termed the "traditional view" is exemplified by cases such as *Stewart* v. *Glasgow Corporation*[21] and *Wilson* v. *Clyde Rigging and Boiler Scaling Co.*[22]

6–20   In *Stewart*, the tenant of a council house sought compensation for the death of her child as the result of an incident allegedly caused by the corroded state of a clothes pole in the back green of her tenement. She wanted to argue that the defenders must have been aware of the state of the pole at the time of the accident. She claimed that this evidence could be found in one of the defender's averments, to the effect that the pole had been inspected and painted five months before the accident. Lord President Clyde in rejecting this submission, relied on the basic statement of law by Lord Sorn in *Lee* v. *N.C.B.* (*supra*) to the effect that an averment which is not admitted has no evidential value until it is proved, and cannot therefore constitute an admission.

6–21   In *Wilson*, a widow sought compensation from the employers of her late husband, who had been killed while assisting in the loading of a cargo of timber into a ship's hold. An important question was whether or not the deceased had been working alone at the time. Apart from eye-witness evidence (which the court on appeal held to be sufficient), the Lord Ordinary (Lord Wheatley) relied on a defence averment to the effect that the deceased had been guiding the load into the hold, which he took to be an implied

---

[20] See *Central Motor Engineering Co. Ltd.* v. *Galbraith*, 1918 S.C. 755; for a more recent authority see *Clark* v. *Clark*, 1967 S.C. 296. See also *Ellon Castle Estates Co.* v. *MacDonald*, *infra*.

[21] 1958 S.C. 28, also dealt with in paras. 16.22–16.31 *infra*, when examining the role of the expert witness.

[22] 1959 S.C. 328.

admission that he had been alone at the time. On appeal, this approach was firmly rejected, again following the authority of *Lee* v. *N.C.B.*

What has given rise to what may be termed the "alternative view" is the **6–22** fact that Lord Sorn qualified the judgment he had given in *Lee* in the partly unreported case of *Dobson* v. *Colvilles Ltd.*[23] In the course of his judgment in *Dobson*, Lord Sorn observed *obiter* that:

> "If pleaders and pleadings were perfect, it would not be necessary to qualify the passage I have quoted[24] but, as things are, it must be recognised that in practice cases occur in which it is right to treat an averment in answer as equivalent to an admission. Whether this should be done must depend upon the particular case and the particular pleadings and I shall only say that I think we have an example here. The pursuer avers that his hand was injured by the guide wheel. Instead of admitting this and going on to give their own explanation of how the accident came about (as strictly they should have done) the defenders reply with a general denial; but in the explanation which follows they too make an explicit averment to the effect that the pursuer's hand was injured by the guide wheel. The case has been conducted on the footing that this was an agreed fact and, although not formally admitted by the defenders, it would not do now to hold that they had put the pursuer to the proof of it."

Lord Sorn's qualifications were applied in *Lord Advocate* v. *Gillespie*.[25] **6–23** This was a case involving an accident between two vehicles. The Lord Advocate on behalf of the Ministry of Defence raised an action against a contractor, alleging that one of his lorries had forced an RAF vehicle off the road. It was not proved in evidence that the lorry had at the time been driven by one of the contractor's employees, but it was averred on behalf of the MoD that the RAF vehicle had encountered, at the crown of the bend, a lorry belonging to the defender and being driven on the wrong side of the road. In answer, the contractor averred that the lorry had been approached on the bend by an RAF vehicle being driven in a reckless fashion.

The sheriff was of the opinion that he was free to choose between Lord **6–24** Strachan's judgment in *Wilson* and Lord Sorn's amended view as expressed in *Dobson*, and opted for the latter, regarding it as "the more realistic approach to the problems both of insufficient evidence and improperly drawn pleadings."[26]

---

[23] 1958 S.L.T. (Notes) 30, unreported so far as concerns Lord Sorn's amended opinion, which is, however, reproduced *per* Lord Wheatley in *Wilson, supra,* at p. 330.

[24] *i.e.* his own judgment in *Lee* v. *N.C.B., supra.*

[25] 1969 S.L.T. (Sh.Ct.) 10.

[26] At p. 12. And see also *Ellon Castle Estates Co.* v. *Macdonald,* 1975 S.L.T. (Notes) 66, followed in *EFT Finance Ltd.* v. *Hawkins,* 1994 S.L.T. 902; and *McNaught* v. *B.R.B.,* 1979 S.L.T. (Notes) 99.

JUDICIAL ADMISSIONS IN CRIMINAL CASES

6–25 There are three contexts in which a judicial admission may arise in a criminal case. These are:

    (i)   as a plea of guilty;
    (ii) in a joint minute between the prosecution and the defence; and
    (iii) in the course of a special defence, which may or may not include a partial admission as to the *actus reus*.

There are also certain statutory situations in which an accused who fails to challenge an assertion may be taken to have impliedly admitted it.

PLEA OF GUILTY

6–26 "A plea of guilty is a solemn judicial confession of fact, and if accepted, may result in an immediate conviction."[27]

6–27 The procedural and evidential consequences of a plea of guilty vary somewhat as between solemn and summary cases, and are now considered separately.

(1) Solemn cases

6–28 Section 77(1) of the Criminal Procedure (Scotland) Act 1995 states that if the accused pleads guilty and the plea is accepted by the Crown, then a written copy of the plea should be signed by the accused, and countersigned by the trial judge. If the plea is to only part of the indictment, and the Crown are not prepared to accept it, then the non-acceptance is also recorded, per section 77(2).[28] There is no obligation on the Crown to accept any plea of guilty, not even one which covers the entire indictment,[29] but they cannot thereafter make any evidential use of the fact that the accused was prepared to plead guilty.

6–29 In *Strathern* v. *Sloan*,[30] Lord Justice-Clerk Aitchison observed, at page 80, that: "Wherever a plea of guilty is tendered and not accepted by the prosecutor, the plea of guilty must under no circumstances be used against the panel, and, where the trial is on indictment, must not be disclosed to the jury."

6–30 In solemn cases[31] if the Crown accepts a partial plea of guilty in respect of an indictment which contains more than one charge, and proceeds to

---

[27] Macphail, *op. cit.*, n. 13, Chap. 2.26.
[28] Previously, similar provisions were contained in s. 103 of the Criminal Procedure (Scotland) Act 1975.
[29] *Peter and Smith* (1840) 2 Swin. 492. See also *Strathern* v. *Sloan*, *infra*.
[30] 1937 J.C. 76 at p. 80. The case is dealt with more fully *infra*.
[31] But not in summary cases.

trial on the remaining charges, they cannot make use of that plea of guilty as evidence against the accused on the remaining charges. The authority for this is *Walsh* v. *H.M.A.*[32]

In *Walsh,* W was charged on indictment with the theft of three cars, and **6–31** at the trial diet he tendered a plea of guilty to the third charge and pleas of not guilty to the first two. The jury were then empanelled, and the sheriff clerk read out all three charges to them. In charging the jury, the sheriff directed them formally to find W guilty on the third charge, and consider whether or not it was relevant to the issue of his guilt on the remaining charges, using the *Moorov* doctrine.[33] W was convicted on all three charges and appealed.

It was held that the jury should not have known about his plea of guilty, **6–32** that the third charge should not have been read out to them, and that they should not have been directed to find him guilty. Irrespective of the operation of the *Moorov* doctrine, it was held that the sheriff had misdirected the jury by suggesting that a plea of guilty to charge 3 was of evidential value on charges 1 and 2, and the convictions were quashed.

Macphail[34] argues that the operation of the rule is "unrealistic" in cases **6–33** in which the *Moorov* doctrine might otherwise be applied. He accepts that in general it is undesirable for a jury to be influenced by being made aware of the accused's plea of guilty to one or more other charges. But he points out that the effect of *Walsh* is to make it "prudent" for the Crown to decline partial pleas when they intend to invoke the doctrine.

The effect of a plea of guilty, once signed and countersigned, is as if a **6–34** formal finding of guilt had been made following trial. The court may proceed to pass sentence following the prosecution's summary of the circumstances of the offence, and the defence plea in mitigation.[35]

The question of whether or not a guilty plea may be withdrawn is dealt **6–35** with below, under "Summary cases", since it is common law based, and the only modern authorities are in respect of summary charges.

---

[32] 1961 S.C. 51.

[33] For which see paras. 7.66–7.81 *infra*. In brief, the *Moorov* doctrine allows an incident spoken to by only one witness to be corroborated by a witness speaking about another incident where the two incidents are strikingly similar, and appear to form a course of conduct.

[34] *op. cit.,* n. 13, Chap. 2.28.

[35] Section 77 of the Criminal Procedure (Scotland) Act 1995. In practice, where the plea is partial only, sentence will be deferred until the end of the trial on the remaining charges.

[36] Section 144 of the 1995 Act. By virtue of s. 146(8), it is not necessary for the prosecutor to prove the accused's guilt of those charges to which he has pled guilty. According to Renton and Brown, *Criminal Procedure* para. 14.30, acceptance by the Crown of a partial plea is equivalent to desertion simpliciter of the rest of the complaint.

(2) **Summary cases**

6–36   In summary cases a plea of guilty, if accepted by the prosecutor, allows the court to proceed immediately to sentence, following the usual representations by the fiscal and the defence agent.[36] As in solemn cases, there is no obligation on the prosecutor to accept any guilty plea, but although the offer of a plea and its rejection will be recorded, the prosecutor may not thereafter make any evidential use of it.

6–37   In *Strathern* v. *Sloan*[37] G and S were charged with the theft of a motor vehicle. At the pleading diet G entered a not guilty plea, but S attempted to plead guilty. The fiscal refused to accept the pleas, and requested a trial diet for both accused. The sheriff refused, and recorded a plea of guilty against S, continuing the case for sentence at a later diet. The prosecution appealed by way of a bill of advocation, and it was held[38] that the fiscal was entitled to lead evidence against S.

6–38   However, in summary cases, it seems that if the prosecutor accepts a partial plea of guilty to certain charges on a complaint, and proceeds to trial on the remainder, where relevant, the prosecutor may then make use of these guilty pleas in proving the guilt of the accused on the remaining charges.[39]

6–39   This emerged in the case of *McColl* v. *Skeen*.[40] This was an appeal against conviction for the offence of producing, on request from the police, a forged test certificate for a motor vehicle. The accused had pled guilty to another charge on the complaint, namely using a motor vehicle without a valid test certificate. It was the fact that the accused had been unable to produce such a certificate to police officers who had stopped the vehicle that had led to the police request that such a certificate be produced at a police station, and the eventual production of a forgery. In the course of finding the accused guilty on the charge of producing a forged certificate, the trial sheriff made use of the fact that a guilty plea had been entered on the charge of driving the vehicle without a valid current test certificate. The accused appealed, but the appeal was rejected. The High Court made the following observations[41]:

> "The plea of guilty to charge 1 was highly relevant to proof of guilt on charge 2 ... There is no statutory prohibition which inhibits a sheriff from taking cognisance and account of a plea of guilty to one charge or two or more in the same complaint when the fact of the

---

[37] 1937 J.C. 76; see *supra* for Lord Justice-Clerk Aitchison's comments on the evidential value of a rejected plea, which covers both solemn and summary cases.
[38] Relying on *Kirkwood* v. *Coalburn District Co-op.*, 1930 J.C. 38.
[39] *e.g.* under the *Moorov* doctrine.
[40] 1980 S.L.T. (Notes) 53.
[41] At p. 54.

admission implied in the plea is, as a fact, relevant to proof of another charge or charges libelled in the complaint."

Some confusion has arisen in recent years over the question of whether, **6–40** having offered a plea of guilty, the accused may then withdraw it. The authorities[42] suggest that it may only, in any case, occur when the accused can show that the plea was tendered as the result of trickery or coercion, or because of a genuine misunderstanding. It was held in *Tudhope* v. *Campbell*[43] that a plea may be withdrawn on one of these grounds before the conviction and sentence have been recorded.

The issue in *Tudhope* v. *Cullen*[44] was whether or not the plea could be **6–41** withdrawn after the recording of the conviction, but before sentence. The accused, having pled not guilty to an assault charge at the pleading diet, turned up at the trial diet without a solicitor and pled guilty. Sentence was deferred for a social inquiry report. At the adjourned hearing, the accused attempted to withdraw his plea of guilty, claiming that he should have been legally represented at the trial diet, but had been let down by his solicitor. After consideration of the background circumstances, the sheriff refused to allow him to withdraw his plea, but held to the view that in some cases it might be possible, even after conviction, basing his decision on the unreported case of *P.F. (Glasgow)* v. *MacCauley*.[45]

In *MacCauley,* the accused had originally been charged with a variety **6–42** of road traffic offences. At the pleading diet he pled guilty to one charge and not guilty to the remainder. Sentence was deferred on the charge to which he had pled guilty, but at the trial diet, the accused appeared with a solicitor and requested leave to withdraw the guilty plea, on the grounds that it had been tendered without the benefit of legal advice. The minute of conviction had by that stage been signed by the clerk, and the prosecution argued that *Tudhope* v. *Campbell* could not therefore be relied upon.

The sheriff concluded that, although the minute referred to a "deferred **6–43** sentence", this was not to be taken as necessarily implying that conviction had taken place, and that the plea was therefore irreversible. This would be the case where sentence followed immediately upon conviction, but in a case such as this, said the sheriff,[46] the court should apply "the wider equitable principle that allows a plea of guilty to be withdrawn in a suitable case." Since both parties were in agreement that the equities of the case demanded it, the guilty plea was withdrawn, and a plea of not guilty recorded.

---

[42] See, *e.g.* Renton and Brown, *op. cit.,* n. 36, para. 14–29, and the cases cited there.
[43] 1979 J.C. 24.
[44] 1982 S.C.C.R. 276.
[45] Reported in full in *Tudhope* v. *Cullen, supra.* But see *Burns* v. *Wilson,* 1993 S.L.T. 809.
[46] At p. 280.

6–44   Once sentence has been recorded, however, it would appear that there can be no possibility of a guilty plea being withdrawn.[47]

6–45   In *Backhurst* v. *McNaughten*,[48] it was held that an accused who makes a credible confession, on oath, to theft, cannot be convicted of reset.

JOINT MINUTES

6–46   Parties to a civil action may elect to minimise the factual issues between them by admitting certain facts in a joint minute.[49]

6–47   In criminal cases, in both solemn and summary proceedings, there were provisions in the Criminal Procedure (Scotland) Act 1975 permitting the lodging of joint minutes of admissions. The purpose is to speed up the court process by not having to spend time proving non-contentious matters. Following the Scottish Law Commission's Report: *Documentary Evidence and Proof of Undisputed Facts in Criminal Proceedings*,[50] the statutory position has been fortified. Section 256 of the Criminal Procedure (Scotland) Act 1995 largely re-enacts the earlier provisions[51] and permits the lodging in court of minutes of admission and minutes of agreement. Documents and copy documents can be admitted using this mechanism.[52] To encourage the use of these provisions, section 257 places a duty on the Crown and the defence[53] to identify facts which are unlikely to be disputed and which if admitted would avoid the need for oral evidence.[54]

6–48   Section 258 goes one step further and entitles a party who considers there are facts which are unlikely to be disputed, to serve on the other party a statement setting out those facts. Unless the receiving party challenges the statement within seven days, the facts "shall be deemed to have been conclusively proved." In terms of s. 258(5) parties are not subsequently excluded from leading evidence relevant to any matter contained in the statement. Any document admitted through the joint minute procedure will be deemed to have been duly proved.

6–49   Joint minutes are appropriate and are frequently used in a variety of situations in which evidence (*e.g.* medical or forensic) is not contentious, or in which the entire evidence of a witness (*e.g.* a police scenes-of-crime

---

[47] *MacNeill* v. *McGregor*, 1975 J.C. 55.
[48] 1981 S.C.C.R. 6.
[49] For the procedure see Maxwell, *op. cit.,* n. 3, and Macphail, *Sheriff Court Practice*.
[50] Report No. 137, published in 1992.
[51] Contained in s. 150 (solemn) and s. 354 (summary) of the Criminal Procedure (Scotland) Act 1975.
[52] s. 256(1)(b).
[53] The duty only applies to an accused who is legally represented.
[54] *Quaere* as to whether the admissions need to be in writing. See *Jessop* v. *Kerr,* 1989 S.C.C.R. 417 and the Commentary following the report.

photographer) is not challenged. However, the intention behind the 1995 provisions is to go further than agreements relating to formal or expert evidence. It is to seek and obtain evidence from an accused which, at the pre-trial stage at least, appears uncontroversial. Both the prosecution and defence can use section 256, but the latter may be reluctant to agree anything other than the most non-contentious evidence on the basis that the accused is entitled to "put the Crown to the test."

It is unclear how these provisions will operate in practice. Only **6–50** represented accused have the duty to agree evidence and it may be that solicitors will adopt the cautious approach typical of judicial examination procedures.[55] Although unrepresented accused are entitled to take advantage of section 256, this will inevitably impose additional work on the prosecutor who will have the responsibility of preparing these minutes.

Any minute of admissions or agreement will be strictly construed. In **6–51** *Evans* v. *Wilson*,[56] in a trial for alleged drunken driving contrary to the road traffic legislation, the parties lodged a joint minute to the effect that certain numbered productions were doctor's and analyst's certificates under section 10 of the Road Traffic Act 1972. The certificates themselves were not produced, and at the end of the trial, after the completion of the evidence, the defence agent argued that since the certificates were not before the court, there was insufficient evidence for a conviction. The sheriff then instructed the fiscal to lay the certificates before the court, and thereafter convicted the accused.

On appeal, the conviction was quashed on the grounds that, (i) since he **6–52** had closed his case before the certificates themselves had been lodged in evidence, it was incompetent for the fiscal to have done so when he did, even on the instruction of the sheriff; and (ii) the joint minute, which simply stated what the productions were, and in no way admitted the facts contained in the certificates, could not remedy the situation.

IMPLIED ADMISSIONS FROM SPECIAL DEFENCES

When an accused lodges a special defence such as self-defence or insanity, **6–53** there is an implied admission of the *actus reus* of the crime charged. The accused is also seeking to escape the normal consequences of the crime by arguing that there was an absence of the necessary *mens rea* for conviction.

The general effect of lodging such a special defence is that the Crown is **6–54** relieved of the burden of proof on the issue of the *actus reus*.[57] There are

---

[55] Where it is commonplace for an accused to say nothing in response to prosecution questioning on, "the advice of my solicitor."

[56] 1981 S.C.C.R. 60.

[57] For burdens of proof generally, see Chap. 2 *supra*.

though some exceptions where the Crown is still required to prove the *actus reus*.

6–55   In *H.M.A.* v. *McClone*[58], an accused charged with a razor assault lodged a special defence of self-defence which originally read that "the panel pleaded not guilty and further that if any wound was received by [the victim] it was inflicted in self-defence in the course of a struggle in which [the victim] was himself the aggressor." The advocate-depute, for the Crown, objected to this wording, since it was in effect saying: "I did not do it, and if I did, I did it in self-defence." The special defence was then reworded to read that "the panel pleaded not guilty and specially that on the occasion libelled he was acting in self-defence, he then having been assaulted by [the victim]."

6–56   The important concession won by the Crown was, of course, the implied admission by the accused that he had committed the act.

6–57   Like all admissions, however, special defences must be taken subject to the qualifications and excuses contained in them. In *Owens* v. *H.M.A.*[59] in which it was held that the evidential burden on the issue of self-defence rests with the accused, Lord Justice General Normand made the following observation[60]:

> "[The Crown] must prove that the fatal act was the accused's, and that it was deliberate or committed with a reckless disregard of the consequences. The panel relieved the Crown of the first part of the burden by himself admitting the stabbing with a lethal weapon, but attached to this admission the explanation of its being done in self-defence in the circumstances explained by him. The Crown cannot, we think, take advantage of the admission without displacing the explanation or at all events presenting to the jury a not less strong case that shows directly or indirectly that the explanation is false."

IMPLIED ADMISSIONS CREATED UNDER STATUTE

6–58   By virtue of section 138(4) and schedule 3 to the Criminal Procedure (Scotland) Act 1995, certain offences when libelled against the accused may contain implicit terms regarding the commission of the offence. Any objection taken to these would require to be by way of preliminary plea prior to the recording of the plea to the charge.[61]

---

[58]   1955 J.C. 14

[59]   1946 J.C. 119

[60]   At p. 124. The persuasive burden of proving the charge of murder remained with the Crown throughout.

[61]   Previously s. 312 of the 1975 Act. See Renton and Brown, *op. cit.*, n. 36, para. 13.54 and all the cases cited there.

Section 280(9) of the Criminal Procedure (Scotland) Act 1995 provides **6–59**
that at any trial, it will be presumed that the person who appears in answer
to the complaint is the person originally charged by the police, and any
contrary assertion must be disposed of by way of a preliminary plea.[62]

---

[62] Which is taken as if it were a plea to the competency or relevancy. The significance of this
provision as a link in a chain corroborating the identification of the accused emerged in
Smith v. *Paterson*, 1982 S.L.T. 437, and is further considered in paras. 7.25–7.47 *infra*.

Chapter 7

CORROBORATION

Introduction

7–01 Corroborative evidence means an item of evidence emanating from an independent source which is available to support another item of evidence. The need for corroboration differs as between criminal and civil cases. As a general rule in criminal proceedings an essential fact cannot be proved by the testimony of one witness alone. Instead that witness's testimony must be proved by corroborative evidence. Corroboration means the testimony should be supplemented, supported and confirmed by independent evidence to the same effect from a second source. That second source need not be another witness—it could, for example, be evidence of a documentary nature. As the Scottish Law Commission Report No.100[1a] pointed out, "in practice it [corroboration] is commonly found in a combination of direct testimony and circumstantial evidence."[1]

7–02 The need for corroboration reflects a genuine concern that a case should not normally be decided on the basis of the testimony of one witness. The evidence of that witness should, instead, be "corroborated" before it receives legal recognition in the form of an appropriate finding of fact. In criminal cases there are various exceptions to the general rule requiring corroboration.

7–03 In civil cases, since the Civil Evidence (Scotland) Act 1988, there is no longer any requirement for corroboration. However, where there is corroborative evidence in a case a party does have more chance of success since the evidence is likely to attract greater weight.

7–04 It is only the "crucial" or essential facts of a criminal case which require corroboration. These must be distinguished from the categories of evidential or procedural facts. The next section addresses these three separate categories.

[1a] In Report on *Corroboration, Hearsay and Related Matters* (1986).
[1] Para. 2.2 quoting Dickson, *Evidence*, para.1808 and 1811.

CRUCIAL AND EVIDENTIAL FACTS DISTINGUISHED

The crucial facts of any case are what were referred to in Chapter 1 as the **7–05** *facta probanda,* or "those matters in dispute between the parties."[2] In a criminal case they are "the facts which ... establish the accused's guilt of the crime charged and must be libelled in an indictment or complaint, expressly or by statutory implication"[3]; while in a civil case they are "the facts which a party must, or ought to, aver in order to make a case relevant to be sent to proof."[4]

They will obviously vary with the substantive law. In *Lockwood* v. **7–06** *Walker*,[5] the accused was charged with lewd and libidinous practices with a girl below the age of puberty, and he was acquitted because the only evidence of the girl's age came from the girl herself. As the Lord Justice-Clerk put it[6]: "No doubt our law does not require that every fact in a case shall be proved by two witnesses, but it most certainly does require that every crucial fact[7] shall be so proved."

In a criminal case the proof of crucial facts must usually be by reference **7–07** to more than one item of evidence. These items of evidence may take several forms. They may, in the simplest possible case, be the eye-witness accounts of two independent witnesses. For example, when two witnesses say they saw X hit Y. Or again, they may take the form of a confession by the accused and either a witness statement which links the accused to the crime, or some forensic report which has the same effect.

Alternatively, evidence may take the form of a statement by a witness, **7–08** A, who was present at an incident into which the court is inquiring, linked with some additional evidence which, while not of itself direct evidence of what actually occurred, nevertheless tends to support the statement of A. They may even consist of two such items of indirect evidence which are independent of each other, but which point towards the same fact and do not require the support of direct evidence. These items, which while not direct evidence of what happened are nevertheless evidence towards it, are referred to as "evidential" facts.

In the vast majority of cases, evidential facts are the same thing as **7–09** circumstantial evidence, which is considered more fully in its own right in Chapter 9. For example, if A tells the court that he saw X running from the scene of a knife attack, B tells the court that he saw X throw something shiny in the river, and C testifies that he saw blood on X's clothes five

---

2   Walker and Walker, *Law of Evidence in Scotland*, para. 4.
3   Walker and Walker, *op. cit.,* n. 2, para. 382.
4   *ibid..*
5   1910 S.C.(J.) 3; see also *McCourt* v. *H.M.A., per* para. 7.16 *infra.*
6   At p. 5.
7   Sometimes referred to as an essential fact.

minutes later, a powerful case has been established against X. A crucial fact (that X committed a stabbing) is capable of being established without a single piece of direct evidence. The evidence so far adduced has been entirely circumstantial, or evidential.

7–10 The significance of this distinction between crucial facts and evidential facts is that whereas a crucial fact requires to be corroborated, an evidential fact does not. Evidential facts can be linked together as in the above example and offered in proof of a crucial fact. It is the relevance of the evidential fact to the crucial one which makes it admissible.

7–11 This relevance often enhances the reliability of the evidence. So, in the example given above, the case against X is built around three separate items of evidence—the running away, the abandoning of the knife and the bloodstained clothing—from three separate witnesses. Hume[8] referred to this process as a "concurrence of testimonies", and added that "the aptitude and coherence of the several circumstances often as fully confirm the truth of the story as if all the witnesses were deponing to the same facts."

7–12 The rationale underlying the "concurrence of testimonies" can explain why only one witness is required to prove an evidential fact which is to be linked to some other item of evidence in order to prove a crucial fact. The crucial fact will ultimately have been proved by two separate items of evidence. The evidential facts which led to the proof of the crucial fact will have been supported by only one each, which is all that the law requires.

7–13 A simple illustration of the use of an evidential fact in corroboration of another item of evidence is afforded by *Patterson* v. *Nixon*[9] a case of theft by housebreaking in which P had confessed to being near the locus dressed for housebreaking, but denied that he had actually committed it. This partial confession required corroboration,[10] and the police took a tracker dog to the locus. It picked up a scent, and when released it went straight to P's house, one of six in a block which it could have chosen. It was held that the behaviour of the dog was enough to provide the required corroboration.

CORROBORATION IN CRIMINAL CASES

GENERAL

7–14 The classic formulation of the requirement for corroboration is that of Lord Justice-Clerk Aitchison, delivering the opinion of a full bench, in *Morton* v. *H.M.A.*,[11] who stated that:

---

[8]　II, 384.
[9]　1960 J.C. 42. See also *Norval* v. *H.M.A.*, 1978 J.C. 70; *Little* v. *H.M.A.*, 1983 S.C.C.R. 56; and *Kennedy* v. *F.*, 1985 S.L.T. 22.
[10]　See paras. 7.48–7.57 *infra*.
[11]　1938 J.C. 50 at p. 55.

"no person can be convicted of a crime or a statutory offence except where the legislature otherwise directs, unless there is evidence of at least two witnesses implicating the person accused with the commission of the crime or offence with which he is charged. This rule has proved an invaluable safeguard in the practice of our criminal courts against unjust conviction, and it is a rule from which the courts ought not to sanction any departure."

The reference to "two witnesses" must not be taken literally, since what is required is two independent items of evidence which may not necessarily be in the form of testimony (*e.g.* a forensic report, or the behaviour of the tracker dog in *Patterson* v. *Nixon* in paragraph 7.13 *supra*), but which point to the crucial fact which needs to be established. In the words of Renton and Brown[12]:

"The basic requirement is that the offence be brought home to the accused by evidence from at least two sources. The question is not whether each of the several circumstances points by itself to guilt of the libel charged, but whether taken together they are capable of supporting the inference of guilt beyond reasonable doubt."[13]

The Crown must, of course, prove that a crime has been committed, and that the accused committed it, and the facts which will require corroboration may vary from case to case. As will be seen in subsequent sections of this chapter, the Crown must always corroborate any identification of the accused as the guilty party, and, with rare exceptions, any confession the accused is alleged to have made, but otherwise the requirement for corroboration will vary with the charge. **7–15**

In most cases the age of the victim is irrelevant but as was seen in *Lockwood* v, *Walker*[14] it is crucial in a sexual offence which is defined by reference to age.[15] In *McCourt* v. *H.M.A.*,[16] M was charged with an offence under the Prevention of Crimes Act 1908 which necessitated him being an habitual criminal over the age of 16. M had admitted to a police officer that **7–16**

---

[12] *Criminal Procedure*, para. 18–52, quoting *Little* v. *H.M.A.*, 1983 S.C.C.R. 56 at p. 61.

[13] *i.e.* a "concurrence of testimonies", *per* Hume, quoted in para. 7.11 *supra*. In *Gracey* v. *H.M.A.*, 1987 S.L.T. 749, it was held that the oral testimony of the complainer in a rape case might be corroborated by evidence from other witnesses as to her distressed condition shortly afterwards, it being a matter for the jury to assess the genuineness or otherwise of that distress: see also *Stephen* v. *H.M.A.*, 1987 S.C.C.R. 570, and paras. 7.82–7.86 *infra*.

[14] *per* para. 7.06 *supra*.

[15] *e.g.* Sexual Offences (Scotland) Act 1976 ss. 3 and 4.

[16] 1913 S.C.(J.) 6, applied in *Herron* v. *Nelson*, 1976 S.L.T. (Sh.Ct.) 42, in which it was held that the fact that D was disqualified from driving was a "crucial" fact which required proof by corroborated evidence for a conviction for driving while disqualified. The extract conviction was not sufficient without evidence which linked the accused to the extract.

he was 44, but his conviction was quashed on appeal because there was no corroborating evidence of his age.[17]

7–17   Similarly, on a charge of "knowingly" making false statements, it must be proved by corroborated evidence that the accused knew the falsity of the statement(s) he was making.[18] Complications sometimes arise from the fact that certain facts which are required to be proved in the course of a criminal trial are what is usually termed "procedural" in nature, and do not need to be corroborated.

7–18   For example, in *Farrell* v. *Concannon*[19] it was held that only one witness was required to the fact that the accused was advised of his rights before consenting to a medical examination. And in *MacLeod* v. *Nicol*[20] the same was said to be true of all the preliminary procedure in an alleged drunken driving charge, up to and including the first positive breath test at the locus.[21] In *Hudson* v. *Hamilton*,[22] it was said that where a tape-recording of an accused's police interview was lodged in court, it was not necessary for a second police officer to listen to the tape to identify it. It was sufficient that the second police officer could confirm that the tape lodged was the tape used.

7–19   Section 277 of the Criminal Procedure (Scotland) Act 1995 permits the prosecution to lodge in court a transcript of any interviews the accused may have had with the police. There is a procedure for certification of the tape as accurate but to use this procedure a copy of the transcript has to be served on the accused not less than 14 days prior to the trial. The accused can then object to the making or accuracy of the tape.

7–20   Where evidence is considered "routine" the Criminal Procedure (Scotland) Act 1995, contains statutory provisions permitting the evidence of only one witness to be sufficient evidence of a fact. In terms of section 280 where a certificate is lodged and signed by an authorised person it is deemed to be sufficient evidence of certain non-contentious issues.[23] In terms of section 281(2) where an autopsy or forensic report is lodged as a production, the Crown, after due notice to the accused and without any objection from him, may call only one pathologist or forensic scientist to give evidence regarding anything contained in their report.

---

[17] And see *Paton* v. *Wilson*, 1988 S.L.T. 634, a prosecution for selling alcohol to an under-age person, where there was insufficient corroboration of a 16 year old's age.

[18] *Townsend* v. *Strathearn*, 1923 J.C. 66.

[19] 1957 J.C. 12, which presumably also extends to evidence of a caution before the taking of a confession.

[20] 1970 J.C. 58.

[21] The case was decided under s. 2 of the Road Safety Act 1967, (now s. 6 of the Road Traffic Act 1988), and Lord Justice-Clerk Grant described the whole section as containing matters which were "clearly procedural and incidental."

[22] 1994 S.L.T. 150.

[23] A wide range of these issues is covered in Schedule 9 of the Act and includes matters relating to firearms, drugs, immigration, pollution, and road traffic.

It is also now well established that no corroboration is required of the **7–21**
modus of a crime or even, apparently, certain elements of any aggravation
of it.[24]

Where the Crown alleges certain facts which rest "peculiarly within the **7–22**
knowledge of the accused",[25] then it is settled law that the prosecution
evidence need establish only a prima facie case against the accused, and it
is then for the accused to produce the evidence which will lead to an acquittal.
The clearest examples arise on charges of driving without a licence, or
without insurance, and the prima facie case against the accused may consist
simply of one item of uncorroborated evidence. Thus, in *Milne* v. *Whaley*[26]
it was held that in such a case, an uncorroborated confession by the accused
is sufficient for a conviction.

Where the prosecution adduce as a witness someone who was involved **7–23**
in the crime along with the accused (a *socius criminis*) then the evidence of
that person does not require corroboration. The trial judge in a trial on
indictment is however entitled to warn the jury to treat such evidence with
special care.[27]

Five particular features of corroboration in criminal cases call for closer **7–24**
study. They are:

    (i)   corroboration of the identification of an accused;
    (ii) corroboration of alleged confessions by an accused;
    (iii) special suspensions of the normal rule requiring corroboration;
    (iv) corroboration of a series of charges under what is popularly
         known as the "*Moorov* doctrine"; and
    (v)   distress as corroboration.

IDENTIFICATION OF AN ACCUSED

The first feature of corroboration to be considered in more detail is **7–25**
identification of an accused. No one may be convicted of any criminal
offence in Scotland unless there are two independent items of evidence
which point to that person having been the perpetrator. The identity of the
accused has been described[28] as being "in a different category from any

---

[24] See, *e.g. Yates* v. *H.M.A.*, 1977 S.L.T. (Notes) 42 and *Stephen* v. *H.M.A., supra*; but see *Lynch and Munro* v. *H.M.A.*, 1986 S.C.C.R. 244, in which it was held that corroboration was required of the personal violence necessary to convert theft into robbery.

[25] For which see paras. 2.80–2.87 *supra*.

[26] 1975 S.L.T. (Notes) 75. When stopped by the police, the accused had admitted that he had neither driving licence nor insurance.

[27] Known as a *cum nota* warning. This is not now mandatory: see *Docherty* v. *H.M.A.*, 1987 S.L.T. 784 where a bench of nine judges held it unnecessary to give such a warning.

[28] In Renton and Brown, *op. cit.*, n. 12, para. 18–54.

other fact in issue." A simple illustration of the rule in action can be seen in *Morton* v. *H.M.A.*[29]

7–26   M was charged with an indecent assault upon a woman whom he had allegedly hustled into a close in order to molest her. He was identified by the victim, both at an identification parade and in court, and she was not cross-examined on her identification. The only other items of evidence were first, that of a neighbour who had seen the assault from within the close, but who could not identify the accused, and second, that of the victim's brother, who spoke only to her distressed state when she arrived home, and her complaint of having been assaulted. It was held that M must be acquitted because there was no corroborated evidence that he was the assailant.

7–27   The rule only comes into play if identification is a live issue. If the accused admits his presence at the *locus*, or admits the *actus reus* but denies *mens rea*, then there will be no need for proof.[30]

7–28   The most straightforward form of corroborated identification of an accused is by two eye-witnesses and the recognised procedure is for the witnesses to point to the accused in court as the person they are referring to in their evidence.[31] In *Bruce* v. *H.M.A.*,[32] B was charged with wilful fire-raising along with D, and the latter, having pled guilty, then gave evidence implicating B and identifying him. None of the other witnesses in the case was asked to point him out in court, although they referred in their evidence to "the accused James Bruce." In acquitting the accused, Lord Wark on appeal pointed out that[33]: "identification of an accused is not a matter which ought to be left to implication. The proper practice is to have the accused identified directly by persons who are speaking to facts which are material to the charge which is under investigation."

7–29   It is, however, by no means uncommon for the witness to be unable to identify the accused in court, particularly if a long period has elapsed since the incident. It is then that the prosecution are obliged to fall back on evidence that the accused was identified by the witness on an earlier occasion, either in the course of an identification parade, or at the scene of the crime, or shortly after the incident. In all these situations, if it is presented correctly, the court will accept such identification.

7–30   The leading case in this area is *Muldoon* v. *Herron*[34] in which three youths were charged with a breach of the peace. Two witnesses who saw the

---

[29]   1938 J.C. 50; see also para. 7.14 *supra*.

[30]   See *Stewart* v. *H.M.A.*, 1980 S.L.T. 245.

[31]   A normal requirement confirmed in *Stewart, supra*, at p. 251.

[32]   1936 J.C. 93, approved in *Stewart, supra*. See also *Wilson* v. *Brown*, 1947 J.C. 81.

[33]   At p. 95.

[34]   1970 J.C. 30. For the increasing latitude allowed in cases such as this, see *Reilly* v. *H.M.A.*, 1987 S.C.C.R. 68; *Gracie* v *Allan*, 1987 S.C.C.R. 364; *Nolan* v. *McLeod*, 1987 S.C.C.R. 558; *Ralston* v. *H.M.A.*, 1987 S.C.C.R. 467; and *Jamieson* v. *H.M.A. (No.2)* 1994 S.C.C.R. 610.

incident, Mr and Mrs M, both identified the three accused to the police as soon as they arrived. At the trial, neither Mr or Mrs M was able to identify any of the accused. However, both agreed that they had, at the time of the incident, pointed out the culprits to the police. Mrs M gave evidence to the effect that the accused in the dock had not been among those whom she had pointed out to the police, but the sheriff disbelieved her. Two police officers gave evidence that the three accused were all among the group identified by both witnesses shortly after the incident and on this evidence the sheriff convicted.

On appeal, the conviction was upheld on the grounds that there were **7–31** two independent items of identification. First, there was the evidence that Mr M identified the accused shortly after the incident (the act of identification being spoken to by Mr M and the identification of the accused as being those pointed out coming from the police); and second, the identical evidence of identification by Mrs M spoken to by police officers, the denial of which on oath by Mrs M the court disbelieved.

In passing, the court gave an official blessing to identification parades.[35] **7–32** In the words of Lord Cameron:

> "The practice, which has in recent years become a common feature of trials, of evidence being led without objection both for the Crown and the defence as to what passed at identification parades appears to me to be competent, and I am of opinion that the evidence so obtained is properly admitted and falls well within the scope of the law as it has been developed."

Muldoon was applied in *Bennett* v. *H.M.A.*,[36] a case similar to *Muldoon*, **7–33** but different in one vital respect. In *Bennett*, during the course of an identification parade following a serious assault, B was identified by the victim and by two other witnesses to the assault. None of the witnesses was able to identify the accused at the trial, and the Crown sought to fill the gap by means of the evidence of one police witness as to what had taken place at the identification parade.

On appeal, it was held that whereas in *Muldoon* the evidence of two **7–34** police officers was enough to complete the chain of identification and provide a corroborated case against the accused, the evidence of the one police officer in the present case supplied only one adminicle of evidence,

---

[35] *Muldoon, ibid.*, at p. 48. *N.B.* however that his Lordship was not prepared to extend this so as to cover statements of identification given to witnesses other than police officers.

[36] 1976 J.C. 1. See also *Smith* v. *H.M.A.*, 1986 S.C.C.R. 135 for a case in which *Muldoon* was applied even though the witnesses stated in evidence that they were not certain at the time, but had picked out the accused anyway. It was said to be a matter for the jury whether or not they believed the identification evidence to have been positive and unqualified at the time of the parade. See also *Neeson* v. *H.M.A.*, 1984 S.C.C.R. 72, and *Reilly* and *Gracey*, *supra*.

and something further was required to identify the accused as the assailant. In the event there was such evidence, and the conviction was upheld. Where a witness has been shown a photograph and the photograph identified the accused by name, the witness's evidence may still be admissible.[37]

7–35 In *Muldoon*[38] it was pointed out in passing that "it is not necessary that identity should be established by visual recognition alone," It has, for example, long been established that an accused may be identified by means of his voice,[39] and as seen in paragraph 7–18 *infra* and in Chapter 9, the courts will accept the evidence of tape-recorded conversations.[40] The underlying assumption in such cases is that the voice may be identified as being that of the accused either by persons present at the recording, or presumably by a witness in court identifying the voice.

7–36 Identification by build may be admissible if taken in conjunction with other positive identification evidence of the accused.[41]

7–37 Increasingly in recent years identification of an accused has been by more scientific means than eye-witness testimony. This simply reflects some of the advances made in identification techniques this century.

7–38 Since *Hamilton* v. *H.M.A.*[42] it has been accepted in Scots law that an accused may be identified by fingerprint evidence, and that there need be no other evidence in order to secure a conviction. In that case, there were two police officers giving evidence as to the identity of the accused via his fingerprints, and they presumably corroborated each other. In *H.M.A.* v. *Rolley*,[43] the only evidence against R was a palm print lifted from the locus of a housebreaking which matched his. Four police forensic officers gave evidence that no two palm prints were ever the same and even the defence had to concede that this would be sufficient evidence in law if the jury accepted it, which they did, leading to R's conviction.

7–39 Section 284 of the Criminal Procedure (Scotland) Act 1995 introduces a new procedure for cases involving finger or palm print evidence. A certificate can be produced signed by two police officers confirming the details of the taking of such prints. The intention is to obviate the need to produce two witnesses in court to give evidence as to where the print was found and two

---

[37] *Howarth* v. *H.M.A.*, 1992 S.C.C.R. 364 and see Renton and Brown *op. cit.*, n. 12, para. 18–56.

[38] *ibid.*, at p. 45, per Lord Cameron.

[39] *McGiveran* v. *Auld* (1894) 21 R.(J.) 69, followed in *Lees* v. *Roy*, 1991 S.L.T. 665; see also *Burrows* v. *H.M.A.*, 1951 S.L.T (Notes) 69.

[40] See, *H.M.A.* v. *Swift*, 1983 S.C.C.R. 204, and s. 277 of the 1995 Act.

[41] *Nelson* v. *H.M.A.*, 1989 S.L.T. 215; *Murphy* v. *H.M.A.*, 1995 S.L.T. 725; and see *Ralston* v. *H.M.A.*, 1987 S.C.C.R. 467, where it was indicated that if there is at least one emphatic positive identification little else is required.

[42] 1934 J.C. 1, also considered more fully in para. 16.36 *infra*.

[43] 1945 J.C. 155. See also *H.M.A.* v. *Dennson*, 1978 S.L.T. (Notes) 79.

witnesses as to the taking of comparison prints from the accused. Two expert witnesses will still be required to speak to the fact that the two sets of prints are the same.[44]

Other scientific processes have been employed in the provision of **7–40** evidence of identification including dental impressions,[45] blood samples and semen stains.[46] In *Hay* the accused in a murder trial was convicted partly on the evidence of a dental impression left on the body of the victim which matched his own. Although the major part of the appeal case rested on the legality of the taking of the dental impression from him (on which point the appeal was refused), there was no suggestion that the evidence thus obtained could not otherwise be used to identify him. In *Preece* v. *H.M.A.*,[47] there was a successful appeal by a convicted murderer against his conviction on the ground that the Crown forensic evidence had been presented in a biased fashion. It was acknowledged that evidence of blood samples and semen stains had been significant in his identification as the alleged culprit.

Handwriting has also for many years been an acceptable means of **7–41** identifying an accused, without the need for further corroborating evidence of identification.[48] In *Campbell* v. *Mackenzie*,[49] C was charged with having written letters under a false signature in which unfounded allegations were made to the police about another person. The only real evidence against him was that of two handwriting experts who testified that the letters were written by him. It was held that it was for the court to assess the evidential value of such testimony, and to convict on the strength of it if they wished, and since there had been no contrary evidence the conviction was allowed to stand.

Identification of an accused by means of a video film is also competent. **7–42** In *Bowie* v. *Tudhope*,[50] B was charged with assault and robbery in a shop. The incident was recorded on a video camera, and at the trial it was not suggested that the film was anything other than a genuine record of the incident. The shop staff were unable to identify B, either on the video or in court, but at a date prior to the trial two police officers viewed the video separately, and were both able to identify him from it. The film was shown at the trial and again the two police officers identified B as the person in it. In rejecting B's appeal, the High Court ruled[51] that:

---

[44] On identification evidence generally, see Renton and Brown, *op. cit.,* n. 12, para. 18–56.
[45] *Hay* v. *H.M.A.*, 1968 J.C. 40.
[46] *Preece* v. *H.M.A.*, 1981 Crim. L.R. 783, referred to in para. 16.42 *infra.*
[47] *ibid..*
[48] Since at least *Richardson* v. *Clark*, 1957 J.C. 7.
[49] 1974 S.L.T. (Notes) 46.
[50] 1986 S.C.C.R. 205 at p. 209.
[51] *ibid.,* p. 209. Presumably there is no reason why the court itself may not view such a video and form its own opinion of the identity of an accused from it.

"we are of opinion that there is no reason in a situation such as arose in the present case why two police officers, who were familiar with the accused, should not have been able to view the video recording and then to give evidence to the effect that one of the individuals appearing in the recording was the appellant."

7–43   In the last decade DNA profiling or genetic fingerprinting has featured regularly in criminal cases.[52] The technique seems attractive for the high degree of certainty which it appears to produce. For example, in *Welsh* v. *H.M.A.* it was suggested by experts that there was a chance of only one in between eighty eight and ninety nine million of the samples not matching. Much debate has been generated about the reliability of DNA profiling. Undoubtedly it has huge potential to provide incriminating—and exonerating—evidence of an accused to a high level, but some critics have questioned the methodology of the testing procedures.[53]

7–44   In summary cases, as indicated at paragraph 6.59 *supra*, the effect of section 280(9) of the Criminal Procedure (Scotland) Act 1995 is that there is a presumption that the person who appears in answer to a complaint is the person who was charged by the police with the offence(s) libelled in it. This provision can occasionally be used to link the accused with the offence, as one link in a chain of identification. This happened in *Smith* v. *Paterson*.[54]

7–45   *Paterson* was charged with a breach of the peace, the witnesses to the incident being two police officers. At the trial they gave evidence of the incident, and of the fact that they cautioned and charged the offender, but neither was asked to identify P in court. He was acquitted for lack of evidence of identification, but on appeal it was held that since at the trial it had not been contested that P was in fact the person who had been charged,[55] nor had it been alleged that the person seen committing the breach was not the person charged by the police, the chain of identification had been completed, and there was sufficient evidence for a conviction. The court was, however, at pains to stress that the subsection did not create a direct presumption that the person charged was the perpetrator of the offence, and that this required to be proved by evidence, as it had been in the present case.

7–46   In many cases there is only one item of direct evidence identifying the accused (*e.g.* only one eye-witness) and the rules of corroboration require some other adminicle of evidence in order to link the crime to the accused. This connecting evidence can take many forms, and over the years the courts

---

[52]   *e.g. Welsh* v. *H.M.A.*, 1992 S.L.T. 193.

[53]   As techniques are being constantly revised and improved, reference is made only to some of the most recent literature: Alldridge, "Recognising Novel Scientific Techniques: DNA as a test case," 1992 Crim. L.R. 687; Redmayne, "Doubts and Burdens: DNA Evidence, Probability and the Courts," 1995 Crim. L.R. 464.

[54]   1982 S.L.T. 437, a case under s. 26(5) of the 1980 Act.

[55]   *N.B.* that the presumption created by s. 26(5) may be challenged by the defence.

have been required to consider a vast variety of items of evidence offered in corroboration.[56]

It is possible for the accused himself, by his subsequent words or actions, **7–47**
to provide the evidence necessary to corroborate the evidence of one good witness against him. In *Nisbet* v. *H.M.A.*,[57] N was charged with reset. The evidence of the thief to the effect that he had sold the goods to N, and that he had been fully aware of their origin, was held to have been corroborated by police evidence of the "awkward story" which N had given as to how he had acquired them. But evidence of an accused's demeanour cannot be treated as corroboration of his confession.[58]

CONFESSIONS BY AN ACCUSED

The second feature of corroboration worthy of separate attention is a **7–48**
confession by an accused.[59] An extra-judicial confession is a confession made outwith the witness box and not on oath. It is usually, but not always, made to a police officer. It is potentially one of the most powerful items of evidence against an accused, and accordingly it is surrounded by legal safeguards.[60] One of these safeguards is that a confession cannot be the sole evidence against an accused, and before there may be a conviction, this confession must be corroborated by other evidence establishing guilt beyond reasonable doubt.[61] As Lord Justice-Clerk Thomson put it in *Sinclair* v. *Clark*[62]:

> "an admission of guilt by an accused is not conclusive against him, unless it is corroborated by something beyond the actual admission. One reason for this rule is to ensure that there is nothing phoney or

---

[56] See, *e.g. Douglas* v. *Pirie*, 1975 J.C. 61; *Wright* v. *Tudhope*, 1983 S.C.C.R. 403; *Proctor* v. *Tudhope,* 1985 S.C.C.R. 39; *Downs* v. *Tudhope*, 1982 S.C.C R 563; and *McNeill* v. *Wilson,* 1981 S.C.C.R. 80. For cases in which the alleged corroboration was insufficient, see *Reilly* v. *H.M.A.,* 1981 S.C.C.R. 201; *O'Donnell* v. *H.M.A.*, 179 S.L.T. (Notes) 64; *Ballantyne* v. *Mackinnon*, 1983 S.C.C.R. 97; *Tudhope* v. *Dalgleish*, 1986 S.C.C.R. 559; and *Megeary* v. *H.M.A.,* 1993 S.C.C.R. 974.

[57] 1983 S.C.C.R. 13; see also *Proctor* v. *Tudhope, supra* (accused running away when challenged), and *Iqbal* v. *Annan*, 1983 S.C.C.R. 332.

[58] *McGougan* v. *H.M.A.*, 1991 S.L.T. 908.

[59] *N.B.* that even admissions made on oath in court require corroboration: *Milne* v. *Whaley*, 1975 S.L.T. (Notes) 75, and the same is true of confessions made during judicial declarations: see Renton and Brown, *op. cit.,* n. 12, para. 18–59. However, a formal plea of guilty does not require such corroboration: see para. 6.26 *supra*.

[60] The rest of which are more fully considered in Chap. 14 *infra*.

[61] Which could, of course, be another item of evidence (such as an eye-witness identification) which itself requires corroboration, the two items coming together to form a corroborated case. Hume 11, 333 and Walker and Walker, *op. cit.,* n. 2, para. 30.

[62] 1962 J.C. 57 at p. 62. And see *Meredith* v. *Lees,* 1992 S.L.T. 802 for discussion of what is required.

quixotic about the confession.[63] What is required in the way of independent evidence in order to elide such risk must depend on the facts of the case, and, in particular, the nature and character of the confession and the circumstances in which it is made."

7–49   The confession itself need not be spoken to by more than one witness,[64] but an accused cannot in law corroborate his own confession, either by confessing to more than one person, or by repeating it on other occasions. A confession, however often made and to whatever number of witnesses, requires corroboration by means of other independent evidence.

7–50   However, this evidence need not be very strong. As was seen in *Patterson* v . *Nixon*,[65] it need be nothing more formal than the actings of a police dog, and more recent cases have served to illustrate that "very little is required to corroborate a confession."[66] The risk of this notion of "very little corroboration" being elevated to a rule was highlighted by Lord Justice-General Hope in *Meredith* v. *Lees*[67] when he explained that if that were to happen, "there will be a weakening of the principle that there must be a sufficient independent check of the confession to corroborate it." What constitutes a "sufficient independent check" will depend on the circumstances of the case.

7–51   *Meredith* was a case involving allegations of lewd, libidinous and indecent practices towards a four year old girl. The accused had given the police a detailed confession of his behaviour. Although the child's description of the events lacked an ideal level of specification and her terminology was somewhat ambiguous, the court undoubtedly took into account her age and that "she was trying to tell the truth." The accused was convicted and appealed on the ground that the child's evidence did not afford sufficient corroboration of the accused's confession. The appeal court refused the appeal pointing to the consistency of the child's account in relation to time, place and circumstance with that given by the accused, combined with the voluntary and genuine nature of the confession. This consistency constituted sufficient corroboration of the unequivocal confession.

7–52   One reason why "very little" corroboration is required is that confessions are statements against interest. As Lord Dunpark explained in *Hartley* v. *H.M.A.*,[68] "the confession of guilt by an accused person is prejudicial to his

---

[63]   *i.e.* that the accused has not been "set up" by the police, and has not, for reasons best known to him, falsely confessed, as happened in *Boyle* v. *H.M.A.*, 1976 S.L.T. 126.
[64]   *Mills* v. *H.M.A.*, 1935 J.C. 77.
[65]   1960 J.C. 42, at para. 7.13 *supra*.
[66]   Sheriff Gordon in his commentary on *Cummings* v. *Tudhope*, 1985 S.C.C.R. 125. For other cases in which very little was held to be required by way of corroboration of a confession, see *Sinclair* v. *Clark*, *supra*, and *Lockhart* v. *Crockett*, 1987 S.L.T. 551.
[67]   1992 S.L.T. 802 at p. 804.

own interests and may therefore initially be assumed to be true." In *Hartley,*[69] H confessed to the murder of a small boy by drowning him in a burn. At his trial he denied his confession, and claimed that he had simply been working in the area in a local authority gardening squad. It was held that there was "ample" corroboration of his confession from (i) the fact that his work did not require him to go near the burn, although he had said that it did; (ii) the fact that another young boy described the victim struggling with someone answering H's general description; (iii) the fact that evidence was led to show that his clothing had been in water that day; and (iv) the fact that H stayed off his work for the week following the murder.

Such a process of cumulative circumstantial evidence may be **7–53** unexceptionable when one is dealing with an unequivocal and clear admission of guilt. But great care is obviously required when the circumstances of the confession give rise to doubts, or the accused is of limited intelligence, as was said to be the case in *Hartley.* As Lord Dunpark asserted in that case,[70] one may initially assume that a confession is true, and then: "one is not ... looking for extrinsic evidence which is consistent with his confession of guilt." This is arguably much more necessary when there is doubt about the quality of the confession.

The "extrinsic evidence" in question often comes from information **7–54** supplied by the accused himself. This may be either by indicating the location of items connected with the crime, or by disclosing information which only the perpetrator of the crime, or someone present during the commission of it, could have known. This is acceptable if there is no question of the confession being anything other than freely and frankly given, since it then minimises the possibility of a bogus confession.[71] It does not, however, guarantee the validity of the confession if it is alleged by the accused that the entire confession—together with the "linking" facts—was invented by the police.

Extrinsic evidence supplied by the accused suggests "inside information". **7–55** This is sometimes described as the "special knowledge" rule. Despite the potential risk of the unreliability of such a confession,[72] the courts regularly accept such evidence as corroboration. One of the most notorious examples

---

[68] 1979 S.L.T. 26 at p. 33.

[69] *ibid..* See too Lord Grieve, at p. 31, who observed that: "It is well settled that where, as here, an accused person has, by means of an unequivocal confession, identified himself with an offence, little is required by way of corroboration to meet the requirements of our law."

[70] At p. 33.

[71] Other than in the rare event of collusion between the accused and the real offender.

[72] See Griffiths, *Confessions*, para. 5.63–5.104 for a critical treatment of modern cases dealing with special knowledge.

was *Manuel* v. *H.M.A.*,[73] in which M, during a confession to a murder, offered to point out to the police the separate spots in a field where he had buried the victim and one of her shoes. His ability to do so later was held to be corroborative of his confession, and this line of reasoning was approved in *Hartley, supra.*

7–56   In *Gilmour* v. *H.M.A.*,[74] the accused gave the police a confession to rape and murder which contained details which, allegedly, only the real offender could have known. The confession also contained discrepancies with the proven facts. In his summary to the jury, the trial judge dwelt only on the consistent facts which could be said to corroborate the confession, stating that the inconsistencies had been effectively rehearsed in the defence speech. It was held on appeal that there was nothing wrong with such an approach, and that when a confession contains both consistencies and inconsistencies, it is for the jury to decide whether or not they feel that the confession is nevertheless corroborated.

7–54   At the end of the day, however prepared a court may be to find that a clear confession has been corroborated, there must be some evidence by means of which they may do so.[75]

STATUTORY EXCEPTIONS TO THE GENERAL RULE IN CRIMINAL CASES

7–58   The third feature of corroboration requiring separate study forms the statutory exceptions to the general rule. They vary widely in nature, and the law is as laid down for each particular situation. Only a few of the more common examples are given here.

7–59   Under section 14(1)(*b*) of the Road Traffic Act 1960,[76] for example, a provision was enacted whereby a motorist charged with failing to comply with a traffic sign could be convicted on the evidence of a single witness. It was applied in *Sutherland* v. *Aitchison*,[77] in which two witnesses spoke to the fact that a car had been driven contrary to a road sign, but were unable to identify the accused as the driver. The accused, who was the owner of the vehicle, had admitted to the police that he was the driver at the material time, and had given a circumstantial account of what had happened. It was held that the effect of section 14(1)(*b*) was that he had been lawfully convicted.

---

[73] 1958 J.C. 41. See also *Allan* v. *Hamilton*, 1972 S.L.T. (Notes) 2; *Torrance* v. *Thaw*, 1970 J.C. 58; *Wilson* v. *McAughey*, 1982 S.C.C.R. 390; *McAvoy* v. *H.M.A.*, 1982 S.C.C.R. 263; *Annan* v. *Bain and Hamill*, 1986 S.C.C.R. 60; *Wilson* v *H.M.A.*, 1987 S.C.C.R. 217; and *MacDonald* v. *H.M.A.*, 1987 S.C.C.R. 581.

[74] 1982 S.C.C.R. 590.

[75] See *Sinclair* v. *McLeod*, 1964 J.C. 19.

[76] Reproduced in s. 36 of the Road Traffic Act 1988.

[77] 1970 S.L.T. (Notes) 48.

These statutory exceptions generally place the burden of proof on a **7–60** particular issue with the accused.[78] In some such cases, instead of the Crown having to produce a corroborated case which negatives the accused's defence, it is for the accused to produce corroboration of any evidence which, he claims, exempts him from conviction.

In *Templeton* v. *Lyons*,[79] L was charged with failing to send his child to **7–61** school, the charge being brought under an Act which gave the accused the burden of proving any "reasonable excuse" in bar of conviction. L claimed that he was unaware of the truancy, since all communications concerning it had been intercepted by his wife. Additionally, the attendance officer, who knew him by sight, had on several occasions passed him on the street without comment. In the course of upholding his conviction, Lord Wark[80] commented that "the onus lay upon him to establish by legal proof[81] the excuse which he alleged in explanation of his failure to see that his child attended school, and that he could not do without leading evidence which to some extent corroborated his own evidence."

In *Farrell* v. *Moir*,[82] M had been convicted of refusing to give a second **7–62** breath test or blood or urine sample. He pleaded that there was a "special reason" in terms of section 93(1) of the Road Traffic Act 1972[83] why he should not be disqualified from driving, in that he had only driven the car because the police had ordered him to move it. There was no corroboration of this claim, but the sheriff ruled[84] that M's uncorroborated evidence (which only had to be proved on a balance of probabilities) was sufficient:

> "The general principle in Scotland is that where there is an onus on a party to prove any essential fact that must be done by corroborated evidence. If this general principle applies to the present case then the accused must fail ... In my opinion in a proof such as this, when the onus is on the accused, his own uncorroborated evidence, if believed, is sufficient."

The appeal court confirmed this approach, *i.e.* no requirement for **7–63** corroborated evidence, in *King* v. *Lees*.[85]

Statutory provisions have also made inroads to the need for corroboration **7–64** in certain matters classed as "routine evidence" in the Criminal Procedure

---

[78] See, generally, paras. 2.61–2.101 *supra*.
[79] 1942 J.C. 102.
[80] At p. 108.
[81] *i.e.* by discharging the legal or persuasive burden by means of corroborated evidence: see paras. 2.61–2.101 *supra*.
[82] 1974 S.L.T. (Sh.Ct.) 89.
[83] Now s. 34 of the Road Traffic Offenders Act 1988.
[84] At p. 90. The sheriff observed that there was no earlier authority directly in point.
[85] 1993 S.L.T. 1184, a decision criticised by Sheldon in his article, "Hip Flasks and Burdens", 1993 S.L.T. (News) 33. See para. 2.75 *supra*.

(Scotland) Act 1995.[86] In routine matters, such as those involving the submission of expert reports and certificates, there is no requirement for corroboration. Sections 281–282 of the Criminal Procedure (Scotland) Act 1995 provides that the evidence of one pathologist or forensic scientist is to be regarded as sufficient to prove any fact or conclusion as to fact contained in any report signed by him and another pathologist or forensic scientist.

7–65   The Criminal Procedure (Scotand) Act 1995 provides for dispensing with corroboration through the use of certification of evidence in cases involving drugs, video surveillance, and (as noted earlier) fingerprints and palmprints. Sections 282–284 detail the procedures which can be used to avoid calling witnesses to court simply to speak to such matters.

THE *MOOROV* DOCTRINE

7–66   The fourth feature of corroboration which justifies special attention is when a person is accused of a series of offences which are "closely linked in time and circumstances,"[87] and a special rule of evidence applies known as "the *Moorov* doctrine". Under this doctrine each of the separate offences need only be proved by the evidence of one witness, and each offence then corroborates the other(s) as if the crimes charged were one single continuing offence.

7–67   This principle, which was recognised by Hume,[88] is now named after the leading case of *Moorov* v. *H.M.A.*,[89] and the facts of that case illustrate the circumstances in which it may be applied. The accused was an employer who was alleged to have committed separate assaults and indecent assaults involving 21 charges and a total of 19 female employees over a period of four years. He was convicted of seven assaults and nine indecent assaults. Corroborative evidence was only available in three of these charges. On appeal to a full bench of seven judges, the conviction was upheld on nine of the original charges, which stretched over a period of some three years, six of these charges resting on the evidence of a single witness. In explaining the circumstances in which such convictions were possible, Lord Justice-General Clyde[90] pointed out that:

> "Before the evidence of a single credible witness to separate acts can provide material for mutual corroboration, the connection between the separate acts (indicated by their external relation in time, character or circumstance) must be such as to exhibit them as subordinates in

---

[86] Discussed in paras. 7.19–7.20 *supra*.
[87] Renton and Brown, *op. cit.,* n. 12, para. 18–63.
[88] II, 385, and quoted in Dickson on *Evidence*, paras. 1807–1810.
[89] 1930 J.C. 68, approved obiter by the House of Lords in *D.P.P.* v. *Kilbourne* [1973] A.C. 729.
[90] At p. 73.

some particular and ascertained unity of intent, project, campaign or adventure which lies beyond or behind—but is related to—the separate acts."

Put more briefly in the words of Lord Sands[91]: "There must be some special circumstances connecting the incidents in order that it may be held that a course of conduct is established." **7–68**

The *Moorov* doctrine has been applied innumerable times and in a wide variety of contexts. For example, in *Begg* v. *Tudhope*,[92] B, a schoolteacher, was accused of indecent assaults on two of his female pupils. The evidence against him consisted of the testimony of the two girls themselves, plus independent evidence of the distressed condition of one of the girls shortly after the incident. Although on appeal it was held that the evidence of the girl's condition (plus a *de recenti* statement made by her to the witness of her condition[93]) was not capable of corroborating her allegation of assault, nevertheless the convictions could be upheld because: "as the sheriff accepted the two complainers as credible and reliable ... he was entitled to apply the principle laid down in *Moorov* v. *H.M.A.* ... and hence to find the appellant guilty on both charges."[94] **7–69**

The *Moorov* doctrine is not restricted to cases of alleged sexual assault,[95] but given the nature of such offences it is most frequently encountered in this context. **7–70**

It is not strictly necessary for all three elements of time, character and circumstance to unite in each case to present an overpowering presumption of guilt on the part of the accused. However, where any of them is absent, it may be unsafe to apply the *Moorov* doctrine. The mere fact that the crimes libelled against the accused are similar in nature is not *per se* sufficient to attract the operation of the doctrine.[96] **7–71**

So far as the element of time is concerned, the key issue is the gap between each of the constituent offences. It will in many ways depend upon the nature of these offences, since: "A man whose course of conduct is to buy houses, insure them, and burn them down, or to acquire ships, insure them, and scuttle them, or to purport to marry women, defraud and desert them, cannot repeat the offence every month, or even perhaps every six months."[97] **7–72**

---

[91] At p. 89.
[92] 1983 S.C.C.R. 32. See also *Scott* v. *H.M.A.*, 1987 G.W.D. 24–871.
[93] On which point this case is considered further in paras. 10.37–10.39 *infra*.
[94] *per* Lord Stott at p. 40.
[95] For example, it was applied in *McCudden* v. *H.M.A.*, 1952 J.C. 86 (two attempts to bribe professional footballers), *H.M.A.* v. *McQuade*, 1951 J.C. 143 (six razor attacks) and *Harris* v. *Clark*, 1958 J.C. 3 (three charges of reset).
[96] See *Ogg* v. *H.M.A.*, 1938 J.C. 152, *McHardy* v. *H.M.A.*, 1982 S.C.C.R. 582 and *Tudhope* v. *Hazelton*, 1984 S.C.C.R. 455.
[97] *Moorov* v. *H.M.A.*, *per* Lord Sands at p. 89.

7–73   There are various recent examples of cases where the time period between alleged offences has been a significant factor. In *Coffey* v. *Houston*[98] a male nurse was convicted of indecently assaulting two girls both aged eleven, in hospital wards in separate hospitals. The time gap was two years and two months which was said by the court to be "comparatively long" but was not fatal to the conviction given the existence of strong links between the offences which were described as "identical assaults."

7–74   By contrast, in *Russell* v. *H.M.A.*,[99] the accused was charged with lewd and libidinous conduct towards two girls who were in a neighbouring household. The alleged offences were three and a half years apart and this was held to be too long for the operation of the *Moorov* doctrine.

7–75   Whatever flexibility may exist on the question of the time gap, there is no doubt that in order for *Moorov* to be applied, the offences with which the accused is charged must be substantially similar.[1] They do not, though, require to be precisely the same.[2] The courts have been willing to interpret "substantially similar", as cases which include charges of a different name but with a broadly equivalent nature. In *Smith* v. *H.M.A.*,[3] two charges of lewd, indecent and libidinous conduct and one of sodomy led to the application of the *Moorov* doctrine because the court held that there was sufficient relation between the offences to provide a connection of the elements of character and circumstance.[4]

7–76   By contrast, in the earlier case of *H.M.A.* v. *Cox*,[5] the court refused to apply the doctrine to two charges of incest and a charge of sodomy which were allegedly committed in the family home against stepchildren (two female and one male), on the grounds, (i) that sodomy and incest were not the same crimes; and (ii) that the two charges of incest were separated by a period of three years.[6]

7–77   However, in *H.M.A.* v. *Brown*,[7] B was charged with a variety of sexual offences against three stepdaughters (the only witnesses against him) all allegedly committed in the family home within a 21-month period. The

---

[98] 1992 S.C.C.R. 265.

[99] 1990 S.C.C.R. 18.

[1] Or, as was described in *Turner* v. *Scott*, 1995 S.C.C.R. 516, "sufficient coherence in character and circumstance."

[2] *e.g. H.M.A.* v. *W.B.*, 1969 J.C. 72 and *P.M.* v. *Jessop*, 1989 S.C.C.R. 324.

[3] 1995 S.L.T. 583.

[4] See too, *Carpenter* v. *Hamilton*, 1994 S.C.C.R. 108 where a charge of indecent exposure was corroborated by a breach of the peace. But in *Farrell* v. *Normand*, 1993 S.L.T. 793 a charge of indecency was not corroborated by a breach of the peace.

[5] 1962 J.C. 27.

[6] The period of three years was mentioned in *Russell* v. *H.M.A. infra*, where it was said that the *Moorov* doctrine had not been applied in any case with a time gap of more than three years.

[7] 1970 S.L.T. 121.

time period was held to be short enough to apply the *Moorov* doctrine since only a period of months separated the courses of conduct with each girl. In the case of two of the victims, a course of lewd and libidinous behaviour was followed by incestuous intercourse, and it was held[8] that:

> "the evidence in regard to incest can validly be used as corroboration in regard to the charges of lewd practices. The greater here includes the lesser. On the other hand, I do not think the contrary is true. Incest is a very much more serious crime than lewd practices and I think that it would be dangerous to treat evidence that a man had committed lewd practices towards Y as indicative of his guilt of incest with Z … On the other hand, as I have already indicated, the *Moorov* doctrine could apply the other way round."

In *Hay* v. *Wither*,[9] the court had to consider whether there was a sufficient **7–78** connection in character and circumstance in two charges of breach of the peace. In both incidents a teenage boy was sexually accosted in a public place in nearby towns by a man driving a van. It was considered that there was the "necessary nexus" in the offences to apply the *Moorov* doctrine.

While each case is very much determined on its own facts, there is perhaps **7–79** a detectable shift in attitude in the application of the *Moorov* doctrine in recent years, particularly in cases concerning children. This may owe something to the greater awareness today of child sexual abuse and to the improvements in arrangements for children giving evidence.[10]

The offences which are used in order to support the *Moorov* doctrine **7–80** must all be "live" ones, in respect of which a finding or admission of guilt has not yet been entered.[11]

It is also essential for the operation of *Moorov* that the accused be clearly **7–81** identified as the culprit in each of the incidents which are being conjoined for that purpose.[12]

It should be noted in conclusion that while the principle exemplified by **7–82** *Moorov* finds its most common expression in criminal cases, the rationale underlying it[13] has also on occasions been employed in civil cases in which corroboration is normally required.[14]

---

[8] *per* Lord Justice-Clerk Grant at p. 122.
[9] 1988 S.C.C.R. 334.
[10] Dealt with in full in para. 11.10–11.21 *infra*.
[11] See *Walsh* v. *H.M.A.*, 1961 J.C. 51, referred to more fully in paras. 6.31–6.33 *supra*.
[12] See paras. 7.106–7.108 *infra*.
[13] See *McRae* v. *H.M.A.*, 1975 J.C. 34.
[14] *i.e.* that "the aptitude and coherence of the several circumstances often as fully confirm the truth of the story, as if all the witnesses were deponing to the same facts": Hume, *op. cit.*, n. 8.

Distress as Corroboration

7–83 The fifth feature of corroboration calling for closer study is when the victim's distress provides corroboration of the offence. In cases of assault, primarily sexual assault, corroboration for a victim's allegations can sometimes be gained from evidence of his or her distressed condition.[15] As in the *Moorov* doctrine, time is of importance and the evidence of distress must not be too remote from the incident complained of. Thus, in *Moore* v. *H.M.A.*[16] no corroboration was found in evidence of distress exhibited some twelve to thirteen hours after an alleged rape. The court laid emphasis on the fact that during this period the complainer had seen her boyfriend and visited two public houses looking for her handbag without apparently showing signs of distress.

7–84 However, in *Cannon* v. *H.M.A.*[17] the evidence of a complainer's distress exhibited some twelve hours after a rape, was held to be corroborative, when there was evidence that the complainer delayed disclosing her distress until she had the opportunity to speak to a close friend.

7–85 If corroboration is to be found in the distress, then the court must be satisfied that the distress is caused by the offence and no other intervening factor.[18] In *McLellan* v. *H.M.A.*[19] the evidence of a child's distress following alleged lewd and libidinous behaviour was held not to be corroborative because it was thought in part due to her fear of getting a row from her mother for visiting the house where the alleged assault occurred.

7–86 Distress as corroboration has come under attack as being insufficient in itself to corroborate an assault. For example, in *Stobo* v. *H.M.A.*[20] defence counsel suggested that distress was merely an adminicle of evidence. This was rejected by the appeal court who affirmed that distress on its own was capable of corroboration of certain assaults. Lord Justice-General Hope accepted though that distress is not appropriate for the corroboration of an assailant's identity, or of the nature of physical injuries sustained, or of penetration in rape cases, or to convert an indecent assault into an attempted rape.[21]

---

[15] *Yates* v. *H.M.A.*, 1977 S.L.T. (Notes) 42; *Stephen* v. *H.M.A.*, 1987 S.C.C.R. 570 and *Moore* v. *H.M.A.*, 1990 S.L.T. 278.

[16] 1990 S.L.T. 278.

[17] 1992 S.L.T. 709.

[18] A factor which was considered in *Cannon, supra.*

[19] 1992 S.L.T. 991.

[20] 1994 S.L.T. 28. For a review and analysis of the case law in this area see Shiels, "Distress as Corroboration", 1994 J.L.S.S. 293.

[21] At p. 33F–G.

CORROBORATION IN CIVIL CASES

GENERAL RULE

Since April 3, 1989, when the Civil Evidence (Scotland) Act 1988 came **7–87** into force, the requirement for corroboration on crucial issues in a civil case has been removed. That Act was a result of the recommendations of the Scottish Law Commission in their Report, *Evidence: Report on Corroboration, Hearsay and Related Matters*[22]

The Scottish Law Commission pointed out that, given modern practice **7–88** in civil cases: "It ... may be inconsistent with justice that a party, though he may have an honest and credible case, must nevertheless necessarily fail if, through circumstances over which perhaps he has no control, corroboration is not available."[23] Accordingly, it recommended[24] that: "The requirement of corroboration in civil proceedings in so far as it still applies should be abolished." This recommendation is now section 1(1) of the Civil Evidence (Scotland) Act.

Prior to the Act there had been other inroads made into the general rule **7–89** that corroboration was required. The Scottish Law Commission had in an earlier report published in 1965,[25] called for the abolition of the corroboration requirement in all civil cases. Political opposition at that stage restricted the recommendation to dispensing with the need for corroboration in cases of personal injury. This was enacted as section 9 of the Law Reform (Miscellaneous Provisions)(Scotland) Act 1968. This section was replaced by provisions of the 1988 Act but the history of its interpretation is valuable in demonstrating how the courts regard the rule dispensing with the need for corroboration. This section is considered in more detail and the chapter concludes with other illustrations of areas of civil law in which the general rule has been modified.

CIVIL EVIDENCE (SCOTLAND) ACT 1988 s. 1(1)

There is still surprisingly little reported case law arising from the operation **7–90** of section 1(1) of the 1988 Act but where a pursuer has relied on that section there is a clear preference for the liberal approach which was one of two approaches emerging from the earlier provision contained in section 9 of the Law Reform (Miscellaneous Provisions) (Scotland) Act 1968. By virtue of section 9, (and now section 1(1) of the 1988 Act), the normal

---

[22] Report No. 100 published in 1986.
[23] *ibid.*, para. 2.8.
[24] *ibid.*, para. 2.10.
[25] Paper No. 4, Report for Reform of the Law relating to Corroboration.

rule of evidence requiring that a party provide a corroborated case was dispensed with in claims for damages or *solatium* in respect of personal injuries, including disease and/or mental or physical impairment. The rule applied whether or not the party claiming was the pursuer, and covered any fact in the case which the court is "satisfied" has been established.

7–91   In the first authoritative consideration of section 9 of the 1968 Act, *Morrison* v. *Kelly & Sons Ltd.*,[26] the Court of Session ruled that it did not eliminate the need for corroboration in those cases in which it was available. In the opinion of Lord President Clyde[27]:

> "There may be cases where owing to the nature of the circumstances corroboration is unobtainable. Such a case may be an appropriate subject for the application of the subsection [2]. But, where corroboration or contradiction of the pursuer's account of the matter is available, a Court would obviously be very slow indeed to proceed on the pursuer's evidence alone ... How could the Court be satisfied if corroborative evidence was available but without any explanation not produced?"

7–92   The ruling was regarded by many as a disappointing start for the new section. However, arguably it merely confirmed that a court will always consider the weight of the evidence presented to it, and conversely, the significance of evidence available but omitted.

7–93   The case itself was not the best vehicle for the application of section 9(2) anyway, since the pursuer produced no corroborating evidence, and his own testimony was contradicted by every other witness in the case, including two of his own. In rejecting the pursuer's claim on appeal, the court was doing no more than reflecting the weight of the evidence.

7–94   A subsequent Outer House case, *Thomson* v. *Tough Ropes*[28] produced a result more in keeping with the spirit of section 9. *Thomson* claimed damages for injuries sustained in the course of her work, allegedly as the result of defective equipment. Her corroborating witness B, was disbelieved by the judge, who did however believe the pursuer, and was at pains not to penalise her because of the poor quality of the evidence from B. Finding that the pursuer's own evidence had established that the accident had occurred as

---

[26] 1970 S.C. 65.

[27] At p. 79. See also *McGowan* v. *Lord Advocate*, 1972 S.C. 68, in which the only other witnesses in the case apart from the pursuer either were not called, or gave evidence contradicting the pursuer. It was held (i) that the pursuer had failed to satisfy the court of his case, and that the question of corroboration did not, therefore, enter into the matter, and (ii) that s. 9 was in any case primarily intended to cover a case in which there were no eye-witnesses other than the pursuer.

[28] 1978 S.L.T. (Notes) 5. See also *Comerford* v. *Strathclyde Regional Council*, 1987 S.C.L.R. 758.

alleged in her averments, Lord Kincraig decided that he could apply section 9 in her favour because:

> "In my opinion, I am entitled to apply s. 9 where the accident occurred in the absence of any credible eye-witness other than the pursuer herself. The fact that there was evidence from an unreliable eye-witness who purported to corroborate the pursuer, should not deprive the pursuer of the assistance of s. 9.[29]

Similarly, in *Ward* v. *U.C.S. Ltd*[30] the court found in favour of an **7–95** uncorroborated pursuer even though at the end of the day it found him to have been contributorily negligent. In a dissenting judgment in *McLaren v. Caldwell's Paper Mill Co. Ltd*,[31] Lord Stott ruled that section 9 was intended to prevent the unjust situation in which an honest and reliable pursuer was denied a remedy on a technical rule of law.

In the case of *McCallum* v. *British Railways Board*[32] the court adopted a **7–96** liberal approach to section 9. Despite a certain lack of corroboration of some aspects and a failure to call potential witnesses, the appeal court said that given the essential facts were proven, the pursuer's apparently credible testimony need not be corroborated.

The Scottish Law Commission[33] argued that section 9(2) had proved **7–97** useful, and had not led to "a flood of weak claims". It therefore recommended that the principle of the section be extended to all other civil actions, and section 1 of the 1988 Act does precisely this.

CORROBORATION IN CONSISTORIAL CAUSES

(1) General rule

No decree will be granted in certain consistorial cases, even if **7–98** undefended, unless the pursuer's grounds are established by evidence.[34] In terms of section 8(2) of the 1988 Act this requirement for evidence applies to actions for divorce, separation or declarator of marriage, nullity of marriage, legitimacy, legitimation, illegitimacy or non-parentage.

Section 8(3) provides that in an action of divorce, separation or declarator **7–99** of marriage, or nullity of marriage, the evidence required to establish the

---

[29] At p. 6. A similar view was expressed in *McArthur* v. *Organon Laboratories Ltd.*, 1982 S.L.T. 425.
[30] 1973 S.L.T. 182.
[31] 1973 S.L.T. 158.
[32] 1991 S.L.T. 5. The case dealt with an accident and judgment at first instance which pre-dated the 1988 Act.
[33] *op. cit.,* n. 22, para. 2.10.
[34] In any other type of civil action, of course, an undefended action will result in a "decree in absence"; see Scottish Law Commission, *op. cit.,* n. 22, para. 2.11.

grounds of an action "shall consist of or include evidence other than that of a party to the marriage".[35] Evidence can come from a source other than another witness, *e.g.* an extract conviction, though even here, a third party will be required to give evidence that the identity of the person to whom the conviction refers is the defender.[36] The reason for retaining the corroboration rule in consistorial cases stems from the courts' reluctance to terminate a marriage except on the strongest of proven grounds.

7–100   The demand for corroborated evidence has even survived the reduction of the standard of proof in divorce actions from that of beyond reasonable doubt to that of a balance of probabilities.[37] This is so even though "one argument against retaining the need for corroboration is that it sits somewhat uneasily with the concept of proof on a balance of probabilities."[38]

(2) Exceptions to the general rule

7–101   Most of the exceptions to the general rule requiring corroboration in consistorial cases have been briefly referred to above, but it is convenient to itemise them again, together with one additional exception which has not yet been touched upon.

(a) *Civil Evidence (Scotland) Act 1988, s.8(4)*

7–102   By virtue of this section, the Lord Advocate has the power to prescribe classes of undefended divorce actions in which corroboration is not required. He has so far done so only in respect of two and five year separations proceeding under "simplified" applications.

(b) *Divorce (Scotland) Act 1976, s. 3(1)*

7–103   Under this provision, a divorce court may "treat an extract decree of separation lodged in process as sufficient proof of the facts upon which such decree was granted." The section excludes adultery-based actions from this rule.[39] In all other cases, the rule operates not only so as to set up a presumption as regards the facts upon which the earlier findings were based,[40] but also so as to obviate the need for any further corroborating evidence.

---

[35] As Clive in *Husband and Wife* at p. 445 points out, "This continues a requirement of the previous law which was designed to guard against the risk of collusion."

[36] *Andrews* v. *Andrews*, 1971 S.L.T. (Notes) 44.

[37] *per* Divorce (Scotland) Act 1976, s. 1(6). See also para. 2.113 *supra*, and generally, Clive, *op. cit.*, n. 35, p. 443.

[38] Scottish Law Commission *op. cit.*, n. 22, para. 2.13.

[39] But they were placed in the same position by virtue of the Law Reform (Miscellaneous Provisions) (Scotland) Act 1968, s. 11 anyway, and that is why they were excluded from s. 3(1); see below.

[40] For which see paras. 3.26–3.31 *supra*.

(c) *Law Reform (Miscellaneous Provisions) (Scotland) Act 1968, s. 11*

As was noted in paragraphs 5.69–5.74 *supra*, the effect of this section is **7–104** to make a finding of adultery in earlier matrimonial proceedings admissible in subsequent proceedings involving at least one of the original parties. As with section 3(1) of the 1976 Act, it sets up a rebuttable presumption.

(d) *Civil Evidence (Scotland) Act 1988 s.8(2)*

Actions of parentage in terms of section 7(4) of the Law Reform **7–105** (Miscellaneous Provisions)(Scotland) Act 1986 establishing paternity no longer require corroboration.[41] The previous law had required corroboration but according to Walker and Walker, "some relaxation of the rules of evidence has always been allowed to a pursuer in such an action."[42]

(e) *The* Moorov *doctrine*

This rule, dealt with in paragraphs 7.66–7.81 *supra*, whereby each of a **7–106** series of related incidents may be spoken to by only one witness, and may then be conjoined into a mutually corroborative chain, has spilled over from criminal cases into consistorial ones.[43] In such cases the normal requirement for a corroborated case is deemed to have been met.

Thus, in *Whyte* v. *Whyte*,[44] Mrs W sought a divorce on the grounds of her **7–107** husband's adultery with a female servant, Y. It was held that the evidence of another domestic servant, H, of W's indecent behaviour with her, corroborated the evidence of Y, and the decree was granted.

The process is subject to the limitations normally imposed when the **7–108** *Moorov* doctrine is involved. Thus, in *Michlek* v. *Michlek*[45] the evidence relied on by the wife in a divorce action based on H's adultery consisted of (i) his alleged acts of incest with a daughter of the marriage, and (ii) his alleged acts of adultery with a stepdaughter. It was held that she was unable to rely on the evidence of each daughter as corroborating the evidence of the other because an interval of five years which separated the two courses of conduct was held to be too long a period.[46]

---

[41] See Wilkinson and Norrie, *The Law Relating to Parent and Child in Scotland*, pp.126 and 159.

[42] *Evidence* at para. 170.

[43] Assisted no doubt, by the fact that until fairly recently the standards of proof were the same in all such cases, *i.e.* beyond reasonable doubt. *N.B.* that the underlying principle is, in any case, much older than *Moorov*.

[44] (1884) 11 R. 710.

[45] 1971 S.L.T. (Notes) 50.

[46] For the significance of which, see paras. 7.71–7.74 *supra*.

(f) *Fatal Accidents and Sudden Deaths Inquiry (Scotland) Act 1976, s. 6(2)*

7–109   This statute permits the sheriff at a fatal accident inquiry to make any finding of fact relating to cause of death and the circumstances surrounding it, once satisfied that the findings of fact have been established by evidence "notwithstanding that that evidence is not corroborated."

(g) *Industrial Tribunals*

7–110   Industrial Tribunals are an example of various tribunals which have distinct regulations for their procedural rules and for the manner in which they receive and treat evidence. There is often a public policy interest to investigate and establish the truth as closely as possible and unhindered by formal technical rules.[47] Their freedom from any requirement for corroboration was firmly established in *Douglas* v. *Provident Clothing and Supply Co.*[48] In that case the Court of Session held on appeal, that an industrial tribunal investigating reasons for a dismissal was entitled to make conclusions of fact based on the uncorroborated evidence of a witness. The reason given was that under tribunal procedure,[49] "a fact may be proved without any sworn testimony at all."[50]

(h) *Children's Hearings*

7–111   Children's Hearings are another example of a form of quasi-judicial proceedings whose rules of procedure are *sui generis*.[51] Although a separate and distinct body, there are frequent referrals from a Children's Hearing to the Sheriff Court, and on points of law to the Inner House of the Court of Session. The nature of the Children's Hearing system, with its emphasis on the care and protection of children, means that the strict rules of evidence, particularly in relation to hearsay and corroboration, are not applied.

---

[47] Notably those relating to hearsay.

[48] 1969 S.C. 32.

[49] For which see now Industrial Tribunals (Rules of Procedure) (Scotland) Regulations 1980 (S.I. 1980 No. 885), Sched. 1, para. 8.1. *N.B.* that a similar consideration can apply in cases before the Lands Tribunal for Scotland under the Lands Tribunal for Scotland Rules 1971 (S.I. 1971 No. 218), paras. 20 and 23; but see *Bell* v. *Inland Revenue Commrs.*, 1985 S.L.T. (Lands Tribunal) 52 to the effect that the Tribunal can, *ex proprio motu*, revert to strict rules of evidence in particular cases.

[50] *Douglas, infra,* at p. 36.

[51] Children's Hearings (Scotland) Rules 1986, S.I.

CHAPTER 8

THE HEARSAY RULE

THE GENERAL RULE DEFINED

The hearsay rule has been defined as: "An assertion other than one made **8–01** by a person while giving oral evidence in the proceedings is inadmissible *as evidence of any fact asserted*."[1] In civil cases, the rule against hearsay was abolished by section 2 of the Civil Evidence (Scotland) Act 1988.

In criminal cases the rule operates generally so as to restrict evidence **8–02** given by a witness in court to an account of what *he or she* perceived with one of their senses.[2] The evidence is also restricted to statements of fact.[3] The hearsay rule preserves both requirements by rejecting as inadmissible any statement by witness A which simply repeats something he was told by B, whether B is called as a witness or not.

To take a simple example—when an assault is witnessed by A, it is A **8–03** who is required to give evidence of what was seen, and not B to whom the incident was recounted. The purported evidence of B is "hearsay", and in accordance with the general rule is inadmissible. Nor is the ban restricted to oral accounts which are passed on in this fashion. The hearsay rule applies also to entries in documents whose authors are not available as witnesses to speak to such entries.[4] It also extends to statements made on previous occasions by persons now giving evidence (at least in so far as such previous statements are offered as evidence of the facts which they contain). What is important to the court is not what the witness may have said in the past, but what is being testified to now.[5]

The remainder of this chapter considers in more detail the nature of a **8–04** statement described as hearsay and then the various exceptions to the hearsay

---

[1] Cross and Tapper, *Evidence*, p.46.
[2] Sight, sound, smell. etc.
[3] And it is for this reason that the "opinion" evidence of a non-expert witness is normally inadmissible: see Chap. 16 *infra*.
[4] Although there are, as will be seen *infra*, many statutory exceptions to the rule *quoad* public and business records.
[5] Where the fact that the statement was made is relevant, then the making of it may be proved: see paras. 8.05–8.10 *infra*.

rule. Finally, the effect of the abolition of the hearsay rule in civil cases is considered.

HEARSAY DISTINGUISHED FROM ORIGINAL EVIDENCE

8–05　A statement will normally only be rejected as hearsay when it is offered as evidence of the truth of its contents. When the important point at issue is the fact that the statement was made[6] then this fact may be proved. As the Judicial Committee of the Privy Council observed in *Subramaniam* v. *Public Prosecutor*[7]:

> "Evidence of a statement ... is hearsay and inadmissible when the object of the evidence is to establish the truth of what is contained in the statement. It is not hearsay and is admissible when it is proposed to establish by the evidence, not the truth of the statement, but the fact that it was made."

8–06　The facts of that case provide a perfect illustration of the distinction. S was charged with being in possession of firearms without lawful excuse, and his defence was one of duress, claiming that Malayan terrorists had threatened to kill him if he refused to hold the arms for them. It was held that, regardless of whether or not the terrorists meant to carry out those threats, in support of his defence, S could testify to the fact that they were made.

8–07　Similarly, in *McLaren* v. *McLeod*[8] M was charged with brothel keeping, and evidence was allowed of a conversation overheard in the premises in question between two people who were not called as witnesses. It was held that the fact that the statements had been made was relevant in that they cast light on the nature of the premises, and the purpose for which they were being used.

8–08　When a statement is spoken to in court simply to prove the fact that it was made, such a statement is known as "original evidence", and is distinguished from hearsay, which is the admission of a statement as evidence of the truth of its contents. A defamation action, for example, involves proof that a certain statement was made,[9] as does a claim for

---

[6]　*i.e.* regardless of whether or not it was true. The fact that it was made must of course be relevant to the case.

[7]　[1956]1 W.L.R. 965 at p. 970, on appeal from Malaya.

[8]　1913 S.C.(J.) 61.

[9]　Its truth or falsity being a matter which may or may not be relevant, according to what defence is offered.

misrepresentation,[10] and in both cases the fact that the statement was made may be distinguished from the question of its veracity.[11]

It is more helpful to use the terms "hearsay" and "original evidence" to distinguish between the two types of evidence than to use the older distinction between "secondary" and "primary" hearsay, and the former distinction is employed throughout the remainder of this chapter. **8–9**

The distinction between a hearsay statement and original evidence is not always easy to draw, particularly when the statement in question takes the form of an implied assertion. Thus, in *Ratten v. R.*,[12] the Judicial Committee of the Privy Council admitted evidence of a telephone call by a murder victim, shortly before her death, in which she asked for police assistance. Although it noted in passing that, had the call been regarded as hearsay, it would have been admissible under the *res gestae* exception,[13] the Privy Council gave as its primary ground for admitting it that it was original evidence of, (i) the fact that it was not the only call from the house that day, as the accused claimed; and (ii) the victim's state of alarm. It is this latter finding which creates the difficulty, since such evidence would only be relevant if it could be regarded as an implied assertion by the victim that she was under threat. This virtually amounts to using the statement as evidence of the truth of its implied contents.[14] **8–10**

THE RATIONALE OF THE GENERAL RULE

It assists understanding of the true nature of the hearsay rule, and the reasons for the exceptions to it, to consider briefly the rationale which underlies it. It was summed up most succinctly by Lord Normand in *Teper v. R.*,[15] who stated that: **8–11**

> "The rule against the admission of hearsay evidence is fundamental. It is not the best evidence and it is not delivered on oath. The truthfulness and accuracy of the person whose words are spoken to by another witness cannot be tested by cross-examination, and the light which his demeanour would throw on his testimony is lost."

---

[10] The falsity of the statement being the ultimate issue; without proof that the statement was made, however, the court need not proceed any further.

[11] A similar distinction is evident in the case of previous consistent and inconsistent statements by witnesses, which when admissible are relevant only to the credibility of the witness. See paras. 10.33–10.47 and 10.74–10.87 *infra*.

[12] [1972] A.C. 378.

[13] As it would be in Scotland: see paras. 8.20–8.33 *infra*. It would also be admissible as a statement by a deceased person; see paras. 8.36–8.44 *infra*.

[14] Under Scots law, it would be admissible in any case under another exception to the hearsay rule relating to physical or mental condition: see paras. 8.34–8.35 *infra*.

[15] [1952] A.C. 480 at p. 486; and for a wider discussion see the Scottish Law Commission's *Report on Hearsay Evidence in Criminal Proceedings*, No. 149, 1995.

8–12   The following elements may be extracted from this rationale.

8–13   (i) The maker of a hearsay statement is not on oath when he makes it, and cannot be subjected to cross-examination. Against this it may be argued that the closer in time the statement is made to the events to which it relates, the more reliable it may be. This consideration underlies the exception to the general rule permitted in those cases in which the statement is part of the *res gestae*.[16]

8–14   (ii) Hearsay statements are not the "best" evidence.[17] They may, however, be the best which is now available, hence the exception which is permitted when the maker of the original statement is now dead.[18] In some cases, a hearsay statement may even constitute the best evidence which could be imagined. As the House of Lords observed of a report on a railway accident made by eyewitnesses, some of whom were available to testify in the subsequent civil action arising from it[19]: "It is clear that the due administration of justice strongly requires disclosure and production of this report; it was contemporary; it contained statements by witnesses on the spot; it would be not merely relevant evidence but almost certainly the best evidence, as to the cause of the accident."

8–15   (iii) There is a risk that a hearsay statement will lose its accuracy through repetition. On the other hand, if it was made in writing close to the events which it describes, that may enhance its reliability, hence the exception to the rule permitted in the case of public and business records.[20]

8–16   (iv) There is a risk that hearsay evidence will be manufactured. This possibility applies to all evidence.

8–17   (v) The court is unable to observe the demeanour of the witness whose evidence is given in hearsay form through the mouth of another. Questions as to that person's demeanour may, of course, be asked of the person now testifying.

8–18   In the past 20 years or so, much of the rationale underlying the hearsay rule has come under question. The English courts were relieved of most of their equivalent rule in civil cases under the Civil Evidence Act 1968, and the Scottish Law Commission in 1986[21] recommended similar legislation for Scotland. This was enacted as section 2 of the Civil Evidence (Scotland) Act 1988, which abolishes the hearsay rule for all "civil proceedings" covered by the Act (including consistorial causes). This permits evidence to be given of any statement made by a person otherwise than in a court of

---

[16] Dealt with in paras. 8.20–8.33 *infra*.

[17] For the "best evidence rule," see paras. 9.56–9.68 *infra*.

[18] Dealt with in paras. 8.36–8.44 *infra*.

[19] *Waugh* v. *British Railways Board* [1980] A.C. 521 at p. 531. *N.B.* the "eyewitness" exception to the general privilege which operates *post litem motam*, *per* paras. 12.50–12.56 *infra*.

[20] Dealt with in paras. 8.57–8.61 *infra*.

[21] Memo. No. 100, para. 3.37.

law when that statement would have been admissible had the person making it done so in the form of sworn testimony (*e.g.* it must be relevant, and the maker must have been a competent witness). At the same time, section 2 continues to permit evidence to be given of the making of such statements where this is relevant as original evidence. "Statements" include all "representations (however made or expressed)", but precognitions are expressly excluded from the operation of section 2.

EXCEPTIONS TO THE HEARSAY RULE

The remainder of this chapter is devoted to an examination of exceptions to **8–19** the hearsay rule. In the main they arise from expediency, and may be regarded as simply one manifestation of the best evidence rule, although some are statutory in origin.

STATEMENTS FORMING PART OF THE *RES GESTAE*

"Evidence is admissible of a statement made contemporaneously with an action or event which is, or forms part of, the fact or facts in issue by a person present at that action or event. The *res gestae* may be defined as the whole circumstances immediately and directly connected with an occurrence which is part of the facts in issue."[22]

The *res gestae* exception is justified on the ground that it represents the **8–20** spontaneous reaction of the person who made the statement. The statement was made before any opportunity existed for reflection, and is therefore likely to be a genuine indication of what really happened. The exception covers not only statements but other physical reactions, such as fainting or vomiting. Included in the *res gestae* category of admissible statements are the express and implied assertions, not only of the participants in the incident themselves, but also of those observing it.

Among the more obvious examples of *res gestae* statements are the **8–21** screams and protests of a rape victim,[23] and the use of nicknames in an unguarded moment by members of a team of hooded armed robbers.[24] Thus in *Murray*[25] the court was considering evidence against M, charged with

---

[22] Wilkinson, *Scottish Law of Evidence*, p. 39.
[23] Thus negativing consent.
[24] Thus, if one of the accused has the same nickname, the use of it by one of the gang to another may be employed in evidence to identify the accused by implication, even if the person who uttered it has never been traced. The statement will be spoken to by the person (*e.g.* the victim) who heard it being made.
[25] (1866) 5 Irv. 232.

ravishing an imbecile girl who was herself deemed incompetent as a witness because of her disability.[26] It was held that her mother might testify as to "the first statement or exclamation she made" when she returned home, which was described as a cry of distress.[27]

8–22   The statement must be sufficiently close in time to the incident as to form part of it, and must relate to it in some material way. This accords with the rationale of the exception, namely that the statement should be forced instinctively from the maker in the heat of the moment. A statement is therefore only part of the *res gestae*: "providing it is made in such conditions (always being those of approximate but not exact contemporaneity) of involvement or pressure as to exclude the possibility of concoction or distortion."[28]

8–23   The facts of *Teper* v. *R.*[29] provide a good example of the fine distinctions which sometimes have to be drawn in this area of law. In the trial of T for an assault by stone-throwing, evidence had been admitted of a statement by an eyewitness, now untraceable, who had pointed to T's door and stated that: "The person who threw the stone went in there." It was held that this statement should not have been admitted, since it was not part of the *res gestae*.

8–24   Lord Normand began by indicating the basic requirements to be met before any statement can be regarded as part of the *res gestae*:

> "It is essential that the words sought to be proved by hearsay should be, if not absolutely contemporaneous with the action or event, at least so clearly associated with it, in time, place and circumstances, that they are part of the thing being done, and so an item or part of real evidence and not merely a reported statement."[30]

8–25   Applying that to the statement in the present case, he ruled:

> "The words were closely associated in time and place with the event, the assault. But they were not directly connected with that event itself. They were not words spontaneously forced from the woman by the sight of the assault, but were prompted by the sight of a man quitting the scene of the assault, and they were spoken to for the purpose of helping to bring him to justice,"[31]

and as such they were not part of the *res gestae*.

---

[26]   See paras. 11.05–11.07 *infra*.

[27]   *N.B.* that although the cry did not strictly accompany the assault, and was therefore more like a *de recenti* statement (for which see below), the circumstances were such that the court felt itself entitled to regard it as being part of the *res gestae*: see *O'Hara, infra*.

[28]   *Ratten* v. *R.* [1972] A.C. 378 at p. 391.

[29]   [1952] A.C. 480.

[30]   At p. 487.

[31]   At p. 488.

However, as was seen in *Murray*,[32] the courts will allow some latitude of **8–26** time in those cases in which the statement in question, although not precisely contemporaneous with the incident to which it relates, is nevertheless clearly made under the continuing psychological pressure of that incident.

The case of *O'Hara* v. *Central S.M.T. Co.*,[33] provides an example of the **8–27** hearsay rule in civil cases prior to the 1988 Act. A statement made by the driver of a bus, accusing a pedestrian of having stepped out in front of him, which although made some minutes after the incident, "was the first opportunity for the discharge of the driver's pent-up emotion" was admitted as evidence.[34] The reactive statement of the pedestrian was also admitted as part of the *res gestae*, although that was perhaps stretching the latitude to the limit.

Res gestae statements are frequently confused with statements made *de* **8–28** *recenti*. As explained in paragraphs 10.37–10.39 *infra*, a statement made *de recenti* is one which was made, by a person now giving evidence, shortly after the incident to which it related. On those rare occasions when such statements are admissible,[35] they serve only to enhance the credibility of the maker as a witness, and are not evidence of the truth of their contents. It is the fact that the earlier statement was made which is of importance, and the admission of such previous consistent statements which were made *de recenti* is merely one example of the general admissibility of original evidence when it is relevant.

The following are therefore the main points of distinction between *res* **8–29** *gestae* and *de recenti* statements.

(i) Statements made *res gestae* are part of the incident to which they **8–30** refer, whereas statements *de recenti* occur shortly afterwards.

(ii) Statements made *res gestae* may be admitted as evidence of the truth **8–31** of their contents; statements made *de recenti* merely enhance the credibility of the maker, who is now a witness.

(iii) Statements made *res gestae* are admissible regardless of who made **8–32** them; statements made *de recenti* are only admissible when the maker is now a witness giving evidence which is consistent with that contained in the *de recenti* statement.

(iv) *De recenti* statements are almost certainly restricted, under modern **8–33** law, to those circumstances in which the victim of a sexual assault is allowed to show consistency in her denial of consent.

---

[32] (1866) 5 Irv. 232.
[33] 1941 S.C. 363.
[34] Walker and Walker, *Law of Evidence in Scotland*, para. 377.
[35] *e.g.* to support a denial by the victim in a rape case that she consented.

SECTION 259 EXCEPTIONS

8–34 Significant changes with regard to hearsay were made to the criminal law following the Scottish Law Commission's *Report on Hearsay Evidence in Criminal Proceedings*.[36] The Commission's recommendations are in broad measure now incorporated into the Criminal Procedure (Scotland) Act 1995, section 259 of which sets out the statutory exceptions permitting hearsay evidence to be admitted to a court. The section provides that evidence other than by oral testimony shall be admissible on five separate grounds. The evidence must be such that it would have otherwise been admissible in oral evidence by a competent witness.

8–35 The five grounds are set out in section 259(2). They are:

    (i)   that the witness is now deceased;

    (ii) that the witness is outwith the UK and it is not practicable to secure his attendance or obtain evidence by alternative means;[37]

    (iii) that the witness has been sufficiently identified, but cannot be found;

    (iv) that the witness declines to give evidence having been advised that it might be incriminating;[38] and

    (v) that the witness refuses to take the oath or to give evidence."[39]

STATEMENTS BY PERSONS NOW DECEASED

8–36 Prior to the 1995 Act, statements by persons now deceased were treated as admissible as evidence of the truth of their contents. The rationale of the rule was that it was now the best evidence which the court had available of the matters contained in such statements.

8–37 In relation to deceased persons, the statutory changes brought about by section 2 of the 1988 Act and section 259 of the 1995 Act will confirm the common law position. Thus, before the rule may be invoked the person now deceased must have been a competent witness at the time at which the statement was made,[40] and the statement will be discounted if at the time

---

[36] Report No. 149 published in February 1995.

[37] *e.g.* evidence on commission, or evidence by live TV link if outside the U.K.: see ss. 272–3 of the Criminal Procedure (Scotland) Act 1995.

[38] This is intended to ameliorate the effects of *Perrie* v. *H.M.A.*, 1991 S.C.C.R. 255 and *McLay* v. *H.M.A.*, 1994 S.L.T. 873, cases where statements made to third parties by an incriminee were hearsay and inadmissible.

[39] See the reforms recommended by Macphail, *Evidence*, Chap. 19.

[40] *e.g.* he or she must not have been a mental defective: see paras. 11.05–11.07 *infra*. See also Dickson, *Evidence*, para. 267. *N.B.* that the Scottish Law Commission, Memo. No. 46, para. T.08, recommended that the date upon which such competency should be tested is the date upon which the statement is tendered in evidence.

when it was made the witness had some self-interest or was contemplating legal action in connection with the subject-matter of the statement. As Lord Watson observed in the *Lauderdale Peerage Case*[41]:

> "the statement of a deceased person, whether oral or written, is not admissible as evidence, when its own terms or the circumstances in which it was made, are such as to beget a reasonable suspicion either that the statement was not in accordance with the truth, or that it was a coloured or one sided version of the truth."

More recently, in *William Thyne (Plastics) Ltd.* v. *Stenhouse Reed Shaw* **8–38** *(Scotland) Ltd.*,[42] a company sued its insurance brokers for negligence. The pursuers were under-insured at the time of a fire, and the defenders sought to adduce an internal memorandum from the manager of the relevant office, now deceased, concerning the instructions given to him by the pursuers. They were refused leave to do so because the memorandum had been sent after it was known that the pursuers were holding them responsible for their losses, and so therefore it "was not a spontaneous account of events written at the time, but a considered version of them after intimation of a prospective claim, and must give rise to a reasonable 'suspicion' that it was a one-sided version of the truth."[43]

Because of the danger of bias creeping in, the courts will likewise reject **8–39** any statement by a person now deceased which takes the form of precognition, for the same reason that such statements are rejected as previous inconsistent statements,[44] namely that they are not the original words of the witness, but have been "filtered through the mind of another."[45]

In *Moffat* v. *Hunter*[46] the court admitted as evidence statements by a **8–40** person (now deceased) who had been a witness to a road accident. The statements had been given in his own words to an insurance inspector. The inspector did not proceed by question and answer, but simply collected the witness's *verbatim* statement. He had done so five months before the writ was issued, and the witness had no clear idea of the insurance company's interest in the case. It was held that in the circumstances, it was not "tainted by interest" and was not a precognition.

Similarly, in *H.M.A.* v. *Irving*[47] the High Court admitted statements made **8–41** to the police by the victim in a theft and rape case, who died shortly

---

[41] (1885) 10 A.C. 692 at p. 707.

[42] 1979 S.L.T. (Notes) 93.

[43] *ibid., N.B.* the similarity of time period (*i.e.* the first intimation of a claim) with that observed in cases involving the privilege *post litem motam*, considered in paras. 12.50–12.56 *infra*.

[44] For which see 10.74–10.87 *infra*.

[45] *Kerr* v. *H.M.A.*, 1958 J.C. 14, *per* Lord Justice-Clerk Thomson at p. 19. The leading case is normally taken to be *Young* v. *N.C.B.*, 1960 S.C. 6, as followed in *Miller* v. *Jackson*, 1972 S.L.T. (Notes) 31.

[46] 1974 S.L.T. (Sh.Ct.) 42.

[47] 1978 S.L.T. 58.

afterwards, because it was held that her statements were in the form of a straightforward complaint and not by way of precognition. But in *Thomson v. Jamieson,*[48] the court rejected a statement made by the now deceased driver of a car which had been in collision with the pursuer's motorcycle because it was made to a claims inspector employed by an insurance company at a time when a claim was in prospect, and took the form partly of a question-and-answer session. That was enough, said the court, to make it inadmissible on the ground that it was "akin to a precognition."

8–42   The common law also recognised exceptional circumstances in which even a statement originally made in the form of a precognition could be admissible after the maker is dead. Again, these will not be affected by the statutory changes. An example of these "exceptional" circumstances was the "dying declaration or deposition" of a witness in a criminal case who has material evidence to give in the case.[49]

8–43   The other possible main exception arises when the statement in question has been given in the form of evidence in another case. Although it has thereby been obtained by the stilted question and answer method akin to a precognition, it has the advantage of having been given on oath and subjected to cross-examination. It is therefore arguably the best evidence now available. The authorities are divided as to whether or not the fact that the witness has not been cross-examined by the opposing party in the present case is fatal to its admissibility,[50] but the Scottish Law Commission[51] recommended that this should affect only the weight to be attached to it.

8–44   The Commission also recommended[52] that if a deceased person's statements are to be admitted, the fact that they are in the form of a precognition should go only to their weight.

REPUTATION IN CASES INVOLVING MARRIAGE, LEGITIMACY, PEDIGREE AND ANCIENT RIGHTS

8–45   In cases involving marriage, legitimacy, pedigree and ancient rights, the common law had long recognised exceptions to the general rule against hearsay. Evidence in such cases was permitted under the best evidence

---

[48] 1986 S.L.T. 72. See also *Hall* v. *Edinburgh Corporation*, 1974 S.L.T. (Notes) 14; *Pirie* v. *Geddes*, 1973 S.L.T. (Sh.Ct.) 81; and *Ferrier's Exr.* v. *Glasgow Corporation*, 1966 S.L.T. (Sh.Ct.) 44.

[49] Adequately vouched for in Walker and Walker, *op. cit.,* n. 34, para. 410, but rarely mentioned in modern case reports. *N.B.* that the witness may be for either the Crown or the defence, is questioned on oath, but need not know himself to be dying. The witness need not be the victim. See Walker and Walker, for further details on procedure. See also Macphail, *op. cit.*, n. 39, Chap. 19.33.

[50] See Macphail, *op. cit.*, n. 39, Chap. 19.32 and *Hogg* v. *Frew*, 1951 S.L.T. 397.

[51] Memo. No. 46, para. T.11.

[52] *ibid.*, para. T.10.

rule, on the ground that the events into which the court was then inquiring occurred so long ago that no witnesses remained who could testify in court. The exception was most clearly developed in those cases involving marriage and legitimacy, and rested on the same rationale as that which permits evidence of marriage by cohabitation and repute.[53] Evidence that two persons cohabited, along with a hearsay statement to the effect that local reputation established them as married, may amount to corroborated proof.[54]

The authority for the statement that reputation evidence is admissible in questions of ancient rights rests upon Stair[55] and Erskine.[56] **8–46**

More recently, in *Brook's Executrix* v. *James*,[57] the House of Lords, in **8–47** considering the legitimacy of a man born in 1868 whose "parents" had not been married until 1871, held it to be proved, in the absence of any presumption, by the positive evidence created by the reputation he had enjoyed at the time as being the legitimate son of the husband. In confirming the existence of this exception to the hearsay rule, their Lordships referred[58] to the fact that: "Where, owing to the passage of time or for other good reasons, there is no other evidence at all, then common reputation ought to be regarded as *prima facie* evidence displacing the onus of proof."

The application of the principle to pedigree claims[59] is limited to the **8–48** reputation evidence which emanates from persons who were specially placed to know the true position.[60] The inconsistency which this creates by comparison with ordinary legitimacy cases[61] has no logical justification.

The application of the exception to peerage cases was recently **8–49** reconfirmed in *Viscountcy of Dudhope and Earldom of Dundee*,[62] but was qualified in so far as it was held[63] that:

"In peerage cases, as in other historical inquiries, family traditions must be received with caution, for they may be only flattering and deceptive myths, and it is never possible to be sure that error has not crept in even when the tradition is unfavourable to the family claims."

---

[53] See Clive, *Law of Husband and Wife in Scotland*, pp. 48–67.
[54] *De Thoren* v. *Wall* (1876) 3 R.(H.L.) 28.
[55] IV,xliii.
[56] IV,ii, 7.
[57] 1971 S.C.(H.L.) 77; see also paras. 3.87–3.94 *supra*.
[58] *ibid*., at p. 81.
[59] Which frequently hinge on issues of legitimacy anyway.
[60] *e.g.* confidential servants, as in *MacPherson* v. *Reid's Trs*. (1876) 4 R. 132.
[61] In which general public reputation is sufficient.
[62] 1986 S.L.T. (Lyon Court) 2.
[63] *ibid*., p. 6. *N.B.* that the point being established was an essentially negative one, namely the extinction of all intermediate collateral heirs.

ABOLITION OF HEARSAY IN CIVIL CASES

8–50 The Civil Evidence (Scotland) Act 1988 resulted from the Scottish Law Commission's *Report on Corroboration, Hearsay and Related Matters*.[64] The purpose of the legislation was to promote the inclusion of all relevant evidence and to reduce the effect of exclusionary rules which prevented the court from considering evidence which might be of assistance in reaching decisions. Section 2(1) of the Act provides:

"In any civil proceedings —

(a) evidence shall not be excluded solely on the ground that it is hearsay;

(b) a statement made by a person otherwise than in the course of the proof shall be admissible as evidence of any matter contained in the statement of which direct oral evidence by that person would be admissible; and

(c) the court, or as the case may be, the jury, if satisfied that any fact has been established by evidence in those proceedings, shall be entitled to find that fact proved by evidence notwithstanding that the evidence is hearsay."

8–51 Sections 1 and 2 of the 1988 Act which respectively abolished corroboration and hearsay are closely connected in effect and the case law to have emerged to date supports this.[65] Many of these cases are appeals from Children's Hearings referrals. Where the case concerns children then there is always a risk that the child will not be found to be a competent witness at the proof (see paragraphs 11.10–11.21 *infra*). The question may then arise as to whether a previous statement made by the child can be admitted in evidence.

8–52 In *F* v. *Kennedy (No.1)*[66] the court held that if a child is not confirmed as a competent witness before the judge or sheriff then any previous statement will be inadmissible.[67] This was on the basis that s. 2(1)(b) only permitted hearsay from a witness of whom "direct oral evidence" would be admissible. As has been pointed out elsewhere,[68] the Act is silent as to when competency as a witness is to be judged—the date of the making of the statement or the date of the proof—though the Scottish Law

---

[64] Report No. 100.
[65] For discussion of some of these cases, see the articles by Edwards, "Better Seen and Not Heard", 1993 S.L.T. 9, and Sheldon, "I Heard it on the Grapevine", 1993 J.L.S.S. 292.
[66] 1992 S.C.L.R. 139.
[67] See too, *Sanderson* v. *McManus*, 1995 S.C.L.R. 902.
[68] See Field's, *Annotations to the Civil Evidence (Scotland) Act 1988*.

Commission[69] had recommended the latter was more appropriate. In the case of a child witness it is hard to see how it could be any other date since the court at any proof involving a child witness must first be satisfied that the child is competent to give evidence. That process of inquiry by a judge or sheriff could not be undertaken at an earlier date.

In the Outer House decision of *P.L.* v. *V.L.*[70] the view of Lord Hamilton   **8–53**
was that the appropriate point for determining admissibility was whether the witness was competent at the time of the proof.

The issue of competency was also raised incidentally in *M* v. *Kennedy*,[71]   **8–54**
and in his commentary to the case Sheriff Stewart suggests that a hearsay statement should be admissible provided a witness would have been competent at the time it was made, "at least … where the incompetence of the witness arises from supervening physical disability." The only difficulty with such a proposal is how competency, even in limited cases, would be established in retrospect.

The case of *F* v. *Kennedy(No.2)*[72] clarified the status of hearsay evidence   **8–55**
in situations where a witness gives direct oral evidence. The court ruled that even though direct evidence is given, this does not prevent hearsay evidence being offered to the court of what that witness said on another occasion.

Despite the broad terms of section 2, there is still a prohibition, contained   **8–56**
in section 9 against evidence given in precognitions. In *Anderson* v. *J.B.Fraser & Co. Ltd.*[73] it was held that what was said to a precognoscer could be distinguished from what was recorded in a precognition. It is competent therefore to lead evidence from a precognoscer as to what was said by the witness, but not what was recorded. However, the weight to be attached to such a statement may be limited.[74]

DOCUMENTARY EVIDENCE UNDER STATUTE

On a strict application of the rule against hearsay, all entries in documents   **8–57**
would be essentially hearsay in nature, since they represent merely what someone has recorded on an earlier occasion. An entry in a document cannot therefore (unless it falls under one of the exceptions to the rule already noted) be evidence of the truth of the facts which it records, and even if the person who made the entry is called, he or she may well not be the person

---

[69] *loc. cit.*
[70] 1995 S.C.L.R. 11.
[71] 1993 S.C.L.R. 69.
[72] 1992 S.C.L.R. 750.
[73] 1992 S.L.T. 1129.
[74] *Cavanagh* v. *BP Chemicals Ltd,* 1995 S.L.T. 1287.

with the knowledge of the truth of the facts recorded.[75] However, rigid adherence to this principle would make many facts almost unprovable, or at best would delay the process of justice to intolerable lengths. For this reason, Parliament has on many occasions, and for many different purposes, decreed that entries in documents may be adduced as evidence of the facts which they contain, subject to certain safeguards.

8–58   Both the Civil Evidence (Scotland) Act 1988, and the Criminal Procedure (Scotland) Act 1995 make further substantial provision for the certification of certain types of documents being provable in evidence without the need for a witness to speak to them. In civil cases, section 5 of the Civil Evidence (Scotland) Act 1988, admits, for the purposes of any "civil proceedings", a document suitably docqueted and purportedly signed by "an officer of the business or undertaking to which the records belong". Such a statement may then be received in evidence without being spoken to by a witness. In terms of section 6, a copy document is similarly admissible if it purports to be authenticated by the person making it. Documents and records are defined broadly in section 9 of the Act and include tapes, discs and computer records.[76]

8–59   In criminal cases, schedule 8 to the 1995 Act provides for the admissibility of copy documents and for the certification of documents, primarily business documents, which if properly authenticated are admissible as evidence of any fact or opinion of which direct oral evidence would be admissible. Document is defined very broadly in paragraph 8 to schedule 8 and includes maps, plans, graphs, drawings, photographs, discs, tapes, and films.

8–60   Apart from these major statutory provisions, other statutes render admissible, for the limited purposes specified in each statute, various other records, mainly of a public nature. For example, section 41 of the Registration of Births, Deaths and Marriages (Scotland) Act 1965 renders extracts or abbreviated certificates issued by the relevant registrar evidence of the facts they record, although it is necessary in practice to produce other evidence in order to identify the persons named in the record.

8–61   There is also general authority for the statement that all public records may be regarded as evidence of the facts which are recorded in them, as may official records kept by a public officer.[77]

---

[75] *e.g.* the Registrar of Births, Deaths and Marriages simply records the information given by the person who conveys the facts.

[76] This replaces an earlier and similar provision contained in s. 7 of the Law Reform (Miscellaneous Provisions)(Scotland) Act 1968.

[77] Dickson, *op. cit.,* n. 40, paras. 1104, 1204 and 1209; Walker and Walker, *op. cit.,* n. 34, para. 219. Entries in the Registers of Sasines, Inhibitions and Adjudications, the Books of Council and Session and court records are all admissible under statutes applicable to them. For further consideration of documentary evidence see paras. 9.21–9.45 *infra*.

CHAPTER 9

TYPES OF EVIDENCE

INTRODUCTION

All evidence may be classified in three very basic ways, namely as: **9–01**

- (i) Oral, Real or Documentary, *or* as
- (ii) Direct or Circumstantial, *or* as
- (iii) Primary or Secondary.

These three classifications, far from being mutually exclusive, are in fact three separate methods of categorising all items of evidence. Thus all evidence, while being oral, real or documentary, may also be classified as either direct or circumstantial, and as either primary or secondary. Each classification serves a different purpose, and each has its own relevance to the conduct of a case.

ORAL, DOCUMENTARY AND REAL EVIDENCE

ORAL EVIDENCE

"Oral" evidence is simply the verbal testimony of a witness in court. The **9–02** law of evidence places great value on the oral testimony of a witness. The witness, ideally, will be describing something which he or she has seen, heard, smelled or felt. If a witness seeks simply to relate what someone else perceived and communicated, then that witness's testimony may well be rejected as hearsay.[1] In criminal cases hearsay evidence is generally inadmissible. In civil cases it is admissible, by virtue of the Civil Evidence (Scotland) Act 1988, but it is not best evidence.

In certain cases, the main purpose of the witness's testimony lies not in **9–03** what was perceived. Instead it is the assistance which the witness is able to give to the court in interpreting facts spoken to by others or objects connected with the matter under investigation.

---

[1] For which see Chap. 8, *infra*. There are, as will be seen, some important exceptions to this general rule.

9–04   An example of this is the oral testimony of the expert witness, who in most cases appears in order to present a report which gives an expert assessment of a situation. In such cases, the entire evidence given by that witness is best regarded as oral evidence, including the report which is presented, and which is incorporated into the testimony by reference.

9–05   The actual content of oral testimony is, of course, capable of further classification. If, for example, witness X states that he saw A hit B, then in an assault trial this is *direct* evidence. If, on the other hand, his testimony is to the effect that he saw A running from the scene of the assault, then his evidence is *circumstantial*. This method of classifying evidence is further considered below and has already been encountered on several other occasions in earlier chapters.[2]

REAL EVIDENCE

9–06   "Real" evidence, has been defined as: "a thing, which may be a human being, any features of the thing which are significant, and the inferences to be drawn from the existence of the thing or from its significant features."[3]

9–07   Real evidence is clearly something tangible and physical, and most such items of evidence are known in the Scots courts as "productions". The court is being asked to examine the production (and any accompanying expert report—see paragraphs 9.02–9.05 *supra*) and draw its own conclusions from it. In crimes of violence with the use of a weapon, the weapon, if available, will be lodged as a production in court. In crimes involving violence against the person or theft by housebreaking, it is the accepted practice for the Crown to produce the clothing of the victim and accused, or stolen items (if recovered) in order that the court may draw from those items such conclusions as it sees fit.

9–08   It is impossible to draw up a comprehensive list of those items which may be produced under the heading of "real" evidence, since many such items are accepted without formal acknowledgment by the courts. Thus, the judge who takes into account the uneasy and prevaricating behaviour of a witness giving oral testimony is making use of real evidence. Equally, when scenes-of-crime photographs are examined to give an understanding of the locus, this is real evidence.

9–09   Real evidence may be offered to a court for a variety of purposes. In some cases, it is made available by one of the parties simply because it features in the case, and not because of any significant new fact which may be deduced from its appearance. For example, in a routine shoplifting case, it is expected that the Crown will produce the items in question[4] but very

---

[2]   See, for example, paras. 1.13–1.21 and 7.05–7.13 *supra*.
[3]   Walker and Walker, *Law of Evidence in Scotland*, para. 416.
[4]   On which point see paras. 9.62–9.68 *infra*.

rarely will they yield any evidence themselves. In a rape case, the items of clothing of an alleged rape victim, are important because of the body fluid stains identified upon them and examined in the experts' reports, but are not in themselves usually significant.

In other cases, however, the item of real evidence itself forms a crucial **9–10** part of the case of either or both of the parties. This may be because of certain deductions which the court can make from its appearance, or its very existence. In *Sandells* v. *H.M.A.*,[5] The important question was whether a cigarette vending machine wrenched from the wall of a social club and removed from the premises had been stolen by one man or two. The appearance and weight of the machine in question was considered to be a crucial issue in the case. Similarly, as was seen in *Patterson* v. *Nixon*,[6] the behaviour of a police tracker dog proved sufficiently important to corroborate a partial confession by the accused.

Often, the significance of an item of real evidence is only apparent with **9–11** the assistance of expert testimony. In a drunk-driving case it is the forensic certificate which accompanies the blood/urine sample which is of significance. The sample—or rather its remains—must always be produced in court, but the focus is on the blood/alcohol reading produced by a small portion of the sample now no longer available anyway because of the destructive nature of the test itself.[7]

Another type of real evidence is the mechanical recording, both audio **9–12** and visual. In *Hopes and Lavery* v. *H.M.A.*,[8] it was held that a tape-recording of an incriminating statement by a blackmailer obtained by "wiring up" the intended victim was "direct" and "primary" evidence[9] and the taping of a confession in a police station was admissible in *Lord Advocate's Reference (No. 1 of 1983)*.[10]

In *Bowie* v. *Tudhope*,[11] the court accepted identification evidence from **9–13** two police officers who knew the accused and who had picked him out on

---

[5]   1980 S.L.T. (Notes) 45.
[6]   1960 J.C. 42, considered more fully in paras. 7.13 *supra*.
[7]   The same is true for fingerprint evidence (see *H.M.A.* v. *Dennison*, 1978 S.L.T. (Notes) 79) and evidence yielded by dental impressions (*Hay* v. *H.M.A.*, 1968 J.C. 40) and body fluids such as semen (*Preece* v. *H.M.A.* [1981] Crim. L.R. 783). These cases were all considered in paras. 7.25–7.47 *supra*.
[8]   1960 J.C. 104.
[9]   Considered in paras. 9.52–9.55 *infra*.
[10] 1984 S.L.T. 337, also considered in paras. 14.30–14.44 *infra*. It was held in this case that a written transcript of the confession should normally be supplied to the court. Section 277 of the Criminal Procedure (Scotland) Act 1995 makes provision for the reception by the court of a certificate signed by the person making such a transcript. A copy thereof must be served on the accused not less than 14 days before his trial, and in the absence of any defence objection not less than six days prior to the trial, the certificate will be regarded as conclusive evidence of the making of the transcript and of its accuracy. Alternatively the oral evidence of the maker will be regarded as having the same effect.
[11] 1986 S.C.C.R. 205, for which see para. 7.42 *supra*.

a video film of a robbery in a shop. It would be competent to allow juries to see such films for themselves and form their own conclusions as to the identities of those shown on them.

9–14   Blood tests may now be used as items of real evidence in a variety of cases. The most obvious covers paternity, and in *Docherty* v. *McGlynn*,[12] the lover of a deceased woman sought to show that a child born during her marriage was in fact his child. He relied upon the results of blood tests, the deceased's blood having been taken before her death for other purposes. In concluding beyond reasonable doubt[13] that the deceased's husband could not have been the father of the child, and on a balance of probabilities that the lover could have been, the court made use of the blood test evidence, the presumptive father having given consent to the test on behalf of the child. It was not, however, the only evidence which supported the lover's case. At an earlier stage of the action it had been successfully argued that blood tests could be carried out and the presumptive father could give consent for the child. Lord President Emslie[14] opened the door to the use of such tests in future cases by ruling that: "the reliability of serological tests of blood for grouping has greatly increased to the point where a particular person's claim to paternity may be excluded to a very high degree of probability."

9–15   The question of consent to the taking of a blood sample was an issue in *Docherty*. It is now regulated by statute. Section 6 of the Law Reform (Parent and Child) (Scotland) Act 1986, provides for the obtaining of consent in civil cases relating to "the determination of parentage."

9–16   Blood tests are still not compulsory. At common law, the court has no power to compel an adult to provide a blood sample to determine paternity whether through blood tests or DNA profiling (otherwise known as genetic fingerprinting).[15] However, section 70(1) of the Law Reform (Miscellaneous Provisions) (Scotland) Act 1990 empowers the court to request a party to proceedings to provide a sample or consent to the taking of a blood sample from a child.[16] Although such blood tests are not compulsory, section 70(2) states that the court may draw adverse conclusions from a refusal to provide such a blood sample.

9–17   In an action of declarator of paternity it has been held that this section extends to the situation where the court may require an executor of a party to provide a blood sample. This happened in *Mackay* v. *Murphy*,[17] where

---

[12] 1985 S.L.T. 237.

[13] This case pre-dated the Law Reform (Parent and Child) (Scotland) Act 1986 which reduced the standard of proof to that of a balance of probabilities.

[14] 1983 S.L.T. 645 at p. 648. See also *Allardyce* v. *Johnston*, 1979 S.L.T. (Sh.Ct.) 54.

[15] *Torrie* v. *Turner*, 1990 S.L.T. 718.

[16] Section 2(4) of the Age of Legal Capacity (Scotland) Act 1991 enables a child under 16 to give such consent provided the nature and consequences of the treatment are understood.

[17] 1995 S.L.T. (Sh.Ct.) 30.

the executor of a deceased soldier was a party to a paternity action raised against the deceased. The executor was the deceased's mother and therefore the alleged grandmother of the child.

In some cases, it is not altogether clear whether or not an item of real **9–18** evidence need be physically produced in court, even though its existence will be referred to in evidence, and will be crucial to the case. There are, for example, practical problems in the case of very large, fixed or perishable items, and this whole issue is examined more thoroughly in paragraphs 9.56–9.68 *infra*, when investigating aspects of what is known as the "best evidence rule."

When real evidence is produced in court, it must be formally lodged as **9–19** a "production" by whichever party is relying upon it. It must be spoken to by at least one witness (or be covered by a joint minute of the parties) in order to make it available as evidence, unless by statute there is no requirement to call such a witness.[18]

Confusion may arise when real evidence takes the form of a document, **9–20** since any document which is adduced for its content falls into a separate class of evidence known as "documentary" evidence. It is only when the document in question has relevance simply because of its very existence that it remains an item of "real" evidence. For example, a document which forms the very basis of the charges because it has been stolen, or forged.

DOCUMENTARY EVIDENCE

"Documentary" evidence may be defined as, "any written or printed matter **9–21** expressed in words and also drawings, plans and maps."[19] In practice, many mechanical recordings are now accepted as evidence of their contents, and since this is precisely the function of documentary evidence, the supposed distinction between real and documentary evidence may be largely academic.[20] However, where a document is adduced in evidence under a statutory provision operating as an exception to the hearsay rule,[21] the distinction is still necessary.

---

[18] For example, *per* s. 16(1) of the Road Traffic Offenders Act 1988, in the case of a certificate relating to a blood or urine sample taken in the course of a drink-driving investigation. This is, though, subject to the provisions of ss. 281–284 of the Criminal Procedure (Scotland) Act 1995 dealt with in paras. 7.64–7.65 *supra*. On the requirement for a witness to speak to a production before it becomes evidence, see *Hamilton* v. *H.M.A.*, 1980 J.C. 66. The jury may not necessarily insist on taking a production into the jury room with them, see *Hamilton* v. *H.M.A.; Sandells* v. *H.M.A., supra*, and *McMurdo* v. *H.M.A.*, 1987 S.C.C.R. 343.

[19] Wilkinson, *The Scottish Law of Evidence*, p. 7. Under s. 9 of the Civil Evidence (Scotland) Act 1988, and for the purposes of that Act, "document" is defined so as to include, in addition to the items listed above, photographs, discs, tapes and films.

[20] In *Carmichael* v. *Ashrif*, 1985 S.C.C.R. 461, the sheriff was clearly of the opinion that a video tape could be equated to a document such as a book or magazine.

[21] Dealt with in Chap. 8 *supra*.

9–22   An early definition of documentary evidence was provided by Lord McLaren in *Jacobs* v. *Hart*,[22] who ruled that before a writing might come within the definition of "documentary" evidence, there must be some fact within it which the contents tend to prove. As his Lordship put it: "Is it necessary that the judge should read the contents of the writing produced, or is it only shown to the witness for the purposes of identification?"

9–23   In the latter case, the writing or paper, as explained in paragraph 9.20 *supra*, will be classified as a production only, but when it is relied on or referred to for its terms, it must either be incorporated in the pleadings or "noted" by the court during the course of the trial. This is so that, in the event of any appeal, the appeal court is able to assess all the evidence on which the first instance judgment was based.[23]

9–24   There are also situations in which the presentation of evidence in documentary form creates special problems, for which special rules of evidence are required. The majority of these have been encountered in previous chapters and can be summarised as follows:

9–25   (i) As explained in paragraph 9.20 *supra*, on occasions a document may constitute "real" evidence, as for example when it is stolen property, or when it constitutes an alleged forgery. It is only when its importance arises from something which is contained in it that it constitutes "documentary" evidence in the true sense.

9–26   (ii) Sometimes only a copy of an original document now remains, and the court is invited to consider the evidence which may be gleaned from that copy under the "best evidence rule." This is considered in paragraphs 9.56–9.68 *infra*, and it will be seen that on occasions it is necessary for the party seeking to rely on the document to "prove the tenor" of the original.

9–27   (iii) Some forms of documentary evidence fall within categories which may be "judicially noted." These were considered in Chapter 4, and include Acts of Parliament (paragraph 4.20) and statutory instruments (paragraphs 4.21–4.29).

9–28   (iv) Some documents, or copies thereof, are admissible as evidence of their contents as an exception to the hearsay rule (see Chapter 8, *supra*). If not, then they are only evidence of their own existence, or the terms upon which the parties reached an agreement, and nothing else. In some limited circumstances, they may also be used to discredit a witness by demonstrating the inconsistency of his or her evidence, although they never become evidence in their own right (see paragraphs 10.74–10.87 *infra*).

9–29   (v) When the document in question takes the form of a record of a previous conviction, or a finding of adultery in a previous case, it may be used in a later case without need for further proof (see Chapter 5 *supra*). If

---

[22] (1900) 3 Adam 131 at p. 140.
[23] Lord MacLaren in *Ogilvy* v. *Mitchell* (1903) 4 Adam 237 at p. 245. For the suggested best procedure in a criminal case, see Renton and Brown, *Criminal Procedure*, para. 14–75.

not, then it is not admissible *in causa* in the case itself, but a previous conviction may be used in considering sentence in a criminal case.

Regardless of the purpose for which a document is to be used, there are **9–30** two general aspects of the law relating to private documents which remain to be considered.

PROVING PRIVATE DOCUMENTS

Private documents may be defined as those which are not maintained or **9–31** compiled for public or official purposes, but which are used in support of a private action between two parties (*e.g.* because they prove the existence of an obligation or because they suggest the existence of a defence or counterclaim).

The Requirements of Writing (Scotland) Act 1995 which came into force **9–32** on August 1, 1995 made radical changes to the law relating to the authentication of deeds.[24] Authentication is the process of prescribing the formalities of execution of documents. The Act provides for a new type of "self-proving" status.

For the purposes of the law of evidence a document can have "self- **9–33** proving" status and be valid if the statutory requirements of subscription have been complied with.[25] Provided a document is subscribed by the grantor, signed by one witness and contains details of the witness's name and address, it will have self-proving status. Writing is required for the effective constitution of certain types of contracts: *i.e.* those relating to heritage, wills, gratuitous unilateral obligations (except where undertaken in the course of a business), and trusts (where the trustor is the sole trustee).[26] Even if the statutory requirements for subscription are not met, then in some cases it may be possible to apply to the court under section 4 for certification of self-proving status.

A document which is not self-proving in terms of the Act or which has **9–34** not been certified as such by a court, may be proved to be authentic by means of any competent evidence as is both available and acceptable to the court. Such evidence may well be that of the person who made the document,[27] or someone who saw it being compiled. Equally, a document which is not self-proving may be challenged as to its authenticity by any admissible means available to the party challenging it, and it is not necessary to do so by means of an action of reduction.

---

[24] See Rennie and Cuisine, *The Requirements of Writing (Scotland) Act 1995.*
[25] Section 2.
[26] Section 1.
[27] *i.e.* compiled it, but not necessarily as the person in possession of the facts recorded in it.

9–35   Section 11(1) of the Requirements of Writing (Scotland) Act 1995 abolished the previous rule of evidence that in relation to certain types of contract, (loans of a limited amount, obligations of relief and innominate and unusual contracts) proof was restricted to the writ or oath of the defender. Such contracts may now be proved by any competent and admissible means.

CHALLENGING THE TERMS OF A PRIVATE DOCUMENT

9–36   As indicated in paragraphs 9.21–9.30 *supra*, when two parties have chosen to record the terms of an agreement in writing, it is regarded as the best possible evidence of what they agreed. In consequence it is not normally open to either of them, at some later date, to adduce any evidence[28] which will have the effect of varying, adding to or contradicting the clear written terms of that agreement. Often referred to as the "parole evidence rule",[29] its rationale was explained thus in the leading case of *Inglis* v. *Buttery*[30]:

> "Where parties agree to embody and do actually embody their contract in a formal written deed, then in determining what the contract really was and really meant, the court must look to the formal deed and to that deed alone. This is only carrying out the will of the party."

9–37   A previous agreement may, of course, be cancelled by a later one which is expressed to have such an effect or which is so regarded in law,[31] but otherwise the general rule is that once completed, a written agreement stands alone on its own terms.

9–38   To this general rule there is a long list of recognised exceptions, which are best considered in other works dedicated to the substantive law.[32] The following are among the best known.

(1) **Evidence to show that the document is not valid**

9–39   It is permissible to prove, by other evidence, that the document is not the valid record which it purports to be. Into this category come allegations that it was obtained by improper execution, fraud, essential error and fear, etc.[33]

---

[28] Even written evidence.
[29] See *e.g.* Walker and Walker, *op. cit.*, n. 3, para. 242.
[30] (1818) 5 R. (H.L.) 87 at p. 102.
[31] *e.g.* "novation" in the law of contract, and the superseding of missives by the formal disposition itself: see *Lee* v. *Alexander* (1883) 10 R.(H.L.) 91 at p. 96.
[32] *e.g.* Gloag and Henderson, *Introduction to the Law of Scotland,* Chap. 6. See also Walker and Walker, *op. cit.*, n. 3, paras. 256 *et seq*.
[33] See Gloag, *Contract*, p. 365, and *Stewart* v. *Kennedy* (1890) 17 R.(H.L.) 25.

(2) **Evidence to show that the document is not operative**

The question may be raised as to whether or not a document has become **9–40** operative (*e.g.* whether or not a prior condition has been purified[34]) or ceased to be operative (*e.g.* because its objective has been exhausted, or rendered impossible) and evidence is admissible on either point, unless it would contradict the document in question.

(3) **Evidence to show that the document does not reflect the parties intentions**

In *Hotson* v. *Paul*,[35] an action over a bond, extrinsic evidence was **9–41** admitted to show that the bond did not record the correct amount advanced, even though the parties could not agree as to what the correct amount was. Similarly, where a pure clerical error has led to the parties' agreement not being correctly recorded, parole evidence can be led to show what the parties had really agreed.[36]

(4) **Evidence to supplement a silent point in a document**

In some cases, extrinsic evidence may be admitted to supplement a **9–42** document on some point which has been left silent. This has been permitted, for example, in cases in which a collateral agreement exists separate from the main one. This situation occurs quite often in the context of missives and the sale of heritage. Provided the collateral agreement is clear and distinct from the main agreement, evidence will be permitted of its existence.[37]

Similar exceptions apply in relation to extrinsic evidence which assists **9–43** in the interpretation of a document, upon which the document itself is silent,[38] or which establishes whether the grantee of a deed was acting in a personal or a representative capacity.[39] Customs of trade may also be proved, where they were intended to apply and are not inconsistent with the document.[40]

(5) **Evidence to clarify a latent ambiguity**

The clear terms of a contract or other agreement will be enforced by the **9–44** courts, even though they may contain an obvious ("patent") ambiguity, such

---

[34] *e.g. Abraham* v. *Miller*, 1933 S.C. 171.
[35] (1831) 9 S. 685.
[36] *Krupp* v. *Menzies*, 1907 S.C. 903.
[37] *See Jamieson* v. *Welsh*, 1900 3F. 176; *Winston* v. *Patrick*, 1980 S.C. 246; and *Porch* v. *MacLeod*, 1992 S.L.T. 661.
[38] See, *e.g. Renison* v. *Bryce* (1898) 25 R. 421.
[39] See, *e.g. Laird* v. *Laird and Rutherford* (1884) 12 R. 294.
[40] See *Tancred Arrol* v. *Steel Co. of Scotland* (1890) 17 R. (H.L.) also referred to in para. 16.21 *infra*.

ambiguity being resolved wherever possible by reference to the rest of the document. Where, however, the ambiguity is "latent" (*i.e.* it does not appear manifest from the wording of the document, but only comes to light when the parties attempt to implement it), then extrinsic evidence will be permitted in an effort to resolve the conflict.[41] There is also case authority for the suggestion that the distinction is not always maintained, and that even patent ambiguities may be resolved by recourse to extrinsic evidence.[42]

(6) Incorporation of other writings

9–45 On occasions, a document may indicate, expressly or by implication, that other documents or writings are meant to be read in association with it, in which case evidence may be admitted of those other documents. For example, a contract of employment may specifically refer to a pension scheme to which an employee will be subject, details of which are available in another document, while a testator may incorporate further instructions given to his executors in a separate paper into the body of the will.[43]

DIRECT AND CIRCUMSTANTIAL EVIDENCE

THE DISTINCTION DEFINED

9–46 "Direct" evidence may be defined as evidence which leads directly to proof of a fact or facts in issue (*facta probanda*), while "circumstantial" evidence is evidence which proves an "evidential" fact on the way to proving a fact in issue. As Walker and Walker put it,[44] circumstantial evidence is "indirect evidence of a fact in issue." Thus, for example the evidence of W to the effect that he saw A hit B is, in an assault case, direct evidence of that assault. On the other hand, W's statement to the effect that he saw A running away from the scene of the assault on B is circumstantial evidence that A committed the assault, in that it proves a fact which itself tends to suggest another fact, which is the fact in issue (*i.e.* the assault). W's statement that he saw A running amounts to indirect evidence of the assault.

9–47 Circumstantial evidence has played a prominent role in several of the civil cases already examined. In *Stewart* v. *Glasgow Corporation*,[45] the pursuer wanted to prove that a clothes pole in a council drying green was known by the landlords to be in a dangerously corroded state at the time of a fatal accident. Evidence was led to show that it must have been in a poor

---

[41] See, *e.g. Cathcart's Trs.* v. *Bruce*, 1923 S.L.T. 722; *McDonald* v. *Newall* (1898) I F. 68; and *Naismith's Trs.* v. *N.S.P.C.C.*, 1914 S.C. 76.

[42] See *e.g. Robertson's Trs.* v. *Riddell*, 1911 S.C. 14.

[43] *Inglis* v. *Harper* (1831) 5 W. and S. 785.

[44] *op. cit.*, n. 3, para. 8.

[45] 1958 S.C. 28, considered in para. 6.20 *supra*.

state five months previously, when it was inspected and painted. Such evidence was circumstantial only. In *Bark* v. *Scott*,[46] the court held that in assessing a driver's capability at a given time, it was competent to consider how the vehicle was being driven shortly before, and shortly after, that time.

One striking example of circumstantial evidence leading to a conviction **9–48** in a criminal case was the behaviour of the police dog in *Patterson* v. *Nixon*.[47] Also, the remarkable set of evidential facts tending to prove the accused's complicity in a robbery in *Norval* v. *H.M.A.*,[48] which Lord Emslie described as "a chain of circumstantial evidence." Evidence of handwriting, fingerprints and dental impressions is also, of course, circumstantial in identifying the accused as the culprit in a criminal trial, as explained in paragraphs 7.25–7.47 *supra*. As such it can be powerful evidence requiring little corroboration.

The analogy of circumstantial evidence giving rise to a "chain" of relevant **9–49** facts is no longer regarded as a valid one, since a chain is no stronger than its weakest link. Or, as described in the case of *R* v. *Exall*, "It is more like the case of a rope comprised of several cords. One strand of the cord might be insufficient to sustain the weight, but three stranded together may be of quite sufficient strength."[49]

Circumstantial evidence can be adduced by either party, and the court **9–50** can be left to establish the truth from nothing but a string of items of circumstantial evidence, some more compelling than others. For example, the Crown in a criminal case may possess several items of circumstantial evidence which point strongly towards the guilt of the accused. In contrast, the accused may have only one such item, an alibi, which, if believed, is enough to negative all the items relied on by the prosecution. As Walker and Walker explain[50]: "Even if the accused's fingerprints are found in the premises which have been broken into, the jemmy used was his, and the stolen goods were found hidden in his bedroom, he must be acquitted of the theft if he was in prison when it occurred."

Evidence of character and of previous convictions, where admissible, **9–51** are also examples of circumstantial evidence, in that they have a bearing on the credibility as a witness of the person to whom they refer. These are considered in Chapter 12, but it may be noted at this stage that such evidence is often excluded on the grounds of public policy, because of its tendency

---

[46] 1954 S.C. 72, considered in para. 1.10 *supra*.
[47] 1960 J.C. 42, considered in para. 7.13 *supra*, and also, of course, an example of an unusual form of "real" evidence: see 9.06–9.20 *supra*.
[48] 1978 J.C. 70.
[49] (1866) 4F. and F. 922 at p. 929, *per* Pollock CB.
[50] *op. cit.*, n. 3, para. 9(a).

to be disproportionately prejudicial,[51] or because it raises an issue which is not sufficiently relevant to the matter in hand.[52]

PRIMARY AND SECONDARY EVIDENCE

THE DISTINCTION DEFINED

9–52   "Primary" evidence is, purely and simply, the best form of evidence which one can find in favour of a particular fact or issue, while "secondary" evidence is, by definition, something less than the best. Thus, the best evidence that A hit B comes from B, and anyone else who happened to witness the assault, while evidence given by X to the effect that B told him what had happened is clearly not the best evidence that one can produce, and will in fact normally be rejected under the hearsay rule.[53]

9–53   Similarly, when A sues B, alleging that he possesses certain rights against B under a contract, then the best evidence in support of that claim is the original of that contract, and not a copy. Once again, where it is alleged that X stole various items from a supermarket, the original items form the primary, or best, evidence, while a photograph of them is inevitably second-best.

9–54   The distinction arises from the "best evidence" rule. The application of this rule has become less rigid in recent years as it has given way to the sort of guiding principles restated by the Scottish Law Commission as expressed in their *Report on Hearsay Evidence in Criminal Proceedings.*[54] Broadly, these were that rules of evidence should aim to achieve reasonable expedition and a reasonable degree of certainty, while avoiding needless expense. The Commission noted that the best evidence rule was rarely applied today.[55] Nonetheless, the rule still has some significance and many other rules of evidence have originated from it.

9–55   For example, the hearsay rule, with all its exceptions, and the general requirement that where the best available evidence is not led, a good explanation is normally required. There is also the more specific rule that in the case of a document which is relied upon as establishing a right of one party against the other, then only the original will do, unless the party relying upon it can "prove the tenor" of it in a separate action. The hearsay rule was considered in its own right in Chapter 8, but the remaining applications of

---

[51]   When it concerns the character or previous convictions of an accused.

[52]   In the case of a witness who is not a party to the proceedings.

[53]   Considered in Chap. 8. *N.B.* that some of the exceptions to the rule (*e.g.* dying declarations and entries in business documents) themselves reflect the fact that in the circumstances, they are the best evidence which the courts can hope for.

[54]   Report No. 149 published in February 1995 paras. 2.26–2.31.

[55]   At para. 3.5.

the best evidence rule in civil and criminal cases are examined below in more detail.

BEST EVIDENCE RULE IN CIVIL CASES

As we saw earlier in *Stewart* v. *Glasgow Corporation,*[56] a crucial issue in the case was the allegedly corroded condition of a clothes pole in a local authority drying green. Several times during the proof, pointed reference was made to the fact that the pole itself was not produced, most notably when the court rejected the evidence of an "expert" witness who had not even examined the pole, but relied upon the verbal description given by another expert who had examined the pole.[57]   **9–56**

Similarly, in *McGowan* v. *Belling & Co*[58] a claim for injuries sustained in a house fire hinged upon the allegedly defective state of an electric fire, which was never made available at any time after the fire. An attempt to adduce expert evidence based on an examination of an appliance allegedly identical to the one involved in the accident, which itself was not lodged as a production, was rejected on the ground that since it was essential to know if the two appliances were identical,[59] the best evidence rule required the production of at least the appliance which had been examined.   **9–57**

In all such cases, clearly it is for the court to assess how much the failure to adduce potential evidence detracts from the overall case of the party who should have adduced it.   **9–58**

The clearest application of the best evidence rule in civil cases is the rule that when a document is fundamental to a claim being made by one of the parties,[60] then the original[60a] of that document must be produced. If the original cannot be produced then the problem can only be overcome if the parties accept a copy of the original. This acceptance should be incorporated into a joint minute by the parties or there requires to be an admission on record to the effect that a document quoted *ad longum* in the averments is genuine.   **9–59**

The absence of such an original is fatal to the party seeking to establish the point evidenced by the document, (if a joint minute or an admission   **9–60**

---

[56] 1958 S.C. 28, considered in para. 6.20 *supra.*
[57] Whose evidence was uncorroborated on this crucial point and therefore rejected.
[58] 1983 S.L.T. 77.
[59] The court apparently being prepared to consider it reasonable for the offending fire not to have been produced.
[60] And does not belong to a class of documents, an extract of which is deemed by statute to be the equivalent of its original (*e.g.* extracts of birth, death and marriage, for which see paras. 8.57–8.61 *infra*). For the consequences of failing to produce the best evidence see *Inverclyde District Council v. Carsewell,* 1987 S.C.L.R. 145.
[60a] Or an authenticated copy of the original, in terms of s. 6 of the Civil Evidence (Scotland) Act 1988. See *McIlveney* v. *Donald,* 1995 S.C.L.R. 802.

cannot be secured), unless the party can prove the contents of the document by means of an action of "proving the tenor" of it, or unless the document was lost or destroyed while in the hands of the other party.[61]

9–61   When the missing document does not constitute the foundation of a party's claim (but is, for example, simply an adminicle of evidence of it), then it is the normal practice for secondary evidence of its terms to be admitted in proof. This is only so if the absence of the document is satisfactorily explained, or if it is in the custody of some person beyond the jurisdiction of the court who refuses to give it up. Whether or not a party will succeed in adducing such secondary evidence will, of course, depend upon the circumstances of the case.[62]

BEST EVIDENCE RULE IN CRIMINAL CASES

9–62   In criminal cases, the best evidence rule operates as the general principle that any production relied on by the Crown must be lodged in court if its absence would be prejudicial to the accused. However, where no such prejudice would arise, and where production would be totally impracticable, then the court may dispense with it.

9–63   The rule was considered in *Hughes* v. *Skeen*,[63] in which H was charged with the theft of 78 newspapers from a consignment of 102 which had been left for collection in a common close. The newspapers themselves were not produced in court, and on appeal against conviction the defence alleged that although H had not been prejudiced by the non-production of the newspapers, the best evidence rule required that they be produced unless to do so was impracticable.

9–64   In rejecting the appeal on the grounds that in the circumstances it was impracticable to produce the papers, and that to have done so would have served no useful purpose anyway, the High Court stated[64] that:

> "it is perfectly true that in a criminal trial the best evidence rule applies to the extent that where it is both convenient and practicable, productions which are referred to, or to be referred to, must be produced or an adequate explanation furnished for their non-production."

---

[61] For modern examples of the continuing applicability of this rule, see *Scottish & Universal Newspapers Ltd.* v. *Gherson's Trs.*, 1988 S.L.T. 109; *Crichton* v. *Wood*, 1981 S.L.T. (Notes) 66; and *Inverclyde D.C.* v. *Carswell* (Sh.Ct.), 1987 S.C.L.R. 145.

[62] See, *e.g. Elliot* v. *Galpern*, 1927 S.C. 29; *Young* v. *Thomson*, 1909 S.C. 529; and *Ritchie* v. *Ritchie* (1857) 19 D. 505.

[63] 1980 S.L.T. (Notes) 13. See also *McLeod* v. *Woodmuir Miners Welfare Society Social Club*, 1961 J.C. 5, and *MacIver* v. *Mackenzie*, 1942 J.C. 51.

[64] *ibid.*.

One of the most common reasons for not lodging potential productions **9–65** is the fact that they are perishable. In *Anderson* v. *Laverock*,[65] salmon seized from the accused were destroyed prior to the trial. In such circumstances, the accused should at least be given the opportunity to examine the items where their condition is crucial to the case.

In *Kelly* v. *Allan*,[66] the issue of "material prejudice" to the accused from **9–66** the failure to produce an item central to the case arose in the context of a stolen vehicle. Whereas it is normal practice not to produce motor cars which are allegedly stolen,[67] in the present case the charge was reset of a motorcycle which, despite missing registration plates, frame and engine numbers, was nevertheless identified by the true owner to the police. K did not deny being in possession of the cycle, and did not challenge police witness descriptions of its condition when found in his possession. He did not deny that it belonged to the true owner. The Crown did not produce the motorcycle at the trial, and they did not even produce photographs. An appeal against conviction was rejected on the grounds that in the circumstances, the failure caused no "such material prejudice as to lead to the conclusion that his conviction represented a miscarriage of justice."

An application of the best evidence rule, in relation to original documents, **9–67** arose in an interesting context in *Nocher* v. *Smith*,[68] a case involving illegal possession of drugs found during a police raid under a search warrant. The warrant itself was not produced at the trial, although it had been shown to N before the search took place, and the defence argued that since the whole of the evidence subsequently discovered depended for its legality on the validity of the warrant, and since the best evidence of a document is the document itself, the absence of the warrant among the Crown productions was fatal to any conviction. In rejecting this argument the High Court gave the opinion[69] that:

---

[65] 1976 J.C. 9. See also *Miln* v. *Maher*, 1979 S.L.T. (Notes) 10 (deer carcase in a case in which the cause of death of the deer was crucial). Note also the standard practice in any homicide case of offering the defence the opportunity to be represented at a post-mortem examination before the body is released for burial.

[66] 1984 S.C.C.R. 186. For another recent case in which lack of material prejudice to the accused seems to have been regarded as the main test of whether or not failure to lodge a production was fatal, see *Tudhope* v. *Stewart*, 1986 S.L.T. 659.

[67] And sometimes not even parts of cars—see *Morrison* v. *Mackenzie*, 1990 G.W.D. 4–174, where tyres alleged to be defective in a prosecution under the Road Vehicles (Construction and Use) Regulations 1986 were not produced in court. The appeal court upheld the sheriff's view that it would be inconvenient for the Crown to have to produce the tyres. For a commentary on this and best evidence in criminal cases, see Nicol, "Best Evidence in Criminal Cases", 1990 S.L.T. (News) 149.

[68] 1978 S.L.T. (Notes) 32.

[69] *ibid.*, relying on the principle that even if evidence is illegally obtained, it may still be admissible: see Chap. 15 *infra*.

"We are in no doubt that in a case of this nature it is desirable that the warrant should be produced, but that does not necessarily mean that its non-production here was per se fatal to the acceptance of the evidence of the police officers as to what they found as a result of the search."

9–68 The distinction between primary and secondary evidence, and the suggestion that the best evidence rule renders the latter inadmissible, continues to appear in a variety of contexts in criminal cases.[70]

---

[70] See, *e.g. Hamilton* v. *H.M.A.*, 1980 J.C. 66 (written confession); *H.M.A.* v. *Dennison*, 1978 S.L.T. (Notes) 79 (fingerprint "lifts"); *Hamilton* v. *Grant*, 1984 S.C.C.R. 263 (photographs of fingerprints); *H.M.A.* v. *Swift*, 1983 S.C.C.R. 204 (tape-recording of confession); and *McLeod* v. *Fraser*, 1987 S.C.C.R. 294 (computer printout of blood/alcohol reading).

CHAPTER 10

THE COURSE OF A TRIAL OR PROOF

INTRODUCTION

The remaining chapters of this book are concerned with the process by **10–01** which evidence is led. Although this is a book on evidence, the rules of procedure determine how evidence is led and some account must be given of these rules. It is intended to provide an outline only of the rules of procedure. For more detailed analysis reference should be made to specific texts on civil and criminal procedure.

THE ORDER OF TRIAL AND PROOF

(1) **Criminal trials**

The rules of evidence have to be applied in the separate contexts of **10–02** solemn and summary procedure. The distinctive features of these two contexts which have consequences for the evidential rules arise from the presence of a jury in solemn procedure, and from the duty placed upon the presiding judge or sheriff to ensure fairness. The actual order in which the evidence is heard is the same in both types of case, and begins when the Crown call their first witness.[1] Unlike the system in England and Wales, there are no opening speeches by either the prosecution or the defence.[2]

In virtually all criminal trials, since the persuasive burden of proof[3] is on **10–03** the prosecution, it is the prosecution which leads its witnesses first. Each witness for the Crown[4] will first of all be examined "in chief" by the prosecutor (paragraphs 10.20–10.22 *infra*), after which the witness is available for "cross-examination" by the defence (see paragraphs 10.53– 10.65 *infra*). Before leaving the witness box, it is also possible that the

---

[1] *N.B.* that whereas, in a summary case, the swearing in of the first witness is officially the "commencement of the trial"; in solemn procedure the trial commences when the jury is sworn in: see Renton and Brown, *Criminal Procedure*, para. 14.47.
[2] The Thomson Committee (Cmnd. 6218), para.41, were against their introduction into Scots criminal procedure.
[3] For which see paras. 2.06–2.14 *supra*.
[4] Called in such order as the Crown may choose: see Macphail *Evidence*, Chap. 8.16.

witness may be "re-examined" by the Crown (see paragraphs 10.106–10.109 *infra*) in those cases in which this is permitted.

10–04 After leading all the witnesses, but before closing the Crown case, the procurator fiscal or advocate depute will place before the court any record of judicial examination of the accused[5] and any joint minute or statements of facts agreed with the defence (for which see paragraphs 6.47–6.53 *supra*), and will have ensured that any productions relied upon by the Crown which are not admissible in their own right have been spoken to by at least one witness (see paragraphs 9.06–9.20 *supra*).

10–05 Once the Crown has closed its case, it is the turn of the defence to call its witnesses, beginning always with the accused if he or she is to give evidence. The roles are then reversed, with the defence agent examining the witnesses in chief, and the Crown subjecting them to cross-examination, the defence having the right to re-examine where appropriate. Defence productions will also, where relevant, be spoken to by defence witnesses, although they can be admitted by means of being put to a prosecution witness during cross-examination.[6]

10–06 Once the defence has intimated that it has led its last witness, and has no further evidence to offer the court, the normal procedure is for the Crown to sum up its case, leaving the defence with the traditional "last word" by way of defence summary. In solemn trials, the final word comes from the presiding judge or sheriff, who in the "charge" to the jury summarises the law and the available evidence before the jury retires to reach a verdict. In both types of case, it is possible that either side may endeavour to place additional evidence before the court after the formal close of its case, or may wish a witness to be recalled after having left the witness-box. These possibilities are considered in paragraphs 10.110–10.141 *infra*.

(2) Civil proofs

10–07 In a civil proof, the order of leading evidence is little different from that described above. The terms "pursuer" and "defender" should be substituted for "Crown" and "defence" respectively. In a civil case, it is the general rule that the party bearing the "ultimate burden" is the one who must lead evidence first. This will normally be the pursuer. Most civil cases are heard before a single judge. In some cases there is a civil proof before a jury of twelve. In a civil jury trial it is the normal practice for counsel for each party to address the jury in general terms concerning what it is hoped to prove before calling witnesses,[7] but otherwise the procedure is as described for criminal cases, with each party examining the witnesses in chief, having them cross-examined, and then re-examining them where appropriate.

---

[5] For which see Renton and Brown, *op. cit.*, n. 1, para. 5.54.

[6] See, *e.g. Hogg* v. *Clark*, 1959 J.C. 7.

[7] See Wilkinson, *Scottish Law of Evidence*, p. 157.

(3) **Judicial questioning**

It is also possible, at any stage of either a criminal trial or a civil proof, **10–08** that the judge or sheriff will wish to ask questions of his or her own, either to clarify a matter which remains obscure, or perhaps to open up another line of inquiry which seems pertinent. Little formal objection is likely to be raised to such a course in a summary criminal trial, or during a civil proof without a jury, but where the judge or sheriff is sitting with a jury, the greatest tact and impartiality must be observed if an appeal is to be averted. Opportunity should also be offered to the parties to cross-examine on any new points raised by such questions from the bench.[8]

OBJECTIONS TO EVIDENCE

At any stage of a trial or proof, the apparently smooth flow of examination, **10–09** cross-examination, etc., may be halted by an objection by one of the parties to a question being asked of the witness, or to an entire line of questioning which is being embarked upon. Two questions then arise under the law of evidence. First, can a party who does not object immediately, be said to have impliedly accepted the admission of that evidence. Second, must a trial judge make a decision there and then about admissibility or can evidence be allowed in "under reservation" of the question of its admissibility.

(1) **Implied acceptance by silence**

(a) *Criminal cases*

In summary criminal cases, the position is largely governed by section **10–10** 192(3) of the Criminal Procedure (Scotland) Act 1995,[9] which states that in a case in which the accused is legally represented, no appeal may be based on the admission or rejection by the sheriff of an item of evidence unless the appropriate objection "shall have been timeously stated at the trial by the Solicitor for the accused." The High Court in *Skeen* v. *Murphy*[10] stated

---

8 See, *e.g. McLeod* v. *H.M.A.*, 1939 J.C. 68; *Lavery* v. *H.M.A.*, 1979 S.L.T. (Notes) 4; *Livingstone* v. *H.M.A.* (Court of Criminal Appeal March 22, 1974), reported in *Tallis* v. *H.M.A.*, 1982 S.C.C.R. 91 in Sheriff Gordon's commentary, and *Nisbet* v. *H.M.A.*, 1979 S.L.T. (Notes) 5. For an example of the same principle in action in a civil case, see *McCallum* v. *Paterson*, 1969 S.C. 85. For the policy to be followed in summary criminal cases, see *Elliot* v. *Tudhope*, 1987 S.C.C.R. 85, and for an example of "unjustified" interference in such a case, see *Cooney* v. *H.M.A.*, 1987 S.C.C.R. 60.

9 Previously, s. 454(1) of the 1975 Act.

10 1978 S.L.T. (Notes) 2. *N.B.* that this was a Crown appeal in which the High Court held that the defence failure to object to the late service of the analyst's certificate, etc., at the time it was tendered in a drink driving case meant that they could not object subsequently. The section clearly covers appeals against acquittal as well as conviction. See also *Tudhope* v. *Stewart*, 1986 S.L.T. 659.

the rationale of this rule to be that: "unless objection to the ... admission of evidence is timeously taken, it cannot be subsequently taken, and, if not, such evidence becomes part of the evidence *in causa*." However, it is to be doubted whether even this clear statutory provision can be used to justify the admission of evidence which is *per se* incompetent.[11]

10–11   There is no equivalent of section 192(3) in solemn cases. However, there are frequent successful appeals against conviction which arise from a decision by a presiding judge or sheriff to admit evidence which is inadmissible, even in the absence of defence objections.[12] These indicate that whether the defence object at the time or not, the wrongful admission of some items of evidence may be fatal to a conviction. A failure to object does not necessarily preclude an accused from using the admission of such evidence as a ground of appeal.[13]

10–12   In summary proceedings, when either party requests it, objections to the admission of evidence must be noted in the record in terms of section 157 of the Criminal Procedure (Scotland) Act 1995. An equivalent rule for solemn cases requires in terms of section 93 that such objections be noted in the shorthand record, though in practice most judicial proceedings are now taped.

(b) *Civil cases*

10–13   In summarising the position in 1987, Sheriff Macphail[14] observed that:

> "It is ... thought that the rule now generally observed in practice in the courts in Scotland ... is that a pursuer may not found on a ground of liability which has not been averred although it may have been the subject of evidence to which no timeous objection has been taken."

---

[11] See Walker and Walker, *Law of Evidence in Scotland*, para. 340, who were of the opinion that this was not possible despite the existence of a similar rule under the Act then in force as the predecessor to the 1975 Act. See also *Handley* v. *Pirie*, 1976 J.C. 65; *McLeary* v. *Douglas*, 1978 J.C. 57; and *Robertson* v. *Aitchison* 1981 S.C.C.R. 149. See also Renton and Brown, *op. cit.*, n. 1, paras. 14–77 and 16–12, and Macphail, *op. cit.*, n. 4, Chap. 8.40.

[12] See Renton and Brown, *op. cit.*, n. 1, paras. 11–36 and 18–03.

[13] But see *McAvoy* v. *H.M.A.*, 1982 S.C.C.R. 263, in which the failure by the defence to object timeously to the admission of a statement by a witness which revealed that A had a criminal record was taken into account as part of the circumstances surrounding the case, but the appeal finding was that, overall, there had been no "miscarriage of justice". Sheriff Gordon, commenting at p. 275, pointed out that: "it is not safe for counsel or solicitor to 'sit back and wait for the Crown to make a mistake' as the professional lore used to have it." In other words, even in solemn cases objections should be made timeously.

[14] *op. cit.*, n. 4, Chap. 8.40.

He was, however, also obliged to concede that, in certain other cases,[15] the failure of the other party to object timeously to the admission of evidence which opened up matters not on record, was held to have the effect of admitting it. The position is still not resolved.

In all civil cases the challenging party is well advised to object to the **10-14** evidence in question as soon as it is sought to admit it.[16]

(2) **Evidence heard "under reservation as to its admissibility"**

(a) *Criminal cases*

In summary cases, it is now well established that the better practice, **10-15** where possible, is for the sheriff to admit the evidence *ab initio*, but to reserve the question of admissibility until the end of the trial.[17]

In solemn cases the position almost certainly is,[18] if only by analogy **10-16** with civil jury trials, that questions of admissibility should be dealt with as soon as they are raised, and presumably outwith the hearing of the jury.[19] However, so far as concerns one of the most important of such issues which is likely to arise in practice—the question of the admissibility of a confession—the ruling in *Balloch* v. *H.M.A.*[20] would tend to suggest a movement towards letting the jury decide for themselves on what is now regarded as a question of fact rather than one of law.

(b) *Civil cases*

The general rule in civil cases heard without a jury now seems to be for **10-17** the judge or sheriff to allow the evidence in "under reservation" of the question of its admissibility, so that the issue may be debated later, and also in order that the evidence is on record for any subsequent appeal court to consider.[21]

---

[15] Notably *McGlone* v. *British Railways Board*, 1966 S.C. (H.L.) 1, and *O'Donnell* v. *Murdoch Mackenzie & Co.*, 1966 S.C. 58, 1967 S.C. (H.L.) 63. See also *Brown's Exr.* v. *North British Steel Foundry Ltd.*, 1967 S.L.T. (Notes) 111, and *Gibson* v. *B.I.C.C.*, 1973 S.L.T. 2, in which the House of Lords criticised the Scottish closed record system for its rigidity.

[16] See, *e.g. McDonald* v. *Duncan*, 1933 S.C. 737.

[17] *Clark* v. *Stuart*, 1950 J.C. 8 at p. 11. See also *Copeland* v. *Gillies*, 1973 S.L.T. 74. *Cardle* v. *Wilkinson*, 1982 S.C.C.R. 33 and *Aitchison* v. *Rizza*, 1985 S.C.C.R. 297.

[18] Although virtually no clear authority can be found for the proposition.

[19] For the system of "a trial within a trial", see paras. 14.40–14.44 *infra*.

[20] 1977 J.C. 23, dealt with more fully in paras. 14–39 *infra*.

[21] See, *McDonald* v. *Duncan*, *supra*, Wilkinson, *op. cit.*, n. 7, p. 165 and Walker and Walker, *op. cit.*, n. 11. But see also *McGowan* v. *Mein*, 1976 S.L.T. (Sh. Ct.) 29, for a case in which the sheriff saw good reason for departing from this practice.

10–18   A failure to follow such a practice will, of course, have the effect in some cases of depriving the court of evidence for all time, and can lead to a successful appeal.[22]

10–19   It is a different matter, however, when there is a jury, since there is then a risk that if a decision on admissibility is not made as soon as the point is raised, the jury will rely on the evidence thus admitted, and may not be swayed by any subsequent instruction by the presiding judge to ignore what they have heard. The appropriate procedure in such cases was stated in *McDonald* v. *Duncan*[23] to be that: "if an objection is taken to the admissibility of evidence, it is for the judge there and then to decide that question and not to hold it up until the conclusion of the whole proof, and then to give a pronouncement on it." This rule still applies in civil jury cases.[24]

EXAMINATION-IN-CHIEF

10–20   Examination-in-chief is the process whereby the counsel or solicitor for a party elicits from a witness called by that party evidence which it is believed will be favourable to that party's case. It should be noted though, that the Crown have a duty to elicit *all* evidence having a bearing on the case, and not just that which is apparently favourable to them.

10–21   This belief will be based on information provided by the witness at an earlier date, in the course of a "precognition". However, experience shows that for various reasons, witnesses do not always live up to their early promise, and the agent for the party calling them may, in varying degrees of desperation, attempt to encourage them to refresh their memories from notes taken at the time. Alternatively the agent may ask "leading questions" or put to the witness statements made by him or her on a previous occasion, or indeed deal with the witness as if he or she were a "hostile" witness called by the other party.

10–22   Each of these possibilities requires separate examination.

REFRESHING MEMORY

10–23   It is a cardinal principle of the law of evidence that a non-expert witness should, when giving oral testimony, be speaking from personal memory of something that witness experienced with one of his or her senses. It may therefore seem odd to suggest that witnesses be allowed to refresh their memory by reference to notes. Nevertheless, this has become the standard practice in many situations, and the only prerequisite would seem to be that

---

[22] As in *Baretdji* v. *Baretdji*, 1985 S.L.T. 126.

[23] *ibid.*, *per* Lord Anderson at p. 744. See also *McCallum* v. *Paterson*, 1969 S.C. 85.

[24] See Wilkinson, *op. cit.*, n. 7, p. 210.

the notes to which the witness refers must either have been made or dictated to someone else at, or shortly after, the time of the events to which they refer.[25]

There are two familiar examples of this process. First the police officers **10–24** in a criminal trial who refer to their notebooks in order to testify as to precisely what the accused said when cautioned and charged. Second, the doctors in the civil proof who refer to their notes in order to advise the court of the precise nature of the pursuer's injuries shortly after the accident. It would seem, however, that refreshment of memory is competent in any case in which the necessary conditions are satisfied.[26] The fact that witnesses have had recourse to such an *aide-mémoire* may, of course, affect the weight to be attached to their evidence.

The documents from which the witness refreshes his or her memory **10–25** "become part of the witness's oral testimony".[26a] In the words of Lord Justice-General Clyde in the leading case of *Hinshelwood* v. *Auld*[27] speaking of the witness who uses notes in order to refresh his memory:

> "If ... when he gives his evidence, he requires to look at the notes in order to enable him to give his account of what occurred, then the notes become part of his oral evidence. They are—so to speak—read into his oral testimony, as a material part of the foundation on which that testimony rests."

If a witness does rely on notes to refresh memory and give oral testimony **10–26** then the notes must be made available to the other party. As Lord Justice-General Clyde pointed out in *Hinshelwood*[28]: "In such a case considerations of fairness compel the production of the notes ... it is obvious that the cross-examiner becomes entitled, not only to see them, but to use them in cross-examination." He added the proviso that: "if the witness does not use his notes to refresh his memory in the witness-box, the notes possess no evidential quality whatever, and production of them cannot be compelled by the cross-examiner."

The type of note to which a witness may validly refer in the course of **10–27** oral testimony must serve simply to *refresh* memory, and may not be used as a total substitute for it. If the witness has no recollection of the events in question then he or she should not be giving oral testimony in the first place, since:

---

[25] See, *e.g.* Walker and Walker, *op. cit.,* n. 11, para. 341(b) and Wilkinson, *op. cit.*, n. 7, p. 162.

[26] *e.g.* the witness to a road accident who writes down the registration number of the offending vehicle, or the housebreaking victim who makes a list of what is missing.

[26a] Walker and Walker, *loc. cit.*

[27] 1926 J.C. 4, at pp. 7–8.

[28] *ibid.*, at p. 8. See also *Niven* v. *Hart* (1898) 25 R.(J.) 89.

> "It is essential to this kind of evidence ... that the witness have some recollection upon the matter to which the [note] refers; for if his memory is a total blank on it, the document is not made part of his deposition, but comes under the rules as to the admissibility and production of written evidence.[29]

10–28　　In cases in which the note is being used to refresh the witness's memory, and is considered part of the oral testimony, it is proper practice for it to be lodged as a production.[30]

10–29　　To summarise, a note used by a witness to refresh memory should be lodged as a production though it need not be in a form which would make it admissible *per se*. But a note which represents a witness's *only* recollection of events must be lodged to even have a chance of being considered admissible.[31]

LEADING QUESTIONS

10–30　A "leading" question is one which either suggests the desired answer, or takes for granted a crucial fact which has yet to be proved. For example, if in an assault charge the witness complainer is asked by the prosecutor, "He hit you, didn't he?", that would be an example of a leading question which suggests a desired answer. If, before the fact of the assault had been established by evidence, the same witness complainer is asked, "What did you do after he hit you?", that would be an example of a leading question which took for granted that a crucial fact had yet to be proved.

10–31　　The general rule is that, whereas leading questions are permissible when put to a witness in cross-examination,[32] they may not be asked of a "witness-in-chief" (*i.e.* a witness called by one's own party). In practice, however, it is acceptable for the agent calling a witness to "lead" him or her through the introductory part of the evidence (name, address, occupation, presence at the locus, etc.,) until the point is reached at which the evidence to be given by that witness is likely to be disputed by the other party. Exceptionally (and normally by prior agreement between the agents) a witness may be led through all, or a large portion of, the evidence, where it is uncontroversial and the parties have not arranged in advance for a joint minute[33] to cover it. A common example is the evidence of a police photographer "speaking to" photographs taken of the locus, or of a casualty doctor speaking to injuries sustained by a road accident victim.

---

[29] Dickson, *Evidence*, para. 1778. See also *McGowan* v. *Mein*, 1976 S.L.T. (Sh.Ct.) 29.
[30] See *Hinshelwood* v. *Auld*, *supra*, and Renton and Brown, *op. cit.*, n. 1, para. 14–75.
[31] *H.M.A.* v. *McPherson*, 2 Broun 450.
[32] For which see paras. 10.53–10.55 *infra*.
[33] For which see paras. 6.05–6.14 and 6.46–6.52 *supra*.

When a leading question is improperly put, it should be objected to, **10–32** although the damage will have been done if the witness has given the desired answer before objection is made. Walker and Walker[34] suggest that the form of the question and answer should be recorded, in order to assist an appeal court to assess the reliability of that evidence. Modern practice tends to leave the question of the weight to be attached to a witness's testimony firmly in the hands of the judge or sheriff at first instance, who may make allowances for the fact that the witness was "led".

PREVIOUS CONSISTENT STATEMENTS BY THE WITNESS

Because of the primacy of oral testimony, special rules have developed for **10–33** the admissibility of statements made by a witness before a civil proof or criminal trial. In civil cases, section 3 of the Civil Evidence (Scotland) Act 1988 provides that a previous statement made by a witness is admissible "in so far as it tends to reflect favourably or unfavourably on that person's credibility."[35] A previous or prior statement must be distinguished from a precognition which is never admissible. Section 9 of the Act defines "statement" so as to exclude a precognition.

In criminal cases, there is a general prohibition against the admissibility **10–34** of previous statements other than in specific exceptional circumstances.[36] The position varies depending on whether or not the prior statement is consistent with what the witness is now saying in the witness box. In both cases there is a recognition that evidence is always admissible of the fact that a statement was *made*, as opposed to evidence of the contents of that statement.

(1) Civil cases

(a) *To bolster the credibility of a witness*

The position with regard to previous statements in civil proceedings is **10–35** less strict than in criminal proceedings. Since the abolition of the hearsay rule in terms of section 2 of the Civil Evidence (Scotland) Act 1988, it is admissible to lead evidence of the *content* of a witness's prior statement. It had always been possible to lead evidence of the making of the statement. As indicated above, section 3 permits the use of previous statements both to support or attack a witness's credibility and to lead evidence of the contents

---

[34] *op. cit.,* n. 11, para. 339(b).

[35] This section adopted recommendations 16 and 17 of the Scottish Law Commission's Report, No. 100, published in 1986.

[36] Since, if related by the witness himself, it simply duplicates his present testimony, and if related by someone else, it is usually struck at by the hearsay rule, for which see Chap. 8 *supra.*

of the statement. As in criminal cases though, statements in precognitions remain inadmissible.[37]

10–36   When it is alleged that the evidence which the witness is now giving is fabricated, and in particular is a recent fabrication, at common law, evidence may be led to show that the same witness told the same story much earlier in the history of the case, in order to negative such an allegation.[38] The evidence of a prior consistent statement can be produced in re-examination, by calling additional witnesses either before the party's case is closed or before the final speeches.[39] The reason for admitting the prior statement is to show that the witness is a more credible or reliable witness by virtue of being consistent with their story.

(2) Criminal cases

(a) *De recenti statements*

10–37   A prior statement may be admitted if it has been made *de recenti*. These types of statements arise in a limited class of cases, namely those in which an accused person is charged with an assault, usually of a sexual nature. In such cases, it is competent to offer support for the complainer's testimony by leading evidence to show that that complainer first made his or her allegation against the accused shortly after the event, and usually to a close trusted friend or relative. This type of early statement—known as a *de recenti* statement[40]—is taken to provide positive evidence in support of the credibility of the complainer.[41] The absence of any early complaint has become regarded as a point in favour of the defence.

10–38   *De recenti* statements can themselves be used in support of the witness's credibility. In *Morton* v. *H.M.A.*,[42] M was accused of dragging his victim up a close and sexually assaulting her. Among the items of evidence offered by the Crown as corroboration was the fact that shortly after the assault, the victim went home to her brother in a distressed condition and complained

---

[37] s. 9 of the Civil Evidence (Scotland) Act 1988.
[38] *Barr* v. *Barr*, 1939 S.C. 696, *Gibson* v. *N.C.R.*, 1925 S.C. 500, and, most importantly, *Burns* v. *Colin McAndrew and Partners*, 1963 S.L.T. (Notes) 71, which was the first to impose the prerequisite that the witness's credibility be first impugned.
[39] Considered in later sections of this chapter.
[40] And as such a recognised exception to the hearsay rule: see Chap. 8 *supra*.
[41] Which, logically, ought not to be required unless and until this is challenged.
[42] 1938 J.C. 50, considered more fully as the *locus classicus* of corroboration in criminal cases in paras. 7.14–7.24 *supra*. See now *Yates* v. *H.M.A.*, 1977 S.L.T. (Notes) 42, *Stephen* v. *H.M.A.*, 1987 S.C.C.R. 570 and most notably *Gracey* v. *H.M.A.*, 1987 S.L.T. 749, in which it was held that the distressed state of a rape victim shortly after the alleged offence was capable of corroborating her complaint.

of being assaulted. Speaking of the practice of allowing such evidence to be heard in assault cases, Lord Justice-Clerk Aitchison[43] stated that:

> "the Court will allow the evidence of complaints or statements *de recenti* made by the injured party, for the limited purpose of showing that the conduct of the injured party has been consistent and that the story is not an afterthought, and, in the case of assaults upon women, to negative consent. A complaint *de recenti* increases the probability that the complaint is true and not concocted, and the absence of complaint where sexual offences are alleged is always a material point for the defence. But it must be clearly affirmed that the evidence is admissible as bearing upon credibility only, and the statements of an injured party, although made *de recenti* of the commission of a crime, do not in law amount to corroboration ... A statement of the injured party *de recenti* is nothing but the statement of the injured party, and is not evidence of the fact complained of."

Such statements are only admissible when they are made as soon after the alleged assault as is reasonable in the circumstances.[44]

The *de recenti* rule was applied in *Begg* v. *Tudhope*,[45] in which the point **10–39** emerged strongly that one potential use for such a statement is to supply the credibility required of a victim/witness in order that her statement may be used as a foundation for the application of the *Moorov* doctrine.[46]

(b) *Reply to caution and charge*

In current criminal practice, even in summary cases, it is normal policy **10–40** for police officers to relate to the court what the accused said when cautioned and charged. In many cases this is incriminating and constitutes a confession.[47] In all cases it is admitted as an exception to the hearsay rule,[48] in so far as it is offered as evidence of the truth of its contents.

Where the accused is giving evidence and part of a prior statement which **10–41** he gave is exculpatory,[49] the admission of such a statement creates another situation in which a previous consistent statement by a witness is being admitted. However, in this context, the statement is evidence, not simply of

---

[43] *ibid.*, p. 53. In fact the evidence was insufficient in this case.

[44] See *Anderson* v. *McFarlane* (1899) 1 F.(J.) 30, and *Hill* v. *Fletcher* (1847) 10 D. 7.

[45] 1983 S.C.C.R. 32, referred to more fully in para. 7.69 *supra*. Once again there was an attempt to use the girl's complaint to a teacher shortly after the alleged event as corroboration of her oral testimony, on the grounds that it was admissible as part of the *res gestae*, for which see below and paras. 8.20–8.33 *supra*.

[46] For which see paras. 7.66–7.81 *supra*.

[47] Dealt with in Chap. 14 *infra*.

[48] Dealt with in Chap. 8 *supra*.

[49] *e.g.* it contains early indication of a now fully developed defence of alibi or self defence.

the accused's consistency as a witness, but as evidence of the truth of *all* its contents—both exculpatory and incriminatory.[50]

(c) *Evidence of previous identification*

10–42   A third situation when a prior statement may be admitted arises when a witness at a trial identifies the accused in court and states that identification was also made of the accused on an earlier occasion, *e.g.* at an identification parade.

10–43   When the witness identifies the accused all over again when in the dock, then the evidence of previous identification (*e.g.* during a formal identification parade) would seem to be superfluous; nevertheless it seems to be a practice which "has existed without objection for many years."[51]

10–44   The practical effect is probably to bolster the credibility of the witness on a crucial matter central to any subsequent conviction. There are times though when a witness, who may have picked out the accused in an identification parade is unable subsequently to identify the accused in court as the person the witness believes committed the crime. In such circumstances the law permits other witnesses (usually police officers) to give evidence that on an earlier occasion it was the accused who was picked out by the witness. Provided the witness confirms that an identification was made earlier, then there is considered to be corroboration of the identification of the accused.

10–45   The Scottish Law Commission pointed out that the courts in England have now held this type of evidence to be inadmissible hearsay. Nonetheless, the rule has been extended on several occasions. In *Muldoon* v. *Herron*[52] it was held that even if the witness at the trial denies having identified the accused previously, if the police give evidence to the effect that identification did occur, the evidence of the police can be relied on as evidence of who in fact was identified. The rule also extends to identification by description given previously to the police.[53]

(d) *Section 260 Criminal Procedure (Scotland) Act 1995*

10–46   The Criminal Procedure (Scotland) Act 1995 enacts a new statutory provision which was intended to embody the *ratio* of the decision in *Jamieson* v. *H.M.A.(No.2)*.[54] The Scottish Law Commission recommended that the principle emerging in *Jamieson* be given legislative effect.[55] In

---

[50]   *Morrison* v. *H.M.A.*, 1990 J.C. 299 and *Brown* v. *H.M.A.*, 1964 J.C. 10.
[51]   Macphail, *Evidence*, Chap. 19.60.
[52]   1970 J.C. 30.
[53]   *Frew* v. *Jessop*, 1990 S.L.T. 396.
[54]   1994 S.C.C.R. 610.
[55]   Report No.149 *supra* at paras. 7.39–7.40.

Jamieson a witness stated in court that she could not remember details of an assault. As part of her examination-in-chief by the Crown she acknowledged that she had made an earlier statement to the police about the incident and that the prior statement was a true statement. A police officer to whom the witness had given the original statement then gave evidence regarding its content. The accused was convicted and appealed on the ground that the police officer's evidence was inadmissible hearsay.

The court applied the principle in *Muldoon* v. *Herron* which they declared **10–47** to be "of wider application and ... not confined to identification evidence."[56] In this case the court considered there were two separate and primary sources of evidence, namely, (i) the evidence of the police officer as to what was said to him by the witness; and (ii) the evidence of the witness that she had made a statement to the police officer and that what she said to him at the time was true.

THE HOSTILE WITNESS

If a witness called by a party does fail to live up to early promise regarding **10–48** the evidence to be given there are various courses of action open to that party. The subtle refreshment of memory, the tactical use of leading questions, and where permissible, the introduction of previous consistent statements can, however, achieve only so much, and on some occasions the agent for the party calling the witness may realise that the witness is doing more harm than good to the case.

There may be many reasons for this, not the least being a hopelessly **10–49** optimistic precognition,[57] and it by no means follows that the witness is now lying, or has been "got at" by the other party. However, the agent for the party calling the witness has to make a fairly urgent decision on how to deal with the situation, and reduce the effect of any damaging evidence which that witness has given. One tactic may be to put to that witness, where this is permitted,[58] the fact that on a previous occasion a statement was made which is inconsistent with the one which is now being made. Another is to switch to cross-examining the witness rather than conducting an examination-in-chief. In the course of the cross-examination the agent can suggest to the witness that he or she is acting out of bias, fear, self-interest, etc. In England, such a witness is termed a "hostile" witness and although the term is not officially recognised in Scotland the effect is the same.

---

[56] *per* the Lord Justice-General at p. 618.
[57] The frequency of which is one of the main arguments against allowing in previous inconsistent statements which take the form of precognitions: see paras. 10.74–10.87 *infra*.
[58] This is considered in paras. 10.74–10.87 *infra*.

10–50   It is for each party to decide how best to use a witness, and when and if to change tactic. Leave of the court is not required.[59] In *Avery* v. *Cantilever Shoe Co.*[60] Lord President Normand explained the Scottish procedure as follows:

> "[It] is for the counsel to make up his mind, subject to the Court's seeing that the witness has fair play, how he will examine his witness, and for the counsel at the end of the day to lay his submissions before the Court, having in view his own method of handling the witness, and, if he so chooses, to ask the Court to disbelieve the witness, provided that he has given him a fair opportunity of answering any charge of unreliability or untruthfulness which may emerge from his evidence."

10–51   The rule applies to both civil and criminal cases. Thus, in *Manson* v. *H.M.A.*,[61] a prosecution witness appeared hesitant and reluctant to give evidence, then admitted in response to a question from the advocate-depute that she had in fact been threatened by M's wife. The question and answer were held to be quite permissible.

10–52   The authorities are in agreement that rulings such as this leave little room for doubt that in criminal cases, as well as in civil, the party calling such witnesses may switch from regarding them as witnesses in chief to treating them as the equivalent of a hostile witness without the leave of the court, and whenever the circumstances warrant.[62] Equally clearly, the questions put to such a witness are only of use in testing credibility. When they concern the character of the witness,[63] they may be kept to a minimum by the court on the grounds that they concern issues which are only "collateral" to the matter in hand. This point is considered further in paragraphs 10.74–10.87 *infra*.

CROSS-EXAMINATION

PURPOSE AND FUNCTION

10–53 According to Walker and Walker,[64]:

> "Cross-examination has two purposes, first to test the veracity of the

---

[59]   Unlike the position in England, where leave of the court must be sought to treat the witness as "hostile".

[60]   1942 S.C. 469 at p. 471.

[61]   1951 J.C. 49. See also *Frank* v. *H.M.A.*, 1938 J.C. 17.

[62]   See, *e.g.* Walker and Walker, *op. cit.*, n. 11, para. 341(c) and Macphail, *op. cit.*, n. 4, Chap. 8.17. *N.B.* that s. 3 of the Evidence (Scotland) Act 1852, and s. 263(4) of the Criminal Procedure (Scotland) Act 1995, which permits the putting of previous inconsistent statements to witnesses, and which is dealt with in paras. 10.74–10.87 *infra*, does not restrict such questioning to cross-examination of the other party's witnesses.

[63]   As they legitimately may: see Chap. 13, and *Green* v. *H.M.A.* in paras. 10.88–10.105 *infra*.

[64]   *op. cit.*, n. 11, para. 342(a).

witness and the accuracy of his evidence, and secondly to obtain from him evidence on points on which he has not been questioned and which may support the cross examiner's case."

This dual role played by cross-examination should never be overlooked, **10–54** since there is a danger of regarding cross-examination simply as a process whereby the evidence given by a witness for the "other side" is neutralised. In fact, skilful cross-examination can yield a good deal of favourable evidence for one's own party and in some contexts it is essential to put certain questions to a witness in cross-examination if a particular line of argument is to be developed later.[65]

This section of the chapter is primarily concerned with those rules of **10–55** evidence which control the cross-examination of a witness called for the other party, but these same rules can also be applied to a witness of one's own who is now being regarded as the equivalent of hostile, as was explained in paragraphs 10.48–10.52 *supra*.

THE RIGHT TO CROSS-EXAMINE

The general rule, in both civil and criminal cases, is that every party may cross- **10–56** examine every witness who is called by the other party, and may also examine that witness in chief if wished. In civil cases, this is established by section 4 of the Evidence Act 1840. In criminal cases the same rule is now applied in both solemn and summary cases by section 263 of the Criminal Procedure (Scotland) Act 1995.[66]

The primary purpose of each section seems to have been to allow the **10–57** opposing party to treat a witness called by the other side as a witness of his own, although it also has the effect of confirming his right to cross-examine every such witness. It is necessary, in terms of the legislation, for the witness to be actually called and sworn in before the opposing party has this right, but in criminal trials it has become the practice for the defence to be allowed to call, and examine-in-chief, any witness who appears on the Crown witness list, even if that witness has not been called and sworn by them. This is in keeping with the more general role to be fulfilled by a witness which was recommended by the Thomson Committee.[67]

---

[65] See *Lee* v. *H.M.A.*, 1968 S.L.T. 155 at p. 157.
[66] Previously, ss. 148 and 340 of the 1975 Act.
[67] Cmnd. 6218, para. 38.22, which found expression, for solemn cases, in s. 82A of the Criminal Procedure (Scotland) Act 1975, now, s. 67(6) of the Criminal Procedure (Scotland) Act 1995. It allows any party (including a co-accused) to examine *in causa* any witness listed by another party. See *Todd* v. *H.M.A.*, 1984 S.L.T. 123 and *Hunter* v. *H.M.A.*, 1984 S.L.T. 434.

10–58   As was seen in paragraphs 10.02–10.06 *supra*, the presiding judge or sheriff in a criminal trial has a right to put questions to a witness, and even though that right should be used sparingly it may serve to elicit new evidence. In *McLeod* v. *H.M.A.*[68] it was held that the party against whom such evidence operates should, in such a case, have a further right to cross-examine, and both Walker and Walker[69] and Macphail[70] argue that the same rule should apply in civil cases.

10–59   Problems can arise in connection with the order in which each of the parties may cross-examine a witness where there is more than one party. Taking civil cases first, the question arises as to the appropriate order for calling the different parties' witnesses. It is more likely that there will be a multiplicity of defenders than of pursuers, and that each of those defenders will have conflicting interests and be separately represented.[71]

10–60   In such a case, each of the pursuer's witnesses will be cross-examined by each of the defenders in turn, in the order in which they appear in the "instance" of the closed record. The first defender's witnesses will be cross-examined first by the remaining defenders in the same order, and then finally by the pursuer. The second defender's witnesses will be cross-examined by the remaining defenders, then the pursuer, and then the first defender and so on,[72] forming a circular order of cross-examination.

10–61   In *Boyle* v. *Olsen*,[73] the Court of Session was faced with an unusual situation in which there was more than one pursuer, and it was held that each pursuer might cross-examine not only the defender's witnesses, but also the witnesses for the other pursuer.

10–62   In criminal cases in which there is more than one accused, and each is separately represented, it was established in *Young* v. *H.M.A.*[74] that the evidence of each accused is admissible against the others, and that therefore: "once one of the accused goes into the [witness] box in support of his separate defence, the door opens for a general cross-examination by his co-accused for the purpose of vindicating their own separate defences."[75]

---

[68]   1939 J.C. 68.

[69]   *op. cit.,* n. 11, para. 338(a).

[70]   *op. cit.,* n. 4, Chap. 8.24.

[71]   If that is not the case, then of course the problem does not arise.

[72]   As Macphail explained it, *op. cit.*, n. 4, Chap. 8.25: "In a civil action by P against Dl, D2 and D3, where the defenders have conflicting interests and are separately represented, P and his witnesses are cross-examined by D1, D2 and D3; Dl and his witnesses are cross-examined by D2, D3 and P; D2 by D3, P and Dl; and D3 by P, Dl and D2." In such cases, it seems from *Ayr Road Trustees* v. *Adams* (1883) 11 R. 326 that all such evidence will be regarded as evidence *in causa*.

[73]   1912 S.C. 1235, a salvage case in which two pursuers conjoined their actions.

[74]   1932 J.C. 63.

[75]   *ibid.*, p. 74. This right is now confirmed and broadened by s. 266 of the Criminal Procedure (Scotland) Act 1995, which is considered in paras. 11.50–11.65 *infra*. *N.B.* that the right applies even when the co-accused have a joint defence, and whether or not D1 has given incriminating evidence against D2.

The same case also confirmed the right of the Crown to cross-examine **10–63** such an accused after the remaining accused have done so. Exactly the same procedure is observed *quoad* the remaining witnesses called for each accused, so that: "in the trial of X, Y and Z, X and each of his witnesses are in turn examined by X's, advocate then cross-examined by Y, Z and the prosecutor; then Y is examined by his own advocate and crossed by X, Z and the prosecutor."[76]

The order in which each of the accused is allowed to take part in this **10–64** rotating system seems to be the order in which each appears on the complaint or indictment, and "this is determined by the Crown on what may be alphabetical, chronological or tactical grounds; or it may be simply a matter of chance."[77]

The presiding judge or sheriff has a discretionary right to alter this order, **10–65** in the interests of justice or clarity.[78]

IMPLICATIONS OF FAILURE TO CROSS-EXAMINE

It is not essential to cross-examine every witness in a criminal trial or civil **10–66** proof, and it will be a question of tactics as to when the opportunity to cross-examine is foregone. There are various circumstances, however, when failure to cross-examine creates difficulties.

In civil cases the position is summarised in the words of Lord Justice- **10–67** Clerk Cooper in *McKenzie* v. *McKenzie*,[79] who, while conceding that it should not be necessary for a party to put every fact averred in his case to every witness called for the other party, nevertheless observed:

> "[The] most obvious principles of fair play dictate that, if it is intended later to contradict a witness upon a specific and important issue to which that witness has deponed, or to prove some critical fact to which that witness ought to have a chance of tendering an explanation or denial, the point ought normally to be put to the witness in cross-examination. If such cross-examination is omitted, the witness may have to be recalled with the leave of the Court, possibly on conditions as to expenses; and in some circumstances the omission may cause fatal damage to the case."

The most obvious situation in which a failure to cross-examine can "cause **10–68** fatal damage to the case" arises where, by allowing the witness to go

---

[76] Macphail, *op. cit.,* n. 4, Chap. 8.25.
[77] Macphail, *loc. cit.*
[78] *Sandlan* v. *H.M.A.,* 1983 S.L.T. 519. See also paras. 10.121–10.141 *infra.*
[79] 1943 S.C. 108 at p. 109. See also *Harrington* v. *Milk Marketing Board,* 1985 S.L.T. 342 for an example of a case in which failure to cross-examine was nearly fatal. *Cf.* also *Walker* v. *McCruther and Marshall,* 1982 S.L.T. 345.

unchallenged, the party against whom he or she is called hereby entitles the court to regard him or her as a credible witness on that point. But this process does not dispense with the need for the other party to provide sufficient corroboration for their own case. In other words, failure to cross-examine does not operate as a corroborating factor.[80]

10–69   In criminal cases, the position is dominated by the fact that the burden of proof is on the Crown to prove the accused guilty beyond reasonable doubt,[81] and that unless this is achieved there can be no conviction. The defence may conduct itself as it best sees fit, and in particular may choose not to cross-examine all or any of the Crown witnesses. The risk which the defence runs in doing so, of course, is that the Crown witnesses will be believed.[82]

10–70   The question of the evidential significance of a failure on the part of the Crown to cross-examine defence witnesses arose, in *Young* v. *Guild*,[83] when neither the accused nor his witness (his wife) were cross-examined by the fiscal. On appeal, it was argued that this failure amounted to an acceptance by the Crown of the defence version of events (an assault) and that the Crown should not then have sought a conviction. It was held that while such a failure might well have "an impact on the weight and value of the evidence," it could not operate as a bar to conviction. The court took its lead from *McPherson* v. *Copeland*, and ruled[84] that:

> "It was for the sheriff to decide at the end of the day on all the evidence before him whether a conviction should result or not. If the unchallenged evidence of the appellant and his wife had even cast a reasonable doubt in his mind about convicting, that would have been enough to warrant an acquittal."

10–71   In short, while the Crown, by not cross-examining, runs a serious risk that the defence witnesses will be believed, they are still entitled to a conviction if they are not.

10–72   Also, at the end of the day, of course, the Crown must produce a corroborated case against the accused, and it was firmly established in *Morton* v. *H.M.A.*[85] that they may not do so solely on the basis that a witness giving evidence of a crucial fact has not been cross-examined on that fact by the defence.

---

[80]   See *Stewart* v. *Glasgow Corp.*, 1958 S.C. 28.
[81]   For which see paras. 2.61–2.101 *supra*.
[82]   *McPherson* v. *Copeland*, 1961 J.C. 74.
[83]   1985 S.L.T. 358.
[84]   At p. 360.
[85]   The *locus classicus* of the law on this point, which is more fully examined in paras. 7.25–7.26 *supra*.

Finally, it should be noted that when it is intended to cross-examine a **10–73** witness on the basis of some document which exists,[86] it may be necessary to lodge that document as a production, at least in civil cases. This is because both the Sheriff Court Ordinary Cause rules[87] and Rules of the Court of Session[88] require that all productions which are to be put in evidence shall be lodged before proof, have been taken to apply even to documents which are intended only for use in cross-examination.[89] In summary criminal cases they may apparently be produced at the last minute,[90] but in solemn cases it is essential to lodge them, to avoid the possibility of being denied the use of them during the course of the trial.

PREVIOUS INCONSISTENT STATEMENTS

In paragraphs 10.33–10.47 *supra*, the focus was on the admissibility of **10–74** prior statements which were consistent with what is now being said by the witness. If there is a suggestion that the witness made a prior statement which is *inconsistent* with the evidence now being given in the witness box, then in criminal cases a different approach is taken.[91] In criminal proceedings the appropriate rule is now that contained in section 263(4) of the Criminal Procedure (Scotland) Act 1995.

In terms of section 263(4),[92] a witness may be examined as to whether **10–75** he has previously made a statement different from the evidence given at the trial. Evidence can be led at the trial to show that indeed a different statement was made previously.

The fact that a witness has, on a previous occasion, made a statement **10–76** which is inconsistent with the one which he or she is now making is clearly of considerable significance, if only to show that the witness is not to be relied upon. Where this is permitted, one would normally expect the allegations of previous inconsistency to be put during cross-examination, by the party against whom the witness is testifying. In some circumstances though it may become necessary for the party calling that witness to do so, when the evidence given turns out not to be that which was expected, and it is felt necessary to undertake "damage limitation".

---

[86] Whether to test his credibility, or to secure new evidence in one's favour.

[87] Rule 29.11.

[88] Rule 36.3.

[89] Macphail, *op. cit.,* n. 4, Chap. 8.32 and *Report on Corroboration, Hearsay and Related Matters in Civil Proceedings;* Scot. Law Com. No. 100, para. 3.10. But see Walker and Walker, *op. cit.,* n. 11, para. 300(b), who suggest that this does not apply to documents which simply test the credibility of the witness.

[90] Since productions do not require to be lodged in advance in such cases anyway; see *Hogg v. Clark,* 1959 J.C. 7.

[91] In civil cases both consistent and inconsistent statements are admissible by virtue of s. 3 of the Civil Evidence (Scotland) Act 1988: see paras. 10.33–10.47 *supra.*

[92] Previously, ss.147 and 349 of the 1975 Act.

10–77   The circumstances in which this may happen, and the process by which the party calling the witness is entitled to change tactics, have been considered in paragraphs 10.48–10.52 *supra*. Also, as will be seen in paragraphs 10.121–10.141 *infra*, the party alleging the previous inconsistent statement may produce evidence of that statement at any time up to the close of his case, and, in the case of the Crown in a criminal trial, at any time up to the speeches with which the parties close their cases.

10–78   This section concentrates simply on the evidential implications of a previous inconsistent statement, whether proved in chief or cross-examination, and regardless of the identity of the party proving it.

10–79   It seems that in both types of case, the party seeking to prove the previous statement must first of all lay a basis for this by putting to the witness the fact that it was made, and giving the witness the opportunity to confirm or deny that fact. Only if it is denied can the evidence of the previous inconsistent statement be led.[93]

10–80   The one exception to the rule is that a witness may not be faced with a prior contrary statement made as part of a "precognition"[94] unless, in the case of a precognition given prior to a trial or proof, it was given on oath.

10–81   This exception applies in both civil and criminal cases, and various reasons have been given for it. The unsworn precognition has been said, for example, to be confidential in nature,[95] and as such in some way covered by a privilege. Alternatively, it has been argued that the ends of justice, and the public interest in obtaining the truth in a criminal case, are better facilitated if the precognition is kept confidential. But perhaps the most cogent reason is that:

> "in a precognition you cannot be sure that you are getting what the potential witness has to say in a pure and undefiled form. It is filtered through the mind of another, whose job it is to put what he thinks the witness means into a form suitable for use in judicial proceedings. This process tends to colour the result. Precognoscers as a rule appear to be gifted with a measure of optimism which no amount of disillusionment can damp."[96]

---

[93]   See Walker and Walker, *op. cit.,* n. 11, para. 343(a) and Renton and Brown, *op. cit.,* n. 1, para. 18–83. See also *Mactaggart* v. *H.M.A.*, 1934 J.C. 33, *Childs* v. *McLeod*, 1981 S.L.T. (Notes) 27 and *Gall* v. *Gall* (1870) 9 M. 177. The process by which the prosecution in a criminal case may lead such evidence after the end of the defence case is considered in paras. 10.121–10.137 *infra.*

[94]   A formal statement given to the agent for either party, as part of the pre-trial preparations of both sides. The distinction is often a fine one. See e.g. *Low* v. *H.M.A.*, 1988 S.L.T. 97.

[95]   By, *e.g.* Lord Justice-General Clyde in *McNeilie* v. *H.M.A.*, 1929 J.C. 50 at p. 53, and Lord Justice-Clerk Thomson in *Kerr* v. *H.M.A.*, 1958 J.C. 14 at p. 19.

[96]   *per* Lord Justice-Clerk Thomson in *Kerr* v. *H.M.A., ibid.. N.B.* that the Thomson Committee (Cmnd. 6218), para. 44.03, opted to retain the ban against using unsworn precognitions in criminal cases as previous inconsistent statements primarily for the final reason.

None of these arguments, however, is applicable when the precognition **10–82**
is given on oath before a sheriff, taken down *verbatim* by a shorthand writer,
read over by the witness and signed by him. The Thomson Committee
recommendation that the rule should be changed in such cases[97] found
sympathy in *Coll, Petitioner*,[98] an unusual case in which a man who had
earlier given a precognition on oath before a sheriff to the procurator fiscal
in the course of the preparation of a High Court indictment presented a
petition to the *nobile officium* of the High Court to have his precognition
(which he had read over and signed at the time) destroyed. His reason for
requesting this was said to be so that he could give his evidence "freely and
without bias" at the trial itself.

In rejecting his petition, the court distinguished between precognitions **10–83**
taken on oath and all other forms of precognition. Speaking of a precognition
"made in the form of a judicial declaration on oath," Lord Justice-Clerk
Wheatley[99] held that:

> "it is obtained subject to safeguards which are calculated to avoid the
> possible defects and unfairness which Lord Justice Clerk Thomson[1]
> had in contemplation … It is difficult to conceive a situation more
> apposite for the invocation of the section 3 procedure.[2] While,
> therefore, each case has to be determined on its own facts, in our
> opinion such a declaration would normally be competent as a basis
> for challenging under that section the evidence of a witness. It would
> only be when it is alleged that the safeguards of the procedure had
> not been observed that a challenge to its use for that purpose could be
> made."

The essential reason for changing the rule in respect of precognitions on **10–84**
oath may perhaps be found in his Lordship's closing observation that:

> "we find comfort in the thought that the clarification of the legal
> position on this point gives legal sanction to a procedure which can
> be invoked to counter one of the deadly blows which is being struck
> at the administration of justice at the present time, namely, witnesses

---

[97] *ibid.*, para. 44.07.

[98] 1977 J.C. 29.

[99] *ibid.*, at pp. 32–33. *N.B.* that "judicial declarations" made by an accused in chambers are
not made on oath; see Criminal Procedure (Scotland) Act 1995, s. 6. They are, however,
admissible anyway, in the manner explained in paras. 10.37–10.41 *supra*, and there is no
apparent reason why they may not be used to discredit the accused as a witness when and
if he gives inconsistent evidence at his trial.

[1] In *Kerr, supra*.

[2] *Quaere* why the court was not referred to the 1975 Act, s. 147, but the effect of the ruling
has been taken to apply to all the relevant sections; see Renton and Brown, *Criminal
Procedure,* para. 18–83. If arrangements could be made in a civil case to precognosce a
potential witness on oath, presumably the ratio of *Coll* would apply with at least persuasive
force.

going back on their earlier statements when giving evidence in criminal trials."

10–85 Since the introduction of section 9 of the Criminal Justice (Scotland) Act 1980, the defence have possessed the same right to precognosce on oath before a sheriff any witness other than a co-accused as had previously been the exclusive right of the prosecution. This right is now embodied in section 291 of the Criminal Procedure (Scotland) Act 1995.

10–86 A statement made to a police officer at a time when the maker is only a potential witness is not regarded as a precognition,[3] nor is a statement made to a friend.[4] Indeed, in both civil and criminal cases the current trend seems to be to allow witnesses to be challenged on the basis of any previous inconsistent statement made other than in the traditional precognition situation.[5]

10–87 In conclusion, it should be emphasised that the principal function of previous inconsistent statement evidence is to suggest to the court that the witness is not reliable and that the testimony which is now being given should be ignored.

CROSS-EXAMINATION AS TO CREDIBILITY

10–88 The previous section considered previous inconsistent statements as a means of attacking the credibility of a witness. In relation to criminal proceedings the Scottish Law Commission canvassed views on whether a prior inconsistent statement might be admissible of its content.[6] They reported that "the weight of opinion was against such a radical reform of the law."[7] One powerful reason against admitting such a statement was the consideration that an "accused could be convicted on the basis of prior statements attributed to witnesses by police officers, even though the witnesses denied having made such statements."[8]

10–89 Questions may be put to witnesses which are designed to undermine their credibility and show that they are of such poor character generally, that they should not be believed. Or it may be suggested that there exists some fact extrinsic to the actual facts of the case in hand which renders the witness unreliable in that particular context. Issues of credibility can be categorised under four main headings.

---

[3] *Aitchison* v. *Simon*, 1976 S.L.T. (Sh.Ct.) 73, also shows that a false denial that such a statement was made can form a satisfactory basis for a perjury charge. See also *Hall* v. *H.M.A.*, 1968 S.L.T. 275.

[4] *Green* v. *H.M.A.*, 1983 S.C.C.R. 42, considered more fully in paras. 10.92–10.93 *infra*.

[5] See, *e.g. Dorona* v. *Caldwell*, 1981 S.L.T. (Notes) 91, and *Low* v. *H.M.A.*, 1987 S.C.C.R 541, in which the statement was later used as the basis for a perjury charge.

[6] Report No. 149, *Report on Hearsay Evidence in Criminal Proceedings*, published in 1995.

[7] At para. 7.11.

[8] *ibid.*.

(1) **Cross-examination as to character generally**

While the general character[9] of a witness may be relevant in assessing **10–90**
veracity, in practice the courts are less likely to discount the evidence of a
witness on the grounds of some moral flaw in his or her character.[10]

The older authorities cite a previous conviction for perjury as an example **10–91**
of poor character which may be used to discredit a witness.[11] Apart from
perjury or some other specific previous conviction, there are a few other
isolated cases which arise when the interests of justice demand that the
general behaviour, or even personality, of a witness be taken into account.
The court is being presented with evidence which may affect a witness's
credibilty and is admitted because of the light which, potentially, it sheds
on the whole of that person's evidence. This is the same consideration which
in some circumstances permits the character of a victim or complainer in a
criminal case to be examined.[12] When that victim gives evidence it can be
almost impossible to distinguish between evidence which shows that the
victim is unreliable as a witness and evidence which goes to the very
credibility of the allegation, and hence the guilt of the accused.

In *Green* v. *H.M.A.,*[13] G and another had been convicted of rape. Their **10–92**
defence had been consent, and evidence had been given by the complainer
herself that she had been sniffing glue on the day of the incident. In the first
case of its kind, the High Court, in hearing the appeal under those provisions
of the Criminal Justice (Scotland) Act 1980 which allow for the introduction
of fresh evidence,[14] heard new evidence to the effect that the complainer
had on previous occasions made false allegations of rape, was suffering
from a psychiatric disturbance which led her to fantasise, and had admitted
to a third party that the present allegations were false.

It was held that this fresh evidence cast such grave doubts on the **10–93**
credibility of the complainer, and had such serious implications for the
original defence of consent, that the accused must be acquitted on the
grounds of a miscarriage of justice.

---

[9] By which is meant "disposition" as shown by previous behaviour, rather than pure reputation, which is rightly regarded as irrelevant.

[10] Under the Criminal Procedure (Scotland) Act 1995, s. 265(1)(a), a witness is not excluded from testifying by virtue of having previous convictions.

[11] Walker and Walker, *Law of Evidence in Scotland*, para. 345(b) and Dickson, *Evidence*, para. 1618. *N.B.* that not even this may be proved by additional evidence when denied by the witness. See *Carey* v. *Tudhope*, 1984 S.C.C.R. 157.

[12] Even when deceased; see *H.M.A.* v. *Kay*, 1970 J.C. 68, *H.M.A.* v. *Cunningham* (quoted by Macphail, *Evidence*, Chap. 16.07) and 13.20–13.21 *infra*. In *Cunningham*, proof by means of extract convictions was allowed, while in the same case, evidence in chief was permitted of previous assaults by the deceased upon the accused.

[13] 1983 S.C.C.R. 42. See also *Marshall* v. *Smith* 1983 S.C.C.R. 156; but see *Allison* v. *H.M.A.*, 1985 S.C.C.R. 409.

[14] Which are considered again briefly in paras. 10.121–10.137 *infra*.

(2) **Cross-examination as to personal interest**

10–94   One of the most important impediments to a witness's credibility could be the fact that he or she has some sort of personal interest in the outcome of the case. This may be in the form of a personal relationship, present or former, to one of the parties or the accused, or it may be that the witness has a financial stake in the subject-matter of the action. As a general rule, however, the relationship of a witness to a party in an action does not disqualify that witness from testifying.[15]

10–95   The type of background circumstances which cannot be ignored include allegations that the person giving evidence in a criminal trial in fact took part himself in the criminal activities with which the accused is now charged. Such persons are known as *sociis criminis*,[16] and in a jury trial, the presiding judge is entitled to draw the jury's attention to the potential question mark against the credibility of the evidence of any *socius criminis*. However, such a warning is not obligatory.[17]

10–96   In *Manson* v. *H.M.A.*,[18] a Crown witness who appeared hesitant and reluctant to give evidence eventually admitted, under cross-examination by her own counsel, that she had been threatened by the accused's wife. It was held that such cross-examination was valid provided that the jury were carefully directed that such matters go only to the credibility of the witness. Arguably this type of personal bias regarding the outcome of a case could become more prevalent, given the increasing incidence of witness intimidation.

(3) **Evidence of the character of the complainer in a sexual offence**

10–97   Reference has already been made to the decreasing relevance of a person's sexual morality in assessing whether or not he or she is a credible witness. Mounting concern over the standard practice of defence counsel in rape cases attacking the general sexual history of the complainer[19] led to the

---

[15]   Evidence (Scotland) Act 1840, s. 1; Criminal Procedure (Scotland) Act 1995, s. 265(3).

[16]   Defined in *Wallace* v. *H.M.A.*, 1952 J.C. 78, *per* Lord Keith at p. 83 as being anyone who has been convicted of, or pleaded guilty to, the offence with which the accused is charged or who gives evidence, on his own admission, as an accomplice in that crime.

[17]   In *Docherty* v. *H.M.A.*, 1987 S.L.T. 784, the practice of giving what is usually referred to as the *cum nota* warning was stated to be a matter of discretion for the trial judge. Corroboration is not required if the witness is believed; see paras. 7.14–7.24 *supra. N.B.* that a co-accused still on trial cannot be treated as *socius criminis*; see paras. 11.50–11.65 *infra.*

[18]   1951 J.C. 49, considered also in paras. 10.48–10.52 *supra* as an example of a so-called "hostile" witness being challenged by the party calling her. See also *Williamson* v. *H.M.A.*, 1978 S.L.T. (Notes) 58.

[19]   *e.g.* Macphail, *op. cit.*, n. 12, Chap. 16.09. Such questioning is admissible at common law, *per Dickie* v. *H.M.A.* (1897) 24 R.(J.) 82 in so far as it reflects upon the credibility of the witness.

passing of section 36 of the Law Reform (Miscellaneous Provisions) (Scotland) Act 1985, which is now contained in section 274(1) of the Criminal Procedure (Scotland) Act 1995.[20]

In terms of section 274(1), no complainer in any of the cases covered by the legislation[21] may be cross-examined[22] as to her previous good character in sexual matters, as to whether or not she is a prostitute, or as to whether or not she has previously engaged with any person in any sexual behaviour[23] which does not form part of the subject-matter of the charge. In terms of section 274(4) none of these restrictions apply to questions being put by the Crown.[24] All of these prohibitions can be modified in the circumstances prescribed in section 275.

10–98

These circumstances are:

10–99

    (i)   that such questions must be asked in order to explain or rebut evidence adduced, or to be adduced, otherwise than by or on behalf of the accused;[25] or

   (ii) that the questions relate to other sexual behaviour which took place on the same occasion as the behaviour with which the accused is charged,[26] or are relevant to the defence of incrimination; or

  (iii) that it would be contrary to the interests of justice to exclude such questions.[27]

Before such questions may even be put in cross-examination the accused must make special application during the course of the trial, but outwith the presence of any jury, the complainer, any person cited as a witness and the public. The court has a wide discretion to allow or to limit the extent of such questioning. In *Bremner* v. *H.M.A.*[28] the appeal court refused to interfere with the trial judge's refusal to allow the complainer to be questioned about

10–100

---

[20] Previously, ss. 141(A) and 346(A) of the 1975 Act.

[21] *i.e.* virtually all sexual offences. The offences of clandestine injury and incest were added by the Criminal Law (Consolidation)(Scotland) Act 1995 to those contained in ss. 141(A)(2) and 346(A)(2) of the 1975 Act.

[22] Nor may any such evidence be led in chief.

[23] *N.B.* not just the accused.

[24] Presumably to the accused, but conceivably to the complainer herself, or to any of the Crown witnesses: see paras. 10.48–10.52 *supra*.

[25] *e.g.* if the complainer alleges that she was a virgin at the time of the offence, or if medical evidence is led for the same purpose.

[26] *e.g.* the accused alleges that certain sexual familiarities were permitted prior to an alleged rape, or that he was only one of several men who had intercourse with the complainer with her consent, or that in fact someone else committed the act with which he is charged. In such cases, the evidence in question will presumably be expected to form part of the *res gestae*, for which see paras. 8.20–8.33 *supra*.

[27] A potentially enormous loophole which subverts the primary aim of the entire legislation.

[28] 1992 S.C.C.R. 476.

her relationship with the accused which had ended some eight months before the rape.

10–101　　Some observers have cast doubt over the effectiveness of the legislation in protecting the character of the complainer from attack. Research carried out in 1992 found that in 32 per cent of sexual offence trials the defence made an application to lead evidence of the previous character of the complainer, and in 85 per cent of these cases the applications were at least partially successful. The research also found that there was a high incidence of breach of the prohibition against leading character evidence (in 24 per cent of cases).[29]

(4) Witness credibility as a collateral issue

10–102　　The main problem which bedevils the entire issue of witness credibility is that it is traditionally regarded as an issue "collateral" to the primary matters into which the court is enquiring. As such it is not relevant to the essential facts and evidence regarding it will be admissible.

10–103　　Evidence suggesting some dubiety about the witness's credibility is regarded as an exception to the general rule that credibility is collateral. But the party attacking credibility is normally only permitted to raise the suggestion that the witness is not to be believed, and leave it at that. It is not permissible to pursue the point and rebut any denial with additional evidence.

10–104　　It is not therefore permissible to produce extracts of previous convictions which relate to a witness.[30] In some cases, further pursuit of the issue is permissible only if the evidence which is to be adduced forms part of the facts in issue.[31] However, as more recent cases[32] suggest, courts may now be prepared to investigate more fully those issues which may have a bearing on the credibility of a witness, particularly in the broader interests of criminal justice.

10–105　　A party seeking to test the credibility of a witness will not, however, be permitted to descend to mere scurrilous abuse,[33] "fishing expeditions" into the witness's past, or a general attempt to annoy or disconcert the witness.

RE-EXAMINATION

Purpose and Function

10–106　The precise purpose and function of re-examination are summarised by Wilkinson[34] as being: "to give the party who has adduced the witness an

---

[29] Brown *et. al.*, *Sexual History and Sexual Character Evidence in Scottish Sexual Offence Trials*, 1992, Scottish Office Central Research Unit Papers.

[30] See *Kennedy* v. *H.M.A.* (1896) 23 R.(J.) 28, and *Dickie* v. *H.M.A., ibid.*, at p. 83.

[31] One of the rationales of the exceptions permitted in sexual cases *supra*.

[32] *e.g. Green, Marshall, Williamson, supra.*

[33] *e.g.* as in *Falconer* v. *Brown* (1893) 21 R.(J.) 1.

[34] *Scottish Law of Evidence*, p. 161.

opportunity of clearing up difficulties or ambiguities which may have emerged from cross-examination or to seek to repair the damage which cross-examination may have done."

The party re-examining the witness must remember that re-examination **10–107** is simply a second chance to examine in chief on matters arising from cross-examination. The normal niceties of examination-in-chief must be observed, and in particular no leading questions may be put.[35]

Problems can arise when, in the course of re-examination, a witness **10–108** goes beyond the questions put to him or her, or the questions put go beyond the normally permitted limits and new matter is introduced upon which the other party has had no opportunity to cross-examine. The authorities seem to be in favour of permitting further cross-examination in such cases.[36] In criminal cases it would certainly be in keeping with the spirit of *McLeod* v. *H.M.A.*,[37] which can be taken as having laid down a general rule that evidence against an accused (from whatever source it originates) is something upon which the accused should always have the right to cross-examine. This applies whether it comes from a witness during examination-in-chief or from the subsequent examination.

It will also be recalled from *Sandlan* v. *H.M.A.*[38] that an accused has the **10–109** right to cross-examine any witness who has given evidence against him, even when that evidence was given in the course of cross-examination by another accused named further down the indictment. By analogy, it may be argued that the same rule of fairness requires that the right to cross-examine be given when such evidence is taken from a witness in re-examination by the Crown.

FURTHER EVIDENCE

INTRODUCTION

After every witness has been taken through the process of examination-in- **10–110** chief, cross-examination and re-examination, it may come to light that there is further evidence which might have been led, but was not. It may be, for example, that a later witness gives evidence which indicates that an earlier witness may not be as credible as was believed at the time, and it may be

---

[35] But see Macphail, *op. cit.,* n. 12, Chap. 8.33, who observed that: "There seems to be fairly widespread practice of asking leading questions in re-examination. It is thought that the practice is objectionable, particularly in jury trials, and should be explicitly declared to be so."

[36] See, *e.g.* Walker and Walker, *op. cit.,* n. 11, para. 338(a), and Macphail, *op. cit.,* n. 12, Chap. 8.34. Macphail in fact goes so far as to advocate a statutory rule to that effect, in the absence of appropriate case law. See also *Gunn* v. *Brown,* 1987 S.L.T. 94.

[37] 1939 J.C. 68; see also paras. 10.02–10.08 and 10.56–10.65 *supra.*

[38] 1983 S.L.T. 519; see also paras. 10.56–10.65 *supra.*

desired to put this suggestion to the earlier witness. Alternatively, a fresh line of evidence may have been opened up by a later witness which it is felt might usefully be explored with a witness who has already testified. Or it may simply be the case that the agent for the party calling the witness forgot to ask an important question.

10–111   In these circumstances, it becomes necessary to ask the leave of the court to recall a witness, or to call completely new witnesses who can supply fresh evidence which is relevant to the case but which has only emerged during the case. This will only be permitted if it is evidence which could not reasonably have been anticipated. Such witnesses may sometimes be called by the court itself, or they may be called by one of the parties. Such action may be necessary either before or after the close of the case for the party seeking to adduce the fresh evidence. The purposes for which such additional evidence will be permitted may also vary from case to case.

10–112   These issues are considered in the final two sections of this chapter.

RECALL OF A WITNESS

10–113 A sharp distinction may be drawn between the common law rules relating to the recall of a witness who has already testified, and the corresponding rules laid down by statute.

10–114   At common law, a witness may only be recalled by the presiding judge or sheriff *ex proprio motu*, though of course it could be done at the request of one of the parties. The recall may be at any stage of the trial or proof, even after both parties have closed their case, but the recall is only ever permitted for the limited purpose of clearing up some ambiguity in that witness's evidence.[39] The recalled witness is classed as the judge's witness, and must be questioned only by the judge.

10–115   When a witness is recalled in this way, at least in a criminal case, then by analogy with the facts in *McLeod* v. *H.M.A.*,[40] either party may claim the right to cross-examine on any new evidence elicited by such questions as may be put by the judge.

10–116   This common law rule is obviously very restrictive in its operation, and offers no assistance to a party who wishes to recall a witness to ask specific questions. However, there is now statutory regulation of the position. Section 4 of the Evidence (Scotland) Act 1852 deals with the civil position, and section 263(5) of the Criminal Procedure (Scotland) Act 1995 with the criminal position.

10–117   Both sets of provision depart considerably from the common law rule, in that the recalled witness remains the witness of the party recalling him

---

[39] *Lindie* v. *H.M.A.*, 1974 J.C. 1.

[40] *supra;* see also Renton and Brown, *op. cit.,* n. 2, para. 18–73.

or her, and the questions which may be put are not limited simply to those which resolve ambiguities. In addition, the party wishing to invoke the section may do so at any time up to the close of their case.[41]

The injustice which could arise from such an interpretation became most **10–118** obvious in *Lindie* v. *H.M.A.*,[42] which gave rise to a good deal of criticism,[43] and the Thomson Committee[44] recommended a whole new approach to fresh evidence which becomes available in a criminal case after the parties have closed their cases. The current statutory provisions are contained in section 268 of the Criminal Procedure (Scotland) Act 1995.[45]

Section 268 allows witnesses to be recalled where a party wishes to lead **10–119** fresh or additional evidence. Various statutory conditions must be met and these are dealt with in paragraphs 10.121–10.141 *infra*. The position in criminal cases therefore now is that:

(i) *before* the close of his or her case, either party may seek leave to recall a witness under section 263(5).

(ii) *after* the close of his or her case, either party may seek leave to adduce additional evidence, including where necessary the recall of a witness, when the conditions of section 268 are satisfied.[46]

These latter provisions may now be considered in the broader context of **10–120** "fresh" evidence generally.

FRESH EVIDENCE

The recall of a witness is simply one means by which a party in either a **10–121** civil or a criminal case may seek to introduce fresh evidence. As was seen in paragraphs 10.113–10.120 *supra*, there are restrictions placed even upon that limited method of raising fresh issues, and it might never have been allowed at all had it not been for the intervention of statute.

There are many reasons why a party may discover, at the last possible **10–122** moment, that evidence is now available which was not available earlier, or

---

[41] For the general effect of the rule, see *Todd* v. *MacDonald*, 1960 J.C. 93, at p. 96. In this case, it was held that the section might be used to allow a party to put a question which he had earlier forgotten to put; for example, as in that case, the Crown could recall a witness in order that he might identify the accused when this was vital to a conviction, and the question had been overlooked in chief.

[42] 1974 J.C. 1; a decision which had to consider the effect of s. 4 of the 1852 Act.

[43] See, *e.g.* Gordon, "*Lindie* v. *H.M.A.*" (1974) 19 J.L.S. 5 and Macphail, *op. cit.*, n. 12, Chaps 8.56 and 8.58.

[44] (Cmnd 6218), paras. 43.05 to 43.13; Recommendations 120 to 123.

[45] Previously, ss. 149 and 350 of the 1975 Act.

[46] This is all, of course, in addition to the common law power of the presiding judge or sheriff to recall a witness for the limited purpose of clearing up an ambiguity; see above. In civil cases, only s. 4 of the 1852 Act operates in addition to the common law, so that a party in a civil case has no right to recall a witness after their case has been closed.

that evidence is now required to rebut issues raised by the other party which no one could reasonably have anticipated. In examining the laws of evidence which deal with this type of situation, it is necessary once again to distinguish between criminal and civil cases.

(1) **Criminal cases**

10–123 As indicated in paragraphs 10.118–10.119 *supra*, the position in criminal law is now dominated by the effects of section 268 of the Criminal Procedure (Scotland) Act 1995.

10–124 The section permits the introduction of "additional evidence" after the close of a party's case but before the speeches begin (in solemn proceedings), and before the prosecutor addresses the judge on the evidence (in summary proceedings).[47] The procedure is open to either party, who must make a motion to that effect to the judge or sheriff. In both cases, the presiding judge or sheriff may only grant the motion where:

10–125 (i) the additional evidence is considered to be prima facie material,[48] *and*

10–126 (ii) it is accepted that at the time when the case was closed, *either* the additional evidence now being introduced was not available and could not reasonably have been made available, *or* the materiality of such evidence could not reasonably have been foreseen by the party now wishing to introduce it.

10–127 The judge or sheriff may permit the additional evidence to be led notwithstanding that a witness must be recalled.[49] In a solemn case, permission may be granted notwithstanding that a witness or a production will now be introduced who or which was not on the original lists served by the parties, and the requisite notice was not given concerning them. In all cases, if the motion is granted, the judge or sheriff may adjourn or postpone the trial before allowing the additional evidence to be led.

10–128 An integral component of the current approach to fresh evidence, is contained in section 269[50] of the 1995 Act which provides that the prosecutor alone may, after the close of the defence case but before the commencement

---

[47] Ironically, if the facts in *Lindie* were to recur there would still be no statutory remedy since in that case the speeches had begun.
[48] Presumably to either the substantive issues of the case or a collateral issue such as the credibility of a witness. If, for example, the sort of additional evidence heard on appeal in *Green* v. *H.M.A.* (for which see paras. 10.92–10.93 *supra*) had been available at the trial, presumably it would have been allowed in before the speeches. *N.B.* also the effect of ss. 149A and 350A considered below, which allow questions relating to the credibility of a defence witness to be raised by the prosecution after the close of the defence case.
[49] For which see paras. 10.113–10.120 *supra*. For a case in which the "reasonableness" test was applied, see *Salusbury-Hughes* v. *H.M.A.,* 1987 S.C.C.R. 38.
[50] Previously, ss. 149A and 350A of the 1975 Act.

of the speeches, move for leave to call additional evidence. This can be for the purpose *either* of contradicting evidence led by the defence which could not reasonably have been anticipated by the Crown, *or* of providing evidence that a witness who has given evidence gave a previous inconsistent statement on some prior occasion.[51]

The reason for the introduction of such a rule is, of course, that the **10–129** Crown will not be in a position to put to a defence witness the fact that he or she has made such a statement, or to bring evidence "in replication" of fresh matters raised by the defence, until after the close of its own case. It would clearly lead to injustice if, purely because of the order in which a criminal trial is conducted, the defence were in a procedural position to counter all the evidence led by the Crown, but the Crown did not have a similar right *vis-à-vis* the defence case.

The same procedural conditions are attached to section 269 as accompany **10–130** section 268, namely that the additional evidence may be led even if it requires the recall of a witness, and even though a new witness called or a fresh production introduced did not appear on the original list for the Crown.[52] As with the previous sections, the presiding judge or sheriff may also adjourn or postpone the trial before allowing in the additional evidence.

The High Court considered the operation of the previous statutory **10–131** provisions (contained in section 149A of the Criminal Procedure (Scotland) Act 1975) in *Sandlan* v. *H.M.A.*[53] *Sandlan* appeared first on an indictment for theft which included K. He was cross-examined by counsel for K first of all, in respect of his movements on the day in question. He claimed to have visited a certain shop on that day, and he was pressed for further details of this in his subsequent cross-examination by the Crown. The Crown then applied for, and were granted, leave under section 149A to lead evidence in replication to show that the visit to the shop in question had in fact occurred two days earlier. S was then allowed to give further evidence to rebut the evidence led in replication, and to call his own solicitor as a witness.

It was held on appeal that the operation of section 149A was not restricted **10–132** to evidence led in chief by the defence, but could in fact apply to evidence elicited from the defence during the course of cross-examination. It is not clear from the report of the case whether this related only to the cross-examination by the Crown, or was thought to extend to cross-examination by a co-accused, and the court also made it clear that the point was being decided *obiter*.[54] No adverse comment was made on the fact that S was

---

[51] For which see paras. 10.74–10.87 *supra*.

[52] As is required in solemn cases—see ss. 67(5) and 78(4) of the 1975 Act.

[53] 1983 S.L.T. 519, also referred to in paras. 10.56–10.65 *supra*.

[54] See Lord Hunter, *ibid.*, at p. 93. *N.B.* that the possibility of the Crown making use of s. 149 appears not to have been considered.

allowed to lead further evidence to rebut the Crown evidence in replication, even though, as Sheriff Gordon points out[55]: "This procedure could theoretically go on for ever."

10–133 To summarise the position in criminal cases regarding the leading of fresh evidence (if necessary by recalling a witness) after the close of one's case, but before the commencement of the speeches:

10–134 (i) either party may do so, with the leave of the court, when the new evidence is material, and either it was not reasonably available at the time or its materiality could not reasonably have been anticipated (section 268);

10–135 (ii) additionally the Crown may do so, with the leave of the court for the purpose either of contradicting defence evidence which could not reasonably have been anticipated, or of proving that a witness who has given evidence[56] has in the past made a statement inconsistent with the one given during the trial (section 269).

10–136 It should be noted in passing that fresh evidence may also be heard by the High Court in the course of hearing an appeal *either* from a solemn trial (*per* section 106 of the 1995 Act)[57] or by way of a stated case from a summary trial[58] (*per* section 175 of the 1995 Act).

10–137 The forerunner to section 106 was section 228 of the Criminal Procedure (Scotland) Act 1975. The interpretation of section 228 has given rise to a number of cases in recent years.[58a] The test for admitting new evidence is a strict one. It must be "important and reliable" and "likely to have had a material part to play in the jury's determination of a critical issue at the trial".[58b] Two of the most recent and controversial cases are those of *Church* v. *H.M.A.*[59] and *Elliott* v. *H.M.A.*[60] These two cases were heard within a fortnight of each other. *Church* was heard first and hailed as a breakthrough in the application of the section. The appeal was continued to allow additional evidence to be heard. In the meantime, the appeal in *Elliott* was remitted to a full bench who disapproved the decision in *Church* and rejected the liberal interpretation of section 228 made there, and to restate the

---

[55] In his commentary on the case: *ibid.*, at p. 96.

[56] *N.B.* not necessarily a defence witness, although presumably the Crown can deal effectively at the time with any such issues as may arise in the course of examining one of their own witnesses.

[57] See, *e.g. Moffat* v. *H.M.A.*, 1983 S.C.C.R. 121 and *Cameron* v. *H.M.A.*, 1987 S.C.C.R. 608. See also *Green, supra.*

[58] See *Moore* v. *Tudhope* 1987 S.C.C.R. 371 and *Moffat* v. *McNaughtan*, 1987 S.C.C.R. 497.

[58a] See, *e.g. Cameron* v. *H.M.A.*, 1988 S.L.T. 169 and *Stillie* v. *H.M.A.*, 1992 S.L.T. 279.

[58b] *Stillie, ibid., per* the Lord Justice-General at p. 284c, approving *dicta* in *Cameron* v. *H.M.A.*, 1988 S.L.T. 169.

[59] 1995 S.L.T. 604.

[60] 1995 S.L.T. 612.

traditionally strict approach to the question of whether additional evidence "was not and could not reasonably have been available at the trial."[61]

(2) Civil cases

In civil cases, the position with regard to the admissibility of fresh **10–138** evidence is far more piecemeal. There is no general rule covering all civil cases, but certain exceptions have been recognised in which the "interests of justice" require that evidence "in replication" of evidence already led should be admitted. In Court of Session cases,[62] the common law position in both Outer House first instance and Inner House reclaiming cases is that fresh evidence may be led after the close of the proof only if it could not have been made available previously by the exercise of reasonable diligence. This normally means that no warning of it could have been gleaned from a careful study of the closed record.[63]

In cases in which the Court of Session is hearing appeals from decisions **10–139** of the sheriff court, the Inner House has the power under section 72 of the Court of Session Act 1868 to hear additional evidence "if necessary" in the interests of justice.[64]

In the sheriff court itself, a sheriff conducting a proof has no power **10–140** to hear fresh evidence after the proof has closed, but the sheriff principal can hear such evidence in any appeal case in terms of section 27 of the Sheriff Courts (Scotland) Act 1907. Such examples as arise in practice are normally in the nature of *res noviter*,[65] which were not known at the time of the original proof.[66]

Once new evidence comes to light after a civil jury trial has been **10–141** concluded, the only way of dealing with it would appear to be via a new trial.[67]

---

[61] See the articles by Scott, "The Cases of *Church* and *Elliott*", 1995 S.L.T. (News) 2, and by Ferguson, "Fresh Evidence Appeals", J.L.S.S. 1995, 264.

[62] For which, generally, see Maxwell, *The Practice of the Court of Session*, p. 550.

[63] See Walker and Walker, *op. cit.,* n. 11, para. 338(a).

[64] See *Gairdner* v. *Macarthur*, 1915 S.C. 589.

[65] "New matters" which could not have been anticipated with the exercise of due diligence. This is the type of matter which at common law can be admitted in Court of Session actions: see above.

[66] See, *e.g. McFarlane* v. *Raeburn*, 1946 S.C. 67. (alibi not disclosed in closed record for affiliation and aliment action).

[67] See Wilkinson, *op. cit.,* n. 34, p. 166, and Maxwell, *op. cit.,* n. 62, pp.337 and 574. For the position in the sheriff court, see Macphail *Sheriff Court Practice*, paras. 16.94–96.

CHAPTER 11

COMPETENCE AND COMPELLABILITY OF WITNESSES

INTRODUCTION

11–01 A witness is "competent" to give evidence on oath or under affirmation when he or she is *allowed* to by law; and "compellable" as a witness when he or she can be *forced* to testify under threat of a charge of contempt of court.[1] The general rule is that every person who is capable of giving intelligible evidence is both a competent and a compellable witness.[2]

11–02 Although most witnesses are required to take the oath before testifying, a witness may choose, for religious or other reasons, to "affirm".[3] The fact that a person is of bad character, has previous convictions, or even has an interest in the outcome of the case does not operate as a bar to their testifying, since "moral turpitude or interest is a ground of criticism not of the admissibility of the witness but of the reliability of his evidence."[4]

11–03 Given the wide applicability of the general rule that everyone is both competent and compellable as a witness, it is only necessary to take note of those exceptions which still exist to this general rule. There are still some classes of persons who are not fully competent as witnesses, and there are others who, while competent, are not compellable. A more detailed study of these exceptional cases takes up the remainder of this chapter, in which, unless indicated to the contrary, the principles quoted apply equally to civil and criminal cases.

11–04 The additional complication arising from the fact that some witnesses, although normally both competent and compellable, may claim a "privilege" against answering certain types of question is considered in Chapter 12.

---

[1] See *H.M.A.* v. *Airs,* 1975 S.L.T. 177 at p. 181. This case is also considered in paras. 12.66–12.67 *infra.*

[2] Walker and Walker, *Law of Evidence in Scotland*, para. 348(a).

[3] Oaths Act 1978. See below for the further alternative of a simple admonition to tell the truth.

[4] *Dow* v. *McKnight,* 1949 J.C. 38 at p. 56. This case contains a comprehensive summary of the development of Scots law in this area. For the possibility of attacking a witness's *credibility* on the grounds of bad character, etc., see paras. 10.88–10.105 *supra* and the Criminal Procedure (Scotland) Act 1995, s. 265(1)(a).

WITNESSES OF LIMITED COMPETENCE

MENTAL INCAPACITY

There is no general rule that a person who is mentally ill, or who suffers **11–05** from mental incapacity, is incompetent as a witness. The test in all cases is whether or not the witness understands the difference between truth and falsehood, appreciates the duty of telling the truth, and can give coherent testimony.[5] It is a question of degree in the circumstances, and, for example, the man who is convinced that he is the reincarnation of John the Baptist may be a perfectly good witness to an assault in a bus station.

When it is decided to make use of such testimony — and the final decision **11–06** is that of the presiding judge or sheriff, if necessary after hearing evidence on that point[6]—the witness may either be sworn in the normal way, or simply admonished to tell the truth. The nature and extent of the disability may of course affect the weight to be given to that witness's evidence.

One possible approach to the problem was suggested by the trial judge **11–07** in *H.M.A.* v. *Stott*,[7] a trial for murder of a nurse in a mental asylum. Evidence was taken from one of the patients, but his Lordship warned the jury that since it was impossible to tell how much of the witness's evidence was a reliable product of his memory, and how much (if any) emanated from a diseased mind, they should not proceed on that evidence except in so far as it was corroborated by other witnesses.

DEAF, DUMB AND INARTICULATE WITNESSES

The only problem which arises in the case of a person with communication **11–08** difficulties is the physical one of obtaining evidence from him or her. A witness who has a hearing or speech impediment is a perfectly competent witness. A witness who does testify should do so on oath. It is competent to use an interpreter,[8] or, a witness may be able to give replies to questions in writing.

A witness will only be deemed incompetent if all reasonable attempts at **11–09** communication are fruitless.

CHILDREN

There is no official age below which a child is incompetent to give evidence. **11–10** The test to be applied is whether the child has a sufficient understanding of

---

5   Walker and Walker, *op. cit.*, n. 2, para. 350.
6   Black (1887) 1 White 365.
7   (1894) 1 Adam 386.
8   Experts in sign langauge may be used by the deaf: see *H.M.A.* v. *Wilson,* 1942 J.C. 75.

the concept of truth, an understanding of the duty to tell the truth, and is able to give coherent testimony. Extreme youth may detract from the weight to be attached to the resultant evidence. The presiding judge or sheriff has a duty to establish the competence of the child, and may hear evidence in order to assist in making the decision.

11–11   Competence has to be established in two stages. First, the judge or sheriff has to be satisfied the child knows the difference between truth and lies, and second the child must be admonished to tell the truth.[9] Where a child remains mute throughout the proceedings these requirements cannot be met.[10] In *Millar*,[11] a child of three was allowed to testify concerning a sexual assault upon her, in respect of which she had made a *de recenti* statement,[12] but in *Thomson*,[13] in the absence of such a statement, a child of three was rejected as a witness in a murder trial.

11–12   The competence of children as witnesses has gained prominence in recent years due to the frequency of cases referred to the sheriff court for proof from the Children's Hearing system. It is left to the discretion of the presiding judge or sheriff whether or not to administer the oath to child witnesses,[14] but it has recently been clarified that children under 12 are simply admonished to tell the truth, children aged from 12 to 14 are sworn by the judge if he is satisfied that they understand the nature of the oath, and children over 14 are sworn as a matter of routine.[15]

11–13   The frequency with which children are appearing in court as witnesses has led to increasing awareness that the formal procedures of the judicial process are not well-suited to assist children to give evidence. This is particularly so when the nature of the evidence which they are giving is of a difficult or embarassing nature. Similarly it is felt that it is especially intimidating for children in cases of physical or sexual abuse to have to give their evidence in a witness box placed a short distance from the alleged perpetrator. In 1990 the Scottish Law Commission published their Report on *Evidence of Children and Other Potentially Vulnerable Witnesses.*[16] A number of recommendations were made, many of which have now been enacted in legislation. The main steps which are now operative to facilitate the giving of evidence from child witnesses are considered next.

11–14   Although the Scottish Law Commission recommended improvements, for some time prior to the 1990 Report many judges and sheriffs had tried

---

[9] *Rees* v. *Lowe*, 1990 S.L.T. 507, followed in *Kelly* v. *Docherty*, 1991 S.L.T. 419.

[10] *F.* v. *Kennedy*, 1993 S.L.T. 1277.

[11] (1870) 1 Coup. 430.

[12] For the nature of which, see paras. 10.37–10.39 *supra*.

[13] (1857) 2 Irv. 747.

[14] *Anderson* v. *McFarlane* (1899) 1 F.(J.) 36.

[15] See *Rees* v. *Lowe infra*, *Kelly* v. *Docherty, infra*, and *M* v. *Kennedy* 1993 S.C.L.R. 69. Also, Macphail, *Evidence*, Chap. 8.03.

[16] Report No. 125.

to alleviate the formality of the court setting by removing wigs and gowns, clearing the court of unnecessary personnel and by re-arranging the furniture so that the judge was not in a distant and elevated position. However, it had been recognised that these voluntary practices did not go far enough.

Following the publication of the Scottish Law Commission's Report in **11–15** 1990, the Lord Justice-General issued a Memorandum on Child Witnesses[16a] which suggested a variety of measures which the presiding judge could take to achieve the general objective of ensuring that "so far as is reasonably practicable, ... the experience of giving evidence by all children under sixteen causes as little anxiety and distress to the child as possible in the circumstances." In addition to the three practices mentioned earlier which some judges had adopted, the Memorandum also suggested permitting the child to be accompanied by a relative or other supporting person.

The Law Reform (Miscellaneous Provisions)(Scotland) Act 1990 enacted **11–16** a major recommendation arising from the Commission's 1990 Report.[16b] That statutory provision is now embodied in section 271 of the Criminal Procedure (Scotland) Act 1995 which provides that a court may authorise the giving of evidence by a child witness by live television link. Section 271(7) states that this can be done "on cause shown", having regard to the possible effect on the child if the application was not granted; whether the child would be "better able to give evidence" if the application was granted; and the views of the child. In considering whether to grant such an application the court may take into account the four factors set out in section 271(8):

    (i)   the age and maturity of the child;
    (ii) the nature of the alleged offence;
    (iii) the nature of the evidence the child is likely to give; and
    (iv) any relationship between the child and the accused.

So far, the response by the courts to these provisions has been quite **11–17** restrictive. In *H.M.A.* v. *Birkett*[17] there was an application to allow five children's evidence to be given by live TV link. Three of the children were witnesses to an attempted murder of their mother. The court permitted evidence to be by TV link in the case of only one of the children as he was said to be frightened of the accused. In the case of the other children the court ruled that cause had not been shown in terms of the Act, but that a subsequent application could be made nearer the time if the circumstances changed.

[16a] Reproduced in Dent and Flin (eds.), *Children as Witnesses,* pp. 148–150.
[16b] s. 56 of the 1990 Act.
[17] 1992 S.C.C.R. 850.

11–18   In the case of *Brotherston* v. *H.M.A.*[18] three children gave evidence by means of a live television link. The quality of the resulting evidence was much criticised by the defence during the trial and in his charge to the jury the judge commented on it. On appeal, the court said that the use of a TV link required a balancing of two interests—fairness to the accused, and avoiding undue distress to the child.

11–19   Section 271(1) also permits a child to give evidence on commission.[19] This is a procedure whereby the court appoints a commissioner (either an advocate or solicitor of 5 years' standing) to take evidence from the child. The child's responses to questions asked by the commissioner are to be recorded on video tape and witnessed by the accused in a separate room. In determining an application made for a child to give evidence on commission, the court has to have regard to the same considerations in section 271(8).

11–20   Another measure designed to protect child witnesses is contained in section 271(6) which permits the use of a screen to conceal the accused from a child witness. The screen must be of a design to allow the accused to watch and hear as the child gives evidence.[20]

11–21   In terms of the Criminal Procedure (Scotland) Act 1995, s. 50(3) in any proceedings relating to indecent or immoral conduct in which a child is called as a witness, the court has the power to order from the courtroom everyone except the parties and their legal advisers, other persons directly concerned with the case, officers of the court and the press.

JUDGES, JURORS AND ARBITERS

11–22 Judges, acting in their private capacity as members of the public are perfectly competent witness to anything they may see or hear. The position regarding their competency as witnesses while acting in a judicial capacity then varies depending on the status of the judge. In *Muckarsie* v. *Wilson*,[21] it was held that a judge of the Supreme Court could not be called as a witness to evidence given before him.[22] On the other hand, judges of the lower courts are frequently called as competent witnesses to cases heard by them,[23] notably when the testimony of a witness heard by the judge results in a subsequent perjury charge.[24] The distinction would seem to be based on the twin

---

[18]   1995 S.C.C.R. 613.

[19]   For details of the procedures involved generally in taking evidence on commission see Maxwell, *Practice of the Court of Session*, and Macphail, *Sheriff Court Practice*.

[20]   Formerly a provision contained in s. 34 of the Prisoners and Criminal Proceedings (Scotland) Act 1993.

[21]   1834 Bell's Notes 99.

[22]   But he could to a physical incident such as a disturbance.

[23]   A practice which was regular even as early as in *Monaghan* (1844) 2 Broun 131.

[24]   *e.g. Davidson* v. *McFadyean*, 1942 J.C. 95.

considerations of the dignity of the office and the fact that senior judges are often sitting with a jury.[25]

Jurors may not testify to matters which arise in the jury room,[26] either in civil[27] or in criminal[28] cases, although in all other matters they remain competent witnesses, *e.g.* to an incident occurring during the trial. **11–23**

It seems that whereas a decree-arbitral[29] must "stand or fall on its own merits,"[30] arbiters are competent witnesses on any matter which could form the basis of a challenge to their awards,[31] even though otherwise evidence of the testimony heard by them is incompetent.[32] **11–24**

PROSECUTORS AND DEFENCE SOLICITORS

It seems from *Mackintosh* v. *Wooster*[33] that procurator fiscals are perfectly competent witnesses to any matter on which they can assist the court, provided that they are not also conducting the case, and if possible have had no personal involvement in its preparation. Perhaps the best guide in this matter comes from Lord Deas in *Ferguson* v. *Webster*,[34] to the effect that: "It would be the duty of anyone so situated to decline from the outset all interference, either official or judicial, in a case in which he knew he had important testimony to give from his own personal knowledge." **11–25**

On the other hand, there is no objection to a defence solicitor, while actually conducting a client's case, testifying as to matters within his or her knowledge.[35] In such cases the client cannot, at least in a criminal case, insist on certain matters being excluded on the grounds of agent-client privilege.[36] **11–26**

---

[25] See Macphail, *op. cit.,* n. 15, Chap. 3.08–3.13.

[26] At least, not so far as concerns their deliberations; see *McGuire* v. *Brown,* 1963 S.C. 107 at pp. 109 and 112.

[27] *Pirie* v. *Caledonian Ry.* (1890) 17 R. 1157 at p. 1161.

[28] Hume, II, 429.

[29] The final ruling of an arbiter, which *quoad* the parties has the force of law.

[30] Macphail, *op. cit.,* n. 15, Chap. 3.15.

[31] *e.g.* bias, failure to exhaust remit, etc.

[32] See *Black* v. *John Williams & Co.,* 1923 S.C. 510; 1924 S.C.(H.L.) 22 at p. 28. For an example of a case in which the arbiter's evidence was heard in an action for the reduction of his award, see *Glasgow City and District Ry.* v. *MacGeorge* (1886) 13 R. 609.

[33] 1919 J.C. 15.

[34] (1869) 1 Coup. 370 at p. 375. The effect of *Mackintosh* is that the only strict bar arises when the prosecutor is actually presenting the case.

[35] *Campbell* v. *Cochrane,* 1928 J.C. 25. The rule extends to defence advocates; see Renton and Brown, *Criminal Procedure,* para. 18–78.

[36] For which see paras. 12.35–12.49 *infra.* This is the effect of s. 265(2) of the Criminal Procedure (Scotland) Act 1995. *Quaere* where it extends to civil cases.

HEADS OF STATE

11–27   There is no direct authority on the competence of the monarch as a witness, but the general assumption seems to be that he or she is competent, but not compellable, as a witness.[37] The remainder of the Royal Family are taken to be both competent and compellable.[38]

11–28   Foreign heads of state, their families and domestic retinue, have the same basic privilege as foreign diplomats, in that they are competent but not compellable as witnesses.[39]

PERSONS PRESENT IN COURT DURING PREVIOUS EVIDENCE

11–29   At common law, there was an absolute bar against the hearing of testimony from a witness who had been in court prior to giving evidence, and had therefore heard some of the previous testimony.[40] This rigid rule has now been partly amended by section 3 of the Evidence (Scotland) Act 1840, which applied to all cases until 1975 (and still applies in civil cases) and section 267 of the Criminal Procedure (Scotland) Act 1995.[41]

11–30   The effect of section 3 of the 1840 Act is that the court has a discretion to admit the evidence of any witness who has been present "without the permission of the court" and "without the consent of the party objecting," when it can be shown that the witness's presence in court was not the result of "culpable negligence or criminal intent" and that "injustice will not be done by his or her examination." The burden of proof on each of these issues rests with the party seeking to adduce the witness.[42]

11–31   The effect of section 267(1) of the 1995 Act is that the court may, on the application of any party to either solemn or summary proceedings, permit a witness to be in court during the proceedings of any part of them before giving evidence, if the court is satisfied that this would not be contrary to the interests of justice. These provisions apply when permission is being sought in advance for a witness to be present during proceedings.

11–32   Where a witness has been in court without permission and a party wishes to call that witness to give evidence then section 267(2) gives the court discretion to admit the evidence provided:

---

[37] See Macphail, *op. cit.,* n. 15, Chap. 3.04–3.06.

[38] Wilkinson, *Scottish Law of Evidence*, p. 154.

[39] The effect of the State Immunity Act 1978, s. 20. Their status is confirmed by a certificate from the Foreign Office: *ibid.*, s. 21.

[40] See Dickson on *Evidence*, para. 1599.

[41] Previously, ss. 139A and 342A of the Criminal Procedure (Scotland) Act 1975.

[42] *Macdonald* v. *Mackenzie*, 1947 J.C. 169 at p. 174. *N.B.* also pp. 175 and 176, where it was held to be the duty of the judge to question the competence of any witness who has been present in court where this is apparent to him.

(i)   that the witness's presence in court was not as a result of culpable negligence or criminal intent; and

(ii) that the witness has not been unduly instructed or influenced by what has taken place; and

(iii) that there will be no injustice by his being heard.

It was finally established in *Campbell* v. *Cochrane*[43] that parties, their **11–33** advocates and agents may testify even though they have been present during the whole of the prior evidence, and this applies equally to the accused.[44] Equally, it has been established since at least the turn of the century[45] that in the absence of any objection, an expert witness[46] may be allowed to remain in court during the hearing of other testimony, except the opinion part of other experts' testimony.[47]

When a witness is allowed to remain in court after giving testimony, but **11–34** is then recalled,[48] it seems that current practice does not recognise any objection to the recall on the ground that the witness has heard some of the testimony, and has almost certainly heard that part of it which has led to the recall.[49]

WITNESS COMPETENT BUT NOT FULLY COMPELLABLE

INTRODUCTION

As has already been noted, the guiding general rule is that a witness who is **11–35** competent is also compellable. In the words of Sheriff Walker[50]:

> "If a competent witness, who has knowledge of the circumstances to be inquired into, is present in court, I can see no inherent objection to his being compelled to give evidence, whether he be a party or not, if the court decides that this is desirable in the interests of justice with a view to the ascertainment of the facts."

---

[43] 1928 J.C. 25; see also paras. 11.25–11.26 *supra* and 11.46–11.48 *infra*. The fact that a party has heard prior testimony can, however, be the subject of judicial comment; see *Penman* v. *Binny's Trs.*, 1925 S.L.T. 123.

[44] *H.M.A.* v. *Ferrie*, 1983 S.C.C.R. 1.

[45] See, *e.g. H.M.A.* v. *Laurie* (1889) 2 White 326.

[46] For which see Chap. 16 *infra*. In some cases, expert evidence may actually be given on the basis of the facts which are established by other testimony.

[47] See Renton and Brown, *op. cit.,* n. 35, para. 18–79 and *H.M.A.* v. *Laurie supra*.

[48] For which see paras. 10.113–10.120 *supra*.

[49] See *Dyet* v. *N.C.B.*, 1957 S.L.T. (Notes) 18.

[50] Sir Allan G. Walker, Q.C., co-author of Walker and Walker, *Law of Evidence in Scotland*, in *McDonnell* v. *McShane*, 1967 S.L.T. (Sh.Ct.) 61, at p. 63.

11–36   This ruling, made *obiter*, arose in the context of a witness who had not been cited, but there can be little doubt that it reflects the modern view.[51] In civil cases, section 1 of the Evidence (Scotland) Act 1852 renders competent witnesses who appear without citation, and a similar rule exists in criminal cases *per* section 265(1)(d) of the Criminal Procedure (Scotland) Act 1995.

11–37   It follows from this that a witness called for one party in a civil case, but not examined by that party, may be called by the other party. This was the point established in *McDonnell* v. *McShane*,[52] in which the witness in question was the defender in an affiliation and aliment action. It was ruled that he could be called as a witness by the pursuer, even though he had not been cited as a witness, since citation simply serves the purpose of securing the attendance of the witness, and thereafter he or she is compellable for either side if competent.

11–38   A similar ruling for criminal cases was laid down in *Todd* v. *H.M.A.*.[53] T objected to the fact that evidence given by a witness for a co-accused, L, was used against her, arguing that evidence by a witness for one co-accused was not, at common law, admissible against another accused when they were running separate defences. On appeal, it was held that the law of evidence had developed and broadened over the years, to the point at which a co-accused may, *per* sections 141 and 346 of the 1975 Act,[54] be called as a witness for another accused.

11–39   The general rule for both civil and criminal cases would therefore seem to be that a person who has appeared at court as a witness, whether cited as such or not,[55] is available as a witness for either side, and is compellable to give such evidence in the interests of justice.

11–40   To this general rule there are certain exceptions, and the remainder of this chapter considers these in turn.

DIPLOMATS AND CONSULAR OFFICIALS

11–41 Under the Diplomatic Privileges Act 1964, the head of a diplomatic mission based in the United Kingdom, and members of the diplomatic staff, while competent to give evidence if they wish, cannot be compelled to do so. The

---

[51] See, *e.g.* Macphail, *op. cit.,* n. 15, Chap. 3.31, and Wilkinson, *Scottish Law of Evidence*, p. 154.

[52] 1967 S.L.T. (Sh.Ct.) 61.

[53] 1984 S.L.T. 123.

[54] The forerunning sections to s. 266 of the Criminal Procedure (Scotland) Act 1995. This point is developed in paras. 11.66–11.75 *infra*.

[55] But *N.B.* The requirement in solemn criminal cases for both parties to give notice to the other of the witnesses they intend to call, *per* s. 65 of the 1995 Act. Generally, for discussion of the previous provisions contained in the 1975 Act see Renton and Brown, *op. cit.,* n. 35, paras. 7.14, 7.15, 7.20, 7.21 and 7.23. There are also exceptions in the case of the accused himself where he intends to give evidence, and co-accused who plead guilty during the course of the trial. These are dealt with *infra*.

same privilege extends to the families and staff of diplomats, and to the families of members of staff, provided in every case that they are not also citizens of the United Kingdom and colonies. The qualification of any given person to claim this form of diplomatic immunity is determined by a certificate from the Foreign Office.

Under the Consular Relations Act 1968 and the Diplomatic and Other **11–42** Privileges Act 1971, similar rules apply to full-time consular officials. All part-time consular officials, however, and their staff, are both competent and compellable, except in relation to matters covered by their diplomatic work. Nor may they be compelled to act as expert witnesses on the law of their home countries.

BANKERS

In criminal proceedings, by virtue of the Bankers Books Evidence Act 1879, **11–43** s. 6, a bank official is competent but not compellable as a witness in matters relating to entries in the bank's books. This extends to appearances or to production of any bank book or record, unless ordered by the court to do so for "special cause" as shown by the party wishing to call him.

Where it is necessary to call a bank witness to testify that a copy of an **11–44** entry in the bank's records is an authentic copy of the original, he is compellable for that purpose.[56]

In civil proceedings, the position is broadly the same, as section 7(2) of **11–45** the Civil Evidence (Scotland) Act 1988 extends the effect of section 6 of the Bankers' Books Evidence Act 1879 to civil matters.

PARTIES AND THEIR SPOUSES IN CIVIL CASES

As was explained in paragraphs 11.01–11.04 *supra*, there has been a gradual **11–46** erosion of the old common law rule whereby a party to a civil action was incompetent as a witness, and it was formerly abolished by section 3 of the Evidence (Scotland) Act 1853. It was also held in *Campbell* v. *Cochrane*[57] that the fact that such parties have been present in court and have therefore heard the testimony prior to their own does not disqualify them as witnesses.

Section 3 did not specifically state whether or not a party was compellable **11–47** as a witness, and indeed in the normal course of things such a question will not arise. It will arise, however, when the party in question is forced into the witness box by the other party, which is what happened in *McDonnell* v. *McShane*.[58] The court held that in such circumstances the party was

---

[56] See *ibid.*, ss. 4 and 5.
[57] 1928 J.C. 25, referred to in paras. 11.25–11.26 and 11.29–11.34 *supra*.
[58] Dealt with in paras. 11.35–11.40 *supra*.

compellable, and this accords with the general rule that competence implies compellability. It is consistent with "the trend which seeks to remove artificial or illogical restrictions from the law of evidence."[59]

11–48 The parties' spouses were also granted competence as witnesses under section 3, while at the same time they were given a privilege against testifying to matters characterised as "any matter communicated (to each other) during the marriage." There is no definition provided of "marital communications."[60] The wording of the section, however, gave rise to some doubts[61] as to the compellability of the spouse in other cases.

THE ACCUSED: GENERAL

11–49 There are three contexts in which the accused person in a criminal trial might find himself in the witness box, namely:

    (i)   as a witness for himself;
    (ii) as a witness for a co-accused; and
    (iii) as a witness for the prosecution.

The accused may be a competent witness, subject to certain safeguards, in all three cases, but special problems surround the circumstances in which he may be called, and his compellability in such cases. Each of these contexts is examined in turn.

THE ACCUSED AS A WITNESS FOR HIMSELF

11–50 At common law, the accused had no status as a witness in his own trial, and had to content himself with an unsworn judicial declaration from the dock. In 1898 he was made a competent witness in his own defence on any charge, and the current law is to be found in section 266(1) of the Criminal Procedure (Scotland) Act 1995.[62] It states that the accused is a competent witness for the defence at every stage of the trial, whether he is tried alone or with a co-accused.

---

[59] Lord Justice-Clerk Wheatley in *Todd* v. *H.M.A.*, in para. 11.38 *supra* at p. 127. See also Macphail, *op. cit.,* n. 15, Chap. 3.31.
[60] This aspect of the law is considered more fully in 12.24–12.32 *infra.*
[61] Which are considered by Clive, *Husband and Wife,* pp. 348–352 and also Macphail, *op. cit.,* n. 15, Chap. 4.04, who suggests a statutory rule making it clear that in civil cases the spouse is both competent and compellable.
[62] Previously, ss. 141(1) and 346(1) of the 1975 Act.

Section 266(11) requires that where the accused is to be called as a witness **11–51** by the defence, he must be the first witness called unless the court directs otherwise.[63]

When giving evidence, the accused is sworn, or affirms, in the normal **11–52** way, testifies from the witness box,[64] and is liable to a perjury charge if he gives false evidence.[65] In solemn cases, although the defence must give advance notice to the Crown of their intention to call all other witnesses, they need not do so in the case of an accused, who may testify at the trial without prior intimation.[66]

Although the right to make an unsworn judicial declaration was lost in **11–53** 1898, the Criminal Justice (Scotland) Act 1980 introduced the concept of judicial examination and the current provisions are contained in section 35(4) of the Criminal Procedure (Scotland) Act 1995. This permits an accused who appears on petition before a sheriff to advance a defence or make any other comment in response to questions put by the prosecutor.[67]

The accused is not on oath during judicial examination, and has the **11–54** right to refuse to answer any questions put to him by the Crown in the course of their endeavours to establish his preliminary response to the charge(s) against him. However, a record of the proceedings (subject to deletions called for in advance by either party, and agreed by the court after hearing both sides) is read out at the trial. This creates the potential for introducing to the jury a statement by the accused on which he cannot be cross- examined if he declines to go into the witness box.

This practice was condemned by Lord Justice-Clerk Wheatley in *Hendry* **11–55** v. *H.M.A.*[68] as "illegitimate", who went on to observe that "the sooner it is stamped out the better." Even so, the appeal court was obliged to hold that such a statement could be used to bolster the credibility of other, independent evidence.

Section 266(2)[69] states that the accused may only be called as a witness **11–56** for himself upon his own application and it follows that in the formal sense, an accused can never be compelled to give evidence on his own behalf. There may be dangers, however, in such a course of action since adverse implications might be drawn from silence on the part of an accused.

---

[63] *Quaere* how this may be reconciled with the plea of "no case to answer" permitted in both solemn and summary cases, after the rejection of which the accused may go on to call witnesses and give evidence himself. Renton and Brown, *op. cit.,* n. 35, para. 18–07 state that the sections have never been enforced in Scotland, and they were criticised by Walker and Walker, *op. cit.,* n. 2, para. 356, and Macphail, *op. cit.,* n. 15, Chap. 5.16–5.19.

[64] Previously ss. 141(1)(*g*) and 346(1)(*g*) of the 1975 Act.

[65] See *H.M.A.* v. *Cairns*, 1967 J.C. 37.

[66] See *Kennedy* v. *H.M.A.* (1898) 2 Adam 588.

[67] For further details of this procedure, see Renton and Brown, *op. cit.,* n. 35, paras. 5.58 *et seq.*

[68] 1986 S.L.T. 186.

[69] Previously, ss. 141(1)(a) and 346(1)(a) of the 1975 Act.

11–57   Until April 1, 1996 the failure of the accused to give evidence was not something upon which the Crown could comment. However section 32 of the Criminal Justice (Scotland) Act 1995 repealed those provisions in the 1975 Act which prohibited comment.[70] The entitlement now to comment is an encroachment on the so-called "right to silence" since any Crown comment is likely to be adverse.

11–58   In a solemn trial, the judge or sheriff is entitled to comment adversely on an accused's failure to give sworn testimony, though if such comment is excessive it can give rise to grounds for appeal, and a reasonable balance should be struck.[71]

11–59   In some cases, adverse comment may be unavoidable if justice is to be done to both sides. There are cases in which an accused is expected to give an innocent explanation of circumstances which imply guilt,[72] and his silence in such cases is an invitation to the jury to draw the most adverse inferences it wishes from the unchallenged prosecution evidence.

11–60   The guidelines to be followed in cases in which evidence ought reasonably to be expected from the accused are those laid down by Lord Justice-General Normand in *Scott* v. *H.M.A.*,[73] who advised trial judges and sheriffs that:

> "Although a comment of the kind is, in my view competent, it should be made with restraint and only when there are special circumstances which require it; and, if it is made with reference to particular evidence which the panel might have explained or contradicted, care should be taken that the evidence is not distorted and that its true bearing on the defence is properly represented to the jury."

11–61   It is an unsettled point whether or not a co-accused can comment on the failure of an accused to give sworn testimony, although the authorities seem to be in agreement that such comment should be allowed.[74] If an accused fails to testify, he cannot of course be cross-examined by that co-accused,[75] and it would seem to be only fair to allow the frustrated co-accused the right to comment on this.

11–62   In the course of giving evidence on his own behalf, it is quite possible that D1 will give evidence which is adverse to, or even incriminatory of,

---

[70] ss. 141(1)(b) and 346(1)(b).

[71] See *Stewart* v. *H.M.A.*, 1980 S.L.T. 245.

[72] See *McHugh* v. *H.M.A.*, 1978 J.C. 12 and *Hardy* v. *H.M.A.* in paras. 2.25–2.44 *supra*; see also Lord Justice-Clerk Grant in *McIlhargey* v. *Herron, ibid.*, who pointed out that "the silent defender does take a risk." See also *Dorrens* v. *H.M.A.*, 1983 S.C.C.R. 407 at 411.

[73] 1946 J.C. 90 at p. 98. See also *Knowles* v. *H.M.A.*, 1975 J.C. 6.

[74] See Macphail, *op. cit.*, n. 15, para. 5.34, and Renton and Brown, *op. cit.*, n. 35, both of whom quote the English authority of *R.* v. *Wickham* (1971) 55 Cr.App.R. 199, which allowed comment by a co-accused in a case under the Criminal Evidence Act 1898, which was the forerunner of the 1975 Act in Scotland.

[75] See paras. 10.56–10.65 *supra*.

D2. The common law rule that the evidence of D1 is not admissible against D2 unless they are running a joint defence was ignored in practice for many years, and was finally laid to rest in *Young* v. *H.M.A.*[76]

It is obviously of crucial importance to every accused to have the right **11–63** to cross-examine a co-accused who gives evidence, but *Young* v. *H.M.A.* arguably only applied when the two accused were running separate defences, and perhaps only when D1 gave evidence adverse to D2. For this reason, section 266(8)(b) of the Criminal Procedure (Scotland) Act 1995 states that an accused may "ask a co-accused any question in cross-examination if that co-accused gives evidence."[77] The effect of this is to place on the widest possible basis the right of D1 to cross-examine D2 when and if he gives evidence on his own behalf. It is not necessary for the defences of each to be separate, or for D2 to say a single word against D1. The very fact that he gives evidence on his own behalf allows D1 to cross-examine him, along of course with the Crown.[78]

When more than one accused appears on the same charge(s), and any **11–64** one of them gives evidence, then *quoad* the remainder, the evidence of each is obviously the evidence of a *socius criminis*.[79] However, it is incompetent and improper to issue the *cum nota* warning to the jury in respect of that evidence because of the prejudicial effect which it may have on a person whose guilt has yet to be established.[80] This is true even though there is evidence to incriminate a co-accused.[81] If an accused pleads guilty to, or is convicted of, the charges in which he is *socius criminis* before the end of the trial, and thereafter gives evidence for the Crown, then the warning may be administered,[82] but it may not be administered until then.

The remaining issues which arise from the position of the accused as a **11–65** witness for himself (*i.e.* questions of privilege, and cross-examination as to character and previous convictions) are dealt with in later chapters.

---

[76] 1932 J.C. 63, considered also in paras. 10.62–10.63 *supra*. This case also established the right of D1 to cross-examine D2 in order to vindicate his own defence. See also *Lavery* v. *H.M.A.*, 1979 S.L.T. (Notes) 4.

[77] Alternatively, *per* s. 266(9)(a), he may call him as a witness with his consent, but he cannot do both; see paras. 11.66–11.75 *infra*. The previous statutory provisions were contained in ss. 141(2) and 346(2) of the 1975 Act.

[78] For the order in which such cross-examinations are to take place, see paras. 10.56–10.65 *supra*.

[79] See para. 10.95 *supra*.

[80] *Martin* v. *H.M.A.*, 1960 S.L.T. 213.

[81] *Slowey* v. *H.M.A.*, 1965 S.L.T. 309.

[82] *Wallace* v. *H.M.A.*, 1952 J.C. 78 at p. 84; see now *Docherty* v. *H.M.A.*, 1987 S.L.T. 784 at paras. 10.95 *supra*.

THE ACCUSED AS A WITNESS FOR A CO-ACCUSED

11–66 At common law, D1 could not competently be called as a witness for D2,[83] but that position was changed by statute in 1980 and the current provisions are contained in section 266(9)(a) of the Criminal Procedure (Scotland) Act 1995. This states that "the accused may, with the consent of a co-accused, call that other accused as a witness on the accused's behalf."[84] It is clear from the outset, of course, that while D1 may be competent as a witness for D2, he cannot be compellable while the two remain co-accused, *i.e.* still facing a verdict on charges on a complaint or indictment in which they are both named.

11–67 That is as far as the law goes while the two remain as co-accused, but the position is more complicated if and when one of the accused has the charges withdrawn, or pleads guilty, after the start of the trial. This is because of the effect of section 266(10) of the 1995 Act which states that:

> "The prosecutor or the accused may call as a witness a co-accused who has pleaded guilty to or been acquitted of all charges against him which remain before the court (whether or not in a case where the co-accused has pleaded guilty to any charges, he has been sentenced) or in respect of whom the diet has been deserted; and the party calling such co-accused as a witness shall not require to give notice thereof, but the court may grant any other party such adjournment or postponement of the trial as may seem just."[85]

11–68 Equally clearly, in such a case, the accused is compellable,[86] and in solemn cases there is no need for his name to have appeared on the defence list of witnesses beforehand.

11–69 Before the subsection may operate, however, it is necessary for all the charges which the former accused faced at the start of the trial diet to have been disposed of by either a guilty plea or an acquittal or a desertion of the diet by the Crown.[87] It is not necessary for the accused to have been convicted or sentenced.

---

[83] See Renton and Brown, *op. cit.*, n. 35, para. 18–17.

[84] It will be recalled from paras. 11.50–11.65 *supra*, that by subs. (9)(*b*) in each case, he may also cross-examine him if he gives evidence, but he may not do both. The previous statutory provisions were contained in ss. 141(2)(a) and 346(2)(a) of the 1975 Act.

[85] Previously, ss. 141(3) and 346(3) of the 1975 Act. The application of the rule to the prosecution is considered in paras. 11.76–11.85 *infra*.

[86] In accordance with the normal rule that competence implies compellability, and by contrast with the wording of s. 266(9)(*a*) *supra*.

[87] Unless the Crown desert these charges *simpliciter* the accused giving evidence for a co-accused enjoys a privilege against answering questions which may incriminate him, even in respect of charges which have been withdrawn: see paras. 12.21–12.23 *infra*. He will, however, come within the purview of the subsection because he will have pled guilty to all the charges "remaining before the court", a phrase clearly intended to make allowance for withdrawals by the Crown.

The point arose in *H.M.A.* v. *Ferrie*,[88] in which a number of accused **11–70** persons appeared in an indictment on a number of charges. One of them, Y, pled guilty to part of one charge, and the Crown accepted it by withdrawing the remaining charges against him from the indictment, the jury being directed to record a not guilty verdict on the remainder of the charge to which he had partially pled guilty. Sentence on him was postponed until the end of the trial and he was held in custody.

The Crown then sought leave to call him as a witness against the **11–71** remaining accused, who objected on the ground that he had not pled guilty to all the charges which remained against him at the time of the making of the plea. It was held that the moment of time at which the subsection was to be applied was the moment at which he was called as a witness, and at that time he had pled guilty to the only charge which remained against him.

Before a person can be classed as the "co-accused" of another for the **11–72** purposes of section 266(9), it is necessary for them both to appear at a trial diet on the same complaint or indictment. Even if they began in this position when first charged, D1 will no longer be classed as the co-accused of D2 if their trials have been separated as the result of some earlier diet prior to trial. In such cases, each will be a competent and compellable witness for the other in their separate trials, whether or not his case has been disposed of.[89] Where the trial proceeds by solemn procedure the potential witness must appear on the witness list of the accused for whom he will be testifying.

It was held in *Monaghan* v. *H.M.A.*[90] that when D1 is originally charged **11–73** along with D2 on an indictment, but pleads guilty by the accelerated procedure available under section 76 of the 1995 Act,[91] he remains a "co-accused" since his name appears on the indictment, and qualifies to be called as a witness for a co-accused by virtue of section 266(10).

The final possibility is that the charges against one of two original co- **11–74** accused are dropped by the Crown prior to the commencement of the trial. In such a case the person concerned is at common law a competent and compellable witness for the remaining accused, but in solemn cases must appear on the defence witness list, and, unless the Crown have deserted *simpliciter*, may refuse to answer any questions which tend to incriminate him *quoad* those charges.

No co-accused giving evidence on behalf of another co-accused can be **11–75** classed as *socius criminis*, a term which is confined to witnesses giving

---

[88] 1983 S.C.C.R. 1. *N.B.* that this was a case in which the former accused was called by the Crown, but the point at issue is the same for both types of case.

[89] *Morrison* v. *Adair*, 1943 J.C. 25. In such a case, of course, the accused called as a witness will enjoy a privilege against self-incrimination in respect of the charges still outstanding against him.

[90] 1983 S.C.C.R. 521, another case in which the co-accused was in fact called for the Crown.

[91] Previously, s. 102 of the 1975 Act. For details see Renton and Brown, *op. cit.*, n. 35, Chap. 8.

evidence *against* another accused, and probably to those who do so as Crown witnesses.[92]

THE ACCUSED AS A WITNESS FOR THE PROSECUTION

11–76 For as long as a person remains on trial on charges which have yet to be proved or admitted he can never be a competent witness for the prosecution, either against himself or against a co-accused. However, since *Young* v. *H.M.A.*,[93] an accused giving evidence on his own behalf may well assist the prosecution by giving evidence adverse to a co-accused upon which the prosecution may rely.

11–77   As we saw in paragraphs 11.53–11.54 *supra,* the process of judicial examination was introduced in 1980 and is now embodied in sections 35 and 36 of the Criminal Procedure (Scotland) Act 1995,[94] whereby an accused may, prior to the final determination of his case, be called upon by the Crown to give some sort of evidence. The accused is invited to make any comment he wishes in respect of:

(i) any of the charges in the petition;
(ii) any defence he may wish to put forward; or
(iii) any confession which he is alleged to have made to the police.

11–78   In this sense, the accused may turn out to have given evidence at the behest of the Crown. Although there is a theoretical right to remain almost totally silent on this occasion, the silence may[95] be made the subject of adverse comment by the Crown, the judge or any co-accused if at the subsequent trial any matter is raised[96] which might appropriately have been raised at the judicial examination.[97]

11–79   Leaving aside sections 35 and 36, the most obvious circumstance in which an accused person may become a witness for the Crown is still that in which he ceases to be an accused, by virtue of having pled guilty or had the charges against him deserted, and is then called as a prosecution witness against a former co-accused. Alternatively, as explained in paragraphs 11.66–11.75 *supra*, the trials of himself and a co-accused may be separated so that each is a competent and compellable witness for the Crown at the trial of the other.[98]

---

[92] *Slowey* v. *H.M.A.*, 1965 S.L.T. 309.
[93] 1932 J.C. 63, and in practice since before then.
[94] For details of this process see Renton and Brown, *op. cit.,* n. 35, para. 5.58 *et seq.*
[95] *per* s. 36(8).
[96] *e.g.* a defence such as alibi or incrimination.
[97] For example, *Alexander* v. *H.M.A.*, 1989 S.L.T. 193 where nothing was said at the judicial examination on the instructions of the accused's solicitor. When a defence of alibi was put forward at the trial, it was held competent for the trial judge to comment on this in his charge to the jury, leaving them to assess what weight to attach to the accused's evidence.
[98] See *Morrison* v. *Adair*, 1943 J.C. 25.

When, during the course of a trial, an accused pleads guilty to all the **11–80** charges against him, or has all such charges dropped, or indeed is dealt with by a combination of these two possibilities (*i.e.* a partial plea of guilt being accepted by the Crown), the situation is covered by section 266(10) of the 1995 Act.[99] It will be recalled from paragraphs 11.66–11.75 *supra* that in such a case, the former co-accused may be called as a witness by either a continuing accused *or* the prosecution. He is then, in the circumstances envisaged by the sections, both competent and compellable for the Crown.

All that was written in paragraphs 11.66–11.75 concerning the effect of **11–81** the subsections in relation to the former accused testifying for a former co-accused applies equally *quoad* evidence given by such a person for the Crown. In particular, it will be recalled that both *H.M.A.* v. *Ferrie* and *Monaghan* v. *H.M.A.*, referred to earlier, were cases in which the former accused appeared as a witness for the Crown. The only important distinction between the two situations is that when the former accused gives evidence for the Crown following a guilty plea, then in accordance with the definition in *Wallace* v. *H.M.A.*,[1] his evidence must be treated as that of a *socius criminis,* whether he has been sentenced or not.

It will also be recalled that when D1 appears as a witness for D2, in **11–82** circumstances in which the Crown have not deserted the charges against him *simpliciter*, he may claim the privilege against answering any question which might incriminate him as to the offences with which he was charged.[2] This cannot arise when he appears for the Crown in those cases in which the Crown has given up the right to prosecute him again on these charges. This occurs whenever he is called specifically as a *socius criminis* in respect of those charges which the remaining accused still faces. The *socius* in such cases is said to have an "immunity" against further prosecution, and this operates to all intents and purposes like a desertion *simpliciter*. The same rule applies when the Crown have secured D1 as a *socius criminis* witness by separating his trial from D2. If, however, D1 is not specifically called as a *socius criminis* the immunity does not apply, and D1 will require to fall back on the privilege against self-incrimination.

A modern restriction of what appears to have been a wider rule in Hume's **11–83** day[3] is illustrated by *O'Neill* v. *Wilson*.[4] In this case, N, a police constable, was charged with assaulting L, but claimed immunity on the ground that on an earlier occasion he had, as a witness for the Crown, given evidence

---

[99] First introduced by s. 28 of the Criminal Justice (Scotland) Act 1980.

[1] 1952 J.C. 78, dealt with in para. 10.94–10.95 *supra*. But see *Scott* v. *H.M.A.*, 1986 S.C.C.R. 346 and *Docherty* v. *H.M.A.*, para. 10.95 *supra*.

[2] The nature of this privilege is considered more fully in paras. 12.21–12.23 *infra*.

[3] In the words of Hume, II, 366–367: "By the very act of calling him as a witness, the prosecutor discharges all title to molest him for the future with relation to the matter libelled."

[4] 1983 S.L.T. 573.

against L on a charge of assaulting him, N. It was held on appeal (i) that the immunity from prosecution applies only to a person expressly called as a *socius criminis* in the crime with which the then accused is charged, and (ii) that such immunity covers only the charges contained in the "libel" in support of which he has given evidence.

11–84   The position, in those cases in which D1 is called by the Crown as a witness against D2 while certain charges remain outstanding against D1 (in that they have not been deserted *simpliciter*), would therefore seem to be as follows. If he is called as a *socius criminis* and the charges which remain against him are also the charges faced by D2, then he acquires immunity from further prosecution on such charges, and cannot claim the privilege against self-incrimination. In all other cases, he has no future immunity, but may claim the privilege. He remains, however, otherwise compellable as a witness.

11–85   It remains to be noted that when D1 is called to testify for the Crown against D2 in circumstances which fall within section 266, he need not appear on the Crown witness list, although the court may grant "such adjournment or postponement of the trial as may seem just." In all other cases, the normal witness notice must be given.

THE SPOUSE OF AN ACCUSED: GENERAL

11–86   At common law the spouse[5] of an accused remains incompetent as a witness for all purposes, except in those cases in which she is the "victim" of the crime with which her spouse is charged. In that event the spouse is both competent and compellable for the Crown, but no one else. The most obvious applications of this rule are in cases of physical assault, but it may also be applied in offences against property, such as theft[6] and forgery.[7]

11–87   Until 1980, there were various complex statutory exceptions to this common law rule.[8] The current provisions are in section 264 of the Criminal Procedure (Scotland) Act 1995:

"(1) The spouse of an accused may be called as a witness—
(a) by the accused;
(b) by a co-accused or by the prosecutor without the consent of the accused.
(2) Nothing in this section shall—
(a) make the spouse of an accused a compellable witness for a co-accused or for the prosecutor in a case where such spouse would not be so compellable at common law;

---

[5]   It has been held that "spouse" means married persons and does not include cohabitees. See *Casey* v. *H.M.A.*, 1993 S.L.T. 33.

[6]   *Harper* v. *Adair*, 1945 J.C. 21.

[7]   *Foster* v. *H.M.A.*, 1932 J.C. 75.

[8]   The complex nature of which is well documented by Macphail, *Evidence*, Chap. 6.

(b) compel a spouse to disclose any communication made between the spouses during the marriage.

(3) The failure of the spouse of an accused to give evidence shall not be commented on by the defence or the prosecutor."

Each aspect of the new rules is now considered in turn.   **11–88**

THE SPOUSE AS A WITNESS FOR THE ACCUSED

It is clear from section 264(1)(a) that, without exception, the spouse is a **11–89** competent witness for the accused. Any doubt which might have remained as to her compellability for the same purpose was removed in *Hunter* v. *H.M.A.*,[9] in which H was charged with assaulting and then murdering his daughter. His wife appeared on the Crown witness list against him, but was not called. The accused, who had lodged a special defence incriminating his wife on the assault charge only, sought to call her as a witness for himself. The trial judge ruled that she need not answer any questions put to her by his counsel if she did not wish. On appeal, it was held that, although the omission of the evidence had not led to a miscarriage of justice (since the evidence in question would only have been to the effect that H had hitherto been a loving father to the child), that the trial judge had erred in his ruling. The wife was said to be a compellable witness for the accused because[10]:

> "The provisions of section 143[11] are symptomatic of the development of the principle that, subject to appropriate safeguards, all relevant evidence should be available to the court at a criminal trial in the interests of justice."

In solemn cases in which the Crown do not call the spouse, and the **11–90** accused wishes to, she must of course appear on the defence witness list in terms of section 67 of the 1995 Act.

If a spouse elects to give evidence (having been warned that she is not **11–91** compellable), then she must answer every question put to her, even if that means incriminating her spouse, the accused. In other words, having agreed to go into the witness box, she cannot then be selective about the questions answered.[12] The only matters in respect of which she cannot be compelled to testify (apart from answering questions which might incriminate *her* in

---

[9] 1984 S.L.T. 434.
[10] At p. 437 *N.B.* that had she been asked questions concerning her alleged involvement in the assault, in line with H's original special defence, she would have been able to claim a privilege against answering any question which might incriminate her: see paras. 12.05–12.20 *infra*.
[11] Now s. 264 of the 1995 Act.
[12] *Bates* v. *H.M.A.*, 1989 S.L.T. 701.

any future charge) are, as indicated by subsection (2)(*b*), those covered by the "marital communications" privilege.[13]

THE SPOUSE AS A WITNESS FOR A CO-ACCUSED

11–92   Section 264(1)(b) makes it clear that while a spouse is always a competent witness for a co-accused, she cannot be compelled to testify except in a case in which she would have been compellable at common law. This is somewhat misleading, since, as explained in paragraphs 11.86–11.88 *supra*, there never was any circumstance in which a spouse was compellable at common law for a co-accused. The confusion seems to have arisen from the desire of the draftsman to include the possibility of a spouse testifying for a co-accused along with the possibility of her testifying for the Crown.[14]

11–93   However, there is nothing to prevent the spouse from testifying for a co-accused if she wishes. The "privilege" against testifying is hers to claim or reject, whether her spouse objects or not.

11–94   The difficult position for a spouse of a co-accused who is called as a witness for the prosecution was considered in *Bates* v. *H.M.A.*[15] In that case, the accused asked in cross-examination certain questions of a co-accused's wife. She declined to answer. On appeal it was held that while she could not be compelled to give evidence, if she chose to go into the witness box, then she must answer all questions put to her.

11–95   In solemn cases, in terms of section 67 of the 1995 Act, the spouse must appear on the witness list of the co-accused unless he or she already appears on another list, and is called by that co-accused because the original party does not call him or her.

11–96   Once again, the privilege against disclosure of marital communications is preserved by section 264(2)(b).[16]

THE SPOUSE AS A WITNESS FOR THE PROSECUTION

11–97   As noted in paragraphs 11.92–11.95 *supra*, section 264 is just as applicable to a spouse called by the Crown as it is to a spouse called by a co-accused. The one exception is in cases in which a spouse may be said to be the "victim" of the crime with which the other spouse is charged. In such circumstances, the victim spouse is compellable under the Act because she is compellable at common law.[17] Again the spouse (who retains the option

---

[13]   Both privileges are considered in Chap. 12 *infra*.
[14]   And, as indicated in paras. 11.86–11.88 *supra*, there are common law cases in which she is compellable for the Crown.
[15]   1989 S.L.T. 701.
[16]   For which see paras. 12.24–12.32 *infra*.
[17]   For which see paras. 11.86–11.88 *supra*.

as to whether or not to testify)[18] must appear on the Crown witness list.[19] Equally again, marital communications remain protected from disclosure.[20]

COMMENT ON THE FAILURE OF A SPOUSE TO TESTIFY

Section 264(3) prevents any comment being made by either the Crown or **11–98** the defence on the failure of a spouse to testify. Reference to *McHugh* v. *H.M.A.*[21] suggests that some departures from that rule may be tolerated in practice,[22] provided that overall there is no miscarriage of justice.

In addition, Sheriff Gordon[23] suggests that the accused might be permitted **11–99** to comment when the Crown might have called his spouse but did not,[24] and of course the subsections do not prevent the trial judge or sheriff from making comment, provided presumably that this is not excessive when it is damaging to an accused.[25]

---

[18] Unless compellable.
[19] As happened in *Hunter* v. *H.M.A.*, considered in paras. 11.89–11.91 *supra*.
[20] For which see paras. 12.24–12.32 *supra*.
[21] 1978 J.C. 12, considered in para. 11.59 *supra*.
[22] *e.g.* comment by the Crown when the spouse could have testified in support of an alibi, but did not.
[23] In his commentary on s. 29 of the 1980 Act in the Criminal Justice (Scotland) Act 1980.
[24] *e.g.* where she is the alleged victim.
[25] *Knowles* v. *H.M.A.*, 1975 J.C. 6.

CHAPTER 12

PRIVILEGE AND IMMUNITY

INTRODUCTION

12–01 When a witness is said to possess a "privilege" against answering a certain question or a series of questions, this means that the law recognises the right not to answer such questions. This applies even if the questions are relevant and competent, and even though the witness may otherwise be compellable. For example, as was seen in paragraphs 11.89–11.91 *supra*, a wife is normally both competent and compellable as a witness for her husband, but even so she cannot, because of a privilege which is granted to her,[1] be forced to disclose the contents of a "marital communication."[2]

12–02 If a witness is able to claim a privilege against answering questions then the normal penalty for refusing to answer a competent question as a compellable witness[3] cannot be enforced. As the information which the witness is refusing to disclose is frequently highly relevant to the matters under consideration by the court, the recognition of such a privilege by the law is clearly a matter of balancing the promotion of confidentiality against the interests of justice.[4]

12–03 The general rule is that the privilege is that of the witness who is being called upon to testify, and he or she may waive that privilege if so wished. If the witness does waive the privilege, the other party has no right to object but may apparently object if the privilege is wrongfully upheld, depriving that party of vital evidence which it was intended to call.[5]

12–04 It is also an open question whether or not the courts can make use of the same information which the privileged witness would have given as

---

[1] And which is considered *infra*.

[2] See paras. 12.24–12.32 *infra*.

[3] *i.e.* a charge of contempt: see *H.M.A.* v. *Airs*, 1975 S.L.T. 177 at p. 181, considered in paras. 12.63–12.68 *infra*.

[4] Significantly, much of what is now known as "privilege" was until fairly recently referred to as "confidentiality": see Walker and Walker, *Law of Evidence in Scotland*, Chap. XXXI.

[5] See *Kirkwood* v. *Kirkwood* (1875) 3 R. 235 at p. 236, and Wilkinson, *Scottish Law of Evidence*, p. 88.

evidence when it comes from another source (*e.g.* a third party who overhears a conversation between spouses). There appears to be no general rule, and such matters are resolved from case to case, and from privilege to privilege.

PRIVILEGE AGAINST SELF-INCRIMINATION: WITNESSES OTHER THAN THE ACCUSED

The special position occupied by a criminal accused who gives evidence at his own trial is considered separately in paragraphs 12.21–12.23 *infra*, and this section deals with all other witnesses, in both civil and criminal cases, who are asked on oath any question which might incriminate them in respect of certain matters. **12–05**

The privilege against self-incrimination arises from what was once described as "a sacred and inviolable principle ... that no man is bound to [in]criminate himself"[6]; and its extent was summarised by Walker and Walker[7] as being that: "A witness is entitled to refuse to answer a question if a true answer may lead to his conviction for a crime or involves an admission of adultery." **12–06**

It will be noted that the privilege is against *answering* the question which has such an effect, and the general rule does not prevent the question being asked in the first place. There are two statutory exceptions to this general rule,[8] under which the question may not even be asked, but in general it is for the witness to claim the privilege if and when the question is put. Macphail has suggested[9] that a new statutory rule should be enacted which prevents the question even being asked. But this would not solve the problem of how to ascertain in advance whether or not a seemingly innocent question may turn out to have incriminatory implications.[10] **12–07**

A witness may not, of course, realise that he or she has a privilege against answering a pertinent question, and for that reason it is regarded as being the duty of the presiding judge or sheriff to advise the witness of the privilege when a particular question seems likely to lead towards a possibly incriminating answer.[11] **12–08**

---

[6] Lord Gillies in *Livingstone* v. *Murrays* (1830) 9 S. 161 at p. 162.

[7] *op. cit.,* n. 4, para. 345(a). An untrue answer can lead to a perjury charge: see *Graham* v. *H.M.A., infra*.

[8] Evidence (Further Amendment) (Scotland) Act 1874, s. 2, dealing with questions which tend to show that the witness has been guilty of adultery, and s. 266 of the Criminal Procedure (Scotland) Act 1995, which apply *quoad* questions asked of an accused in a criminal trial, for which see paras. 12.21–12.23 *infra*.

[9] Macphail, *Evidence*, Chap. 18.05.

[10] See Wilkinson, *op. cit.,* n. 5, p. 89, and Scottish Law Commission, Memo. No. 46, para. S.02, who recommended simply that the question and answer be expunged from the record if the question is improperly asked.

[11] Dickson, *Evidence*, para. 1789.

12–09   It is quite possible that only the witness would be aware of the incriminatory nature of the only truthful answer that can be given. There should, therefore, ideally be some process whereby the genuinely incriminatory nature of such an answer may be established. If all that is required is that the witness state an objection, without need for further inquiry, then many awkward questions may be avoided by the unscrupulous or the unwilling.[12] As Cross and Tapper state: "the secret must be told in order that the court may see whether it ought to be kept."[13] At present there is no procedure to achieve this.

12–10   If for some reason a witness does not succeed in claiming a privilege against answering a particular question[14] or chooses to waive it, then the answer given is perfectly admissible for all purposes, even if the witness is a party to the action. This is because: "The common law interposes to protect the witness, not to give an advantage to the defender."[15] There is no authority to prevent the answer in fact providing the initial information which leads to the witness's subsequent trial for a crime which has been admitted, or to prevent a statement being used against the witness in that trial.[16] In *O'Neill* v. *Wilson*,[17] for example, it was firmly reasserted that a failure to warn a witness of his or her privilege does not affect liability to subsequent prosecution.

12–11   The privilege, as originally formulated, seems very wide in its application, but in practice it has been narrowed down to the point at which it can only safely be considered as a privilege against answering questions which would incriminate the witness *quoad* a criminal offence. In particular, the following limitations on the privilege are recognised.

12–12   (i) It is not applicable when the witness is no longer "in peril" of conviction of the offence revealed by the answer, if given. If, for example, an accused has already pled guilty, or been convicted of the offence in question, or has been granted immunity by the Crown because he or she is to be used as a *socius criminis* witness by them,[18] then the witness may no

---

[12] In the same way as the American practice of "taking the Fifth Amendment" has ground many an interesting inquiry to a halt.

[13] *Evidence*, p. 247, quoting *R.* v. *Cox and Railton* (1884) 14 Q.B.D. 153 at p. 175.

[14] *e.g.* because of a lack of awareness of its existence, or because it is denied it by the trial judge.

[15] Or indeed either party: Lord President Inglis in *Kirkwood* v. *Kirkwood* (1875) 3 R. 235 at p. 236.

[16] For which see paras. 14.10–14.12 *infra*. *N.B.* that if a statement was forced from a witness by a denial of the privilege, it would be classed as "involuntary," and therefore inadmissible as a confession.

[17] 1983 S.L.T. 573; see also paras. 11.76–11.85 *supra*. In *Graham* v. *H.M.A.*, 1969 S.L.T. 116, it was held that a witness who is not advised of his privilege, and who then goes on to give a false answer to the question, cannot hide behind the failure to advise him of his privilege in any subsequent perjury trial.

[18] For which see paras. 11.76–11.85 *supra*.

longer refuse to testify as to guilt.[19] A finding of not guilty will presumably also rob the witness of privilege because the matter is then *res judicata*[20] and a desertion *simpliciter* by the Crown will presumably have the same effect.

(ii) A witness cannot, in all probability, claim the privilege against **12–13** answering a question which will reveal the commission of an offence under foreign law.[21] Although it is felt by many[22] that in principle the privilege should extend to such questions, the point remains unsettled under Scots law. The House of Lords in the English appeal case of *Rio Tinto Zinc* v. *Westinghouse Electric Corporation*[23] allowed the privilege to be invoked against disclosure of documents which might expose the defenders to various fines under EC Regulations, but *quaere* whether, given the terms of the Treaty of Rome, this could be regarded as a matter of "foreign law" anyway.[24]

(iii) The privilege may not be claimed in respect of any question the **12–14** answer to which might expose the witness to a civil action.[25] This creates a grey area of uncertainty in those cases in which a future action, although civil in form, can result in penalties which are quasi-criminal in nature. An example is, of course, the system of fines which operates as the penalty for breaches of EC Regulations, and as the *Rio Tinto Zinc* case shows, the English courts are prepared to extend their equivalent privilege.[26] There is, however, no Scots law on the point.

(iv) The privilege does not extend to those questions which might **12–15** incriminate the witness's spouse, although English law has been extended to incorporate such a privilege.[27] It has been argued[28] that it is "repellant" to force a witness to incriminate his or her spouse, but Macphail[29] observes that: "It may be ... that the matter is of small practical importance in Scotland, and any such extension could not, of course, include the evidence

---

[19] *MacMillan* v. *Murray*, 1920 J.C. 13.

[20] See paras. 5.75–5.93 *supra*.

[21] Which in this context includes English law.

[22] Including Macphail, *op. cit.*, n. 9, Chap. 18.13 and Wilkinson, *op. cit.*, n. 5, p. 91, both of whom, however, concede the practical difficulty of the presiding judge having to become acquainted with the law in question.

[23] [1978] A.C. 547.

[24] See paras. 4.43–4.46 *supra*. See also *H.M.A.* v. *Entwhistle* (1980), unreported, *per* Macphail, *op. cit.*, n. 9, Chap. 18.13A, in which a witness in the High Court was allowed the privilege against answering a question which might render him liable to prosecution in England.

[25] Other than that of adultery. It seems that the rule never did have this effect: see Dickson, *op. cit.*, n. 11, para. 1787.

[26] Under the Civil Evidence Act 1968, s. 14(1)(*a*).

[27] Under s. 14(1)(b) of the 1968 Act.

[28] By the Law Reform Committee for England and Wales, whose report led to the 1968 Act.

[29] *op. cit.*, n. 9, Chap. 18.12.

of a spouse testifying at the trial of her husband, whether for the Crown or the defence."[30]

12–16   (v) The privilege may now be limited in its application to allegations of adultery. The broader rule was formulated at a time when adultery was a criminal offence anyway, and it has been argued[31] that when adultery ceased to be a crime, the privilege should have ceased to apply to questions concerning adultery. That this was not the case is evident from the Evidence (Further Amendment) (Scotland) Act 1874, section 2 of which placed the privilege on a statutory footing in "any proceedings", and prevented such questions even being asked of the witness.

12–17   The two questions which remain are whether or not the operation of the 1874 Act should be limited to proceedings in respect of adultery, and in fact whether or not the privilege should be abolished altogether. The total abolition of the privilege has been advocated since as long ago as 1886[32] in Scotland, and between 1912 and 1967 four Law Reform Committees made the same recommendation for English law. The privilege was abolished *quoad* allegations of adultery in England in 1968,[33] and Macphail[34] advocates a similar fate for the rule in Scotland.

12–18   In *Sinclair* v. *Sinclair*[35] it was held that in an undefended divorce action in the sheriff court on the grounds of the defender's adultery, there could be no objection to the use of affidavits, in which both the defender and the paramour admitted adultery, on the ground that the witnesses were not warned of the privilege. It was held that there was no rule of law which required a prospective witness deponing by affidavit to receive such a warning, and no evidence in the present case that the statements had been anything but voluntary. It may be, though, that the prudent course of action is to include a statement *in gremio* in the affidavit that the witness has been warned of his or her right not to incriminate themselves as to adultery.[36]

12–19   (vi) In certain cases, the privilege is removed by statute in circumstances in which it is felt that the personal right to privacy from self-incrimination is outweighed by the public interest in the securing of justice. Among the more common examples is section 172 of the Road Traffic Act 1988, which requires a potential witness/accused to answer police questions concerning the identity of the driver of a motor vehicle owned by the witness, such answers being admissible in evidence later. Many other statutes contain

---

[30] Because it would defeat the object for which she was called as a prosecution witness and make her evidence too one-sided if called for her husband; see generally, Chap. 11 *supra*.
[31] By Wilkinson, *op. cit.*, n. 5 p. 93.
[32] By Lord Trayner, in "The Advances of a Generation" (1886) 2 S.L.R. 57 at p. 91.
[33] By s. 16(5) of the Civil Evidence Act 1968.
[34] *op. cit.,* n. 9, Chap. 18.18.
[35] 1986 S.L.T. (Sh.Ct.) 54. But see *Cooper* v. *Cooper*, 1987 S.L.T. (Sh.Ct.) 37.
[36] *ibid.*.

provisions in like vein where it is felt that public interest outweighs private privilege.[37] In terms of the Bankruptcy (Scotland) Act 1985, s. 47(3), a bankrupt must answer "all lawful questions" which may be put to him in his public examination, even if they incriminate him in a crime, subject to the important proviso that his answers may not be used against him in any subsequent criminal proceedings.

When a witness claims the privilege against self-incrimination, that **12–20** should not be used to create any adverse inference against the witness.[38] But it is always possible that the use of the privilege may detract from the credibility of the witness, since: "an innocent man is far more likely to answer with an indignant denial than to avail himself of his privilege."[39]

PRIVILEGE AGAINST SELF-INCRIMINATION: THE ACCUSED

Since 1898 an accused person has possessed the right to give sworn **12–21** testimony at his own trial, a right which is now to be found in section 266(1) of the Criminal Procedure (Scotland) Act 1995. Clearly, though, an accused cannot be allowed to claim the normal witness privilege against self-incrimination which was examined in paragraphs 12.05–12.20 *supra*. The proceedings would otherwise be rendered farcical if the accused could give evidence-in-chief, and then refuse to answer any questions in cross-examination on the grounds that they tended to incriminate.

On the other hand, it is essential that the accused be protected from **12–22** questions which are designed to show the commission of other offences. Such a disclosure would be prejudicial. To this extent an accused must be treated more favourably than a normal witness.[40]

This compromise is reflected in sections 266(3) and (4) which **12–23** respectively provide as follows:

"(3) An accused who gives evidence on his own behalf in pursuance of this section may be asked, any question in cross-examination notwithstanding that it would tend to incriminate him as to the offence charged:

(4) An accused who gives evidence on his own behalf in pursuance of this section shall not be asked, and if asked shall not be required to answer, any question tending to show that he has committed, or been

---

[37] See, *e.g.* Explosive Substances Act 1883, s. 6(2), and Representation of the People Act 1983, s. 141(1) and (2).

[38] Macphail, *op. cit.*, n. 9, Chap. 18.05: see also paras. 12.21–12.23 *infra* in relation to silence at a judicial examination.

[39] Dickson, *op. cit.*, n. 11, para. 1790.

[40] Who may, subject to the privilege, be asked questions which impugn credibility as a witness. See paras. 10.88–10.105 *supra*.

convicted of or been charged with, any offence other than that with which he is then charged, or is of bad character, unless —..."

Each section then goes on to prescribe certain circumstances in which an accused may forfeit the "shield" of subsection (4), and these are examined in more detail in Chapter 13 *infra*.

MARITAL COMMUNICATIONS

12–24 Once spouses were rendered competent witnesses in law[41] the question arose of whether or not one spouse could claim a privilege against answering questions which related to communications made by the other spouse during the course of the marriage. The intention of the legislature seems to have been to preserve the sanctity of marital communications. If there is to be such a rule it is not clear[42] why only communications in marital relationships, as opposed to other forms of intimate relationships should be protected. The civil and criminal provisions relating to marital communications are quite different and are considered separately.

(1) **Criminal cases**

12–25 In criminal cases, the privilege against disclosing marital communications is now to be found in section 264 of the Criminal Procedure (Scotland) Act 1995,[43] which reproduces the privilege first introduced in 1898,[44] and states at section 264(2)(b) that nothing shall "compel a spouse to disclose any communication made between the spouses during the marriage."

(2) **Civil cases**

12–26 In civil cases, the privilege against disclosing marital communications is to be found in section 3 of the Evidence (Scotland) Act 1853, which states that:

> "nothing herein contained shall in any [civil] proceeding render any husband competent or compellable to give against his wife evidence of any matter communicated by her to him during the marriage, or any wife competent or compellable to give against her husband evidence of any matter communicated by him to her during the marriage."

---

[41] For which see paras. 11.46–11.48 (for civil cases) and paras. 11.86–11.99 (for criminal cases).
[42] Other than for the usual historical ones.
[43] See paras. 11.86–11.99 *supra*.
[44] See *Hunter* v. *H.M.A.*, 1984 S.L.T. 434 at p. 437.

The problems created by the wording of this section arise from the use **12–27** of the phrase "competent or compellable", thus implying that the spouse was not even competent to give such evidence, whether he or she wished to or not, making it in effect the privilege of the other spouse.[45] Taken to its logical extreme, this interpretation could be used as authority for the submission that the evidence could not be given even if both parties wished. Macphail[46] recommends that it be abolished[47] on utilitarian grounds, or at least reduced to the point at which it becomes the privilege solely of the communicator and not the recipient.

It is clear that in such cases, the privilege is that of the witness spouse **12–28** alone, and he or she is free to waive it if so desired.[48]

(3) **General**

In both criminal and civil cases, the privilege appears to apply to any **12–29** form of communication, written, oral or other.[49] However, some exceptions have been recognised to the right to claim the privilege, as in civil cases in which the court is investigating the behaviour of one spouse towards another,[50] and under certain statutes.[51]

The court can hear, from some other source, the same evidence which is **12–30** covered by the privilege. For example, a witness who overheard the conversation in question, or a third party who intercepted a letter.[52] The privilege relates only to the spouse as a witness, and to no one else.

It is unclear whether or not the privilege ends with the marriage, and **12–31** whether, for example, a former spouse can claim the privilege in respect of a communication made during the existence of the marriage. Walker and Walker[53] claim that it does, but more modern observers[54] challenge this view, on the grounds both of utility and the wording of the relevant sections.

The wording of each section clearly envisages that one of the spouses is **12–32** a party to the action in which the privilege is claimed. It is therefore doubtful whether the privilege can be claimed if this is not the case.

---

[45] *i.e.* the party, who could invoke the privilege him/herself by insisting that it was incompetent to inquire into the matter by means of questions put to the witness.

[46] *op. cit.,* n. 9, Chap. 4.06 and 4.07.

[47] As happened in England *per* s. 16(3) of the Civil Evidence Act 1968.

[48] See *H.M.A.* v. *H.D.*, 1953 J.C. 65.

[49] See Walker and Walker, *op. cit.,* n. 4, para. 355, and the cases cited there.

[50] *e.g. Mackay* v. *Mackay*, 1946 S.C. 7, in which the privilege was held not to apply to a letter written by a husband confessing adultery, the contents of which the wife would not otherwise even have been competent to relate: see *supra*.

[51] *e.g.* Bankruptcy (Scotland) Act 1985, s. 47(3).

[52] See Walker and Walker, *op. cit.,* n. 4, para. 355(b).

[53] *op. cit.,* n. 4, para. 355, quoting Dickson, *Evidence*, para. 1660.

[54] *e.g.* Wilkinson, *op. cit.,* n. 5, p. 103; Clive, *Husband and Wife* p. 351; and Macphail, *op. cit.,* n. 9, Chap. 4.10.

MARITAL INTERCOURSE

12–33 A rather curious privilege was introduced into Scots law by virtue of the Law Reform (Miscellaneous Provisions) Act 1949, s. 7, which enacts that:

> "(1) Notwithstanding any rule of law, the evidence of a husband or wife shall be admissible in any proceedings to prove that marital intercourse did or did not take place between them during any period.

> (2) Notwithstanding anything in this section or any rule of law, a husband or wife shall not be compellable in any proceedings to give evidence of the matters foresaid."

12–34   This statutory provision was intended primarily to overrule the decision in the English case of *Russell* v. *Russell*,[55] which had never been adopted into Scots law anyway,[56] and was therefore unnecessary in Scotland. The privilege has never apparently been judicially considered in Scotland,[57] even though it is drafted widely enough to apply not only to all civil proceedings, but to criminal proceedings as well. Ironically, it has been abolished under English law by virtue of section 16(4) of the Civil Evidence Act 1968,[58] and its abolition *quoad* Scots law would seem to be long overdue.[59]

PRIVILEGES IN AID OF LITIGATION

LEGAL ADVISER-CLIENT PRIVILEGE

12–35 Since at least the days of Stair,[60] communications passing between a legal adviser and his client have been privileged from subsequent disclosure in evidence. This is because: "it is essential for the administration of justice that persons should be able to consult their legal advisers freely without the subject matter of their discussions being under risk of disclosure."[61]

12–36   This is true whether litigation is in contemplation or not,[62] and the privilege (or "confidentiality" as it is perhaps more properly called) covers solicitors and advocates, and their clerks and other staff.[63] It is, however,

---

[55] [1944] A.C. 57, in which it was held that a spouse could not give such evidence of non-access as would tend to render illegitimate a child born in wedlock.

[56] See *Brown* v. *Brown*, 1972 S.C. 123.

[57] Macphail, *op. cit.,* n. 9, Chap. 4.12.

[58] For civil proceedings only. *N.B.* that only the privilege was abolished, and that competency remains.

[59] Macphail, *op. cit.,* n. 9, Chap. 4.13.

[60] IV, xliii.

[61] Wilkinson, *op. cit.,* n. 5, p. 94.

[62] See *McCowan* v. *Wright* (1852) 15 D. 229 at p. 237.

[63] Macphail, *op. cit.,* n. 9, Chap. 18.20.

most commonly referred to as "the solicitor and client privilege", and is limited to qualified legal advisers. It will not extend, for example, to accountants giving legal advice in the course of their work.[64] The privilege appears to be that of the client, so that the legal adviser may disclose the communication if authorised by the client, and the privilege is lost if the client calls that legal adviser as a witness.[65]

Before the privilege will cover a particular communication, it must have **12–37** been made in circumstances in which the relationship of legal adviser and client was at least in contemplation between the parties. It is uncertain what the precise position is when a solicitor receives the communication and then declines to act. In *H.M.A.* v. *Davie*[66] such evidence was admitted under reservation,[67] although it was unnecessary to consider the point on appeal. However, doubts have been expressed as to whether this represents Scots law,[68] and it does not apply in England, where the privilege is invoked as soon as the relationship is fairly in contemplation.[69]

At the other end of the timescale, the privilege ends when the relationship **12–38** ends, and communications made after that are not covered. However, communications made during the relationship continue to attract the privilege.[70] The death of the legal adviser clearly ends the privilege, and in most cases so does the death of the client, although when the communication relates to some item of property in which the client's executors have an interest, it seems that the privilege transfers to them, but cannot be invoked to deny a third party rights in the succession.[71]

There are limitations to the extent of the privilege, and they may be **12–39** listed conveniently as follows:

(i) The privilege covers only those matters formally communicated by **12–40** the client to the legal adviser, and not those facts which the latter may observe for himself or herself. As Wilkinson puts it[72]: "A solicitor must refuse to say whether his client confessed to a crime but must answer if asked whether he came to him wearing blood-stained clothing."

(ii) The privilege does not apply when the very matter into which the **12–41** court is inquiring is whether or not the communication was made. Thus, in *Anderson* v. *Lord Elgin's Trustees*,[73] the question arose as to whether or not the pursuer had delayed in bringing his action, as the defenders averred,

---

[64] Dickson, *op. cit.,* n. 11, para. 1665.
[65] See Walker and Walker, *op. cit.,* n. 4, para. 393.
[66] (1881) 4 Coup 450.
[67] See paras. 10.15–10.19 *supra*.
[68] Walker and Walker, *op. cit.,* n. 4; Macphail, *op. cit.,* n. 9, Chap. 18.21.
[69] *Minter* v. *Priest* [1930] A.C. 558.
[70] Dickson, *op. cit.,* n. 11, para. 1664.
[71] See *Mackenzie* v. *Mackenzie's Trs.,* 1916 1 S.L.T. 271.
[72] *op. cit.,* n. 5, p. 95.
[73] (1859) 21 D. 654. See also *Kidd* v. *Bunyan* (1842) 5 D. 193.

and it was held to be competent to adduce correspondence between the defenders and their solicitors which referred to an earlier claim.

12–42 (iii) The privilege will not cover communications which reveal the true nature of the relationship between the parties, where this is in dispute. In *Fraser* v. *Malloch*,[74] for example, the pursuer raised an action against a solicitor who had acted for a client in a previous action, claiming that he had done so without instructions. The pursuer was allowed to recover correspondence passing between the defender and the alleged client in order to shed further light on the relationship.

12–43 (iv) The privilege will not cover communications which have passed between a solicitor and a client who is alleged to have performed some illegal act when it is argued that the solicitor was directly involved in the carrying out of the very act itself. This is an old common law exception to the general rule,[75] which is usually expressed as covering the situation in which the communication is made "in the furtherance of" some criminal purpose.

12–44 In *Micosta S.A.* v. *Shetland Islands Council*,[76] the pursuers brought an action against the local authority for alleged abuse of statutory powers. They successfully obtained commission and diligence to recover certain documents which had passed between the defenders and their law agents. This recovery was despite a claim of privilege, because the documents related directly to the alleged abuses, and were indicative of the defender's state of mind at the time. The court was, however, at pains to stress that such refusal of privilege applies only when the legal adviser has been directly involved in the action complained of.

12–45 There is, however, a valid distinction between a communication made in the furtherance of an unlawful purpose[77] (which is not privileged), and requests for legal advice afterwards on possible defences to legal action, and indeed requests for advice *ab initio* as to whether or not a contemplated course of action will be lawful. Both of the latter attract the privilege.

12–46 (v) The effect of section 47(3) of the Bankruptcy (Scotland) Act 1985 would appear to be that while, during his public examination, the bankrupt himself may not claim the privilege against disclosure of communications which have passed between him and his legal adviser, he need not disclose matters communicated to him by that adviser unless the latter is himself called for examination.

12–47 There are many situations in which statute has preserved the privilege even though it might be argued strongly that it is in the public interest that

---

[74] (1895) 3 S.L.T. 211 (O.H.).
[75] See, *e.g. McCowan* v. *Wright, supra.*
[76] 1983 S.L.T. 483, especially at p. 485.
[77] Whether the agent was aware of the purpose or not.

all the client's dealings be brought into the open.[78] However, Macphail points out[79] that EC Regulations are not so protective, and that on at least one occasion[80] the legal adviser/client privilege has been waved aside in the interests of the enforcement of the Treaty of Rome.

There remains the question of whether or not the court may make use of **12–48** privileged communications which have become available from another source (*e.g.* the overheard conversation or the intercepted letter). There is no Scottish authority on the position when the information is obtained illegally, although Macphail[81] is of the opinion that it should be subject to the normal rules relating to illegally obtained evidence.[82]

In *McLeish* v. *Glasgow Bonding Co. Ltd.*,[83] the information became **12–49** available through an innocent mistake but it was held that it was admissible for the purposes of cross-examination. This ruling is not a helpful precedent for those supporting the rationale of the privilege as promoting public confidence in the legal system together with the fair and proper administration of justice.

COMMUNICATIONS POST LITEM MOTAM

A communication *post litem motam* is one made in circumstances in which **12–50** it is in the mind of a party that litigation may be pending. Any such communication, whether between legal adviser and client or anyone else and a potential party, is generally privileged.

This privilege is clearly wider in scope than the legal adviser/client **12–51** privilege, and is not limited simply to situations in which a writ has been issued. In one sense, however, it is narrower than the legal adviser/client privilege in that the latter covers all communications made at any time, while for a communication to be *post litem motam* it must be made at least when litigation is in contemplation. Thus, it was held in *Admiralty* v. *Aberdeen Steam Trawling and Fishing Co.*[84] that a communication *post litem motam* is one made not "merely after the summons has been raised, but after it is apparent that there is going to be a litigious contention."

The rationale of the privilege was described by the Lord President in **12–52** *Johnstone* v. *National Coal Board*[85] in the context of an industrial accident

---

[78] See, *e.g.* Restrictive Trade Practices Act 1976 s. 37(6); and Data Protection Act 1984, s. 3(2).
[79] *op. cit.,* n. 9, Chap. 18.20.
[80] *AM & S Europe Ltd.* v. *Commr. of the European Communities* [1983] Q.B. 878.
[81] *op. cit.,* n. 9, Chap. 18.22.
[82] Considered in Chap. 15 *infra.*
[83] 1965 S.L.T. 39.
[84] 1909 S.C. 335 at p. 340.
[85] 1968 S.L.T. 233 at p. 235, quoting Lord Walker in *Young* v. *N.C.B.*, 1957 S.L.T 266 at p. 268 and adopted in *More* v. *Brown & Root Wimpey Highland Fabricators Ltd.*, 1983 S.L.T. 669 at p. 670.

claim, as being that: "after an accident and even before any claim has been made, each party having a possible interest should be entitled to pursue his own investigations into the cause of the accident, free from the risk of having to reveal his information to the other side."

12–53   In *More* v. *Brown & Root Wimpey Highland Fabricators Ltd*,[86] it was held that the privilege operated so as to prohibit the recovery, by the pursuer, of photographs taken by the defenders' safety officer shortly after the accident. A similar ruling was given in *Anderson* v. *St Andrews Ambulance Association*.[87] In distinguishing between those communications which are made *post litem motam* and those which are not, Lord Hunter in *Marks & Spencer* v. *British Gas Corporation*[88] ruled that: "the contrast is between reports which are designed to put the person concerned in possession of the true facts, on the one hand, and reports made in contemplation of judicial proceedings, on the other."

12–54   A communication *post litem motam* does not cease to have confidential status on the completion of the case for which it was prepared.[89]

12–55   There is one type of post-accident report which has always been regarded as forming an exception to the general rule. A report made to an employer by an employee who was present at the scene of an accident, and which was made at or about the time of the accident concerning it, is not protected by the general privilege normally afforded to statements *post litem motam*. This is even though it must be obvious that litigation will result. There is little logic to the exception which has been applied in the most extreme of cases.[90] The rationale of the exception appears to be that:

> "if such a report is made as part of routine duty, and as a record of the reporter's immediate reaction before he has had the time, opportunity or temptation to indulge in too much reflection, it may well contain an unvarnished account of what happened and consequently be of value in the subsequent proceedings as a touchstone of truth",[91]

and as such it is similar to the underlying rationale for admitting *de recenti* statements.[92] This overlooks, however, the primary reason for allowing

---

[86] *ibid.*.

[87] 1942 S.C. 555 at p. 557.

[88] 1983 S.L.T. 196 at p. 197.

[89] *Hunter* v. *Douglas Raeburn & Co. Ltd*, 1993 S.L.T. 637.

[90] *e.g.* reports made to insurance companies when litigation was clearly in contemplation, and which contain lists of potential witnesses in such litigation. See, *e.g.* *MacPhee* v. *Glasgow Corp.*, 1915 S.C. 990.

[91] Lord Justice-Clerk Thomson in *Young* v. *N.C.B.*, *supra* at p. 270. This rationale was also approved in *More* v. *Brown & Root Wimpey*, *supra*, in which the exception was affirmed as still representing the law of Scotland.

[92] For which see paras. 10.37–10.39 *supra*.

privilege to attach to communications *post litem motam* in the first place, and the exception has been criticised[93] as anomalous.

When a party seeks to make use of one item in a course of correspondence **12–56** or other communications passing between himself and another party, it seems that he may thereby be taken to have waived any privilege which might otherwise have been claimed *quoad* the entire course of correspondence. Thus, in *Wylie* v. *Wylie*,[94] a pursuer founding on one letter passing between his solicitor and himself was held to have waived his privilege[95] in respect of other letters in the same course of correspondence passing at about the same time and dealing with the same legal action. The rationale appears to be that of preventing a party from selecting only favourable items from a wider collection, with the risk of distortion which might result.[96]

COMMUNICATIONS IN AID OF SETTLEMENT OF LITIGATION

A general privilege exists in respect of communications passing between **12–57** the parties to an action and their respective solicitors with a view to settling that action out of court. These communications may also be covered by the solicitor/client privilege. This is true even if the communication consists of, or includes, an admission. The privilege was said by Dickson[97] to arise from "mutual concessions". It is clearly in everyone's interests that extra-judicial settlements should be encouraged in this manner. The result of the existence of the privilege is that concessions may be offered by either or both parties to a dispute without fear that they may be used against them in court should the attempted settlement fail.[98]

The existence of the privilege explains the tendency of solicitors **12–58** attempting to settle a dispute to head their correspondence "without prejudice", although the phrase is not the term of art which it is under English law.[99] The effect of the phrase has been considered recently in two Outer

---

[93] By, *e.g.* Macphail, *op. cit.,* n. 9, Chap. 18.26, and Walker and Walker, *op. cit.,* n. 4, para. 395. A proposal to abolish this exception was, however, rejected by the Scottish Law Commission, Memo. No. 46, para. S.26.

[94] 1967 S.L.T. (Notes) 9.

[95] *i.e.* both solicitor/client and *post litem motam.*

[96] See *Marks & Spencer, infra,* in which the defenders were not allowed to waive confidentiality on part only of a report when this was not clearly severable from the rest of the report. In England there is recent authority that privilege may be claimed for part only of a document, see *G.E. Capital Corporate Finance group Ltd v. Bankers Trust Co.* [1995] 2 All E.R. 993.

[97] See Dickson, *op. cit.,* n. 11, para. 305; Macphail, *op. cit.,* n. 9, Chap. 18.28; Walker and Walker, *op. cit.,* n. 4, para. 29.

[98] See Macphail, *op. cit.,* n. 9. See also the Civil Evidence (Family Mediation)(Scotland) Act 1995 *supra.* And in terms of s. 133 of the Employment Protection (Consolidation) Act 1978, any statement made to an ACAS officer mediating in labour relations disputes is privileged, but the privilege may be waived by the communicator.

[99] See Cross and Tapper, *Evidence,* pp. 500–503.

House decisions. In *Bell* v. *Lothiansure Ltd.*[1] Lord McCluskey held that the general rule applied and that nothing written or said under the cloak of "without prejudice" should be looked at unless both parties consented.

12–59   In *Daks Simpson Group plc.* v. *Kuiper*[2] Lord Sutherland, in distinguishing *Bell*, said that, "if offers, suggestions, concessions or whatever are made for the purposes of negotiating a settlement, these cannot be converted into admissions of fact." However, he went on to say that if someone made a clear and unequivocal admission or statement of fact, then "I see no objection in principle to a clear admission being used in subsequent proceedings."[3] Both this case and *Gordon* v. *East Kilbride Development Corporation*[4] suggest a fairly strict approach will be taken to the application of the privilege.[5]

12–60   The phrase "without prejudice" may not, however, cover the entire correspondence between the parties, where such correspondence shows that one of the parties was prepared to settle on terms which have subsequently been awarded by the court. In such circumstances, Macphail argues that fact should be brought to the attention of the court when determining expenses.[6]

12–61   There is another limit to the extent of the privilege, namely that it is strictly applied only to those matters which are the subject of the negotiations in hand, and may not be extended to any other matter which may appear in the correspondence. In *Ware* v. *Edinburgh District Council*[7] the distinction was made that:

> "the words 'without prejudice' inserted in correspondence may not cover with the cloak of confidentiality all portions of a particular letter which do not strictly relate to a proposed settlement ... Nevertheless, they do cover actual negotiations and, in particular, negotiation figures for a settlement."

The privilege may apparently be invoked by either party to the dispute, whether that party was the maker or the recipient of the communication.

COMMUNICATIONS IN SETTLEMENT OF MATRIMONIAL DISPUTES

12–62 One special form of negotiation for settlement may arise from a matrimonial dispute, as for example in an offer of terms for a separation agreement.

---

[1]   1990 S.L.T. 58.
[2]   1994 S.L.T. 689.
[3]   At p.692B–C and D.
[4]   1995 S.L.T. 62.
[5]   *ibid.,* at p. 64C where Lord Caplan said the privilege should only apply "where the communication in question is clearly eligible for it."
[6]   See Macphail, *Evidence,* Chap. 18.28.
[7]   1976 S.L.T. (Lands Tr.) 21 at p. 24.

When such communications arise between legal advisers and their clients, then they are part of the wider privilege considered in paragraphs 12.57–12.61 *supra*.[8] The Civil Evidence (Family Mediation) (Scotland) Act 1995 accords privilege as to "what occurred during family mediation".[9] Various exceptions are set out in section 2 and the ethos of the Act is to encourage a frank exchange of views in mediation without concern that anything said can be used in subsequent court proceedings.

OTHER CLAIMS TO PRIVILEGE

GENERAL

There are many other relationships which in popular parlance could be **12–63** regarded as "confidential", and from time to time a court will be faced with the refusal of a particular witness to disclose the contents of a particular statement made to him or her on the grounds that it was made "confidentially." Two obvious examples are communications between doctors and their patients and between bank managers and their customers.

However, except on those rare occasions in which a refusal to disclose **12–64** is supported by statute,[10] and with the possible exception of communications between clergyman and penitent considered in paragraphs 12.69–12.71 *infra*, all such claims to confidentiality have been firmly refused by the Scottish courts, and the only privileged communications which exist are those which have already been considered in this chapter.

The position in those cases in which a witness feels bound by conscience **12–65** to keep a confidentiality is that while that witness may remain silent until ordered by the court to speak, he or she must then disclose the communication or face a charge of contempt of court. This is so even though the breach of confidence may thereby expose the witness to legal action for breach of confidence.

The first point was well exemplified by *H.M.A.* v. *Airs*,[11] in which a **12–66** journalist on the *Daily Record* was fined £500 for contempt of court in refusing to disclose details of a conversation he had allegedly had with one of the accused in the "Tartan Army" trial. It was held that except in the rare case in which a judge may excuse a witness from answering on the ground of conscience, which would not be likely to occur when the evidence in

---

[8] But see Macphail, *op. cit.*, n. 6, Chap. 18.31, in which it is argued that there can be no strict comparison between the settlement of commercial disputes and the settlement of matrimonial disputes, because the latter involve issues about which the court must learn the truth, if necessary by admission, particularly when the welfare of children is in dispute.

[9] s. 1(1).

[10] *e.g.* under the Bankers' Books Evidence Act 1879, as indicated in paras. 11.43–11.45 *supra*.

[11] 1975 S.L.T. 177.

question was highly material to the case in hand, no one could be excused from the duty to answer a competent and relevant question, and that punishment for contempt would be inflicted on anyone who refused. In the words of the High Court[12]:

> "Now that all possible causes of misapprehension have been dispelled, any witness, including any journalist witness, who declines to answer a competent and relevant question in court must realise that he will be in contempt and be liable to incur severe punishment."

12–67   This view may have to be tempered in future cases where journalists claim a privilege as the European Court of Human Rights has recently found the United Kingdom to be in breach of the Human Rights Convention for imposing a fine on a journalist for refusing to reveal his source of information.[13] Certainly the English courts deal with claims of privilege from journalists on a regular basis.[14]

12–68   The second point emerged in *Santa Fe International Corp.* v. *Napier Shipping S.A.*,[15] in which S were suing N for alleged infringement of a patent, and called for recovery of certain documents which had passed between N and third parties.[16] N refused on the ground that to do so would reveal certain technical information which they were bound by contract with those third parties not to reveal, and disclosure of which would render them liable to an action for breach of contract. In holding that N must yield up the documents, it was emphasised by the court that except in "special circumstances", private promises of confidentiality must yield to the public interest in justice and truth.

CLERGYMAN AND PENITENT

12–69   There is some authority for the proposition that a privilege exists in the "confessional" situation in which a parishioner gives confidential information to his or her spiritual mentor. These are considered by Macphail,[17] who describes an unreported case in 1960 in which the High Court upheld the confidentiality of the Catholic confessional in a homicide trial.

12–70   The position, however, is not clear, and has been described[18] in any case as being "of little practical importance." The same view was taken by the

---

[12] *ibid.*, p. 181.
[13] The case of the journalist Bill Godwin, reported in *The Scotsman*, March 28, 1995.
[14] See Cross and Tapper, *Evidence*, pp.498–500.
[15] 1985 S.L.T. 430.
[16] *N.B.* that the specification excepted those communications prepared for or in contemplation of the present action; see paras. 12.50–12.56 *supra*.
[17] *op. cit.,* n. 6, Chaps. 18.38 and 18.39.
[18] Macphail, *op. cit.*, n. 6, Chap. 18.42.

Scottish Law Commission when refusing to recommend that the privilege be formalised.[19] Instead, it was suggested that each case be taken on its merits in the exercise of a general judicial discretion to uphold confidences except where the interests of justice dictate otherwise.

In England there is some authority to suggest such a privilege exists.[20] **12–71**

PUBLIC INTEREST IMMUNITY

DEFINITION AND EXTENT

There are some cases in which it is argued that "public policy" requires that **12–72** certain information remain confidential. In such cases the person or body holding that information may claim an immunity against disclosing it in a court of law. This is a process formerly known as "Crown privilege", but its modern application is much wider merely than Government departments, and has been held to extend to local authorities, police authorities and similar bodies. The term "public interest immunity" has been applied in England,[21] and it was held by the House of Lords in *Conway* v. *Rimmer*[22] that the law of England should be harmonised with that of Scotland in this area. English authority since 1968 has therefore possessed additional weight in Scotland.[23]

The underlying rationale of the immunity is that, in some circumstances, **12–73** private justice must take second place to national security, or confidentiality of official records. The appropriate procedure is for the public officer responsible for authorising or withholding disclosure to grant a certificate or other document in which the court is advised of the general ground upon which immunity is being claimed (national security, confidentiality, etc.). A classic example of the type of case for which the immunity was considered appropriate was *Duncan* v. *Cammell Laird & Co. Ltd*.[24] This was an English case in which the Minister of Defence, during wartime, successfully resisted the production of plans of a British submarine in an action by the relatives of those who had died in it.

In that case, the Minister who claimed Crown privilege was said to have **12–74** the ultimate discretion and it was held that his certificate was conclusive. The case should not, however, be regarded as part of the law of Scotland. In *Glasgow Corporation* v. *Central Land Board*[25] it was held by the House of Lords that the Scottish courts have the power to go behind a ministerial

---

[19] Memo. No. 46, para. S. 32.
[20] Cross and Tapper, *op. cit.* n. 14, p.496.
[21] See *Burmah Oil Co. Ltd* v. *Bank of England* [1980] A.C. 1090 at pp. 1122 and 1130.
[22] [1968] A.C. 910 at p. 990, in which the English authorities to that date are extensively reviewed.
[23] See Macphail, *op. cit.,* n. 6, Chap. 18.54.
[24] [1942] A.C. 624.
[25] 1956 S.C.(H.L.) 1.

certificate and decide for themselves whether or not a particular item of evidence is deserving of immunity, after weighing private interests against public.[26] However, as the Scottish Law Commission observed[27]: "Although this power to overrule ministerial directions is now recognised in both jurisdictions, courts on both sides of the Border have been slow to exercise it."

12–75   There are two types of case in which the immunity may be claimed. The first arises when the document or information called for contains items which it is believed should be withheld (the so called "contents" cases). The second arises where the document itself, while perhaps not containing anything immediately sensitive, belongs to a class of documents which is normally withheld (the "class" cases). Both are, however, subject to the same tests, and in recent years there has been an expansion in the type of document or other information which may be subject to the immunity. As was observed in *D.* v. *N.S.P.C.C.*[28]: "The categories of public interest are not closed and must alter from time to time whether by restriction or extension as social conditions and social legislation develop."

12–76   Much can depend upon the extent to which the party seeking disclosure can show that the information required is vital to the case, since the stronger the private interest in disclosure, the stronger must be the public interest against it. In *Park* v. *Tayside Regional Council,*[29] a foster mother who claimed she had contracted hepatitis B from a child she had fostered, sought to recover hospital and social work records relating to the child. In noting that there had been no case in Scotland in which public interest privilege had been extended beyond departments of national government or of the Lord Advocate, Lord Sutherland went on to say that in this case, "the public interest in seeing justice done far outweighed the public interest in favour of confidentiality."[30]

---

[26] This also became the law in England by virtue of *Conway* v. *Rimmer, supra,* and it was by this means that the law of the two jurisdictions was harmonised.

[27] In Memo. No. 46, S.39.

[28] [1978] A.C. 171 at p. 230, a case in which immunity was successfully sought against disclosing the identity of the person who had made a complaint to the society concerning D's ill-treatment of his child. A similar ruling was handed down in *Rogers* v. *Secretary of State for Home Dept.* [1978] A.C. 388, in which the pursuer sought damages for defamation in respect of a report on him sent by the police to the Gaming Board. Disclosure of the report was refused on the ground that its production might jeopardise the working of the public service. For a recent unsuccessful claim to the immunity by a Scottish local authority *quoad* a social work file, see *Strathclyde R.C.* v. *B*, unreported, *per* Macphail, *Evidence*, Chap. 18.54C.

[29] 1989 S.L.T. 345.

[30] At p. 348D.

The nature of the remedy sought, and the moral worthiness of the party **12–77** seeking disclosure, may also have a bearing.[31] In particular, courts in recent years have displayed a reluctance to go behind the appropriate certificate claiming immunity in cases in which a former accused or suspect is seeking a civil remedy against a police authority.

Thus, in *Friel, Petitioner*,[32] the "victim" of a fruitless police search under **12–78** warrant to search for stolen goods sought to bring a civil action against the person who had informed on him to the police. To do this he required to know his identity, and he petitioned the court for an order for recovery of the relevant police records. This was opposed by the chief constable and the Lord Advocate on the ground that the document in question fell within a class of documents which must be withheld in the interests of crime detection. Against this it was argued that if such claims were upheld, members of the public in F's position would find themselves denied access to the courts.

It was held that in such cases the Lord Advocate's objection to disclosure **12–79** could only be overridden by another public interest (which might take the form of the interests of justice to the individual) which was more pressing. The denial to an individual of the possibility of bringing a civil action for malicious slander was held not to outweigh the general public interest in law enforcement.[33]

An interesting observation concerning the use of "public interest **12–80** immunity" documents arose in *Anderson v. Palombo*,[34] in which A, a police officer, sought damages for defamation against P, who had allegedly made an unfounded complaint concerning his behaviour. In his averments, A made reference to previous unfounded complaints by P against police officers, and a history of incidents in which P had proved abusive and unco-operative with the police. P sought to have these averments struck out as irrelevant and incapable of proof because the relevant police records relating to them would be immune from disclosure. In allowing proof before answer, Lord MacDonald observed that this would not necessarily be the case, the

---

[31] Compare, *e.g. Norwich Pharmacal Co.* v. *Customs and Excise Commrs.* [1974] A.C. 133 with *Alfred Crompton Amusement Machines Ltd* v. *Customs and Excise Commrs.* [1974] A.C. 405, the difference between which appears to have been the fact that in the first case, the party whose identity would have been revealed by disclosure was himself a wrongdoer, while in the second he was not.

[32] 1981 S.L.T. 113, also reported sub. nom. *Friel* v. *Chief Constable of Strathclyde*, 1981 S.C. 1.

[33] *Friel* was applied in *P. Cannon (Garages) Ltd* v. *L.A.*, 1983 S.L.T. 50, when the court refused to order the production of a blood sample taken from an alleged drunken motorist, together with the relevant certificates, for use in a civil action by the owner of a car damaged in the resulting accident. Once again the Lord Advocate opposed production on the "class" argument, and it was held that the private interest involved did not generate sufficient public interest to outweigh the public interest in the administration of criminal justice.

[34] 1984 S.L.T. 332.

implication being that circumstances can clearly have a bearing on the balance between public and private interests.

12–81   The immunity applies as much in criminal cases as in civil actions, but in criminal cases the interests of justice to the individual accused must weigh heavily against any routine denial of information simply because that information belongs in a "class" which is normally immune. In *Rogers* v. *Secretary of State for Home Department*,[35] for example, it was observed *obiter* that the police would not be entitled to protect the identity of an informer when his identification might establish the innocence of an accused, and a conviction on this ground was quashed in *Thomson* v. *Neilson*.[36]

---

[35] *supra*.
[36] (1900) 3 F.(J.) 3.

CHAPTER 13

CHARACTER EVIDENCE

INTRODUCTION

For the purposes of the law of evidence, a person's "character" must be **13–01** taken to include not only his known disposition from previous actions, but also his general reputation in society.[1] As such, it is classed as a "collateral" issue in all but a minority of cases, and as a general rule is therefore inadmissible.[2] The reason for excluding collateral issues is that:

> "Experience shows that it is better to sacrifice the aid which might be got from the more or less uncertain solution of collateral issues, than to spend a great amount of time, and confuse the jury with what, in the end, even supposing it to be certain, has only an indirect bearing on the matter in hand."[3]

There are, of course, some cases in which the character of one of the **13–02** parties constitutes the very "matter in hand", in which case it will no longer be considered as collateral, but will be provable as a main issue. In cases of alleged defamation of character, for example, it is the reputation of the pursuer, but not specific acts performed by him, which is the main issue, and in *C*. v. *M*.[4] the defender was allowed to adduce evidence to show that the pursuer was well-known for having a loose and immoral nature, but would only have been allowed to put suggestions of specific acts of adultery by way of cross-examination as to credibility, had fair notice been given.

A person's character may be a main issue in a criminal action, as for **13–03** example when an accused is charged with driving while disqualified by reason of a previous conviction.[5] In *Wallace* v. *Mooney*,[6] W sued M, a police

---

[1] Renton and Brown, *Criminal Procedure*, para. 18–12; Wilkinson, *Scottish Law of Evidence*, p. 22.

[2] Dickson, *Evidence,* para. 6. For an example of the exclusion of another type of collateral issue, see *Lancashire Textiles* v. *Shepherd,* 1986 S.L.T. 41. The collateral nature of character evidence is also considered in paras. 10.88–10.105 *supra*.

[3] Lord President Robertson in *A*. v. *B*. (1895) 22 R. 402 at p. 404.

[4] 1923 S.C. 1.

[5] On which point, see paras. 13.28–13.41 *infra*.

[6] (1885) 12 R. 710.

constable, for an assault arising from his forcible ejection from a racecourse. M had instructions to remove all persons of bad character, and it was held that he could adduce evidence of W's bad character to justify his actions.

13–04 But in the vast majority of cases, both civil and criminal, a person's character (using the term in its widest sense) is not a main issue. As a collateral issue, it is something which may only be proved in evidence in exceptional circumstances in which it is felt that it has a material bearing on at least one of the main issues, permitting it to be treated as an exception to the general rule against admissibility. These exceptional circumstances are examined in the remainder of this chapter, but may be conveniently listed as follows:

> (i)   Similar fact evidence in criminal cases.
> (ii) Similar fact evidence in civil cases.
> (iii) Character of victim of crime.
> (iv) Character of witness.
> (v)   Character of a criminal accused.
> (vi) Character of other persons.

SIMILAR FACT EVIDENCE IN CRIMINAL CASES

13–05 "Similar fact evidence" has been defined as:

> "evidence of the character or of the misconduct of the accused on other occasions … tendered to show his bad disposition, (which) is inadmissible unless it is so highly probative of the issues in the cases as to outweigh the prejudice it may cause."[7]

13–06 The rationale behind the acceptance of "similar fact evidence" in criminal cases is an exception to the general rule that in assessing the guilt or innocence of a person in a criminal trial it is sometimes impossible to overlook their behaviour on a previous occasion. For example, in the notorious case of *Makin* v. *Attorney-General for New South Wales*,[8] Mr and Mrs M were charged with the murder of a baby which had been unofficially fostered by them in return for money, and whose body had been found buried in the back yard of their house. Their defence that it had died accidentally was rebutted by evidence of the discovery of the bodies of three other babies at the same locus, together with evidence that the accused had initially (and falsely) insisted that they had only fostered one baby.

13–07 In cases such as these, the evidence of the previous misdeeds is admitted, partly because of the similarity of circumstance, and partly because it suggests that the accused is more likely to be guilty of the offence with

---

[7] Cross and Tapper, *Evidence*, pp.362–3.
[8] [1894] A.C. 57.

which he or she is now charged, but mainly because it negatives some innocent explanation of the present charge which the accused is putting forward.

The so-called "rule in *Makin* v. *Attorney-General for New South Wales*" **13–08** has had a complex and unhappy history under English law,[9] but was adopted by approval into Scots law in *H.M.A.* v. *Joseph*,[10] in which Lord Murray held that:

> "Evidence in regard to another incident of a similar character may be admitted in proof of a crime charged notwithstanding that this evidence may incidentally show, or tend to show, the commission of another crime, provided there be some connection or 'nexus' which in the opinion of the court is sufficiently intimate between the two 'incidents'."

This is, of course, very similar to the rationale of *Moorov* v. *H.M.A.*,[11] **13–9** the essential difference being that whereas under the *ratio* of the latter, similar charges on the same complaint or indictment may be spoken to by only one witness in order to produce a corroborative chain of "continuous conduct", in the *Makin* type of case reference is being made to behaviour on the part of the accused with which he is *not* now charged[12] in order to rebut some sort of defence which he is raising to the present charge.

Before such a prejudicial step may be taken, the "nexus" between the **13–10** present crime and the previous act must be a strong one, and it must be

> "relevant to an issue before the jury, and it may be so relevant if it bears upon the question whether the acts alleged to constitute the crime charged in the indictment were designed or accidental, or to rebut a defence which would otherwise be open to the accused."[13]

Remarkably, the principle appears to have featured little in Scots law **13–11** since *Joseph*,[14] though it has appeared frequently in England.[15] At least

---

9 For which see Cross and Tapper, *op. cit.*, n. 7, pp.363–367, and *R.* v. *Selvey* [1970] A.C. 304.

10 1929 J.C. 55 at pp. 56–57. In this case, a fraud committed by J abroad was held to have been competently libelled in an indictment, although not subject to the court's jurisdiction, in order to show the fraudulent intent with which the present offence had been committed.

11 Considered in paras. 7.66–7.81 *supra*.

12 And may never have been charged, as in *Makin* itself.

13 Lord Herschell in *Makin*, *supra* at p. 65.

14 *e.g. Booth* v. *Tudhope*, 1986 S.C.C.R. 638, in which it was held that on a charge of contempt of court against a witness who failed to turn up at a trial diet, the court might validly consider evidence of his failure to appear at an earlier diet in the same case. See also *Griffen* v. *H.M.A.*, 1940 J.C. 1 and *McIntosh* v. *H.M.A.*, 1987 S.L.T. 296.

15 See cases referred to in Cross and Tapper, *op. cit.*, n. 9, p.361 *e.g. D.P.P. v. Boardman* [1975] A.C. 421; *R.* v. *Wilson* (1973) 58 Cr.App.Rep. 169; and *Thompson* v. *R.* [1918] A.C. 221.

under Scots law, it would seem that the link between the present charge and the previous act must be as strong as that required for the operation of the *Moorov* doctrine, with which, of course, it is generically linked.[16]

13–12 The only other context in which similar fact evidence may have a bearing in a criminal case arises when an alleged sexual offender, in order to support a defence of consent, adduces evidence of similar acts involving the complainer in the past to which she did not object. There are, though, restrictions placed on this type of evidence, in terms of section 274 of the Criminal Procedure (Scotland) Act 1995.[17]

SIMILAR FACT EVIDENCE IN CIVIL CASES

13–13 There is no equivalent rule to *Makin* in civil cases, and the general rule is that what may or may not have happened in other incidents is of no relevance in the present action, not even if it sheds light on the character of one of the parties.

13–14 In *A. v. B.*,[18] a pursuer seeking civil damages for rape was not allowed to adduce evidence of the defender's alleged attempts to rape two other women, while in *H. v. P.*,[19] where the main issue in a slander action was whether or not H had committed adultery with P, it was held that P could not lead evidence to show that H had committed adultery with X.

13–15 In both cases, however, it was held that such questions might be put to test the party's credibility as a witness, provided that fair notice had been given. This remains the case today,[20] although doubts have been expressed about the current value of such a practice,[21] and the Scottish Law Commission has recommended the abolition of cross-examination on issues of chastity which cannot be tested by evidence in chief.[22]

13–16 Despite the absence of any general rule, there is authority to the effect that a party's behaviour on some previous occasion may be relevant to the case in hand, and provable in chief, when it appears to form a "course of conduct" with the behaviour currently in issue. *Whyte v. Whyte*[23] is regarded as an early example of this principle in action, when in an action for divorce on the grounds of adultery with a female servant, Mrs W was allowed to adduce evidence of W's indecent behaviour with another female servant.

---

[16] See *H.M.A. v. Pritchard* (1865) 5 Irv. 88 for a case in which it was held that an accused's previous misconduct gave rise to a motive for murder, and was admissible as evidence of such.

[17] And see paras. 13.19–13.22 *infra*.

[18] (1895) 22 R. 402.

[19] (1905) 8 F. 232.

[20] See paras. 10.88–10.105 *supra*.

[21] See Macphail, *Evidence*, Chap. 16.05, and *Duff v. Duff*, 1969 S.L.T. (Notes) 53.

[22] Memo. No. 46, para. Q.04.

[23] (1884) 11 R. 710, considered in paras. 7.106–7.108 *supra*.

Another example was *Roy* v. *Pairman*, although like *Whyte* it may be **13–17**
regarded as a special case in an area of law in which corroboration is difficult
to come by. Of more general application is the authority of *Knutzen* v.
Mauritzen,[24] in which K, in an action for damages against M for the delivery
of poor quality goods, was allowed to adduce evidence that another delivery
from the same consignment, made to a third party, was also of poor quality.[25]

This last case does not, of course, relate strictly to a question of character, **13–18**
but the principle involved is the same. Where the similar fact (or similar
act) belongs in what may fairly be called the same course of conduct with
an alleged act into which the court is now inquiring, it is sufficiently relevant
to be promoted from the status of a mere collateral issue into a main issue
which may be proved by evidence in chief.

The Character of the Victim of Crime

On some occasions, the character of the victim of a crime can be a material **13–19**
issue, whether the victim is called as a witness or not, and an obvious
example arises when an accused on an assault charge pleads self-defence,
or an alleged murderer pleads provocation. The general rule in all such
cases is that if the character in question is materially relevant to the defence,
then it is admissible. When the "character" consists of the victim's behaviour
at the time of the alleged offence, then no special notice is required, but if
the accused intends to attack his victim's character on general grounds,
then it is.[26]

Until recently, it was believed that while an accused might lead evidence **13–20**
of specific acts of violence by the victim on the occasion into which the
court is inquiring, and evidence concerning the victim's character generally,
he might not cite specific acts of violence on other occasions.[27] However,
doubt has been cast on this proposition by the High Court in *H.M.A.* v.
Kay,[28] in which K was charged with the murder of her husband, the
indictment also libelling previous indications of malice and ill-will on the
part of the accused towards the deceased. Her special defence of self-defence
took the form of a belief on her part that she was about to be assaulted by
the deceased, and she was allowed to lead evidence of previous assaults
upon her by the deceased. Lord Wheatley[29] ruled that:

---

[24] 1918 1 S.L.T. 85. See also *Morrison* v. *McLean's Trs.* (1862) 24 D. 625.
[25] Though the evidence to be adduced had to be direct evidence and not merely circumstantial.
[26] See Walker and Walker, *Law of Evidence in Scotland*, para. 20, and *Dickie* v. *H.M.A.* (1897) 24 R.(J.) 82.
[27] Walker and Walker, *loc. cit.*; Wilkinson, *op. cit.*, n. 1, p. 30.
[28] 1970 J.C. 68, also referred to in para. 10.91 *supra*.
[29] *ibid.*.

> "I consider that it would be unfair to allow detailed evidence by the Crown in support of that part of the indictment which alleges that the accused had previously evinced malice and ill will towards the deceased, without allowing the accused the opportunity of proving in turn by detailed evidence that she had reason to apprehend danger from the deceased."

13–21   The Scottish Law Commission,[30] in approving this ruling, widened it as follows:

> "We do not see how an accused can readily prove that the victim was a violent person unless he is permitted to cite specific violent actings on the part of that person ... The arguments against allowing such evidence are that it prolongs criminal trials and can also confuse juries. We do not consider either of these arguments sufficiently weighty to justify the *status quo*, and propose that in cases of murder or assault the accused should be entitled by citing specific acts of violence to prove that the injured person was of a violent or quarrelsome disposition."

This argument is equally applicable to battered women who kill,[31] of whom there have been a number of recent, highly publicised cases. It is essential to the defence of these women that their special defences of diminished responsibility should include evidence of the violent characters of their deceased partners.

13–22   One of the most controversial applications of the law in relation to the character of a victim remains that of a victim of rape or sexual assault. Under common law an accused could attack his victim's general reputation for chastity. The mounting public concern which surrounded the alleged abuse of this rule led to the passing of the Law Reform (Miscellaneous Provisions) (Scotland) Act 1985, section 36 (now section 274 of the Criminal Procedure (Scotland) Act 1995) which was intended to control types of questions relating to the sexual character of the victim. This is considered more fully in paragraphs 10.97–10.101 *supra*, but its general effect is to restrict such evidence to those cases in which it is directly and materially relevant to the offence with which the accused is charged.[32]

---

[30] Memo. No. 46, para. Q.05. See also *H.M.A.* v. *Cunningham* (1974), unreported, cited in Macphail, *op. cit.,* n. 21, Chap. 16.07, in which an accused in a similar position to *Kay* was allowed to prove the deceased's previous conviction for culpable homicide.

[31] See, for example, *R.* v. *Ahluwalia* [1992] 4 All E.R. 889, and *R.* v. *Thornton* [1992] 1 All E.R. 306.

[32] For a summary of the provisions of s. 36, see Macphail, *op. cit.,* n. 21, Chap. 16.10.

The Character of a Witness

This topic was dealt with in paragraphs 10.88–10.105 *supra*, when **13–23** considering the process of cross-examination as a whole. Basically the position is that, in all but extreme cases, the character of a witness is regarded as purely collateral, going only to his or her credibility as a witness and that while questions relating to character may be put to the witness for this limited purpose, the matter may not be pursued by means of evidence in chief. When the witness is also a party or a victim, of course, then the position is governed by those rules which relate to this special status, and the party or victim is not regarded as an ordinary witness.

THE CHARACTER OF A CRIMINAL ACCUSED

General

The character of a criminal accused obviously raises special issues. On the **13–24** one hand, it is crucial to a fair trial that the court (and particularly a jury) should not be influenced in its decision as to the accused's guilt of the offence with which he is now charged by evidence of his misdeeds on previous occasions. On the other hand, it is equally important that an accused should not be allowed to make false claims to having a good character, or to malign the character of those who are testifying against him, without the court being advised of his true character. At the same time, there may be some incident in the accused's past which cannot logically be ignored, given the nature of the present charge, whether the accused has put his character in issue or not.

At common law, it is always open to an accused to put his own character **13–25** in issue. This will normally take the form of evidence of his own good character, which he may raise as an issue of his own volition.[33] His right to do so predates the 1898 Act which first made him a competent witness in his own defence, and it therefore follows that such evidence may take the form, not only of testimony by the accused himself, but also of testimony from other character witnesses called by him.[34] When the accused raises the issue of his character and then goes on to give evidence himself, then, as is explained in paragraphs 13.42–13.68 *infra* he may well find that the prosecution exercise their statutory right to cross-examine him on the question of his character. When, on the other hand, the accused remains out of the witness box, and arranges for his good character to be spoken to by other witnesses, then the normal rule is that the prosecution must stand

---

[33] Dickson, *op. cit.,* n. 2, para. 15.
[34] Or conceivably from prosecution witnesses, by means of cross-examination.

impotently by, unable to lead evidence which they may have concerning his real character.[35]

13–26   On rare occasions it may be necessary for an accused person to use his *bad* character in his own defence, as for example where his alibi defence consists of the fact that he was in prison at the material time. He is free to do so, but must not be forced into such a drastic step by the nature of the prosecution attack on him.[36]

13–27   Until fairly recently, the main problem area concerning the character of a criminal accused was the set of restrictions placed upon the prosecution against cross-examining him on his character when he chose to testify. In the past few years, however, an increasing amount of case law has highlighted those situations in which an accused's character has been regarded as so relevant to the issues in hand that the prosecution have been allowed to adduce evidence of it in chief, regardless of whether or not the accused chooses to give evidence. Additionally, there is the situation where one accused attacks the character of a co-accused in order to exculpate himself. These and other issues are considered in the sections which follow.

PROSECUTION EVIDENCE IN CHIEF OF THE ACCUSED'S CHARACTER

13–28   It is still a firm general rule that the prosecution may not, in the course of its own evidence in chief, lead evidence of the accused's bad character as evidenced by his misdeeds in the past, or by any other inference.[37] So far as concerns previous convictions the general rule finds statutory expression in sections 101 (for solemn cases) and 166 (for summary cases) of the Criminal Procedure (Scotland) Act 1995.[38]

13–29   The apparent strictness of these rules is, however, tempered by a line of cases in which previous convictions have been placed before the court accidentally, and it has been held that no substantial prejudice occurred to the accused and that the conviction could stand. Thus, in *H.M.A.* v. *Corcoran*[39] Lord Anderson ruled that: "Where a witness in good faith, and in answer to a competent question fairly put by the prosecutor, incidentally discloses the existence of a prior conviction, I do not think that a contravention of the statute takes place." This view was endorsed *obiter* in

---

[35] The presiding judge, but not the prosecution, may however comment on an accused's failure to testify; see Criminal Procedure (Scotland) Act 1995, s. 266. and generally paras. 11.50–11.65 *supra*.

[36] See *Carberry* v. *H.M.A.*, 1975 J.C. 40 at p. 46. considered more fully in paras. 13.28–13.41 *infra*.

[37] Dickson *op. cit.*, n. 2, para. 15. Neither may a co-accused: see *Slane* v. *H.M.A.*, *infra*.

[38] Previously ss. 160 (solemn) and 357 (summary) of the Criminal Procedure (Scotland) Act 1975. And see *Forsyth* v. *H.M.A.*, 1992 S.L.T. 189 where there was held to have been a miscarriage of justice though not based on statutory provisions.

[39] 1932 J.C. 42.

Carberry v. *H.M.A.*,[40] while in *Johnston* v. *Allan*[41] the same view was taken of a previous conviction contained on a computer printout from the DVLC which was handed to the sheriff in error, with no improper motive on the part of the fiscal depute.

These rulings appear to proceed upon the basis that there was no **13–30** deliberate attempt by the prosecution to prejudice the accused, and that there was no active intent to lay the previous conviction before the court. However, in most cases this will not reduce the prejudicial effect for the accused, and the more important question on appeal should be whether or not this prejudice was material.

The consequences of a deliberate breach of either section will normally **13–31** be an acquittal on appeal, or a desertion of the diet *ex proprio motu* by the presiding judge. An example of this was *Smith* v. *H.M.A.*,[42] in which a police witness, asked in chief if he recognised the accused, not only acknowledged him but gratuitously informed the court that he knew him as a housebreaker. The subsequent conviction was quashed.

In *Cordiner* v. *H.M.A.*,[43] C was charged on an indictment which libelled **13–32** three charges. On the date upon which one of these was alleged to have occurred, C had been serving a prison sentence in respect of a previous conviction, and he intimated this to the Crown in his special defence of alibi. This was readily confirmable by the Crown, who instead allowed the special defence to be read to the jury, and then later in the trial withdrew the only charge to which it related. The convictions *quoad* the remaining charges were quashed, the Crown having conceded that forcing C to disclose his prison sentence was equivalent to the prosecution having laid a previous conviction before the court.

Notwithstanding the normal application of the general rule, subject to **13–33** those cases examined above in which breach of the sections was held to have been accidental, there are three identifiable circumstances in which even a deliberate and open breach of either section 101(1) or section 166(3) will be competent.

---

[40] 1975 J.C. 40 at p. 46; this case is considered below.
[41] 1983 S.C.C.R. 500; for a similar case, see *O'Neill* v. *Tudhope*, 1984 S.C.C.R. 276; see also *Moffat* v. *Smith*, 1983 S.C.C.R. 392.
[42] 1975 S.L.T. (Notes) 89. See also *Graham* v. *H.M.A.*, 1983 S.C.C.R. 314, in which an accused charged with assaulting his wife and various other offences was acquitted on appeal after a police witness read out a reply to caution and charge which consisted of the words: "That cow's got me the jail again!" The appeal court went so far as to accuse the fiscal depute of having engineered the breach of the statute without justification. See also *McCuaig* v. *H.M.A.*, 1982 J.C. 59 and *Binks* v. *H.M.A.*, 1985 S.L.T. 59.
[43] 1978 J.C. 64; *N.B.* however, that the defence must make timeous objection to any breach of the section: *Jackson* v. *H.M.A.*, 1982 J.C. 117.

(1) **When disclosure is essential to the charge**

13–34   In certain exceptional circumstances, the Crown cannot effectively libel the charge(s) against an accused without making reference to a previous conviction. For example, a charge of driving while disqualified by its very nature implies a previous motoring offence, and the Crown cannot obtain a conviction without proving both the disqualification and the offence which gave rise to it.[44] In such cases, the disclosure is in practice regarded as an essential exception to the general rule if it is performed with the minimum of prejudice to the accused, and is probably covered by the wording of the proviso to each of the sections which refers to such evidence being led "in support of" the charge.[45]

13–35   Two examples of the principle in action are *Varey* v. *H.M.A.*[46] and *Murphy* v. *H.M.A.*[47] In *Varey*, V was charged with prison-breaking, and the indictment libelled the length of the sentence which he had been serving and the offence for which it had been imposed. Despite a defence challenge, the court held that the indictment was relevant, since it was essential to the Crown case to prove the date and length of the sentence, and the fact that such detention proceeded upon lawful cause.

13–36   In *Murphy*, M was charged with perverting the course of justice by giving his solicitor false information concerning his private life in mitigation of sentence on two separate occasions upon which he had pled guilty to charges. He had previous convictions, which he had admitted on each occasion, and the Crown called as witnesses the sheriff and justice who had sentenced him on each occasion, to testify that but for the false representations the sentences would have been more severe. It was held that the Crown could not competently narrate the charges without including reference to the previous convictions, and the disclosure was therefore competent.

(2) **Where disclosure is competent in support of the charge**

13–37   Provisos to both sections 101(2)(b) and 166(8)(b) allow previous convictions to be disclosed in circumstances in which it is competent to do so in support of the charge.[48] This proviso certainly covers the *Varey* and *Murphy* type of case considered above, but arguably it is wider in its operation than that.

---

[44] See *Moffat* v. *Smith, supra*.

[45] The difficulty in *Moffat* v. *Smith, supra*, was the fact that although obliged to libel one previous conviction, the Crown had inadvertently proved two.

[46] 1985 S.C.C.R. 425.

[47] 1978 J.C. 1.

[48] See *Russell* v. *H.M.A.*, 1993 S.L.T. 358, a case decided under the previous statutory provisions: ss. 160 and 357 of the 1975 Act.

It is submitted that when the accused's previous misdeeds are admissible **13–38** under the rule in *Makin* v. *Attorney-General for New South Wales*,[49] then the proviso to each section preserves the effect of the doctrine, and allows such evidence in. Both sections refer in any case only to previous convictions, and on facts such as those in *Makin* itself, as explained in paragraphs 13.05–13.12 *supra*, the evidence would be admissible as an exception to the more general common law rule against disclosure of an accused's bad character. Only when the previous behaviour takes the form of previous convictions will it be necessary to invoke one of the provisos so as to adduce evidence in chief of those previous convictions.

The right to adduce evidence of an accused's previous convictions "in **13–39** support of the charge" may also occasionally be found under statute, as in section 19 of the Prevention of Crimes Act 1871, which allows a prosecutor who has proved an accused's possession of stolen property to adduce evidence of previous convictions implying dishonesty which are less than five years old in support of the *mens rea* of guilty knowledge. Such cases must be taken to operate under the provisos.

(3) Where disclosure is relevant to a defence raised by the accused

On rare occasions, the Crown cannot adequately rebut a defence put **13–40** forward by the accused without revealing that he has previous convictions, and in such cases it seems that they may be permitted to do so. Examples are *Carberry* v. *H.M.A.*[50] and *Gemill* v. *H.M.A.*[51]

The principle embodied in sections 101 and 166 extends to exclude **13–41** disclosure of A's previous convictions by a co-accused B. This was established in *Slane* v. *H.M.A.*,[52] in which S was on trial with two others. During the course of the Crown case, counsel for a co-accused, M, asked a Crown witness questions expressly designed to show that S had a criminal record. It was held that although this was not technically a breach of the statute, it was contrary to its spirit, since "those accused of crime are entitled to enjoy the presumption of innocence throughout their trial and ... information as to their criminal past should not be disclosed to the court or the jury."[52a] Holding that ordinarily, such an "inexcusable" breach of

---

[49] Considered in paras. 13.05–13.12 *supra*. In *McIntosh* v. *H.M.A.*, 1987 S.L.T. 296, it was held to be competent to adduce evidence in relation to one charge on an indictment which had been dropped prior to the trial commencing in support of a second charge which was still "live", because this evidence was relevant to the second charge. See also *Carmichael* v. *Monaghan*, 1987 S.L.T. 339, and *Clarke* v. *Allan*, 1987 S.C.C.R. 33.

[50] See n. 39 *supra*.

[51] 1979 S.L.T. 217.

[52] 1984 S.C.C.R. 77, the first direct case on the point; see Sheriff Gordon's commentary, *ibid.*, at p. 80.

[52a] *ibid.*, at p. 79.

procedural ethics would give rise to a miscarriage of justice, the court was
nevertheless able to uphold the resulting conviction because of the weight
of the other evidence against S.

Cross-Examination of the Accused on Issues of Character

13–42 As explained in paragraphs 13.24–13.27 *supra*, a criminal accused is in an
anomalous situation when he exercises the right given to him under section
266 of the 1995 Act to give sworn evidence in his own defence. On the one
hand, he could not in all fairness be allowed to claim the normal privilege
against self-incrimination which an ordinary witness may claim, and
subsection (3) takes away this privilege *quoad* the offence(s) with which
he is presently charged.[53]

13–43 On the other hand, the effect of disclosing to the trial court that the
accused has previous convictions, or has misbehaved in the past, would be
unduly prejudicial to a fair trial unless the accused has given evidence which
in some way raises the issue of character, or which maligns the character of
those giving evidence against him. This is true even if character evidence is
being adduced merely to impugn the accused's credibility as a witness,
since an accused's character is virtually indivisible in such cases. Evidence
tending to impugn credibility as a witness will invariably go to suggest
guilt of the charge. As was explained in paragraphs 13.28–13.41 *supra*, an
accused who puts his own good character in issue cannot, however, complain
if the prosecution then lead evidence to contradict that, and section 101(2)
and 166(8) of the 1995 Act expressly permit this.[54]

13–44 Section 266(4)(b) deals with the possibility of the prosecution seeking
to redress the balance of the evidence relating to the accused's good character
by cross-examining the accused himself as to his character if he chooses to
give evidence:

> "(4) An accused who gives evidence on his own behalf in pursuance
> of this section shall not be asked, and if asked shall not be required to
> answer, any question tending to show that he has committed, or been
> convicted of, or been charged with, any offence other than that with
> which he is then charged, or is of bad character, unless—
>
> (a) the proof that he has committed or been convicted of such
> other offence is admissible evidence to show that he is guilty of the
> offence with which he is then charged; or
>
> (b) the accused or his counsel or solicitor has asked questions of
> the witnesses for the prosecution with a view to establishing the

---

[53] This aspect of s. 266 is dealt with more fully in paras. 12.21–12.23 *supra*.
[54] And see s. 285 for the procedure for proving a previous conviction by means of a certificate
signed by the Chief Constable.

accused's good character or impugning the character of the complainer, or the accused has given evidence of his own good character, or the nature or conduct of the defence is such as to involve imputations on the character of the prosecutor or of the witnesses for the prosecution or of the complainer; or

(c) the accused has given evidence against any other person charged in the same proceedings."[55]

Only when the accused has brought himself within one of the circumstances listed above may the prosecution cross-examine on his character,[56] and even then it is the proper practice for them to seek the leave of the court before doing so.[57] Otherwise, it will be noted, such questions may not even be asked.

A breach of subsection (4) will normally lead to a successful appeal if **13–45** not carefully corrected by the trial judge in a solemn case when charging the jury, and will be almost automatically fatal in a summary trial. In *McLean* v. *Tudhope*,[58] M was charged with a breach of the peace, and in the course of being cross-examined he stated that he was an honest man. Without seeking the leave of the court, the fiscal depute then referred to a previous conviction, and in re-examination M was obliged to give details of it by way of a damage limitation exercise. On appeal, it was held that since credibility was vital in the case, the reference to the previous conviction required the conviction to be quashed.[59]

An almost identical provision to subsection (4) in England[60] has led, in **13–46** that jurisdiction, to many test cases and much controversy. The position in Scotland was settled by the full bench decision in *Leggate* v. *H.M.A.*[61] This decision overruled previous case law governing the circumstances in which an accused would lose the statutory immunity against attacks against his character. *Leggate* is best considered in the light of the previous case law, both English and Scottish.

Section 266(4) makes the general position clear—the accused shall not **13–47** be asked any question "tending to show" that he has committed, been convicted of or been charged with previous offences. In *Jones* v. *D.P.P.*,[62] it

---

[55] Previously, similar provisions were contained in ss. 141 and 346 of the 1975 Act.

[56] *N.B.* that "character" for the purposes of ss.(4) is not restricted to previous convictions.

[57] *O'Hara* v. *H.M.A.*, 1948 J.C. 90. This case was over-ruled in relation to other aspects by *Leggate* v. *H.M.A.*, 1988 S.L.T. 665 *infra*.

[58] 1982 S.C.C.R. 555.

[59] The fact that M had apparently put his character in issue appears not to have been considered: see Sheriff Gordon's comment on the case, *ibid.*, at p. 557.

[60] Under the Criminal Evidence Act 1898, which applied in Scotland until 1975. See Cross and Tapper, *op. cit.*, n. 7, p.430.

[61] 1988 S.L.T. 665.

[62] [1962] A.C. 635; which considered the equivalent provisions in English law; followed in *Dodds* v. *H.M.A.*, 1988 S.L.T. 194.

was held that the words "tending to show" must be interpreted as meaning "tending to show for the first time". The effect of this is that if the court becomes aware of, for example a previous conviction, by other means,[63] then he may be cross-examined on it.

13–48   In *Maxwell* v. *D.P.P.*,[64] it was held that even though the accused may throw away his immunity by giving evidence of the type now prescribed by (a), (b) and (c) of subsection (4), the prosecution may even then only adduce such evidence of his character as is relevant in the circumstances. In particular, the House of Lords doubted whether there would be many cases in which the fact that the accused had been charged with a previous offence but acquitted would be relevant to the present charge.

13–49   In *Stirland* v. *D.P.P.*,[65] it was held that "charged" meant "charged in court", and the court in that case went on to rule that a person's "character" is indivisible, so that once his character is in issue, all relevant aspects of it may be considered.[66]

13–50   Also, in *Jones* v. *D.P.P.*,[67] the House of Lords pointed out that the statutory protection refers only to questions asked in cross-examination, and does not prevent the question being put to an accused by his own solicitor or counsel during examination-in-chief. When this occurs, of course, the prosecution may then cross-examine on it because such later questions will not "tend to show for the first time" that the accused has a "past", but in *McLean* v. *Tudhope*[68] it was demonstrated that when an accused is forced to go into detail concerning a previous conviction only because of an inadmissible question in cross-examination by the Crown, this does not homologate the asking of the original question so as to make it admissible.

13–51   If the accused uses section 266(4) to set up his own good character or to attack the character of others, the prosecution cannot attack the accused's character unless the presiding judge permits this in terms of subsection 5. In all cases except under s. 266(4) the prosecution must seek the leave of the court, outwith the presence of the jury, before proceeding to cross-examine the accused as to his character. But a co-accused against whom evidence has been given is not affected by these restrictions.[69] Four such separate situations need to be considered.

---

[63]   *e.g.* if the accused makes reference to it, or even if a prosecution witness refers to it by accident: see *H.M.A . v. Corcoran* in para. 13.29 *supra*.

[64]   [1935] A.C. 309. See Lowson v. *H.M.A.,* 1943 J.C. 141, and *Lindie* v. *H.M.A.,* 1974 J.C. 1.

[65]   [1944] A.C. 315; [1944] 2 All E.R. 13.

[66]   On which point see *Leggate* v. *H.M.A.,* 1988 S.L.T. 665, discussed *infra*.

[67]   [1962] A.C. 635; [1962] 1 All E.R. 569; followed in *Dodds* v. *H.M.A.,* 1988 S.L.T. 194.

[68]   1982 S.C.C.R. 555.

[69]   See *McCourtney* v. *H.M.A.,* 1977 J.C. 68 at p. 72, considered *infra*.

(1) Subsection (4)(a): Accused's character relevant to the charge

As was seen in paragraphs 13.28–13.41 *supra*, there are circumstances **13–52** in which, notwithstanding the general rule against adducing evidence of the accused's character in chief, the prosecution may rely on such evidence when it is "relevant" to the charge which the accused now faces. Subsection (4)(a) allows the Crown to cross-examine the accused along these lines, but it may strictly speaking be superfluous in this context, given the ratio of *Jones, supra*, that subsection (a) does not apply when the court has already learned of the accused's bad character by other means.

Thus, in cases such as *Varey* v. *H.M.A.*[70] and *Murphy* v. *H.M.A.*,[71] the **13–53** prosecution could presumably not only adduce evidence of the accused's previous convictions in chief, but could cross-examine him on them if he chooses to give evidence. *Quaere* whether or not this will be the case when the accused's character is relevant only to his defence,[72] but given the ratio of *Jones, supra*, once the court is aware of the character in question anyway, there would seem to be nothing to prevent cross-examination on it.

When "similar fact evidence" is relevant under the rule in *Makin* v. **13–54** *Attorney-General for New South Wales*,[73] cross-examination on it would seem to be permitted under ss. (4)(a).

(2) Subsection (4)(b): Accused gives evidence "of his own good character"

When the accused sets out to establish his own good character, either by **13–55** cross-examining witnesses for the prosecution concerning it, or by giving such evidence on oath himself[74] then the Crown are entitled, with the leave of the court, to counter such evidence by questions in cross-examination which are designed to show that the accused's character is not as spotless as he would have the court believe. It is uncertain whether or not, if the accused denies the accusations made against him, the Crown may go on to prove them by recalling a witness or calling fresh evidence altogether.[75]

There are also problems which arise when the good character evidence **13–56** is obtained by one co-accused from another co-accused or his witness, and where as a result the latter wishes to cross-examine the former as to his character. Since A has "set up" his character it may only be fair to allow B

---

[70] Examined more fully in para. 13.35 *supra*.
[71] Examined more fully in para. 13.36 *supra*.
[72] As in *Carberry* v. *H.M.A.* and *Gemmill* v. *H.M.A.,* referred to in para. 13.40 *supra*.
[73] Considered in paras. 13.06 and 13.38 *supra*.
[74] But not, curiously enough, by adducing defence witnesses as to character, or by asking questions of witnesses for a co-accused; see Walker and Walker, *op. cit.,* n. 26, para. 358(c). This was presumably an oversight by the draftsman; see *R.* v. *De Vere* [1981] 3 W.L.R. 593.
[75] See generally, paras. 10.113–10.137 *supra*.

to set the record straight by cross-examining A as to his misdeeds in the past.

13–57   This is particularly true where the two are running what is popularly known as a "cut-throat" defence (*i.e.* each is impeaching the other) and the issue of credibility is crucial. There is, not surprisingly, no direct authority on the point, since in most such cases each accused will go on to "give evidence against" the other, and thus invoke subsection (4)(c).

13–58   There is not even any authority for the relatively simple situation in which A has set up his own character by his own evidence, and B wishes to exercise the same right as the prosecution to cross examine in rebuttal.

(3) Subsection (4)(b): "Nature and conduct of defence involves imputations on character of prosecutor, prosecution witnesses or complainer."

13–59   The basic rules of fair play suggest that when the accused sets out, either in chief or in cross-examination,[76] to impugn the character of the prosecutor[77] or the Crown witnesses or the complainer,[78] then the court should also be advised of any stains on the accused's own character. At the same time, an accused is entitled to a fair opportunity to develop a genuine defence which may, incidentally, involve imputations against the prosecution witnesses.[79] A balance has to be struck between these two considerations.

13–60   Until the case of *Leggate*[80] the practice was to grant an accused whose defence necessarily involved casting aspersions on the character of Crown witnesses some degree of statutory immunity.[81] This immunity prevented him from then having his own character attacked and previous convictions disclosed if he gave evidence. *Leggate* was a full bench decision which overturned a line of case authority from the case of *O'Hara* v. *H.M.A.* in 1948,[82] and including a five judge decision in *Templeton* v. *McLeod*.[83]

13–61   The appeal court in *Leggate* decided that when an accused attacks the character of a Crown witness, even if this is necessary to establish his defence, he does not retain any immunity from attack on his own character. It was recognised that there might be situations where this was unduly prejudicial to an accused so the trial judge has discretion to ameliorate the consequences of an attack on character. Section 266(5) requires the

---

[76]   *N.B.* that there are no restrictions on the form which such evidence may take.
[77]   See *H.M.A.* v. *Grudins, infra.*
[78]   The addition of the complainer to this list is an extension of the statutory provisions as contained in ss. 141 and 346 of the 1975 Act.
[79]   *e.g.* a provocation defence which involves allegations of homosexual advances to the accused by the victim, as in *Selvey, infra.*
[80]   1988 S.L.T. 665; see para. 13–46 *supra.*
[81]   In terms of ss. 141(1)(f) and 346(1)(f) of the 1975 Act.
[82]   1948 J.C. 90.
[83]   1985 J.C. 12.

prosecution to apply to the court for permission to cross-examine on character. The application must be made outwith the presence of the jury. The judge can refuse leave to cross-examine the accused on his character.

The search for a balance between developing a genuine defence and **13–62** imputations against Crown witnesses has led to a confusing and often contradictory mass of case law in England, culminating in *R.* v. *Selvey.*[84] In that case, the House of Lords refused to give the benefit of the doubt to an accused who cannot mount a fair defence without impugning the character of prosecution witnesses.

When one co-accused attacks the character of another co-accused or his **13–63** witnesses, then as will be seen in paras. 13.65–13.68 *infra*, by virtue of subsection (4)(c) the statutory protection will be lost.

In *H.M.A.* v. *Grudins,*[85] it was held[86] that the accused does not lose the **13–64** statutory protection when the character which is being attacked is not that of a witness. In *Grudins*, the accused on a murder charge did not lose her immunity when she attacked the character of the deceased.[87] The wording of subsection 4(b) indicates that the statutory protection is not lost if the accused attacked the character of a defence witness who proved "hostile".[88]

(4) Subsection (4)(c): "Accused gives evidence against a co-accused"

Section 266(4)(c) applies in respect of any two accused who appear on **13–65** the same complaint or indictment, regardless of the charges against them. When subsection 4(c) comes into play, an accused may be cross-examined as to his character not only by the prosecution but also by a co-accused.

In *Murdoch* v. *Taylor,*[89] the House of Lords, in an English case, held that **13–66** giving "evidence against" a co-accused could consist of either giving evidence which supports the prosecution's case against him in some material respect, or giving evidence which undermines the defence being put forward by that co-accused. In addition, it held that such evidence could be given either in chief or in the course of being cross-examined, and that it was not necessary for the accused to have any hostile motive, since the test of whether or not evidence is given "against" a co-accused is objective and not subjective.

Both rulings were adopted in *Burton* v. *H.M.A.,*[90] in which the court **13–67** added that there was no distinction to be drawn between the case in which

---

[84] [1970] A.C. 304.
[85] 1976 S.L.T. (Notes) 10.
[86] Applying the previous provisions contained in the 1975 Act.
[87] See *H.M.A.* v. *Kay,* in paras. 13.19–13.22 *supra*.
[88] See paras. 10.48–10.52 *supra*.
[89] [1965] A.C. 574.
[90] 1979 S.L.T. (Notes) 59. Some doubts were cast, *obiter*, on the accuracy of the first interpretation in *Sandlan* v. *H.M.A.*, 1983 S.C.C.R. 71, *supra*.

an accused gave evidence against a co-accused expressly, and that in which an attack on the co-accused might be inferred from the evidence given, or arises by implication. In *Sandlan* v. *H.M.A.*[91] it was held that an accused who has been incriminated by a co-accused has a right to cross-examine that accused on the incriminating evidence. This may entail a second cross-exanination. And in *Todd* v. *H.M.A.*[92] it was held that evidence by one co-accused is evidence *in causa* generally, and may be used against another co-accused even if not intended for that purpose.

13–68   In *McCourtney* v. *H.M.A.*[93] it was held that once an accused has given evidence against a co-accused in terms of subsection (4)(c), the judge has no discretion to exclude the disclosure of that accused's bad character, because when one accused gives evidence against another, he "is in the same position as a witness for the prosecution so far as the co-accused is concerned, and nothing must be done to impair the right of a person charged to discredit his accusers."[94]

13–69   The circumstances described above regarding the operation of s. 266(4) only come into play if the accused gives evidence. The 1995 Act introduced a new provision in s. 270 which enables the prosecution to lead evidence of an accused's character (in response to evidence led on his behalf of good character or to evidence impugning character of prosecution witnesses) and to do so even if the accused does not go into the witness box.

CHARACTER OF OTHER PERSONS

GENERAL

13–70 Occasionally it can become important for the court to consider the character of a person who is not a party to the case, nor a witness, nor the victim of a crime. Provided that such evidence is relevant, it may apparently be admitted.

13–71   In *Gracie* v. *Stuart*[95] it was held that, in a reset trial, the Crown could prove that the person from whom the accused admitted having obtained a stolen watch was in fact a dealer in stolen watches, while in *MacPherson* v. *Crisp*,[96] on a charge of brothel-keeping, the Crown were allowed to show that certain persons observed entering the accused's premises were known by them to be prostitutes.

---

[91]   1983 S.L.T. 519.
[92]   1983 S.C.C.R. 472, considered in para. 11.38 *supra*.
[93]   1977 J.C. 68.
[94]   Cross and Tapper, *op. cit.*, n. 7, pp. 373–374.
[95]   (1884) 11 R.(J.) 22.
[96]   1919 J.C. 1.

CHAPTER 14

ADMISSIONS AND CONFESSIONS

INTRODUCTION

Admissions and confessions should, strictly speaking, be referred to as **14–01**
"extra-judicial" admissions and confessions. This is because they are
statements made by a person against his or her own interests outside a
court of law. They are statements made by someone who is later to become
either a party to a civil action or the accused in a criminal trial. When such
statements are made formally in court, as part of the judicial process, they
are known in both civil and criminal cases as "judicial admissions." These
were considered in Chapter 6, from which it will be recalled that they are
binding upon the maker once they are made.

Extra-judicial admissions and confessions, however, **14–02**

> "are not by themselves conclusive against the party making them as
> in the case of judicial admissions. Evidence of them is relevant either
> because it may throw light on the party's credibility as a witness or as
> an adminicle of evidence in the cause, which may be important or
> unimportant, and which must be considered along with all the other
> evidence led."[1]

When the party who made the statement in question also gives evidence **14–03**
in the case, then this admission or confession may clearly have relevance
to that person's credibility as a witness if it conflicts with the evidence
which is now being given.[2] Where the party does not give evidence, then
the admission or confession may be admissible as an exception to the hearsay
rule.[3] However, because of the obvious importance of such statements as
items of evidence in their own right, they command a chapter of their own.

It is traditional to refer to statements against interest made by parties to **14–04**
a civil action as "admissions", and similar statements by criminal suspects
as "confessions". The general rule, though is the same in both cases. The

---

[1] Walker and Walker, *Law of Evidence in Scotland*, para. 29.
[2] On which point, see paras. 10.88–10.105 *supra*.
[3] Considered in Chap. 8 *supra*.

statements are admissible in evidence because they are made against the interests of the person making them, and are therefore more likely than not to be true.[4]

14–05   In criminal cases, admissions and confessions can normally never be the sole evidence in a case, because of the general rule which requires corroboration,[5] but their precise probative value will vary from case to case. Thus, in *Buick* v. *Jaglar*,[6] Sheriff Wilkinson observed that:

> "It is true, no doubt, that a statement against interest, made coolly and after reflection, is stronger evidence against its maker than a statement made by a person who is in a greatly distressed condition. It is also no doubt true that such a statement is stronger evidence if it never be contradicted or it be contradicted only after a long interval than if it is contradicted shortly after it is made."[7]

14–06   Various issues common to both admissions and confessions may be considered first, before the special rules applicable to the admissibility of confessions are examined.

JUDICIAL ADMISSIONS IN PREVIOUS CASES

14–07   As has already been noted, a *judicial* admission made by a party to a civil action is conclusive against that party for the purposes of that action.[8] It also operates as an extra-judicial admission in any subsequent civil cause to which he or she is a party, even though that other party is different from the other party in the first action.[9]

14–08   However, like any other extra-judicial admission it will not be conclusive, and the party making it may, in the later case, seek to argue it away. It must also be taken along with any qualification, excuse or proviso which accompanied it, and the court is entitled to look closely at the circumstances and context in which it was made before deciding how much weight to attach to it. Independent evidence will also be required before a corroborated case will have been established.

14–09   A formal plea of guilty in a previous criminal case also operates as an extra-judicial admission in any subsequent civil action to which the former

---

[4]   Dickson, *Evidence*, para. 297.
[5]   Considered in Chap. 7 *supra*.
[6]   1973 S.L.T. (Sh.Ct.) 6 at p. 8.
[7]   See also Lord Kincraig in *Liquid Gas Tankers Ltd* v. *Forth Ports Authority*, 1974 S.L.T. (Notes) 35, who approved the statement in Walker and Walker, *loc. cit.*, that "in each case the probative weight to be attached to ... an admission must depend upon the circumstances of the particular case."
[8]   See paras. 6.05–6.14 and 14.01–14.06 *supra*.

accused is a party,[10] although of course it will only operate as one adminicle of evidence. There would in principle seem to be no good reason why the reverse should not be true, so that an admission of liability made on the record of a civil action could be used as an extrajudicial confession of guilt in any subsequent criminal trial, assuming the test of voluntariness to have been satisfied.[11]

ADMISSIONS AND CONFESSIONS BY WITNESSES IN PREVIOUS CASES

A person who gives evidence in a case (other than as a party to it), is also **14–10** covered by the principle considered in paragraphs 14.07–14.09 above. In other words, the principle has been extended so that any statement made on oath by that witness will be regarded as an extra-judicial admission or confession for the purposes of any later case to which he or she is a party in which that statement is relevant.[12] Where possible, of course, the witness should be warned before giving such evidence of any privilege against self-incrimination which may apply.[13]

In *Banaghan* v. *H.M.A.*[14] B was charged with sending a threatening letter, **14–11** and the Crown were allowed to adduce evidence of the fact that in a previous civil action to which B had not been a party, he had admitted to having been the writer of the letter. In *Edmison*,[15] the same rule was applied *quoad* a confession of guilt made by E at the criminal trial of another person charged with that offence. It is because of the admissibility of such statements in later cases that the need exists for a privilege against self-incrimination.

It has been held that even though some formal record of the case in **14–12** which the admission was made may be available,[16] reliable oral evidence may be sufficient to prove the making of the statement.[17]

IMPLIED ADMISSIONS AND CONFESSIONS

An admission or confession may sometimes be implied. This might occur **14–13** from a person's silence or other reaction when confronted with an allegation

---

[9] So that *res judicata* does not apply; see paras. 5.57–5.74 *supra*. The leading authority is *Jackson* v. *Glasgow Corporation*, 1956 S.C. 354, especially at pp. 359, 362 and 365.

[10] *e.g.* a guilty plea to careless driving followed by a reparation action by the driver of the other vehicle. See Dickson, *op. cit.,* n. 4, para. 293 and *Mackay* v. *Bolton* (1897) 4 S.L.T. 321. And see paras. 5.101–5.112 *supra*.

[11] For which see paras. 14.30–14.44 *infra*.

[12] Walker and Walker, *op. cit.*, n. 1, para. 33. quoting Dickson, *op. cit.*, n. 4 para. 288.

[13] For which see paras. 12.05–12.20 *supra*.

[14] (1888) 15 R.(J.) 39; (1888) 1 White 566.

[15] (1866) I S.L.R. 107; (1866) 5 Irv. 519.

[16] *e.g.* the shorthand transcript, or the sheriff's notes.

[17] See *McGiveran* v. *Auld* (1894) 21 R.(J.) 69 at p. 72.

which would ordinarily call for some sort of reply, such as a denial. As Walker and Walker put it[18]: "Since an admission or confession may in some cases be inferred from a party's silence or inaction in response to a statement made to him orally or in writing, evidence of such statements is relevant and admissible for this purpose." However, because it would conflict with the so-called "right of silence", the principle is not applied merely because an accused remains silent in the face of a charge or accusation, or offers a flat denial.[19]

14–14 This does not, however, totally eliminate the possibility of the court inferring some sort of confession from the fact that an accused reacted in a particular way to a statement made in his or her presence and/or hearing which could be said to call for a response. For this reason "statements made in the presence of an accused" are regularly admitted as an exception to the hearsay rule[20] in order to cast light on the accused's reaction to them, be it silence or some action such as bursting into tears or turning pale.

14–15 One special form of this process arises when two accused persons are being interviewed by the police, and one of them makes an incriminating statement which the other "adopts" by failing to deny it. In *Annan* v. *Bain and Hammill*,[21] for example, two suspects who had been chased to a standstill by police officers from the point at which they had abandoned a stolen car, made statements there and then. One of them made a reference to a "white car" (which only the thieves might have been expected to know) and the other was held to have adopted this reference by silence. It proved crucial in providing corroboration.

14–16 Such implied admissions by adoption must however be approached with extreme care, and in particular very close regard must be had to the context in which the original statement was made. Thus, in *Hipson* v. *Tudhope*,[22] H had been a passenger in a stolen car which had been chased by police after it failed to stop. The car collided with a railing and stopped, and when the police asked whose car it was, another accused, in the presence of H, stated that it was stolen. It was held on appeal that the failure of H to dissociate himself from this confession did not amount to a new confession by him, and that in view of his explanation that he did not know the car to be stolen when he accepted a lift in it, he could not be convicted of reset.[23]

---

[18] *op. cit.*, n. 1, para. 34, quoting Dickson, *Evidence*, para. 368.

[19] See Walker and Walker, *op. cit.*, n. 1, and *Robertson* v. *Maxwell*, 1951 J.C. 11 at p. 14.

[20] For which see Chap. 8 *supra*.

[21] 1986 S.C.C.R. 60, considered on another point in para. 7.55 *supra*. See, however, *H.M.A.* v. *Davidson* in 14.20–14.29 *infra*, where the point was made that the police will not be permitted to force two accused into this sort of confrontational situation.

[22] 1983 S.L.T. 659.

[23] See also *Clark* v. *H.M.A.*, 1965 S.L.T. 250.

The courts are more prepared to accept implied admissions in civil cases, **14–17**
notably when normal business practice is involved.[24] In *Potter Cowan &
Co.* v. *Allen*,[25] P sued A for non-payment for goods supplied by him. It was
held that the court could take into account, by way of an implied admission
of receipt of part of the consignment, the fact that the relevant invoices had
been paid without question. Decree was granted despite the fact that A
claimed that the goods had not been received.

ADMISSIONS AND CONFESSIONS IN WRITINGS

There is no distinction made between oral admissions and confessions and **14–18**
those which may be reduced to writing, and both types of statement against
interest are subject to the same rules of admissibility. While there may be
some justification for claiming that when such statements appear in writing
they are more reliable, care must be taken to ensure that they genuinely
emanated from the alleged maker, and that they are his own words and not
simply something concocted for him to sign.[26]

There is old authority to the effect that an admission or confession which **14–19**
is in writing will not be admissible until it has been "uttered" by its author,[27]
but this was doubted in *Watson* v. *Watson*,[28] in which the court accepted as
evidence of adultery a torn-up draft letter in the defender's writing.
Macphail[29] argues that while such a document may not be evidence of
"concluded intention", it might still be sufficient to prove "the writer's
knowledge or state of mind."

VICARIOUS ADMISSIONS AND CONFESSIONS

(1) **General rule**

As a general rule, an admission or confession made by A will not be **14–20**
admissible against B. This is particularly true when A and B are co-defenders
or pursuers, or co-accused in a criminal trial. This can lead to some illogical

---

[24] See, *e.g. Dowling* v. *Henderson* (1890) 17 R. 921 and *Smith* v. *Maxwell* (1833) 11 S. 323.
[25] 1983 S.L.T. (Sh.Ct.) 42.
[26] Which is often the case with confessions made to police officers. Anything approaching a
precognition will fail the admissibility test: see paras. 10.74–10.87 *supra*, and *Carmichael*
v. *Armitage*, 1982 S.C.C.R. 475, in which the High Court rejected as inadmissible a
declaration made by A before a sheriff which had been prepared for him by his solicitor,
since the court viewed it as being more in the nature of a precognition than a statement by
the accused himself.
[27] Dickson, *op. cit.*, n. 4, para. 303.
[28] 1934 S.C. 374. See also *Creasey* v. *Creasey* in paras. 14.20–14.29 *infra*.
[29] *Evidence*, Chap. 20.05.

results, as in *Creasey* v. *Creasey*,[30] in which the court admitted as evidence of adultery by C an entry made by her in her diary. The same entry was not, however, deemed admissible against the paramour, X. The finding of the court was therefore that C had committed adultery with X, but that X had not committed adultery with C.

14–21   The same principle also ensures that a statement made by a husband will not automatically be admissible against his wife or vice versa, simply because of their relationship,[31] although it may be if the parties are also in some other relationship (*e.g.* agent/principal) in which vicarious admissions are possible.

(2) Exceptions in civil cases

14–22   There are various permitted exceptions to the general rule in civil cases in which an admission by A will be deemed to be admissible against B. Such exceptions follow the normal rules of agency, on the basis that an agent is really the alter ego of the principal, at least on those matters which relate to the purpose for which the agent was engaged.[32] In *Industrial Distributions (Central Scotland) Ltd* v. *Quinn*[33] this principle was extended into criminal procedure when it was held that certain statements made to VAT inspectors by two company directors were admissible against their company.

14–23   Statements made by an employee will be admissible against an employer if the making of such statements can be regarded as part of the job description, or if the normal principle of implied agency by "holding out" applies.[34] If, for example, the manager of a shop admits having received certain deliveries, this admission may be used against the owner of the shop in any action for non-payment by the supplier. This principle will not apply, however, when the employer is being sued for the negligence of an employee, since although employers are vicariously liable for any such negligence, the employee is not employed to make admissions of liability.[35]

---

[30] 1931 S.C. 9. See *Watson* v. *Watson* in para. 14.19 *supra*. s. 2 of the Civil Evidence Act 1968 makes an admission by one party to a civil action admissible against the other in England, and the Scottish Law Commission, Memo. No. 46, para. T.33, recommended the same for Scotland.

[31] *Jackson* v. *Glasgow Corporation*, 1956 S.C. 354, in which it was held that an admission of liability by a husband who was one of the drivers involved in a collision was not admissible against his passenger wife in a later case in which she sought damages from the other driver. For general discussion of privilege as it affects spouses see paras. 11.86–11.87 *supra*.

[32] See Walker and Walker, *op. cit.*, n. 1, para. 36 and the cases quoted there.

[33] 1984 S.L.T. 240.

[34] Walker and Walker, *op. cit.*, n. 1.

[35] See, *e.g. Livingstone* v. *Strachan, Crerar and Jones*, 1923 S.C. 794; *Scott* v. *Cormack Heating Engineers*, 1942 S.C. 159.

Section 2 of the Civil Evidence Act 1968 makes all such statements by **14–24** employees admissible against employers under English law, and a similar rule has been recommended for Scotland.[36] It will be recalled from paragraphs 12.50–12.56 *supra* that a report by an eyewitness employee to his employer, at or shortly after the time of an accident, concerning it, is admissible as an exception to the normal *post litem motam* privilege. It seems, however, that it is a prerequisite that the report be made as part of the employee's normal duties.[37]

There are various other situations in which the representative role **14–25** occupied by A *quoad* B will be sufficient to render A's admissions admissible against B.[38] To take two such examples, an admission by a partner is admissible against the firm to the extent that it relates to the firm's affairs,[39] while an admission by a cedent prior to assignation will be admissible against the assignee, in line with the maxim *assignatus utitur jure auctoris*.

(3) Exceptions in criminal cases

As has already been noted, the general rule is that a confession by the **14–26** first defender (D1) is not admissible against the second defender (D2). There are two well-recognised exceptions to this general rule. First, where it is shown that the accused were acting in concert, and second, when the statement by D1 was made in the presence of D2, and might reasonably be regarded as having required some response from D2.

"Concert" means simply that the accused were acting together with a **14–27** common purpose. Before any confession by D1 will be admissible against D2 it must relate to that common purpose. There are relatively few cases on the point,[40] but an example of the principle in operation was *H.M.A.* v. *Docherty*.[41] D was charged with corruption in the public office which he occupied, his alleged corrupter being a person J who was dead by the date of the trial. The Crown sought to adduce evidence of incriminating statements made by J in the furtherance of corrupt acts involving D. It was held that if the jury came to the conclusion that D and J were acting in concert, then since D would be answerable for actions performed by J it was permissible for the jury to be made aware of J's contemporaneous statements concerning those actions. In short, J's statements were part of the *res gestae*,[42] and D was bound by them in so far as the two were acting in concert.

---

[36] By Macphail, *op. cit.*, n. 29, Chap. 20.07.
[37] See *Young* v. *N.C.B.*, 1957 S.C. 99 at p. 105, and *More* v. *Brown & Root Wimpey Highland Fabricators Ltd*, 1983 S.L.T. 669.
[38] These are listed in Walker and Walker, *op. cit.*, n. 1.
[39] Partnership Act 1890, s. 15.
[40] See, however, *Young* v. *H.M.A.*, 1932 J.C. 63.
[41] 1980 S.L.T. (Notes) 33, quoting the authority of Walker and Walker, *op. cit.*, n. 1, para. 37.
[42] For which see paras. 8.20–8.33 *supra*.

14–28   As was seen in paragraphs 14.13–14.17 *supra*, a statement made by D1 in the presence of D2 may be regarded as having been adopted by the latter if he fails to dissociate himself from it.[43] However, this will not apply when the second accused may be said to have been compelled to listen to the statement in question against his will. In *H.M.A.* v. *Davidson*,[44] D had been cautioned and charged and lodged in a police cell. Shortly afterwards he was brought to the charge bar to hear what a co-accused, C, said when cautioned and charged. He was given no reason for being there, and was not warned of what was to happen, or the consequences for him. It was held that the confession by C was in no way admissible against D in these circumstances, which amounted to a breach of D's fundamental right to silence after caution and charge.

14–29   Where it is not shown that D1 and D2 were acting in concert, and it is not the case that the statement of D1 was fairly made in the hearing of D2, then the general rule applies, and D2 is not incriminated by anything said by D1.[45] In *Jones* v. *H.M.A.*[46] the High Court, in reaffirming this general principle, emphasised the need for trial judges to make it plain beyond doubt to juries that in normal cases, a confession by one accused[47] is not admissible against any other.

ADMISSIBILITY OF CONFESSIONS: GENERAL TEST

14–30 A confession by an accused person, whether or not he subsequently gives evidence at his own trial, is potentially the most powerful item of evidence which can be adduced against him. It is also, by the same token, one of the most prejudicial against him, and one of the most easily fabricated or misunderstood. For these reasons the courts have over the years been wary of confessions. Before being admitted the confession has to meet a general test of fairness. Putting the test at its simplest, a confession will not be admissible if it was obtained "unfairly."

14–31   The modern test is that laid down, by Lord Justice-General Emslie in *Lord Advocate's Reference (No. 1 of 1983)*[48] in ruling that:

> "A suspect's self-incriminating answers to police questioning[49] will indeed be admissible in evidence unless it can be affirmed that they have been extracted from him by unfair means. The simple and

---

[43] See *Annan* v. *Bain and Hammill*, considered there.
[44] 1968 S.L.T. 17.
[45] See, *e.g. Black* v. *H.M.A.*, 1974 J.C. 43.
[46] 1981 S.C.C.R. 192.
[47] Who, in the case in question, had already pled guilty and had been dealt with, and was not therefore on trial.
[48] 1984 S.L.T. 337 at p. 340.
[49] *N.B.* that the rule is applicable in other contexts, as will appear below.

intelligible test which has worked well in practice is whether what has taken place has been fair or not ... In each case where the admissibility of answers by a suspect to police questioning becomes an issue it will be necessary to consider the whole relevant circumstances in order to discover whether or not there has been unfairness on the part of the police resulting in the extraction from the suspect of the answers in question. Unfairness may take many forms."

Among the "many forms" of unfairness which have rendered a confession **14–32** inadmissible in the past are "third degree" forms of interrogation[50] and so called "questions" which were little removed from aggressive assertions of guilt designed to "break" the suspect into a confession.[51] Threats or inducements will also be classed as unfair, and will deprive any subsequent confession of any utility which it might have had as an item of evidence.

Equally unacceptable are tricks which result in a suspect unwittingly **14–33** incriminating himself in circumstances in which his statement has no guarantee of having been voluntary.[52] In this type of situation, however, the courts have in recent years been prepared to tolerate a certain degree of deviousness on the part of the police in circumstances in which no pressure has been put upon a suspect.

In *H.M.A.* v. *O'Donnell*[53] an accused in a police cell shouted certain **14–34** incriminating remarks to a co-accused in another cell, which were overheard by police officers. It was held by the sheriff at the subsequent trial that the officers in question could testify as to the contents of the remarks because they had been made voluntarily, no inducement had been offered to the accused to make them, the officers listening in to them had done so spontaneously and had not been deliberately listening in, and indeed did not even have any knowledge of O'Donnell's involvement in the case.

In coming to this conclusion, the sheriff felt that he could not rely on the **14–35** conflicting authority of *H.M.A.* v. *Keen*[54] (where, in similar circumstances, the statement was rejected as evidence), which was not in any event followed in *Welsh and Breen* v. *H.M.A.*[55] The Thomson Committee[56] preferred the *Welsh and Breen* and *O'Donnell* approach, and recommended that such

---

[50] *H.M.A.* v. *Friel*, 1978 S.L.T. (Notes) 21, and *Boyne* v. *H.M.A.*, 1980 J.C. 47.
[51] *H.M.A.* v. *Mair*, 1982 S.L.T. 471.
[52] See, *e.g. H.M.A.* v. *Davidson* in para. 14.28 *supra*, and *Tonge* v. *H.M.A.* in para. 14.49 *infra. N.B. H.M.A.* v. *Campbell* in para. 14.63 *infra.*
[53] 1975 S.L.T. (Sh.Ct.) 22.
[54] 1926 J.C. 1.
[55] Nov. 15, 1973, High Court, unreported but referred to in Macphail, *Evidence*, Chap. 20.22 and *O'Donnell.*
[56] Cmnd. 6218 (1975), para. 7.20.

overheard conversations be put to the accused at judicial examination.[57] The Scottish Law Commission also upheld the view expressed in *O'Donnell*,[58] and it would seem that the courts are no longer prepared to carry fairness to the accused to the length of ignoring safe and highly relevant evidence.[59]

14–36 The courts will, however, be particularly vigilant when the accused is either very young or of limited intelligence.[60] In *Hartley* v. *H.M.A.*[61] the court warned that the confession of a young person of limited intelligence must always be examined with particular care. In *H.M.A.* v. *Gilgannon*[62] the court rejected as inadmissible, because it was unreliable, a confession to attempted rape by G, who had been examined by a police surgeon a few hours previously, and who had been categorised as mentally subnormal. The police themselves were unaware of this assessment, and in fact simply noted the contents of a statement which G volunteered to make. Nevertheless, and despite the fact that the police behaviour could not be faulted, the confession was rejected because:

> "it comes as an at least possibly if not probably incomplete narrative from one who is not only mentally subnormal but unable to give a coherent and complete and therefore accurate account of an incident in which he himself played a principal part."[63]

14–37 In that case Lord Cameron gave[64] as the underlying reason for rejecting the confession the fact that:

> "I am not ... prepared to accept the rigid proposition that the matter of fairness is confined to the detailed circumstances in which the voluntary statement is obtained; that is the questioning itself or the pressures put on the maker of the statement. The mental or physical state of the maker may well be an important and relevant circumstance in determining the issue of admissibility. Once, as here, a suspect is under arrest even before he has been formally charged he is under and is entitled to the protection of the court and therefore it is proper

---

[57] *ibid.*, para. 8.18b. *N.B.* that s. 36 of the Criminal Procedure (Scotland) Act 1995 makes provision for this.

[58] Memo. No. 46, para. T.45.

[59] By the same token, the courts will also accept as evidence the contents of intercepted prisoners' letters; see *H.M.A.* v. *Fawcett* (1869) I Coup. 183, approved by the Scottish Law Commission, *op. cit.*, n. 58, para. T.46. See also *Ming* v. *H.M.A.*, 1987 S.C.C.R. 110.

[60] See *B* v. *H.M.A.*, 1995 S.L.T. 961 where the accused was said to be mentally impaired and suggestible.

[61] 1979 S.L.T. 26, considered more fully in paras. 7.48–7.57 *supra*. *N.B.* that the confession in that case was nevertheless admitted.

[62] 1983 S.C.C.R. 10.

[63] Lord Cameron, *ibid.*, at p. 12.

[64] *ibid.*, at pp. 11–12.

that the circumstances in which the statement is taken should be regarded as well as the manner itself in which the statement is obtained and elicited. The physical or mental state of an accused at the time of making a statement may be such as to make it unfair on him."[65]

This reasoning reveals the true rationale behind the "fairness" test, namely **14–38** that it is important to be as certain as possible that the confession is true. This is normally achieved by ensuring that it is "voluntary",[66] which is the principal reason for the "fairness" test. There is an assumption that a confession which is fairly obtained is likely to be voluntary, and therefore likely to be true. The confession which is unfairly obtained may still be true, but it is contrary to public policy, and unsafe, to rely on any confession so obtained.

At one time, the main test of admissibility for a confession was that it be **14–39** "voluntary",[67] and the transition from a test of "voluntariness" to one of "fairness" may be seen in *Balloch* v. *H.M.A.*[68] In that case, B made a highly incriminating statement to police officers after several hours of questioning, during which he had come under strong suspicion of guilt, and shortly after being shown, for a second time, the clothing and belongings of the deceased, with whom he had lodged. The statement was made without caution, and after being asked if he was sure he was telling the truth. In upholding the trial judge's decision to allow the confession to be put to the jury, the High Court ruled that:

> "a Judge who has heard the evidence regarding the manner in which a challenged statement was made will normally be justified in withholding the evidence from the jury only if he is satisfied on the undisputed relevant evidence that no reasonable jury could hold that the statement had been voluntarily made and had not been extracted by unfair or improper means."[69]

Balloch also marked an important departure from the hitherto accepted **14–40** practice by which objections to confessions were considered. In the days after *Chalmers*[70] it was the practice for the jury to be asked to withdraw, and for the trial judge to determine the admissibility of the statement by

---

[65] His Lordship quoted *H.M.A.* v. *Aitken*, 1926 J.C. 83 and *H.M.A.* v. *Rigg*, 1946 J.C. 1 as his authorities.
[66] Although this will not eliminate the deliberately false confession; it is left to the corroboration rule to do this see Chap. 7 *supra*.
[67] See, *e.g. Chalmers* v. *H.M.A.*, 1954 J.C. 66 *per* Lord Justice-Clerk Thomson at p. 82, who defined a voluntary statement as being "one which is given freely, not in response to pressure and inducement and not elicited by cross-examination."
[68] 1977 J.C. 23. See too the importance of "fairness" in the decision in *H.M.A.* v. *B. and M.*, 1991, S.C.C.R. 533.
[69] *ibid.*, at p. 28.
[70] 1954 J.C. 66, at p. 80.

means of a "trial within a trial". Only if it was deemed admissible was the returning jury allowed to consider it as one item of evidence, the truth of which it was a matter for them to assess.

14–41   The practice was frequently criticised in later years,[71] and increasingly ignored.[72] In *H.M.A.* v. *Whitelaw*[73] Lord Cameron ruled that:

> "Evidence as to statements of a possibly incriminating character alleged to have been made by an accused person is prima facie of the highest relevance and the jury's function should not be in fact usurped and unless it is abundantly clear that the rules of fairness and fair dealing have been flagrantly transgressed it would be better for a jury seized of the whole evidence in the case and of all the circumstances, under such guidance as they should receive from the presiding judge, themselves to take that decision as to the extent to which, if at all, they will take into account evidence of statements ... given by a suspect after due caution."

14–42   The final blessing was given to the current practice *in Lord Advocate's Reference (No. 1 of 1983),*[74] in which Lord Emslie reminded all trial judges that:

> "a judge who has heard all the relevant undisputed evidence bearing upon the admissibility of answers by a suspect, under caution, to police questioning, will normally only be justified in withholding the evidence of the alleged answers from the jury if he is satisfied that no reasonable jury could hold upon that evidence that the answers had not been extracted from the suspect by unfair or improper means."

14–43   The Scottish Law Commission[75] recommended an end to the "trial within a trial" system in all but a limited number of special cases.

14–44   The admissibility of a confession may, as was seen above, depend upon a variety of factors, not the least being the circumstances in which it was made. It is therefore appropriate to consider these in more detail.

STATEMENTS MADE PRIOR TO CHARGE

14–45 There are basically two situations in which an accused may find himself making an extra-judicial statement, prior to actually being charged with an

---

[71]   See, *e.g. Thompson* v. *H.M.A.*, 1968 J.C. 61, and *Hartley, supra.*

[72]   *Mair, Gilgannon and Whitelaw* (*infra*) were all cases in which no such trial within a trial was held.

[73]   1980 S.L.T. (Notes) 25 at p. 26, approved in *Tonge* v. *H.M.A.*, 1982 J.C. 130 *and Lord Advocate's Reference (No. 1 of 1983), supra.*

[74]   *ibid.,* at p. 341.

[75]   Memo. No. 46, para. T.55.

offence. The first is where the police are merely carrying out inquiries into the offence, and the accused has not yet become a suspect. The second is when suspicion has begun to harden against him, but the point has not yet been reached when the police ought fairly to caution the suspect and formally charge him with the offence. At both stages the accused is entitled to remain silent, except in so far as, being a potential witness, he must at least supply his name and address.[76] However, a failure at this stage to give an innocent explanation of, *e.g.* his possession of recently stolen property, may create problems of credibility for an accused at any later trial.[77]

At the earliest stages of a criminal investigation, the police should not **14-46** be hampered in their work by having to take into account the fact that a person they are now questioning may subsequently turn out to be an accused. For that reason the mere fact that an accused is charged following questioning does not render his answers to those questions inadmissible.[78] In *Costello* v. *MacPherson*,[79] for example, it was held that police officers were perfectly entitled to stop a person seen carrying goods in suspicious circumstances and question him as to his possession of them. His answers to those questions were admissible.

And in *Thompson* v. *H.M.A.*,[80] while T was being kept at the police **14-47** station and blurted out, without prompting or caution: "It was her or me" his subsequent full confession, after caution, was held admissible. The key factor is whether there has been any unfairness to the accused. In *Johnston* v. *H.M.A.*[81] the accused's answers to police questioning after his arrest and caution, but before charge, were admissible because there was said to be no unfairness in the procedures.

But generally, when suspicion has begun to harden on the accused, it is **14-48** expected that the police will administer a caution to their suspect. At common law[82] there is no prescribed formula of words which must be used, provided that it is made clear to the suspect that he is under no obligation to speak, but that if he does, his statement will be recorded and may be used in evidence in any subsequent trial. Nor is there any given moment at which the caution must be administered, but the absence of such a caution in

---

[76] Criminal Procedure (Scotland) Act 1995, s. 13(1)(a), previously s1(1)(a) of the Criminal Justice (Scotland) Act 1980. *N.B.* also the provisions of s. 14(9) of the 1995 Act.

[77] See *Cryans* v. *Nixon*, 1955 J.C. 1, and paras. 3.113–3.119 *supra*.

[78] *Chalmers* v. *H.M.A.*, 1954 J.C. 66 at p. 81, *per* Lord Thomson. Any such answers, though, will be treated with care.

[79] 1922 J.C. 9.

[80] 1968 J.C. 61.

[81] 1994 S.L.T. 300.

[82] The statutory caution required under the Criminal Procedure (Scotland) Act 1995 is set out in s. 14(9). Previously the provisions were contained in s. 2(7) of the Criminal Justice (Scotland) Act 1980.

circumstances in which a court later feels that it should have been given may render any subsequent statement inadmissible.

14–49   The dangers of failing to observe the rules scrupulously were well illustrated by the now leading case of *Tonge* v. *H.M.A.*[83] in which T and two others were detained under section 2 of the Criminal Justice (Scotland) Act 1980[84] on a charge of rape. T was given the information which by virtue of section 2(7) he was entitled to receive at the start of the detention,[85] but was not given the standard common law caution. Later in the course of his detention, and without caution, T was accused of the crime by investigating officers, whereupon he made an incriminating statement. While not going to the length of laying down a rigid rule that all detainees under section 2 should receive the full caution, the High Court, in ruling that T's alleged confession should not have been left to the jury, found that the allegation made against him amounted to a charge of rape, and that: "To charge an accused person without cautioning him is to put pressure upon him which may induce a response."[86]

14–50   In summarising the requirements of the common law in regard to suspects in a police station, Lord Cameron[87] pointed out that:

> "It is of course well established that police officers are entitled to question a suspect as to his possible complicity in a crime which they are investigating, and that his replies will be admissible in evidence if they have not been extracted or compelled by unfair or improper means including threats, intimidations, offers of inducements, or cross-examination designed or intended to extract incriminating replies, but it is equally well recognised that in the case of one on whom suspicion of responsibility or complicity has centred, in order that his replies should be admissible in evidence, it is proper practice that any further questioning should be preceded by a caution in common form."

14–51   The Lord Justice-General[88] issued the following warning:

> "I would strongly urge police officers throughout Scotland who proceed to accuse a detainee or to question him or to take from him a voluntary statement, to rely not at all upon the efficacy of the warning described in section 2(7), and to appreciate that if any use is to be made in evidence of anything said by a detainee in these circumstances

---

[83]   1982 J.C. 130. See also *Wilson* v. *Robertson*, 1986 S.C.C.R. 700.
[84]   Now s. 14 of the Criminal Procedure (Scotland) Act 1995.
[85]   Namely that he was obliged by law to say nothing apart from giving his name and address.
[86]   At p. 140.
[87]   At p. 147.
[88]   At pp. 145–146.

the ordinary rules of fairness and fair dealing which have been developed by the common law should be strictly observed. The wise course will be, inter alia, to administer to the detainee in the events which I have mentioned a full caution in common law terms. The omission to give such a caution will, by itself, at the very least place the admissibility of anything said by the detainee in peril."

When an accused is given a caution in relation to one charge and **14–52** questioned about other related charges, the answers to the related charges will be admissible provided there is no unfairness to the accused.[89]

So far as concerns the wording of the caution, there are two important **14–53** constituents, neither of which may be omitted. The accused must be left in no doubt that he has the right to remain silent, and in *H.M.A.* v. *Von*[90] a confession was rejected after the accused was told merely that any answers he gave to police questions might be used in evidence, and he was not advised that he need say nothing to incriminate himself. At the same time, informing the accused of his right to remain silent is insufficient by itself if he is not also warned of the potential evidential significance of anything he chooses to say.

Very shortly after the administration of the caution, and preferably along **14–54** with it,[91] the accused should be charged. The reason for this is that it will be regarded as unfair for the police to continue to extract incriminating information from an accused once they have collected sufficient information to make him a "chargeable suspect."[92] Once a person reaches this stage, then as Lord Cameron pointed out in *H.M.A.* v. *Gilgannon*,[93] he comes into a new category in which he is "under and ... entitled to the protection of the court."

STATEMENTS MADE AFTER CHARGE

Once a person is formally charged, his immediate reaction to the charge is **14–55** admissible,[94] but no further statements by him will be admissible unless they are totally spontaneous. In particular, there may be no more police questions designed to elicit new incriminating material from the accused. Where practicable, even a spontaneous statement should be interrupted by

---

[89] *Wilson* v. *Heywood*, 1989 S.L.T. 279, distinguishing *Tonge*, *supra*, because in that case there had been no caution at all of one of the suspects.

[90] 1979 S.L.T. (Notes) 62. See also *H.M.A.* v. *Docherty*, 1981 J.C. 6.

[91] Certainly not before it: see *Tonge*, *supra*.

[92] See Renton and Brown, *Criminal Procedure*, para. 18–33, and *Johnston* v. *H.M.A.*, 1994 S.L.T. 300.

[93] 1983 S.C.C.R. 10, considered in paras. 14.26–14.38 *supra*.

[94] Conveyed to the court by police witnesses who recite to the court what the accused said "when cautioned and charged".

a repeated caution, and taken down by officers unconnected with the case.[95] Particular care must be taken when the accused is mentally subnormal,[96] and any suggestion that pressure or inducements have been applied to persuade the accused to make further statements will render any such statement inadmissible.

14–56   Once charged, an accused should, if possible, be granted the services of a solicitor, but a failure to do so is not necessarily fatal, being simply one factor to be taken into account when assessing the overall "fairness" of the circumstances in which the confession was made.[97]

14–57   Although it is preferable for any reply to caution and charge to be noted *verbatim* in the notebook of the police officers to whom it is made,[98] oral evidence from those officers as to what the accused said is admissible as direct evidence.[99] Tape-recorded confessions were finally approved in *Lord Advocate's Reference (No. 1 of 1983),*[1] in which it was held that they are subject to the normal admissibility tests applied to all confessions, and that while inadmissible parts of the transcript of such interviews[2] must be deleted in just the same way as they must be erased from the original tape, there is no ground for excluding the rest of the transcript from the jury.

CONFESSIONS MADE TO OTHER PERSONS

14–58   So far it has been assumed that a confession made by an accused person has been made to police officers. In fact, many officials have the power to interview persons suspected of contravening a variety of statutes, and H.M. Customs and Excise, H.M. Inspectors of Taxes and D.S.S. officials are three such examples. In addition, criminal accused who are assisting the police with their inquiries, or who have been detained pending a court appearance, sometimes make statements to persons in authority such as prison officers or police surgeons.

14–59   Assuming that in each case the official concerned has the statutory right to ask the questions (and if not, then any resulting confession may well be

---

[95] See *Tonge* v. *H.M.A.,* 1982 J.C. 130 at p. 137; but *cf.* also *Aiton* v. *H.M.A.,* 1987 S.C.C.R. 257; *Custerson* v. *Westwater,* 1987 S.C.C.R. 389 and *MacDonald* v. *H.M.A.,* 1987 S.C.C.R. 581. No adverse inference may be drawn from the fact that the accused exercises his right of silence: *Robertson* v. *Maxwell,* 1951 J.C. 11; *Douglas* v. *Pirie,* 1975 J.C. 61.

[96] *H.M.A.* v. *Gilgannon,* 1983 S.C.C.R. 10, in paras. 14.36–14.37 *supra.*

[97] *H.M.A.* v. *Cunningham,* 1939 J.C. 61. *N.B.* the detainee's right to have "some person" informed of his detention, now in terms of s. 15(1)(b) of the Criminal Procedure (Scotland) Act 1995: *see H.M.A.* v. *McCrade and Stirton,* 1982 S.L.T. (Sh.Ct.) 13.

[98] From which it may be read directly to the trial court: see paras. 10.23–10.29 *supra.* It must, however, be in the accused's own words: see paras. 14.18–14.19 *supra.*

[99] *Hamilton* v. *H.M.A.,* 1980 J.C. 66, considered in paras. 9.19 and 9.68 *supra.*

[1] 1984 S.L.T. 337, and the admissibility of taped interviews is now embodied in s. 277 of the Criminal Procedure (Scotland) Act 1995.

[2] *e.g.* in which the accused refers to previous convictions: see paras. 13.28–13.41 *supra.*

inadmissible) or the person to whom the statement is made is lawfully in the presence of the accused, then the principle which applies is exactly the same as that applicable to confessions made to police officers. It is admissible provided it was not obtained "unfairly".

The leading case is *Morrison* v. *Burrell*,[3] in which a sub-postmaster **14–60** suspected of having abused his position to post off fraudulent bets was interviewed by Post Office officials, and in the course of that interview admitted certain transgressions. In ruling that his confessions were admissible, the High Court was particularly influenced by "the circumstances under which the investigation was conducted and to the absence of any hint or trace of impropriety, unfairness or misuse by the investigators of their position — a factor of vital importance in all cases of this kind."[4]

In *H.M.A.* v. *Friel*,[5] the "fairness" test which subsequently became the **14–61** main test for all confessions per *Lord Advocate's Reference (No. 1 of 1983)*,[6] was applied to questions and answers during an investigation by Customs officers. In such investigations the absence of a caution is one factor to be considered in the wider context of fairness.

In *Pennycuik* v. *Lees*[7] incriminating answers given by a person being **14–62** interviewed by DSS officers were admissible despite the lack of a caution as the questions were fair and proper and there was no suggestion of unfairness or deception on the part of the interviewers. In contrast, in *Oghonoghor* v. *Secretary of State for the Home Department*[8] the statements of a suspected illegal immigrant were held inadmissible when given in the absence of a caution.

In *H.M.A.* v. *Campbell*,[9] C offered to give an interview to a journalist in **14–63** return for money, and when the meeting took place in a public house, the journalist was accompanied by a plain clothes police officer who did not reveal his identity until after C had made certain incriminating statements. It was held that these statements were inadmissible because they had been obtained by a trick.[10] Gordon[11] is of the opinion that such statements would be admitted today. They certainly seem to have been "voluntary".[12]

---

[3] 1947 J.C. 43.
[4] *ibid.*, *per* Lord Justice-General Cooper at p. 49.
[5] 1978 S.L.T. (Notes) 21.
[6] Considered in paras. 14.30–14.44 *supra*.
[7] 1992 S.L.T. 763.
[8] 1995 S.L.T. (Notes) 733.
[9] 1946 J.C. 80.
[10] And similarly, see *H.M.A.* v. *Graham*, 1991 S.L.T. 416 where evidence obtained through police officers "wiring up" a third party was held inadmissible because had equivalent questions been asked in a police station then a caution would have been required.
[11] Renton and Brown, *Criminal Procedure*, para. 18–28.
[12] See paras. 14.30–14.44 *supra*.

14–64   Even when a statement is made to a private person such as a friend, the court will wish to ensure that it was "fairly" made and is therefore voluntary, As Lord Cameron observed[13]:

> "confession to a private party will be admissible unless the circumstances in which it has been made or extracted are such as to raise doubt as to whether it has been falsely made in order to escape from further pressures or in response to inducements offered, and ... this is an issue which is essentially for the jury to determine upon the evidence laid before them. A case could also be figured when, by arrangement with police officers, a private person could be used to exercise upon a suspect pressures which would be fatal to the admissibility in evidence of a confession extracted by them by the use of such pressures: in such a case it cannot be doubted that any confession so obtained would be inadmissible."

STATEMENTS BY ACCUSED PERSONS OVERHEARD BY POLICE

14–65 When police officers overhear a conversation between an accused and another person, perhaps a co-accused, then that conversation will be admissible provided it has been made voluntarily and not as a result of any entrapment.[14] Where there is a suggestion of entrapment then it is likely the evidence will be inadmissible.

STATEMENTS BY ACCUSED PERSONS IN RELATION TO OTHER CHARGES

14–66 Where an accused faces more than one charge, and the facts which gave rise to both charges are the same, can an incriminating statement in respect of one charge be used against him as a confession *quoad* a different charge? The cases are reviewed in Renton and Brown,[15] and the conclusion reached is that such a process may be used when the first charge is more serious than the second, but that the position remains uncertain when the reverse is true.

14–67   In *Willis* v. *H.M.A.*[16] the court had little hesitation in admitting, on a charge of culpable homicide, an incriminating statement made in respect of a murder charge. However, in *James Stewart*[17] the trial court in a murder trial refused to admit evidence of S's declaration given earlier when the

---

[13] " Scottish Practice in relation to Admissions and Confessions by Persons Suspected or Accused of Crime", 1975 S.L.T. (News) 265 at p. 268.

[14] *H.M.A.* v. *O'Donnell*, 1975 S.L.T. (Sh.Ct.) 22, approved in *Jamieson* v. *Annan*, 1988 S.L.T. 631, and considered in para. 14.34 *supra*.

[15] *op. cit.*, n. 11, para. 18–45.

[16] 1941 J.C. 1.

[17] (1866) 5 Irv. 310.

charge was assault to the danger of life. But, in the later case of *H.M.A.* v. *Cunningham*[18] the court saw nothing wrong in allowing in such a statement in identical circumstances.

It seems that Cunningham has now become the leading authority, since **14–68** in *McAdam* v. *H.M.A.*[19] the court allowed in evidence statements made by M on what was originally a charge of assault to severe injury, even though by the date of the trial the Crown had raised the charge to one of attempted murder. Lord Justice-General Clyde[20] ruled that the important test in such cases was that:

> "each of the charges must substantially cover the same *species facti*. I say 'substantially' because all the articles which have been stolen may not have been ascertained, when the earlier charge is made, or the full extent of the injuries to the victim may not be known. None the less, justice demands that the jury be informed of the reply given, after caution, to the limited charge originally made."

McAdam was followed in *H.M.A.* v. *McTavish*[21] in which M, a nursing **14–69** sister, had made certain incriminating statements concerning her administration of an injection to a patient at a time when she was charged only with assault. The patient died, and the court held that her statement was admissible on a charge of murder because the *species facti* were substantially the same on the assault charge as they were on the murder charge.

The principle laid down in *McAdam* was also approved by the Scottish **14–70** Law Commission,[22] which added only that the two charges must fall into the same general category (dishonesty, personal violence, etc.).

---

[18] 1939 J.C. 61, in which *Stewart* was not cited.
[19] 1960 J.C. 1, in which both *Stewart* and *Cunningham* were cited.
[20] At p. 4.
[21] 1975 S.L.T. 27. *N.B.* that M's conviction was quashed on other grounds.
[22] Memo. No. 46, para. T.40.

CHAPTER 15

ILLEGALLY OBTAINED EVIDENCE

INTRODUCTION

15–01 Problems can arise when evidence which is undoubtedly relevant to a case[1] is obtained without lawful authority.[2] It is not automatically inadmissible, even though the person from whom it was obtained may possess certain civil remedies[3] in respect of the manner in which it was obtained from him. Instead, the courts will examine the facts of each case individually, in order to assess whether or not the manner in which the evidence was procured may be justified, with hindsight, to the extent of allowing the evidence in.

15–02 As was seen in Chapter 14, a confession which is obtained unfairly will normally not be admitted, and confessions could legitimately be considered along with the other items in this chapter were it not for the many other factors which make confessions a distinctive case. Other special considerations may arise if a confession which is deemed inadmissible, generates certain information which links the confessor to the crime.[4] The question then arises whether the discovery of this additional evidence may be disclosed to the court, and, more significantly, whether or not it may be linked with the original statement by the accused.

15–03 It is currently necessary to treat illegally-obtained evidence differently *quoad* civil and criminal cases, because of the different criteria of admissibility which are applied. Macphail has suggested that the rules should be harmonised to provide one body of law on the subject.[5] There is little doubt that the civil law has been influenced to some extent by the test currently in use for criminal cases. The latter is considered first.

---

[1] *e.g.* the fact that a suspect has stolen property in his possession, or the fact that certain items proved to have been used in a robbery are found in the accused's house.

[2] *e.g.* after search without warrant, or under a warrant which did not cover the property discovered.

[3] *e.g.* an action for assault or unlawful arrest: see *Dahl* v. *Chief Constable, Central Scotland Police*, 1983 S.L.T. 420.

[4] *e.g.* he may direct them to where the victim's clothing may be found.

[5] See *Evidence*, Chap. 21.01.

CRIMINAL CASES

One of the earliest influential cases in this area was *H.M.A.* v. *McGuigan*,[6] **15–04**
in which Lord Justice-Clerk Aitchison observed that "an irregularity in the
obtaining of evidence does not necessarily render that evidence
inadmissible." This observation was perhaps *obiter*, since the police had
acted in accordance with their undoubted common law powers when, after
arresting M on a charge of murder, they searched the tent in which he had
been living for evidence.[7]

However, in the *locus classicus* of the modern rule, *Lawrie* v. *Muir*,[8] **15–05**
Lord Justice-General Cooper adopted the *McGuigan* approach, and cast it
in a broader principle which has been applied ever since. The facts of the
case were that, acting under warrants issued by the Milk Marketing Board
for the inspection of premises occupied by milk distributors under contract
to the Board, two inspectors searched the premises of the accused. The
search was with her permission, but outwith the terms of the warrant, since
the accused was not a S.M.M.B. distributor. She had believed that the
warrants covered the search, as did the inspectors, but it was argued that
the evidence of the discovery of stolen bottles could not be led because of
the false representation of authority.

In holding that the evidence was indeed inadmissible, Lord Cooper **15–06**
highlighted the two conflicting interests which every court must weigh
together in every such case, namely:

> "(a) the interests of the citizen to be protected from illegal or irregular
> invasions of his liberties by the authorities, and (b) the interests of
> the State to secure that evidence bearing upon the commission of
> crime and necessary to enable justice to be done shall not be withheld
> from Courts of law on any merely formal or technical ground."[9]

These principles have been applied ever since, and *Lawrie* v. *Muir* has **15–07**
proved influential in other jurisdictions which have sought a general test
with which to meet similar problems.[10] It has not, however, passed without
criticism in Scotland.[11]

---

[6] 1936 J.C. 16 at p. 18. Applied in *Edgley* v. *Barbour,* 1995 S.L.T. 711.
[7] For details of this common law power of search, see Renton and Brown, *Criminal Procedure*,
    para. 5–34.
[8] 1950 J.C. 19.
[9] *ibid.*, at p. 26.
[10] See Macphail, *op. cit.*, n. 5, Chap. 21.06.
[11] See, *e.g.* Macphail, *op. cit.*, n. 5, who observed that "it seems inconsistent to exclude a
    confession obtained by illegal means but to countenance the admission of real evidence
    obtained by illegal means."

15–08   Among the more recent applications of *Lawrie* v. *Muir* is *Bulloch* v. *H.M.A.*,[12] in which a warrant granted to the Inland Revenue under the Finance Act 1972 was held to have been unlawfully used because it was undated. In *H.M.A.* v. *Cumming*[13] the objection to the warrant granted under the Misuse of Drugs Act 1971, and the evidence obtained under it, was that it failed to specify the premises to be searched or the officers authorised to search, while in *H.M.A.* v. *Bell*[14] the reason for rejecting a similar warrant was that it was unsigned.

15–09   In *Smith* v. *Innes*,[15] fingerprint evidence was rejected after the court held that the warrant under which it had been taken had been wrongly granted, while in *McGovern* v. *H.M.A.*,[16] decided shortly after *Lawrie* v. *Muir*,[17] the court rejected evidence obtained from fingernail scrapings taken from an accused under suspicion of safe-blowing, but not then charged.

15–10   In the last case, the necessary evidence could have been obtained quite lawfully, either by applying for a lawful warrant or by arresting the suspect,[18] and all the cases quoted so far have one important factor in common, namely that the evidence in each case was rejected because the authorities had made a simple but inexcusable procedural error. In such cases, the courts will not turn a blind eye, and the evidence will be inadmissible.[19]

15–11   However, as Lord Justice-General Cooper observed in *Lawrie* v. *Muir*, there are situations in which the police do not have the luxury of time in which to turn in an immaculate performance under some tortuous statutory procedure, but have to act in an emergency in order to preserve vital evidence which may otherwise be lost. As *McGuigan* shows, such urgent actions may be authorised at common law anyway, but in other similar cases the courts have shown a willingness to exercise leniency in the admission of evidence obtained in an "urgent" situation.[20]

15–12   In *McHugh* v. *H.M.A.*,[21] M was charged with robbing a shop. After his arrest, the police searched both his person and his house. On his person were found certain numbered banknotes which tied in with the robbery, but the accused maintained that the search had taken place before he was charged

---

[12]   1980 S.L.T. (Notes) 5.
[13]   1983 S.C.C.R. 15.
[14]   1985 S.L.T. 349.
[15]   1984 S.C.C.R. 119.
[16]   1950 J.C. 33.
[17]   *supra.*
[18]   See Renton and Brown, *op. cit.*, n. 7, para. 5–30.
[19]   See, however, *Smith* v. *Ross*, 1983 S.C.C.R. 109, in which an irregularity which rendered the arrest of a suspected drunken driver unlawful for the purposes of s. 6 of the Road Traffic Act 1972 did not invalidate the evidence of his condition which was spoken to by a police doctor for the purposes of a s. 5 charge.
[20]   See, *e.g. Allan* v. *Milne*, 1974 S.L.T. (Notes) 76.
[21]   1978 J.C. 12.

and without his consent.[22] Although the appeal court was persuaded on the evidence that the search had been lawful, it went on to find that even if it had not been, the evidence would have been admissible because it had been obtained as a matter of urgency.

Similarly, in *Cairns* v. *Keane,*[23] C objected to the admission of all **15–13** evidence relating to the taking of breath and blood samples from him on the grounds that when the breath sample had been taken, the police had been trespassers in his house, having chased him up the drive to his house and in effect made a forced entry to the house behind him. The sheriff, having observed[24] that:

> "the 'rule of law in Scotland concerning the right of a constable to enter any premises for any purpose' was that, except when investigating serious crime, police officers are no more entitled than any other member of the public to enter upon private property without a warrant and without the consent of the owner; and that if they do so they must be prepared to justify their conduct by reason of special circumstances before any evidence so obtained can be rendered admissible,"

went on to find that such special circumstances existed, and the High Court rejected C's appeal against conviction without even delivering any opinions.

In reaching his finding, the sheriff refused to accept that the common **15–14** law power given to police officers to act in an urgent situation was affected by the statutory provisions relating to the taking of breath and blood samples. In *MacNeill*[25] the High Court went further, and ruled that such powers may in fact only be taken away by clear express statutory provisions designed specifically to do so. In that case the court held that the power given to the procurator fiscal under common law to obtain a search warrant before charging anyone with an offence was not affected by the fact that the Civic Government (Scotland) Act 1982, which makes it unlawful to deal in obscene material, makes no provision for the granting of search warrants. It was also held that such powers may be used *quoad* statutory offences.

The presence or absence of urgency can lead to some fine distinctions **15–15** on the facts. Two frequently-quoted contrasting cases in this regard are *H.M.A.* v. *Turnbull*[26] and *H.M.A.* v. *Hepper.*[27]

In *Turnbull*, T's premises were searched under a warrant alleging tax **15–16** frauds, and a large consignment of papers was removed and passed on to

---

[22] And if so, it was unlawful: see Renton and Brown, *op. cit.*, n. 7.
[23] 1983 S.C.C.R. 277.
[24] *ibid.*, at p. 281.
[25] 1984 S.L.T. 157.
[26] 1951 J.C. 96.
[27] 1958 J.C. 39.

the Inland Revenue without being examined by the police. The Revenue examined them, and found evidence of further offences not covered by the original warrant, and further charges were brought against T as a result. In rejecting the evidence obtained during the search, the court was primarily influenced by the fact that the search had not been carried out as a matter of urgency, and that this was not a case of evidence accidentally coming to life, but simply a general "fishing expedition".

15–17   In *Hepper* on the other hand, the accused had consented to a search of his house in respect of one charge, and in the course of that search a briefcase was found which was taken away in the belief that it related to that charge. It turned out to contain evidence relating to another offence entirely, but the court held that the evidence was admissible on the new charge because the original search had been lawful, the discovery of the briefcase had been incidental, and the consideration of urgency justified its removal.

15–18   Subsequent cases involving unlawful searches, or lawful searches which exceed their remit, tend to be grouped behind one or other of *Turnbull* and *Hepper*, with the determining criterion being either whether the evidence was recovered as a matter of urgency or accidentally.

15–19   In *Leckie* v. *Milne*,[28] L was arrested on petition in respect of a charge of theft from a doctor's surgery, and the sheriff granted the usual search warrant *quoad* articles connected with that offence. Armed with that warrant, police persuaded D, who lived with L, to allow them to search the house, and in the course of that search they discovered evidence which led to L's conviction on new charges of theft from a school and an office. In quashing the convictions, the High Court followed *Turnbull* in holding that the search had been unlawful, being authorised by neither the warrant nor any implied consent from D (who was assumed to have consented only to the extent authorised by the warrant). It was, said the court, more in a way of a random search,[29] and the fruits of it were therefore inadmissible.[30]

15–20   In *McNeill* v. *H.M.A.*,[31] on the other hand, the court followed *Hepper* and used the "urgency" principle to justify the reception in evidence of the fruits of a search of a house in Liverpool under an Excise warrant to search for drugs following the discovery of drugs on a yacht moored in the Clyde. The court was not convinced that the search was unlawful but held that even if it was, it was justified by the urgency of the situation.

15–21   Another example of improperly recovered evidence being admitted under the "urgency" principle is the case of *Burke* v. *Wilson*,[32] where a number of

---

[28] 1981 S.C.C.R. 261.
[29] *N.B.* that the officers who conducted the search were not made aware of the contents of the petition, did not have the warrant with them, and appear simply to have been instructed to search for evidence of theft.
[30] See paras. 15.24–15.28 *infra*.
[31] 1986 S.C.C.R. 288.
[32] 1988 S.L.T. 749.

pornographic videos were recovered during a lawful police search of shop premises for "pirate" videos. The court held that the pornographic videos were admissible evidence as, if they had not been seized as a matter of urgency, they could easily have disappeared.

Examples of "accidental" recovery of evidence (otherwise improperly **15–22** obtained) include *Drummond* v. *H.M.A.*[33] and *Baxter* v. *Scott*[34] In the latter case, police officers discovered stolen goods while checking the boot of a car belonging to a driver they had arrested. The Crown argued that the police had a general power to check the contents of vehicles in their temporory custody and that stolen goods recovered from such a search were legitimately recovered. The court agreed.[35] The case law indicates that a fine line divides evidence recovered properly from that recovered improperly. It is very much a matter of the specific circumstances of the case.

Neither the Thomson Committee[36] nor the Scottish Law Commission[37] **15–23** called for any radical change in the present law.

THE FRUITS OF THE POISONED TREE

Where further evidence is discovered as a result of statements made by an **15–24** accused person which are later deemed inadmissible because of the way in which they were obtained, the question arises as to the status of that further evidence. Even although the statements or information which led to that discovery are themselves inadmissible, can the additional facts unearthed be admitted? Or, to adopt the terminology of the American courts,[38] may the court consume the fruits of the poisoned tree?

In Scots law the question has only been partly answered, and that in the **15–25** context of evidence revealed by inadmissible confessions. The answer in such cases is in the negative. Thus, in *Chalmers* v. *H.M.A.*,[39] C made a full confession to murder which the court later deemed to be inadmissible. During the course of that confession he offered to take the police to the place where he had hidden the victim's purse, and evidence was led to the effect that he had done so. On appeal, it was held that the evidence of the visit to the *locus* (a cornfield) was inadmissible because it was "part and parcel of the same transaction as the interrogation and if the interrogation

---

[33] 1993 S.L.T. 476.
[34] 1992 S.C.C.R. 342.
[35] But see, *Graham* v. *Orr,* 1995 S.L.T. 30.
[36] Cmnd. 6218 (1975), paras. 4.19–4.24.
[37] Memo. No. 46, para. U.04.
[38] See, *e.g. Olmstead* v. *U.S.* (1928) 277 U.S. 438.
[39] 1954 J.C. 66.

and the 'statement' which emerged from it are inadmissible as 'unfair,' the same criticism must attach to the conducted visit to the cornfield."[40]

15–26 The problem which arises from this is that of making the court aware of an important fact (*e.g.* that the accused knew where the victim's purse was buried) which only someone involved in the crime might be expected to know[41] without relating it in any way to the inadmissible statement which led to it. The court in *Chalmers* seemed to be suggesting that the fact that the accused was able to take the police to the *locus* could not be revealed to the jury because he had first offered to do so during an inadmissible confession. Perhaps this is putting the position too strongly. For while a statement made under psychological stress is rightly questionable, an extrinsic fact is not.

15–27 As Gordon comments[42]: "The situation may be different where the whereabouts of the property themselves incriminate the accused." He was referring to the situation in which the accused is found to be linked with the property, as for example where it is found in his house. The same could perhaps be said of property to which the accused leads the police, and the distinction may not be one of substance.

15–28 Macphail,[43] the Thomson Committee[44] and the Scottish Law Commission[45] all favour a more flexible test which would allow the court to make use of the fruit of the poisoned tree provided that it was not of itself obtained by unfair means,[46] and the Crown do not disclose the origin of the information.[47] The Scottish Law Commission[48] were of the opinion that this might already be the law.

CIVIL ACTIONS

15–29 The sole test of the admissibility of illegally-obtained evidence in civil cases has traditionally been simply that of whether or not it is relevant. The leading case—and the one which set an uncomfortable precedent for later courts to follow—is *Rattray* v. *Rattray*,[49] in which a letter sent by the

---

[40] At p. 76. *N.B.* that the Thomson Committee (Cmnd. 6218), para. 7.26, agreed with this ruling.
[41] For the importance of this type of evidence in corroboration of other evidence, see paras. 7.48–7.57 *supra*.
[42] In Renton and Brown, *op. cit.*, n. 7, para. 18–31. But see *Leckie* v. *Milne*, in para. 15.19 *supra*.
[43] *op. cit.*, n. 5, Chap. 21.04.
[44] (Cmnd. 6218), para. 7.27.
[45] Memo. No. 46, para. U.02.
[46] Which begs the whole question anew.
[47] *Quaere* whether the origin of the information could be said to be the accused himself, or the inadmissible statement, or both.
[48] *op. cit.*, n. 45.
[49] (1897) 25 R. 315.

defender to the co-defender in a divorce action based on adultery was stolen from the Post Office by the pursuer, and used by him in evidence. On appeal, although it was held that there was insufficient evidence of adultery *in toto*, the court ruled that the letter had been rightly admitted in evidence, on the ground *inter alia* that "the policy of the law in later years (and I think a good policy) has been to admit almost all evidence which will throw light on disputed facts and enable justice to be done."[50]

The ruling was essentially *obiter*, and there was dissenting opinion.[51] **15–30** Furthermore, any application of the principle to criminal cases was eliminated by *Lawrie* v. *Muir*,[52] and it is only in civil cases that it may still be possible to cite *Rattray* as authority for the alarming suggestion that even evidence obtained by criminal means is admissible.

Later courts have, however, felt obliged to follow *Rattray* because it **15–31** was a ruling by a full court of the Second Division, and no other opportunity to reverse or reconsider the full implications of it has occurred before that court since then. Certainly, in so far as evidence has been obtained by underhand means which fall short of being criminal, the courts appear to admit it routinely without objection being taken. In *MacNeill* v. *MacNeill*[53] and *Turner* v. *Turner*,[54] for example, no objection was raised to the use in evidence of letters passing between defenders and paramours which had been intercepted by both pursuers, while in *Watson* v. *Watson*[55] it was held that the pursuer might found upon a torn-up draft letter by the defender to the paramour which he found in an open desk in the drawing-room.

In *McColl* v. *McColl*,[56] Lord Moncrieff was clearly unhappy at being **15–32** obliged by what he felt to be the clear authority of *Rattray* to admit in evidence a letter from the defender to the paramour which had been intercepted by criminal means, while in *Duke of Argyll* v. *Duchess of Argyll*,[57] Lord Wheatley admitted that: "I must confess that I find the reasoning of Lord Trayner [in *Rattray*] ... difficult to follow ... but ... I feel bound by the decision if unconvinced by the reasoning in that case."

In *Argyll*, certain diaries were admitted in evidence which belonged to **15–33** the Duchess and which were acquired by the Duke by theft. Because adultery was historically treated as a quasi-criminal offence,[58] Lord Wheatley felt

---

[50] At pp. 318–319, *per* Lord Trayner.
[51] The precise grounds for doubting the binding nature of the case as a later authority are well laid out by Macphail, *op. cit.*, n. 5, para. 21.08.
[52] See paras. 15.04–15.23 *supra*.
[53] 1929 S.L.T. 251.
[54] 1930 S.L.T. 393.
[55] 1934 S.C. 374, also considered in para. 14.19 *supra*.
[56] 1946 S.L.T. 312.
[57] 1962 S.C. 140, at pp. 141–142.
[58] And at the time the standards of proof of crime and adultery were the same, namely beyond reasonable doubt: see now paras. 2.102–2.131 *supra*.

himself entitled to treat *Lawrie* v. *Muir* as applicable to a modern divorce case, and he added that:

> "There is no absolute rule, it being a question of the particular circumstances of each case determining whether a particular piece of evidence should be admitted or not. Among the circumstances which may have to be taken into account are the nature of the evidence concerned, the purpose for which it is used in evidence, the manner in which it was obtained, whether its introduction is fair to the party from whom it has been illegally obtained and whether its admission will in fairness throw light on disputed facts and enable justice to be done."[59]

15–34　　The principle of subjecting illegally obtained evidence in civil cases to the same tests as that in criminal cases has found favour with other commentators,[60] and it may well be that in future cases, using the rule laid down by Lord Wheatley, private parties to civil cases will find the courts less lenient than they are to the police in criminal cases, in which at least there may be said to be some public interest to be served in making all relevant evidence available.

---

[59]　1963 S.L.T. (Notes) 42; this is the report of the eventual proof.
[60]　See, *e.g.* Macphail, *op. cit.,* n. 5, Chap. 21.14; Wilkinson, *Scottish Law of Evidence*, p. 118; Scot. Law Com., Memo. No. 46, para. U.06.

CHAPTER 16

OPINION EVIDENCE

INTRODUCTION

As a general rule, when a witness is called to give evidence, the court is **16–01** interested in hearing only of those facts of which he or she has personal knowledge or experience of and which are relevant to the case. It is not interested in the witness's opinion of what might have happened, or suggestions from the witness as to how the facts being given in testimony should be interpreted. This is because such conclusions as may be drawn from the facts should be drawn by those who have been charged with the duty of adjudicating on the facts — the judge, sheriff, magistrate or jury. It is not for the witness to pre-empt that function by, in effect, giving the court an opinion on how it should assess what it has heard.[1]

It is therefore sometimes stated to be a firm rule that "opinion evidence" **16–02** is not admissible in a court of law, and that the only opinion which is relevant at the end of the day is that of the court. However, there are many circumstances in which a court will, consciously and willingly, hear opinion evidence.

These circumstances may be classified into two main categories. First **16–03** of all, an increasing number of cases coming before the courts involve matters so technical or otherwise beyond everyday human experience that the tribunal of fact requires guidance before it may reach an informed conclusion on the facts as a whole. Obvious examples are the evidence of cause of death in a murder trial, and evidence of the condition of a vehicle's brakes in a reparation action. This guidance normally comes from a person called as an "expert" witness. This type of witness gives an opinion based on facts which have either been personally observed (*e.g.* the condition of the deceased at the time of the post mortem, or the condition of the brakes when the vehicle was examined in the workshop) or, more rarely, facts which are put to the expert in the form of an hypothesis, and proved by other witnesses.

---

[1] "The general rule is that it would be quite wrong, and inadmissible, to put a witness into the witness box to tell the jury what the evidence they have been listening to ought to convey to them": Lord Sorn in *Hopes and Lavery* v. *H.M.A.*, 1960 J.C. 104 at pp. 113–114.

16–04   In the second category of cases, the person giving an opinion is not an expert at all. Rather it is a witness testifying to the circumstances of something personally experienced and which necessarily includes some element of personal opinion. For example, the witness who identifies the accused as the person who assaulted him is in effect telling the court that in his *opinion* the person who assaulted him and the person now sitting in the dock are one and the same. It is an opinion based on his powers of observation (which may well be challenged by the defence), and since he was uniquely placed to make the comparison between the two, his opinion is acceptable as an item of evidence.

16–05   In both categories of case, the court will be prepared to receive the opinion, but only under important safeguards, considered in the remainder of this chapter.

THE ROLE OF THE EXPERT WITNESS

16–06 The precise role of the expert witness in any case, whether civil or criminal, and the limitations placed by law on that role, were summarised by Lord President Cooper in *Davie* v. *Magistrates of Edinburgh*.[2] He said of expert witnesses:

> "Their duty is to furnish the Judge or jury with the necessary scientific criteria for testing the accuracy of their conclusions, so as to enable the Judge or jury to form their own independent judgment by the application of these criteria to the facts proved in evidence."

16–07   The expert witness is only required in order that certain facts may be assessed and understood in their specialist (usually scientific) context. The standard of proof to which an expert gives evidence on an essential fact is on a balance of probability.[3] The facts themselves must still be established by evidence (usually that of the expert himself), may be challenged, and may even be discarded, as indeed may the opinion itself if the court is not satisfied with it for some reason.

16–08   On occasions, a case is overturned on appeal when expert evidence should have been led but was not;[4] alternatively a court will refuse to make a finding on a particular point where expert evidence is required but is not made available.

16–09   In *The Nerano* v. *The Dromedary*,[5] a case concerning a collision between two vessels during a thick fog on the Clyde, the trial court refused to draw

---

[2]   1953 S.C. 34 at p. 40.
[3]   *Hendry* v. *H.M.A.*, 1988 S.L.T. 25.
[4]   See, *e.g. U.S. Shipping Board* v. *The St Albans* [1931] A.C. 632.
[5]   (1895) 22 R. 237. See also *Muir* v. *Stewart*, 1938 S.C. 590, where a reparation action against a pharmacist failed for lack of evidence of the relevant professional standards of care.

inferences concerning the speed of one of the vessels at the time of the collision from the nature and extent of the damage to the other because no expert evidence was led on the point, and although the court was sitting with a nautical assessor, it was held to be incompetent simply to invite his opinion.

With scientific advances, there is increasing emphasis on reducing **16–10** uncertainty and establishing the truth or otherwise of certain allegations through the use of technical processes. This forces the courts to rely on expert testimony especially when the advances made are not yet "generally accepted" in the scientific community or involve complex technological issues. Courts have traditionally been reluctant to give too much prominence to expert witnesses and the role of the expert in Scottish courts is very different from the expert in the American system. There is an anxiety that the traditional judicial process should not simply be replaced by a system of trial by experts. As Lord President Cooper put it, in *Davie, supra*: "The parties have invoked the decision of a judicial tribunal, and not an oracular pronouncement by an expert."[6]

Both the Scottish and English courts have kept comparatively strict **16–11** controls on the use of expert evidence.[7] As science and technology develop new complexities there is a commensurate growth of expert opinion. For example, the use of DNA profiling has required specialist forensic experts to give evidence in this field, and the current focus on the defence of battered women's syndrome as a basis for a plea of diminished responsibility for battered women who kill their partners, has required expert testimony from psychiatrists and psychologists.

ESTABLISHING THE EXPERTISE OF THE EXPERT WITNESS

Clearly it would be both unsafe and unfair for a party to a case to seek to **16–12** influence the tribunal of fact by evidence from a person who claims to be an expert, but is not. For this reason, the credentials of the expert must be established before any opinion is given in evidence. In the normal course of things, the expert witness will belong to a profession or a branch of the sciences. In such cases, it is normally only necessary for the party calling the expert to establish the witness's identity and then enumerate the degrees, diplomas and professional membership held by the witness. On occasions, however, as in *Davie, supra*, it is necessary to prove a particular specialist knowledge claimed by an expert.[8]

---

[6] See also *Hendry* v. *H.M.A.* in para. 16.19 *infra*.
[7] Unlike, for example, the United States, where there is a proliferation of expert testimony on every conceivable subject, resulting in what some commentators have described as the introduction of "junk science" into the courtroom.
[8] 1953 S.C. 34.

16–13   In *Hewart* v. *Edinburgh Corporation*,[9] for example, the Court of Session held that it would be competent to ask a police officer and three council employees whether they believed a particular hole in the road to be dangerous because it was their duty to report such dangers. In *Hopes and Lavery* v. *H.M.A.*,[10] Lord Sorn was prepared to hold that a typist might have become an expert on the authenticity of a transcript from a tape recording on which she had worked, since there was "no rigid rule that only witnesses possessing some technical qualification can be allowed to expound their understanding of any particular item of evidence."

16–14   What matters is not so much the academic qualification or the formal recognition, as the expertise. It does not matter where this comes from, provided that the court is satisfied that it exists, and that the person called as an expert witness is fit to guide the court in an area beyond its experience. In an early English case,[11] for example, a solicitor was allowed to give expert evidence on handwriting, a matter in which he had acquired expertise as a skilled amateur.

16–15   It also follows from this general principle that although a person may be an expert for one purpose, opinions must not be offered on matters outwith that person's expertise, even if those matters are closely related to the matter on which the expert is testifying.[12] However, it may be permissible for an expert to refer to literature in a related field provided the literature has a bearing upon the subject in which the witness has expertise.[13]

16–16   A witness may not testify as to matters which are well within the knowledge and experience of the court, for:

> "The fact that an expert witness has impressive scientific qualifications does not by that fact alone make his opinion on matters of human nature and behaviour within the limits of normality any more helpful than that of the jurors themselves; but there is a danger that they may think it does."[14]

16–17   In the case from which this quotation is taken, a young man was charged with the murder of his girlfriend in a blind rage induced by her sexual taunts and admissions of infidelity. His defence was that of provocation,[15] and psychiatric evidence was led to the effect that while the accused was perfectly normal mentally, the sort of experience to which he had been subjected might provide intense provocation even to a normal person. It was held on appeal that once the psychiatrist had advised the jury that the

---

⁹ 1944 S.C. 30.
¹⁰ 1960 J .C. 104 at p. 114. See also *Haq* v. *H.M.A.*, 1987 S.C.C.R. 433.
¹¹ *R.* v. *Silverlock* [1894] 2 Q.B. 766.
¹² As for example in *U.S. Shipping Board* v. *The St Albans* [1931] A.C. 632 in which it was held that land surveyors could not testify to a diagram constructed from a photograph.
¹³ *Main* v. *McAndrew Wormald Ltd.*, 1988 S.L.T. 141.
¹⁴ *R.* v. *Turner* [1975] Q.B. 834 at p. 841.

accused was mentally normal, he had no further expert evidence left to give, for: "Jurors do not need psychiatrists to tell them how ordinary folk who are not suffering from any mental illness are likely to react to the stresses and strains of life."[16]

PRESERVING THE MAIN ISSUE FOR THE COURT

The function of the expert witness is to assist the tribunal of fact to come to **16–18** a decision on the main issue presented to it, and not to make that decision for the tribunal. However closely tied up with the ultimate outcome of the case the evidence of the expert may be, a clear distinction must be maintained between the expert's role as a guide through a specialist area and the role of the tribunal as the ultimate arbiter of fact. This latter function is normally jealously preserved by the courts, even at the expense of discounting the expert evidence altogether.

In *Gellatly* v. *Laird*[17] a magistrate was held to have correctly refused to **16–19** hear expert evidence on whether or not books were indecent or obscene, since that was "the very matter remitted to the opinion of the magistrate."[18] Similarly, in *Meehan* v. *H.M.A.*[19] the High Court refused to arrange for an accused to be examined under a "truth drug," because in respect of any resulting statement, "The medical man would take the place of the jury as a judge of credibility."

There appears to be no clear statement under modern civil law to the **16–20** effect that an expert witness may not give an opinion on the main issue before the court. The nearest to it is a statement by Lord Justice-Clerk Inglis in *Morrison* v. *Maclean's Trs.*,[20] a case in which it was alleged that a testator had been in a state of "facility" at the time when he signed his will. The medical witnesses in the case had been asked to comment on his mental state, and no objection had been taken to this line of questioning by counsel for the executors. Nevertheless, the jury were carefully directed by the trial judge that the issue of capacity to sign was a matter for them, and not the medical witnesses.

A similar consideration lies behind the technical rule found in the law of **16–21** contract that unless a contract employs technical words which create a need

---

[15] Which has the same function under English law as under Scots, in that it reduces a murder charge to the lesser charge of "manslaughter", the equivalent of culpable homicide.

[16] *R.* v. *Turner loc. cit.*

[17] 1953 J.C. 16. This case was followed in *Ingram* v. *Macari*, 1983 S.L.T. 61, but *cf. H.M.A.* v. *McGinlay*, 1983 S.L.T. 562. In *Hendry* v. *H.M.A.*, 1988 S.L.T. 25, it was held that the jury in a murder trial must decide for itself whether or not the causal link between assault and death is proved beyond reasonable doubt, and that it is improper to invite an expert witness to usurp the function of the jury by expressing his opinion on this question.

[18] At p. 27.

[19] 1970 J.C. 11 at p. 14.

[20] (1862) 24 D. 625 at p. 631.

for specialist technical interpretation, then the terms of that contract are to be interpreted by the court, using the normal everyday meaning given to each word used by the parties, and without the aid of experts.[21]

LAYING A BASIS OF FACT

16–22 Even when the opinion of an expert is deemed to be admissible on a particular point, it will be meaningless and should not be considered, unless the facts upon which it is based are also proved to the satisfaction of the tribunal of fact, and to the appropriate standard of proof.

16–23 In the great majority of modern cases, in fact, expert testimony is a mixture of fact and professional opinion. The expert has been called in to make an examination, or conduct a series of tests, and the court is receiving the evidence not just as a pure opinion but also as evidence of the physical condition of something. Obvious examples are the evidence of pathologists describing post-mortem examinations on the deceased, police surgeons describing the results of examinations of rape victims and psychiatrists giving evidence of the mental state of patients in their care.

16–24 In civil cases, experts are frequently called in to describe the state of some object or other, and may regularly be seen in court in reparation actions arising from road accidents, describing the scene of the accident and/or the state of the vehicle.

16–25 It is important for the party leading an expert witness to ensure that a basis of fact has been laid for the opinion evidence of the expert. There is otherwise a danger that the expert evidence will be excluded. In *Blagojevic* v. *H.M.A.*[22] an accused on trial for murder did not give evidence but, unsuccessfully, tried to lead evidence from a clinical psychologist that he would have been suggestible under pressure at the police interview. The court ruled the expert's testimony inadmissible as no foundation in fact had first been laid for it.

16–26 Whether the facts upon which an opinion is based are spoken to by the expert or by other witnesses, they must be proved to the satisfaction of the court before the opinion which relates to them will even be relevant, let alone admissible. In *Stewart* v. *Glasgow Corporation*,[23] for example, the tenant of a council house sought compensation from the local authority for the death of her child as the result of an accident allegedly caused by the corroded state of a clothes pole in the back green of the tenement in which she lived. The accident had occurred in October, 1953, and the pole was examined by an expert witness for the pursuer in January, 1954. He stated

---

[21] See *Tancred, Arrol & Co.* v. *Steel Co. of Scotland* (1887) 15 R. 215; affd. (1890) 17 R.(H.L.) 31.

[22] 1995 S.L.T. 1189.

[23] 1958 S.C. 28, considered at para. 9.56 *supra*.

in evidence that in his opinion, based upon his examination of the pole, it must have been in a manifestly dangerous state for at least the previous six months, and was not cross-examined on this point.

The pursuer had sought to have the pole examined by a second expert **16–27** witness, but the defenders had failed to produce it for this purpose, and the second expert simply gave his opinion (which agreed with that of the first expert) on the assumption that the pole was in the state described by the first expert at the date of his examination of it. It was held that since the fact that the first expert had not been cross-examined did not of itself corroborate[24] the evidence of that expert as to the actual state of the pole in January, 1954, there was insufficient evidence in law upon this factual point to form a basis for any expert opinion, and the pursuer's case was lost.

Similarly, in *Forrester* v. *H.M.A.*,[25] the accused was acquitted on appeal **16–28** after the High Court held that the jury at his trial for safe-blowing should not have heard evidence relating to a small piece of cotton bedspread material which was allegedly found in his pocket. Although forensic scientists concluded the sample found corresponded with material from such a bedspread used in the crime, the Crown failed because they had not satisfactorily established that the sample was found in the accused's pocket.

This important rule—that the opinion of expert witnesses must be **16–29** grounded in proven fact—was applied in the case of *McGowan* v. *Belling & Co.*,[26] which involved the "best evidence rule."[27] Various people who had been injured in a house fire sued *inter alia* the manufacturers of an electric fire which, it was alleged, suffered from certain defects in design and manufacture which had caused it to catch fire. The heater in question was not available either at the civil proof or at any time after the fire, but expert evidence was given by two witnesses who had examined another fire of this type on earlier occasions (three years and one year previously) and who testified that the design of this type of heater made it susceptible to cable overheating. The heater which the two experts had examined was not proved to be identical to the heater in question, although it was still available at the university where they had both examined it, and could have been lodged in production.

It was held that since it was vital to know if the heater which had been **16–30** examined was identical to the one at the centre of the action (particularly in the matter of the cable connectors), the "best evidence rule" required its production, and without it the expert evidence was useless. As the court put

---

[24] On the need for corroboration generally, see Chap. 7. The point which required corroboration was of course the actual state of the pole, and not the expert opinion which was based on that.

[25] 1952 J.C. 28. See also *Ritchie* v. *Pirie*, 1972 J.C. 7 and *Russell* v. *H.M.A.*, 1946 J.C. 37.

[26] 1983 S.L.T. 77.

[27] For which see para. 9.57–9.58 *supra*.

it: "An oral description of its condition in its absence was inadmissible, and any expert evidence based on its alleged condition was also inadmissible."[28]

16–31 In seeking to lay a factual basis for their opinions, experts occasionally find themselves caught up in "collateral" issues, and with the principle that a court should not pursue every remote issue which might conceivably have a bearing on the case in hand. However, the courts seem to allow a greater latitude where it can be shown that the apparent departure from the main issue will allow a more accurate, or more informed, expert assessment to be made.[29]

CHALLENGING THE EXPERT WITNESS

16–32 An expert witness, although giving a professional opinion which must command attention and respect, is at the end of the day only one witness in a court action. Like all witnesses the expert is open to challenge, both as to the validity of his or her opinion and the accuracy of the facts or assumptions on which it is based. It is not unusual for experts to be ranged on both sides, and to be called for both parties in such a way that their expert opinions conflict with each other. This is particularly true when the specialism which they represent is one which admits of diversity of assessment, such as psychiatry.[30] Nor is it by any means unheard of for expert witnesses called by the same party to contradict each other.[31] The function of the expert witness is to assist the court in coming to a conclusion, and not to proclaim some set of universal truths.[32] Even if the expert gives evidence which is not contradicted, the court is not bound to accept the evidence even if it appears credible and reliable.[33]

16–33 The most significant grounds upon which the opinions of experts have been challenged by non-experts are twofold. First, a failure to lay a suitable basis of fact for the opinion (dealt with in paragraphs 16.22–16.31 *supra*), and second, the making of fundamental assumptions on assumed facts.[34]

16–34 An expert witness may seek to support the evidence being given by referring to documents such as books and learned treatises. In doing so the passages which are thus "adopted" become part of the expert's evidence,

---

[28] *ibid.*, p. 78.
[29] See, *e.g. Swan* v. *Bowie*, 1948 S.C. 46 and *Houston* v. *Aitken*, 1912 S.C. 1037.
[30] The ultimate in the U.K. courts having perhaps been reached in the trial of the so-called "Yorkshire Ripper," Peter Sutcliffe; see Kenny, "The Expert in Court", 99 L.Q.R. 197.
[31] See, *e.g. Davie* v. *Magistrates of Edinburgh*, 1953 S.C. 34.
[32] *Dempster* v. *Motherwell Bridge and Engineering Co.*, 1964 S.L.T. 353.
[33] *Beaton* v. *H.M.A.*, 1994 S.L.T. 309.
[34] For two examples of the rejection of evidence on this latter ground, see *S S. Rowan* v. *S.S. Malcolm*, 1923 S.C. 316 and *Gardiner* v. *Motherwell Machinery and Scrap Co.*, 1961 S.C.(H.L.) 1.

and part of the general body of evidence available to the tribunal of fact. But the remainder of such a book or treatise is not evidence, and may not be relied upon, even to challenge that expert witness's opinion.[35]

The opinion of the expert does not require corroboration,[36] although the **16–35** facts upon which that opinion is based may well do.[37]

In criminal cases, the evidence is seldom clear-cut, principally because **16–36** the main item of evidence against an accused is frequently scientific. The witnesses who give evidence as experts are, at the same time, providing the crucial facts leading to conviction. It is now well established that an accused may be convicted solely on evidence relating to fingerprints,[38] palm prints,[39] handwriting[40] and DNA profiling[41] and in such cases the witnesses who give their opinions also speak to the facts upon which they were based.

For this reason, it is a rule of practice that in any criminal case where **16–37** expert evidence is to be led, there will be two experts available, the second normally corroborating the first on a joint report which bears their signatures.[42] The statutory provisions contained in sections 280–284 of the Criminal Procedure (Scotland) Act 1995 relating to the use made of expert evidence of this nature, have already been mentioned (see paragraphs 7.25–7.47 *supra*).

The effect of these sections (gathered together in the statute under the **16–38** heading "Routine Evidence") is that reports become documents spoken to by only one witness unless the defence give prior intimation that they require both witnesses to be called. These provisions reflect the fact that in reality, formal forensic reports are not often challenged as to their accuracy, and that if the defence can disprove or cast doubt upon a conclusion contained within such a report by cross-examining the main witness, this will suffice for them. The heading employed in the statute of "Routine Evidence" clearly implies that the process prescribed by those sections will only apply where the evidence in question is non-contentious.

Section 280(4) states that *any* report "purporting to be signed by two **16–39** authorised forensic scientists shall ... be sufficient evidence of any fact or conclusion as to fact contained in the report and of the authority of the signatories." In such a case, it will not be necessary to call witnesses to

---

[35] For which see *Davie, supra*.

[36] See, *e.g.*, *M* v. *Kennedy*, 1993 S.C.C.R. 69.

[37] As in, *e.g. Stewart* v. *Glasgow Corpn.* and *Forrester* v. *H.M.A.*, dealt with in paras. 16.22–16.31 *supra*. For corroboration generally, see Chap. 7.

[38] *Hamilton* v. *H.M.A.*, 1934 J.C. 1; see also paras. 7.25–7.47 *supra*.

[39] *H.M.A.* v. *Rolley*, 1945 J.C. 155.

[40] *Richardson* v. *Clarke*, 1957 J.C. 1; *Campbell* v. *Mackenzie*, 1974 S.L.T. (Notes) 46; see also paras. 9.06–9.20 *supra*.

[41] *Welsh* v. *H.M.A.*, 1992 S.L.T. 193.

[42] Following the general requirement for corroboration in criminal cases explained in *Morton* v. *H.M.A.*, 1938 J.C. 50 at p. 55, and dealt with more fully in Chap. 7 *supra*.

speak to the report, but the prosecution have the same duty to notify the defence of their intentions, and the defence have a right to object within a specified time limit. The emphasis is once again on the efficient disposal of items of expert evidence which are non-contentious, while at the same time preserving the defence right of challenge when there is something concerning the report with which they disagree.

16–40   Apart from the 1995 Act, there are other statutes which allow expert evidence to be taken in certificate form, the certificate being probative in effect if it is unchallenged. One of the most commonly used is now found in section 16 of the Road Traffic Offenders Act 1988, which allows the court to regard as probative the certificate issued following an analysis of the blood or urine of a person accused of a drink/driving offence, showing the level of alcohol or drug found in that person's blood or urine, and the certificate of the police doctor that a blood sample was taken from that person with consent. In both cases, the qualifications of the expert signing the certificate will also be taken as established by the very certificate itself. In all cases the prosecution is required to serve a copy of the certificate on the accused. The accused may challenge it and require the attendance as witnesses of the forensic scientist or police doctor, and the accused must, at the time of the taking of the sample, be provided with one-half of it for his own analysis.[43]

16–41   Perhaps the most fundamental challenge which may be made against opinion evidence is to question the expert's competence. This may be done diplomatically, for example by suggesting that the expert does not have sufficient experience to form an opinion in the particular case. This was done in a series of appeals in the 1970's and 1980's involving the evidence given by a leading Home Office forensic scientist. It was suggested that his evidence was tainted by bias, and did not display the level of objectivity required of a person in his position.

16–42   The process began with a Scottish appeal, *Preece* v. *H.M.A.*,[44] in which a man who had already served seven years of a life sentence for murder had his conviction quashed after it was learned that forensic evidence involving blood samples and seminal stains, which had played a significant part in his conviction, could have been interpreted in such a way as to lessen its prejudicial effect on the accused. The expert in question had failed to advise the jury of this (although, in fairness to him, he was never asked), and this lapse was regarded as fatal to the conviction since it fell short of the standards of accuracy and objectivity required of an expert witness.

---

[43]   *ibid.*, s. 10(3) and (5). See Chaps. 8 and 9 *supra*.
[44]   [1981] Crim.L.R. 783.

THE OPINION EVIDENCE OF NON-EXPERTS

At the start of this chapter, the point was made that sometimes the court is **16-43** hearing opinion evidence from a witness who is not an expert. This is because:

> "Unless opinions, estimates and inferences which men in their daily lives reach ... as a result of what they have perceived with their physical senses were treated in the law of evidence as if they were mere statements of fact, witnesses would find themselves unable to communicate to the judge an accurate impression of the events they were seeking to describe."[45]

The most obvious example of this process arises in the context of **16-44** identification. Every witness who is asked to identify a person or an object is in fact being required to assert his or her opinion that the person or object which is now being identified is the same as the person or object seen before. Even if there exists a special means by which a witness is able to identify an object (*e.g.* because of a signature on a document or label, or because of initials scratched on the back of an object), what is actually being offered is an opinion that the signature, etc., is that of the witness, by means of observation and familiarity.

Similarly, the best evidence of handwriting comes from the person who **16-45** actually wrote it, confirming that it is his or her handwriting. The second best is the evidence of someone well acquainted with the writing of the alleged author.[46] In the latter case, the court is receiving what in effect is the opinion of the witness.

Apart from questions of identification, there are occasions upon which **16-46** the opinion of a non-expert constitutes an important item of evidence, either because it is the very matter into which the court is inquiring (as in the case of the defence of error in criminal law),[47] or the court needs to know, for some other reason, what opinion the witness formed from the circumstances in which he found himself.[48]

For example, police officers in a drink/driving case are asked as a matter **16-47** of routine whether or not they formed the impression that the accused had been drinking (in order to show the "reasonable cause" necessary before

---

[45] 17th Report of the Law Reform Committee, Cmnd. 4489 (1970), para. 3.
[46] Or someone who actually saw the author perform the writing in question.
[47] See *Owens* v. *H.M.A.*, 1946 J.C. 119, and generally Gordon, *Criminal Law*, Chap. 9.
[48] As in *Ward* v. *Upper Clyde Shipbuilders*, 1973 S.L.T. 182, a reparation action arising from back injuries sustained at work, when a worker only fit for "light" duties was asked to perform heavier tasks, and was allowed to give evidence to the effect that he got the impression that he would be dismissed if he did not.

they may ask him to take a breath test), while witnesses to a road accident are regularly asked questions such as: "Would you say that the car was travelling fast?" Only rarely will exception be taken to that sort of question, whereas the question, "Do you think that X was exceeding the speed limit?" should lead to an objection from the other party.

16–48 In *Wilson* v. *Wilson*,[49] a divorce action for adultery, evidence was given by a lamplighter that he passed the defender lying on a common stair with a lady, in circumstances which he took to indicate immorality, although he did not actually see anything immoral taking place. His evidence was accepted as leading to the conclusion that they were there for an immoral purpose, although as it transpired there was insufficient corroboration for a finding of adultery.

16–49 The relevance and admissibility of non-expert opinion is almost entirely a question of circumstance and degree, and there are situations when it is accepted, largely for practical reasons which outweigh any strict rule of law.

---

[49] (1898) 25 R. 788.

BIBLIOGRAPHY

Alison, *Principles of the Criminal Law of Scotland* (1989) (Edinburgh: Law Society of Scotland, Butterworths)

Anton, *Private International Law* (2nd ed., 1990) (Edinburgh: W. Green)

Brown, *see* Renton and Brown

Brown, *et al.*, *Sexual History and Sexual Character Evidence in Scottish Sexual Offence Trials* (1992) (Edinburgh: Scottish Office, Central Research Unit)

Clive, *The Law of Husband and Wife* (3rd ed., 1992) (Edinburgh: W. Green)

Cross and Tapper, *Evidence* (8th ed., 1995) (London: Butterworths)

Cuisine, *see* Rennie and Cuisine

Dent and Flin (eds.) *Children as Witnesses* (1992) (Chichester: John Wiley & Sons)

Dickson, *Evidence* (3rd ed., 1887) (Edinburgh: T. & T. Clark)

Dobie, *Sheriff Court Practice* (1986) (Collieston: Caledonian Books — reprint of 1948 edition, Glasgow: Hodge)

Field, *Annotation to the Civil Evidence (Scotland) Act 1988* (1988) contained in Scottish Current Law Statutes, volume 2, 1989, Edinburgh: W. Green)

Gloag, *Contract* (2nd ed., 1985) (Collieston: Caledonian Books — reprint of 1929 edition, Edinburgh: W. Green)

Gloag and Henderson, *Introduction to the Law of Scotland* (10th ed., 1995) (Edinburgh: W. Green)

Gordon, *Criminal Law*, (2nd supplement to 2nd ed., 1978) (Edinburgh: W. Green)

Griffiths, *Confessions* (1994) (Edinburgh: Butterworths)

Halsbury's Laws of England, (Hailsham ed.) (4th ed.) (London: Butterworths)

Harper and McWhinnie, *The Glasgow Rape Case* (1983) (London: Hutchinson)

Henderson, *see* Gloag and Henderson

McBryde, *The Law of Contract in Scotland* (1987) (Edinburgh: W. Green)

MacDonald, *Criminal Law of Scotland* (5th ed., 1948) (Edinburgh: W. Green)

MacLaren, *Court of Session Practice* (1916) (Edinburgh: W. Green)

Macphail, *Evidence* (1987) (Edinburgh: Law Society of Scotland) Macphail, *Sheriff Court Practice* (1988) (Edinburgh: W. Green)

McWhinnie, *see* Harper and McWhinnie

Maxwell, *The Practice of the Court of Session* (1980) (Edinburgh: Scottish Courts Admnistration)

Norrie, *see* Wilkinson and Norrie

Rennie and Cuisine, *The Requirements of Writing (Scotland) Act 1995* (1995) (Edinburgh: Law Society of Scotland, Butterworths)

Renton and Brown, *Criminal Procedure* (5th ed., 1983) (Edinburgh: W. Green)

Robinson, *The Law of Interdict* (2nd ed., 1994) (Edinburgh: Law Scoiety of Scotland, Butterworths)

Stair Memorial Enclyclopedia, *The Laws of Scotland* (1989) (Edinburgh: The Law Society of Scotland, Butterworths)

Tapper, *see* Cross and Tapper

Twining, *Rethinking Evidence: Exploratory Essays* (1990) (Oxford: Blackwell)

Walker, *Delict* (2nd ed., 1981) (Edinburgh: W. Green)

Walker and Walker *Law of Evidence in Scotland* (1964) (Edinburgh: Hodge)

Wigmore, *Evidence* (1935) (Brooklyn Foundation Press)

Wilkinson, *The Scottish Law of Evidence* (1986) (Edinburgh: Law Society of Scotland, Butterworths)

Wilkinson and Norrie, *The Law Relating to Parent and Child in Scotland* (1993) (Edinburgh: W. Green)

INDEX